Sanumá Memories

New Directions in Anthropological Writing
History, Poetics, Cultural Criticism

George E. Marcus
Rice University
James Clifford
University of California, Santa Cruz

General Editors

Alcida Rita Ramos

Sanumá Memories

Yanomami Ethnography in Times of Crisis

The University of Wisconsin Press

The University of Wisconsin Press
1930 Monroe Street, 3rd floor
Madison, Wisconsin 53711-2059

3 Henrietta Street
London WC2E 8LU, England

www.wisc.edu\wisconsinpress

Printed in the United States of America

Library of Congress Cataloging-in-Publication Data
Ramos, Alcida Rita.
    [Memórias sanumá. English]
    Sanumá memories: Yanomami ethnography in times of crisis /
Alcida Rita Ramos.
    368 p.   cm. — (New directions in anthropological writing)
    Includes bibliographical references (p. 332) and index.
    ISBN 0-299-14650-2.   ISBN 0-299-14654-5 (pbk.)
    1. Yanomamo Indians.   2. Yanomamo Indians — Social conditions.
I. Title.   II. Series.
F2520.1.Y3R3413   1995
305.898 — dc20   94-39614

ISBN-13: 978-0-299-14654-2 (pbk: alk. paper)

To the Kadimani people,
survivors of a catastrophe

Contents

Illustrations — ix
Maps — x
Figures — xi
Tables — xiii
Preface to the American Edition — xv

Introduction — 3

Part 1. Space and Time

1. Sanumá Spaces — 19
2. Time as Space Organizer — 56
3. Diachrony and Leadership — 96
4. The Marriage-Go-Round — 127
5. Sanumá Times — 154

Part 2. Names

6. Names under Erasure — 181
7. For Name-Sakes — 199
8. To Hunt a Name — 215

Part 3. Others

9. A Rumor on Stage — 235
10. The Sanumá's Others — 258
11. The Age of Gold and Misery — 271

Epilogue — 313
Notes — 323

viii   Contents

Bibliography   332
Acknowledgments   340
Index   341

Illustrations

Grating manioc	24
A mature garden	26
Dry season fishing with stunning vine	31
Childless couples usually sleep in the same hammock	38
In the dry season the Auaris River turns into a playground	50
Lucio and one of his young wives	107
Taking *sakona*	112
Jorge and Zeca visit the Maiongong village during a feast	120
Elderly woman feeds her pet	174
Olivier Parisot of Médecins du Monde at the microscope in Olomai	301
Health team and crew leave Olomai for Tucushim	304
Fording the rapids	305

Maps

1. Distribution of Yanomami   20
2. Distribution of Sanumá villages studied   33
3. The route to Boa Vista   238
4. Yanomami area under siege   290

Figures

1.1	Auaris 1974	47
2.1	Recurrence of names	57
2.2	The internal divisions of the sibs	71
2.3	Inside the *higadili* sib	72
2.4	The *kadimani dɨbɨ* subdivisions	75
2.5	Genealogic connections between *lalawa dɨbɨ* and *soboshidili dɨbɨ* lineages	82
2.6	The *nimtali dɨbɨ*	83
2.7	The *mosonɨwɨ dɨbɨ*	84
2.8	The *kadimani dɨbɨ*	86
2.9	The "fathers beyond" of the *higadili dɨbɨ* sib	87
2.10	The *tototobɨdili dɨbɨ* and the *saulagɨdili dɨbɨ*	93
3.1	The developmental cycle of Sanumá lineages	100
3.2	Relationships at Kalioko's community	118
4.1	Terms of reference — men speaking	135
4.2	Terms of address — men speaking	135
4.3	Terms of reference — women speaking	136
4.4	Terms of address — women speaking	136
4.5	Postmarital terms of reference — men speaking	137
4.6	Postmarital terms of reference — women speaking	137
4.7	Terms of reference — third person	138
4.8	Dumont's "encompassing of the contrary"	139
4.9	Sibling groups at Mosonawa	144
4.10	Sibling groups at Kadimani	145
4.11	Classificatory relationships with known connection	147
4.12	Distribution of marriages between communities	153
5.1	Age sets	160
5.2	Recycling of life and death	172
5.3	Sanumá population pyramid	177
6.1	Teknonymy in the family	191

6.2	Uterine siblings	194
7.1	Individual identification	211
10.1	Identity categories I	262
10.2	Identity categories II	265
11.1	Incidence of diseases at Surucucus and Paapiú after 1987	278

Tables

1.1	Sanumá population of the upper Auaris River valley	34
2.1	Sib distribution per community	61
2.2	A model of marriage exchanges	64
2.3	Relations between sib clusters	65
2.4	Marriages between sibs related as kin or affines	66
2.5	Lineage distribution per community	70
4.1	Distribution of spouses per community	146
4.2	Marriages	149
6.1	Extended teknonymy	193
8.1	Who's who in the *humabi* name	222
8.2	Who's who in a non-*humabi* name	223
11.1	Yawarib losses	272
11.2	Malaria in Auaris	293

Preface to the American Edition

Between 1974 and the publication of the Portuguese version of *Sanumá Memories* in 1990, I did not return to the location of my research among the Sanumá, a subgroup of the Yanomami Indians in northern Brazil. This was an extremely traumatic period for the Yanomami. In three years—from 1973 to 1976—the people of the Ajarani and Catrimani River valleys suffered repeated flu and measles epidemics contracted from hundreds of workers employed in the construction of the aborted North Perimeter (Perimetral Norte) Highway. The indigenous population of these areas was devastated: four Ajarani communities lost 22 percent of their members in the first two years of work on the road, while 50 percent of the people of four communities of the upper Catrimani died in a 1978 measles epidemic, two years after construction had been discontinued. Further north, in the hilly region of Surucucus and Couto de Magalhães, the discovery of tin ore and gold sparked a wave of invasions by prospectors.

After two and a half years of voluntary exile in Great Britain, in January 1980, I was on my way back home via New York. Penniless, I was particularly inclined to notice the soaring prices of gold on the world market. With the sale of a small bracelet I cheerfully paid for my trip back to Brazil. Little did I know that the same boom that helped complete my repatriation was to bring disaster to the Yanomami and involve me in one of the most harrowing episodes of my professional life (Chapter 11).

That same year, about two thousand gold miners (*garimpeiros*) invaded the Furo de Santa Rosa region on the upper Uraricoera River, the northeastern corner of Yanomami territory in Brazil. The 1980s saw the ruthless escalation of the gold rush and the marks it left on the lives of the Yanomami. Virtually all sixty-nine hundred Indians in the state of Roraima were affected by epidemics and acts of violence brought about by the invaders.

In the years between the writing of *Memórias Sanumá* and its re-writing as *Sanumá Memories*, more than a thousand Yanomami died, most of them victims of repeated malaria epidemics. The upper Auaris River valley, the Sanumá country where I did fieldwork in the 1960s and 1970s, had not yet been affected by malaria on the same scale as the Central Yanomami. In 1990 there had been an armed conflict between Indians and *garimpeiros*, but otherwise news from the area did not portray the horror reported for villages such as Paapiú, Homoshi, or Shidea where entire communities had either been wiped out or reduced to a fraction of their former size.

With the beginning of the gold rush, in 1987 until late 1990, the military and the National Indian Foundation prohibited medical personnel, Catholic missionaries, and all researchers, including anthropologists, to go into the Yanomami area. But in 1989, as a Yanomami expert and activist in the cause of indigenous rights, I was allowed to accompany foreign diplomats and Brazilian congressmen on two separate short inspection trips to what was then the *garimpeiro* epicenter, the airstrip at Paapiú. The constant landing and takeoff of small aircraft and helicopters turned the once placid Paapiú into a deafening and unrelenting pandemonium. This mud airstrip, nearly a kilometer long, skirted by shacks covered in bright blue tarpaulin, continuously plowed up by airplanes, trampled by interminable waves of *garimpeiros*, by owners ("bosses") of airplanes and mining sites, traders, prostitutes, and Yanomami of both sexes and all ages, was the stage for one of the most tragic chapters in the short history of Yanomami contact with the outside world. The apocalyptic scene before our eyes made one congressman gasp, "This is a Vietnam!" By then pictures of dying Indians, of children in the last stages of malnutrition, and of corpses found in jungle trails had made their way into world news, which led to charges against Brazil for genocide.

As the gold rush expanded and more Yanomami perished, I had the disconcerting fantasy of being aboard a time machine on a journey back to the seventeenth century from which I was forced to watch the massive collapse of the coastal Tupinambá, a numerous indigenous population that was extinct before the eighteenth century dawned. Was it possible the Yanomami were to be the Tupinambá of the twenty-first century? I can well imagine what a Tupinambá intimate ethnographer might have felt. This time, however, the plight of the Indians was being closely observed and reported by both anthropology and the electronic media.

As I could not return to the Auaris area from mid-1987 to late 1990, the aftermath of the gold rush became an unwritten chapter in the original version of *Memórias Sanumá*. This English translation has given me a second chance, so to speak, to report the extent to which the Sanumá have been caught in the grip of the gold fever. When I finally went back to the Auaris region, we all had lost our innocence: the Sanumá, like virtually all Yanomami, had known the white man at his worst, and I had relinquished the chimera of returning to my own private ethnographic paradise.

November 1990. Almost seventeen years after my last two months among the Sanumá, I met them again. During the first ten days in Auaris I was divided between the pleasure of meeting old friends and the vexation of confronting a milieu much more squalid than I could remember. I recoiled at the sight of soiled and shabby clothes, especially women's skirts. In my mind these tattered skirts became the epitome of squalor. There were no longer beaded or cotton aprons to be seen. Western clothing had made its definitive entry among the Sanumá, all the way to the intimate confines of underwear. My negative reaction to this new ungainly appearance was prompted not by a residue of "imperialist nostalgia" (Rosaldo 1989), but by a sense of aesthetic impoverishment.

Nevertheless, a whole new generation of Sanumá was roaming about doing much the same things I had seen their parents do. The children reacted to me as if they had heard about me and were curious to see how real I was. There was no shock on their part, but there was on mine. My culture shock gave way to "time shock," an extremely disorienting sense of déjà vu. What had I missed in the flow of life while young people grew old and others were born? I felt as if I had been robbed of years of my life, a similar feeling to that of waking up from general anesthesia. What happens to time during oblivion? Confused and unsettled, I decided to take a couple of weeks' break from the field. When I returned from Boa Vista, the capital town of the state of Roraima, my mind had accommodated to the changes, and I enjoyed my stay with the Sanumá as never before.

It was surprising to discover how little the Sanumá had really changed despite almost thirty years of exposure to missionaries. Apparently the latter's work had not made a dent. Below the surface of Western clothing, of dependence on a larger assortment of trade goods, and a certain nonchalance regarding outsiders, the Sanumá were still monolingual, still displayed a keen sense of humor, and guided their actions by much the same principles and expectations as I had known in the 1970s. Through open conflicts with placer-miners they had learned that gold has the power to drive whites to murder, while a few had already grasped the correlation between the presence of *garimpeiros* and the diffusion of contagious diseases.

Invaders notwithstanding, when I reencountered my old hosts and their children, most were healthy, well fed, and good-humored. As it turned out, this was but an ephemeral interlude.

March 1991. I returned to Auaris not as a researcher but as interpreter and cultural translator for a medical team of the National Health Foundation. A malaria epidemic had killed five people at the Olomai community. The most lethal strain of malaria, *Plasmodium falciparum*, was raging through village after village in the entire Yanomami territory. It was not exceptional to find communities with an infection rate of over 70 percent, sometimes going as high as 90 percent. The communities near the Auaris mission, despite being close to medical aid, were no exception.

In that year, a whole Sanumá village—the same Kadimani that plays such a central role in this book—got very close to being wiped out by one of the most virulent outbreaks of malaria known to the medical teams in the entire Yanomami area. Had we arrived a few weeks later, perhaps only four or five out of more than 130 people would have survived. In addition, from far-off villages all around our headquarters at the mission, we received constant calls to assist people reported to be severely undernourished and very ill with malaria, while others had already died. With reduced personnel (one doctor, one laboratory technician, and one anthropologist) and no efficient means of transportation, it was impossible to meet such a vast demand. Some villages were so devastated that rearrangements in residence were already under way. Orphaned children moved in with uncles and aunts; widowers settled in with distant relatives; young women with no parents, husband, or children wandered from place to place, frequently exposed to sexual abuse.

May 1992. My last trip to the Yanomami area was a continuation of the work of the previous year. Our itinerant team of a medical doctor, a microscope technician, an Indian guide, and an anthropologist had some nerve-wracking experiences, such as a long canoe trip paddling through countless rapids complete with capsizing and loss of supplies, and a high-risk flight in a precarious helicopter laden well beyond its capacity. We visited three communities on the middle course of the Auaris River—Olomai, Tucushim and Shikoi—that had received medical treatment some months before. Yet we found the incidence of *falciparum* malaria to be still as high as 60 percent. Several people had died between the two medical visits. We treated the sick and left their villages with the nagging suspicion that more people would die after our departure, as the risk of reinfection was still very high.

It was the first time I had visited the communities of Tucushim and Shikoi and met their inhabitants. There was no common history between us, and it showed. The stares, the distrust, the difficulty in communication—and I don't mean linguistic, but social—were reminiscent of my first encounter with the Sanumá of the upper Auaris. The cold distance that separated me from the Tucushim and Shikoi inhabitants was in stark contrast to the sheer joy of reencountering old acquaintances at the mission, Kadimani, and Olomai. With these people I exchanged memories and new experiences, the young generation were amused with my knowledge of intimate details of their lives, and my overall feeling was that I had returned to the secure ground of a shared past. The memories we had in common gave me a sense of comfortable belonging, and I realized more than ever that I was part of their lives as much as they were part of mine.

November 1993. The advantage of being one's own translator is that the *traduttore, traditore* motto does not apply, or, if it does, is one's own risk and responsibility. In fact, it gives the author-translator the welcome opportunity to rectify errors, to clarify vague ideas, to resolve ambiguities, to introduce updates, and to improve the style. These bonuses more than compensate for the time consumed in translation. As a matter of fact, I don't feel I have translated a book so much as composed a new one. Parts II and III have been substantially changed, and Chapter 11 has been especially written for this edition. What was a standard monograph in the Portuguese version, focusing almost exclusively on the analysis of Sanumá society, has gained an extra breadth with the inclusion of the more recent events that have brought the Yanomami to world attention. While I was away from the field, Western history definitely caught up with the Yanomami.

The title of this book is a double tribute. It is a tribute to the strength of the Yanomami in general and the Sanumá in particular, for their resilience and capacity to endure the most intense hardships without losing their sense of humor. It is also a tribute to that remarkable human capacity that we call memory; that ability to be there without being there, to turn the past into the always already present, to render absence as presence. *Sanumá Memories* encompasses both my remembrances of the Sanumá of my youth and my recalling of these remembrances as I wrote the book. Prohibited to return to the field as a researcher, I tried to grasp the flow of Sanumá life while I was away through reports I collected from missionaries in town. It was my attempt to create memories in the absence of lived experience. But *Sanumá Memories* also means the memories of the Sanumá themselves, then and now, for, after all, every narrative, explanation, or commentary flows from one's memories of things personal and social. When, in the 1990s, Sanumá parents tell their children details of my life among them, they are merging their memories with mine. Bringing back old times is my quasi-Proustian homage to those times as remembered.

Sanumá Memories

Introduction

Sixteen years after finishing my Ph.D. dissertation, I decided to undertake the uneasy task of rewriting it. Drastically changed, it became *Memórias Sanumá*, the 1990 Portuguese version of the present book. Why I did not publish it before is a question with no easy and quick answer, for it takes me to professional and existential landscapes that reach out much further than a mere editorial decision.

The writing of the thesis back in 1971 was hampered with ill feelings and frustration, not only due to erratic interactions with my supervisory committee, but because I had neither the necessary time nor leisure for prolonged thinking over complex ethnographic material. I ended up writing it in the absurd span of two and a half months, defended it in draft form, and rushed off to my first job. In less than a month I moved from the effervescent student ambience of the University of Wisconsin in Madison to the austere surroundings of the National Museum in Rio de Janeiro where I was to spend a year teaching at the recently created graduate program in social anthropology.

Moreover, the theoretical style at that time commended dry and detached analyses of social systems as if life were not lived by flesh and blood human beings. I acceded to it even though my ethnographic data evaded the canons that social life of indigenous lowland South America was supposed to follow. I was not prepared to seek an alternative idiom that might be more appropriate to express unorthodox intricacies. The result was a stiff, arid, and unconvincing piece of work, composed in English, a language that seems to accentuate (more than Portuguese, for instance) the quest for impartiality, favoring a drier and more impersonal tone, especially in kinship studies. In spite of the distance that separates me from that first effort, the central point of the thesis still stands and continues to be part of my understanding of how Sanumá society works. The dissertation was writ-

3

ten on the basis of data collected during the first twenty-three months, between March 1968 and September 1970, of which eighteen months were spent without interruption in Sanumá villages. There were two other short trips to the field, two months in 1973 and two months in 1974, this time to study the intertribal relationships between the Sanumá and their Carib-speaking neighbors, the Maiongong (also known as Yekuana or Makiritare). These field trips resulted in a number of articles and a book, but my reluctance to further explore the Sanumá social system continued.

In all these years I have been gradually refining my field experience. As in a prolonged cooking process in which disparate ingredients are combined with seasoning to produce a harmonious and distinct flavor, I kept my ethnographic data in mental infusion until the time came to either serve them or discard them. What precipitated that crucial moment is one of those *imponderabilia* which we may conjecture about, psychoanalyze, or attribute to pure chance. Be that as it may, the decision to rewrite it was prompted not by a single, outstanding event, but rather by an overdetermination consisting of a number of both internal and external circumstances that came to the surface during many hours of conversation with Bruce Albert and Ken Taylor, two Yanomamologists committed to extracting the long-overdue "Sanumá book" from me. Whether it was white magic or sheer persuasion, the fact is that, almost despite myself, a mental and emotional process was triggered off. It was effective but not exactly painless. Going back to field diaries, interviews, photographs, cards, and other frozen mementos of a very special portion of my life history was like drilling a hole into the past. I had to reconcile myself to the fact that what was will never be again. I had changed and so had the Sanumá, but the most overwhelming change was in social context, as the Yanomami were now under siege from thousands of gold prospectors who were invading their lands in alarmingly increasing numbers.

In the process of rewriting my doctoral dissertation, I often found myself entranced for hours as I read diary after diary in search of some tiny fragment of information to be converted into a strategic detail that would authenticate my analysis. The mixture of pleasure and sadness in this imaginary return to the field had the effect of leaving me paralyzed, blankly facing the text to be written. Since 1987, the Brazilian military had barred all anthropologists from Yanomami territory, as they did not want any witnesses to the disastrous impact the gold rush was having on the Indians. Yet, even if I had been able to return to the area, and live with the Sanumá again, what would it be like to meet them after fifteen years, to face absences caused by death, to see children transformed into grown-ups, to observe how outside influences had changed a cultural face so familiar to me? This ambiguity of memory, this being there without being there, was the spirit that stood with me during the eight months of shaping the first part of the book.

In keeping with the proverbial ethnographic tradition, fieldwork was for me a sort of initiation with its attendant anxieties and revelations. Even at the risk of falling into a hyperbolic heroic romanticism, I might say that my field experience produced some considerable existential reverberations. Twenty-seven months of exposure to a bombardment of drastic otherness had as a perhaps inevitable consequence abandoning a few mental habits, refashioning others, and acquiring new ones. With the Sanumá I learned to admire—albeit not always imitate—their wisdom of taking truths and lies as relative stances; their patience in dealing with children in their worst tantrums; their ability to aim their anger exclusively at its object, thus sparing the rest of the world; and their lavish joy of life and inexhaustible taste for drama. As in a mirror, I saw reflected in the Sanumá my own intolerance when faced with frustrated expectations, impatience with the local slow tempo, irritability with lack of peace and quiet, and, for that matter, alarm over my own reactions. I envied the little girls who, still so culturally unfinished, went about so completely at ease, in charge of the situation, making me see myself as a mere fragment of being. No wonder that *sanima dibi*, i.e., "human beings," are they and only they!

I descended to the bottom of the well of humility and slowly came up again, admiring their subtlety all the more. I was astounded when they confessed that, months before, they had told me simple half truths because, had they told me the whole story, I would have understood nothing. I burst with pride when they complimented me for my progress in language learning, comparing me to a five-year-old child.

Such angles and perspectives of the ethnographic experience undoubtedly become visible only because they are distant. At the time, my greatest wish was to go home, leave behind the exaggerated Sanumá conviviality, and indulge in the luxuries of hot showers and glasses of ice water.

Nevertheless, that is where the so-called ethnographic data come from, data that take on different colors and flavors whether they are worked on as "green," recently picked raw material still stiff with the roughness of what is immediate, or as seasoned witnesses of acts and words that have been steeping in an ongoing, slow process of under-standing. Which leads one to ponder the nature of ethnographic data, painstakingly gathered, wrapped in good and bad memories, prone to apparently inexplicable sublimations, suppressions, and reinter-pretations. The fact that they are *data* ("given") does not mean they are instantly *taken*, if one is not ready to *receive* them. My fieldnotes since 1968 contained precious information on political matters, life and death, puberty, and other topics. Yet, no matter how much I looked at them, they said precious little to me until I was prepared to "read" them. Renato Rosaldo (1980) describes something similar re-garding the endless stream of dull reports that the Ilongots obliged him to record, and which turned out to be central to his ethnography.

My trouble with the data on Sanumá social organization was first to understand what they were "saying," and then to transmit it. Sanumá lineages, for example, have such a tenuous existence that they cannot retain all men and women of that society. What sort of lineages were those that did not fit into anthropological expectations? What reading had I made of the *data* so as to render them so rebellious to ethnological good sense? Moreover, to talk about descent and lin-eages on the South American ethnographic continent, as I had done in my 1972 dissertation, had become synonymous with old-fashioned and theoretically unsophisticated approaches, since over the course of the 1970s, South Americanists struggled for their conceptual de-colonization by declaring their independence particularly from Afri-canist influences.

I crossed that period of turbulence by letting my Sanumá data lie fallow, as it were, without especially changing my original percep-tions. Through the years Sanumá social organization, the untamed shrew that refused to bend to anthropological understanding, began to be domesticated. Finally, its uncertain contours and fragments re-solved themselves in an intelligible configuration. I found myself making forays into the self-conscious meanderings of reflexive an-thropology in order to shift the axis of analysis from the skeletonlike dissertation to the flesh and blood of ethnography. Thus, lived expe-rience acquired as much space in my text as did analytical retro-spection—sometimes more. Sanumá society was no longer a mere ex-cuse for the demonstration of theoretical models. The Sanumá resumed their essence as people, as they had always been in my all-absorbing life in the field. This trajectory of mine, by the way, echoes the trend that Ruth Behar has so perceptively identified.[1]

The text oscillates between synchrony and diachrony due to the fact that its material refers to various moments and passages of time.

The long initial period of twenty-three months in the field, between March 1968 and September 1970, yielded my Ph.D. dissertation. Following two months in 1973, and then two more in 1974, I wrote an updated Portuguese version in 1988–89. In scanning my memory, there were moments when I froze the text into a photographic report and other moments when the span of nearly twenty years set the tone. As a consequence of the alternation between a telescopic and a chronometric stance, the tenses of the narrative shift.

It was harder still to negotiate the 1989 updates without my having returned to the field. These data were collected indirectly, in the town of Boa Vista, during interviews with Donald Borgman, a member of the Unevangelized Fields' Mission (UFM) who has worked among the Sanumá since the mid-sixties. The information he gave me, being secondhand, has a different character from the rest. Yet what he told me has proved extremely useful to elucidate previously perceived tendencies, refute certain possibilities, and provide the analysis with welcome new perspectives. I therefore decided to maintain the body of the text limited to my six years of research, between 1968 and 1974, and place the 1989 data as a counterpoint in notes.

The problem grew more complex with the English translation in 1993. By then the Brazilian government's ban on anthropological work in the Yanomami area had been lifted and I returned as an interpreter for medical teams who were engaged in the difficult task of controlling recurring malaria epidemics. I was back in the field and lived through some of the most dramatic situations facing the Yanomami. I also had the opportunity to witness the effects of over two decades of their contact with non-Indians. Different periods of time are thus presented simultaneously in the same narrative without, I hope, breaking up its flow. Were I to write in the Sanumá language it might be possible to avoid such difficulties, given its fine gradation of actions and verb tenses. In dodging these impasses I have opted to simply alert the reader to the oscillation between past and present tenses. My only justification is that the exercise of memory and retrospection has reasons unknown to realistic reason.

I believe that neither I nor anybody else can transmit to the reader the totality of an ethnographic field experience. A good part of it gets transmuted into subliminal impressions, some things are thoroughly suppressed from memory, and others go on appealing to the senses in such a way as to elude our capacity to put them in writing. On the other hand, to attempt to compress a daily routine of over two years into a few pages is to challenge all laws of both physics and good sense. One has, therefore, to be selective. For the present purpose, I have opted to focus not so much on a day-by-day description of village life as on certain aspects of living with the Sanumá which more aptly bring out the flavor of our ethnographic encounter.

Prefieldwork anxiety that in various ways and degrees attacks every ethnographer turned into a paralyzing migraine when, back in 1968, still deafened by a two-hour flight in a noisy single-engined machine, I stepped out onto the tiny Auaris airstrip that served the UFM mission station. I let myself be led by my field companion, Ken Taylor, to the nearest hammock in the mission guest house as if shrouded in a fog that protected me from dozens of eyes and nearly as many hands that searched for sensorial information about who I was. The missionaries were away, so the Indians were all ours, or rather we were all theirs.

As the months went by, naturally, that initial curiosity diminished, but it never disappeared altogether. There was always an observer about to record our habits and report to neighbors in extensive detail. Never were we "adopted," never did we stop being *setenabi dibi*, or "whites." Though we forever remained foreigners on display, we could also appeal, with few hard feelings, to the convenient fact that we were *tiko dibi*, "others," when we wished to keep a little distance from our hosts. Our meals, which for months had been taken as if onstage before an audience eager for comedy, thus became rather private affairs as a way to preserve ourselves from so much publicity.

When the missionaries returned to Auaris, the Sanumá made it clear that to them not all white interlopers were the same. By exploiting the perceived differences between the missionaries and us, the Sanumá took, or at least tried to take, full advantage of both sides. During the frequent rounds of bargaining for trade goods, one of their most common stratagems was to play white against white by declaring that whoever happened to be absent was always better, always more generous, always more ready to please. When the missionaries resisted an uncertain deal, Sanumá would say that we, anthropologists, were the good ones. In turn, in our presence, they praised the missionaries for their largesse, declaring us *umi*, "stingy," or "mean." Though never uttered as irreparable offenses, such accusations invoked one of the Sanumá key values. To be stingy is to be antisocial, to deny the inviolable reciprocity that governs relationships between people. To breach such reciprocity was to trigger sorcery accusations, or bad feelings, to say the least.

The Sanumá, both men and women, grown-ups and children

alike, are great lovers of trade goods. Among the most prized products of Western factories are glass beads (especially Czech-made) which serve as a yardstick to measure exchange and even sentiments. When I returned to Auaris in 1973 and 1974, amidst effusive professions of welcome, a woman insisted that she had missed me very much, that she cried and cried in longing for me. She then stretched out her hand, demanding beads in exchange for her longing. She had expressed affection and expected recompense. My immediate reaction, as I suppose might have been that of any Westerner who expects to keep friends and business apart, was to play down her claim as no more than a ploy to extract the beads from me. In retrospect, and after having given much thought to the nature of appearances and hidden meanings, I reached the conclusion that, in stark contrast to our ethos that nourishes "uninterested" feelings, that Sanumá woman employed her most cherished symbol of value to convince me that she really was glad to see me again.

Similarly, I learned to reappraise, or rather translate culturally and not simply linguistically, the phrase *iba de pio*, "I want it." Sanumá use the phrase when someone, usually a child, covets something, be it a piece of clothing, a tool, or anything else. As I saw this line played out in context after context, it became clear that these requests were ways of saying: "It is so nice that I want it myself." As Sanumá omit the first notion ("it is so nice") and stress the second ("I want it myself"), I realized how the inverse is so often true in the West, when we voice only the former, but really mean the latter. So much for cultural relativism.

I cannot say that the only motivation the Sanumá had to accept us was the trade goods we carried around like ethnographic passports. A close and prolonged association such as ours generates its own affective dynamics. But, no doubt, our baggage of knives, cloth, pots and pans, and beads contributed a great deal to our acceptance as welcome outsiders. When, in an attempt to do in Rome as the Romans do, Ken decided to fetch our own firewood, we were met with a surprising reaction: instead of approval, the Sanumá frowned, for we were taking away from them an important opportunity for trading. We immediately gave up our attempt at being energetically self-sufficient.

The personal side of human beings engaged with other human beings was never lost on us, with all the subtleties and shades that set personalities apart from each other. There are those people we like, those we prefer to keep at arm's length, and those to whom we are simply indifferent. In this sense, being in the field as a couple showed us how distinct are the ways Sanumá men and women deal with foreigners. While Ken had to go through phases of coping with the mask of bravado put on by certain men from whom he was collecting data, I, working almost exclusively with women, enjoyed the spirit of tranquillity, good humor, and receptivity that most of them transmitted. Having nothing to prove besides being themselves, the women represent the affable, serene, and poised side of Sanumá life. The men, burdened with the onus of having constantly to show competence in hunting, in shamanism, or in visiting rituals, find themselves caught up in existential traps that lead them into implicit as well as explicit virility contests with occasional duels and much anxiety.

An integral part of their vigorously exercised ethos is a taste for both drama and comedy. If I were to select one single trait as the most representative of Sanumá ethos I would promptly evoke their sense of humor, to the point of being tempted to borrow Bakhtin's words for a European trait as displayed in early novels:

> the right not to understand, the right to confuse, to tease, to hyperbolize life; the right to parody others while talking, the right to not be taken literally, not "to be oneself"; the right to live a life in the chronotope of the entr'acte, the chronotope of theatrical space, the right to act life as a comedy and to treat others as actors, the right to rip off masks, the right to rage at others with a primeval . . . rage—and finally, the right to betray to the public a personal life, down to its most private and prurient little secrets. (Bakhtin 1981:163)

Owing to the often excessive Sanumá sense of humor, we developed the strategy of holding interviews with one person at a time. Whenever we tried to have a generalized conversation about any subject on which we were obviously neophytes, it unfailingly turned into a circus of jokes, witty cracks, and puns that said a lot about the comic abilities of the participants, but very little about the topic we wanted to discuss. In both villages where we lived, we had a shelter built for interviews. The interview sessions became part of the village routine and everybody understood their purpose, strategically if not anthropologically speaking. Most of the time we invited people to talk to us in the interview shelter, but there were occasions when the Sanumá spontaneously offered to come for interviews so as to tap one more source of trade goods. Few lasted longer than two hours at a sitting, but they were often repeated many times with people who were especially good at giving us information. Otherwise, every minute in the village or on trips with the Sanumá generated the most varied kinds of "data," often raising new topics for research and for further solitary interviews.

It is worth making a commentary about styles of fieldwork. In the sixties, one often found a cult of the mimetic ethnographer, who tried to insert him or herself into native life by participating in all the appropriate activities: female anthropologists consumed their energies in carrying heavy loads of bitter manioc, while male anthropologists got into emotional crises provoked by the use of hallucinogens, all in the name of a mystical participant observation. I was not surprised, then, when Ken and I were severely criticized during a talk at the University of Durham, England, in the late 1970s, when our conspicuous interview shelters came to the fore. How could we pretend to know that society when we used the formality of interviews instead of throwing ourselves into work in the gardens, into hunting, or into the all-night shamanic seances? Our critics preferred examples of model ethnographers stoically going native, irrefutable demonstrations of the correct way of going to work in the fields of anthropology. It did not occur to anybody to ask about the not so trivial possibility that such physically draining routines might have the effect of blunting ethnographic sense and curiosity.

But, just as everything that changes loses the flavor of being absolute, so the style of fieldwork followed new paths. Between a total immersion and a complete detachment there is space for alternatives. Anthropologists who did their fieldwork in the seventies, judging by some examples from Brazilian ethnography (see, for example, Albert 1985 and Viveiros de Castro 1986), abandoned that mimetic quest to adopt the attitude that, after all, they were there to ask questions and not to produce clumsy imitations of the Indians' actions. Getting involved in some things and distancing themselves from others, ethnographers need not renounce their own being in order to strive to understand the people they are studying. In fact, I suspect the Sanumá specifically and the Yanomami in general would find any attempt on our part to go native, pretending to be what we are not, quite ridiculous.

Strange as it may seem, the styles of ethnographic writing are often the reverse of fieldwork practices: mimetically inclined ethnographers ended up writing extremely impersonal and distant ethnographies, almost exclusively emphasizing formalist analyses (for instance, Christine and Stephen Hugh-Jones's 1979 books); in contrast, ethnographers who explicitly embraced their role as academic researchers produced texts that are much more interactive and interpretive, even when they were inspired by formal analyses such as structuralism.

In my case, I was left with the professional rhetoric of the sixties and the style of fieldwork of the seventies. Neither of these, however, reflects the intensity of interaction I had, as an anthropologist and human being, with those who accepted my company for months on end, in the name of our profession, but also in the spirit of existential experience.

On what sorts of experience do we base ethnographic texts? Whether we are aware of it or not, what happens in the field usually disappears in the very act of capturing the fleeting information and rarely appears in the written text. Behind each cold and impersonal analysis, however, there are situations suffused with emotional innuendos that often serve as impetus to further probing and new queries, but which, due to decorum or to methodological demands, remain invisible to the reader. More often, the moments and ideas which lead to a finished work of anthropology lie, if at all, in the recesses of field diaries. And different circumstances produce different kinds of knowledge. There are, for instance, those writings that are the result of long and painstaking discipline on the part of both the ethnographer and the ethnographed, tied to a specific professional problem and therefore addressed to the initiated. Chapter 2, "Time as Space Organizer," is an example. But there are also other texts which originated in totally unpredictable research situations that yielded rich material by pure chance, such as Chapters 8, "To Hunt a Name," and 9, "A Rumor on Stage."

I confess that my attraction to Sanumá personal names was due to their secrecy, in a typical attitude of savoring forbidden fruit. What I had not anticipated was to find a subtext as unexpected as was the "making of the coccyx." When I first heard the expression my bewilderment was so great that I caused my interlocutor, a very patient woman, to launch into a torrent of repetitions in a tone of voice that got louder and louder as if my problem were merely one of hearing. Baffled to the point of not even knowing how to ask coherent questions, I fumbled my way through the subject matter until, several conversations later, I began to make some sense of what it was to "make the coccyx." At each of my dumbfounded facial expressions, the woman would smile, remove the tobacco wad from her mouth, sigh with a complacent *minaga!* ("just listen," "it's as follows") and try to pierce through the wall of my obtuseness. My memories of that phase, around 1969, bring back the woman's amused expression and my feeling of incompetence and embarrassment for not getting the point. The thing was so completely out of my research expectations and so absent from everything I had read that it took a concentrated effort to see what had been glaring at me all along. Yet none of this appears in the written product, first published in *Ethnology* in 1974. In fact, there is an enormous distance between the lived experience of long hours sitting alone with that woman and with other people poking into the "making of the coccyx," and the finished text, clean of the doubts, frustrations, and confusions strewn along the way of data collecting. But, in spite of my chaotic perception, or because of it, I had more than enough motivation to pursue the subject, not only as a naming procedure, but also as an indicator of relationships between people, nature, and spirits, as spelled out in Chapter 5, "Sanumá Times."

In contrast, regarding "Rumor," all I had to do in the field was literally lie in my hammock and watch the unfolding of a drama, improvised *ma non troppo*, that turned out to reveal some hidden or subdued dimensions of the interaction between the Sanumá and their Carib-speaking neighbors, the Maiongong, and of images of the white man and the outside world. The ease with which the "data" came to me — people would come to tell me the latest development of the rumor — was reflected in the agility with which I wrote the rumor article.[2] Here there were no puzzled grimaces. The rumor was a public affair from the beginning, involving Sanumá, Maiongong, missionaries present and absent, hypothetical whites, and the anthropologists of the moment (my assistant and myself). Willingly or not, all of us were implicated. Directly or indirectly, we contributed to the birth and growth of that interesting monster of intertribal rhetoric. The original article was in part inspired by Lévi-Straussian myth analysis, even though its emphasis was on process rather than on structure. Now it appears in a new cloak. Following the lead of the original paper about the Sanumá taste for drama, I rewrote the piece as a play, something I would not have dared in the seventies.

The second part of the book is a series of three previously published articles that have been substantially rewritten. They highlight the critical role of personal names as elements joining together such diverse social spheres as descent, individual and collective identity, proximity between kin, and beliefs binding together humans, animals, and spirits. Chapters 6 and 7 were originally published in Portuguese (*Anuário Antropológico 76, 77*), while the former also appeared in English under the title "Personal names and social classification in Sanumá (Yanoama) society" (Ramos 1979). Even after the thorough revision I made for the Portuguese version of the book, these two articles were typical representatives of that phase in my life when anthropological austerity was favored at the expense of intersubjective understanding. Personal names were treated as tools for dissecting things social, and as a result, their individual expression appears as a mere accessory to assemble the sociological frame. Even so, these articles represented for me a way out of traditional kinship studies. Common to all three pieces in Part II is the acknowledgment that the Sanumá create concepts and fashion social idioms out of their own actions when they employ, for instance, naming devices as clues to what remains unsaid. Sanumá names, being very private if not even secret, are especially interesting for what they reveal in the very act of hiding. They are an example of what Jacques Derrida (1976) did with concepts that should not be used, and yet cannot be left out; they are indispensable concepts that should be kept *under erasure*. Sanumá personal names are also fundamental for the construction of certain social domains even though they are secluded in privacy. They are, as it were, "crossed out" of the public sphere, yet they reveal this public sphere all the more emphatically precisely because they spill over the private domain.

The third part, with two previously published chapters and a third newly written, examines the interface between Sanumá and non-Sanumá, particularly the Maiongong and whites. Chapter 9, "A Rumor on Stage," thoroughly rewritten, presents the ramifications of a rumor about the imagined death of Sanumá and Maiongong men during a trip home from the town of Boa Vista. It focuses on a well-known leader who was later murdered by whites. Chapter 10, "The Sanumá's Others," handles a politically motivated discussion of the ontological sense of the concept of "Indian." The contrast between ethnic categories as defined by the Sanumá and those originated in the interethnic field dominated by the rhetoric of the whites leads to political, ethical, and moral considerations about what it means to be an "Indian." Both chapters are the result of an intermediary phase when my theoretical interests were more sociological than phenomenological. In turn, Chapter 11 presents the devastating consequences of encroachment by whites upon the Yanomami in general and the Sanumá in particular. It describes the health crises that followed in the wake of a massive gold rush in the 1980s. It is the only chapter I wrote after returning to the field in 1990 and portrays the immense suffering inflicted on the Yanomami for the last twenty years. The Epilogue brings a brief discussion on memory as a region where past and present meet, individual and collective experiences are processed, and interpretations are shaped and reshaped as social time unfolds into history. The title of the book is, therefore, a tribute to this fascinating realm of human imagination.

This book is yet another demonstration that there is no true and definitive description of a people's life (Ramos 1987). More drastic than to compare the work of two or more ethnographers on the same group is to contrast the writings of the same researcher about the same people at different moments of his or her trajectory. Whoever read my doctoral dissertation will probably ask what its author has in common with the author of this book. But I will leave this to any reader who might care to comment.

Part 1
Space and Time

1
Sanumá Spaces

The Guiana shield, watershed of the Orinoco and Amazon basins, is almost entirely covered in tropical rain forest with occasional clearings, small savannas of uncertain origin.[1] From the mountain ridges down to the plains that spread toward the big rivers, the deceptive uniformity of the landscape hides a great variety of natural resources. Although its soil fertility is extremely low, this vast country is ecologically very diversified; each of its levels of altitude has its own specific faunal and floral species. Whereas, for instance, in the uplands of the Parima and Pacaraima ranges the absence of large- and medium-size fish is compensated by a great variety of edible caterpillars, fruits, and nuts found nowhere else, down in the lowlands of the Catrimani and Ajarani Rivers one finds Brazil nut and palm trees that do not exist up in the mountains. Far from being a uniform expanse, to the minimally trained eye the forest displays a rich diversity underneath its great green mantle which seen from an airplane presents itself as endlessly the same.

Throughout the centuries the Yanomami, originally from the Parima range, have spread up toward river valleys on the plains both to the south in Brazil, and to the north in Venezuela. Today their territory covers a 9,500 square kilometer area in Brazil, and nearly 10,000 square kilometers on the Venezuelan side, within a rectangle encompassed between 0 and 5 degrees north, and 61 and 67 degrees west. Of a total population estimated to be around 22,000 people, the Brazilian Yanomami number a little less that 10,000.[2] The Yanomami territory straddles the Brazilian-Venezuelan border in approximately 80 percent of its length (see Map 1).

The Sanumá, who call themselves *sanima dibi* (*sanima*, "people"; *dibi*, "plural, more than two"), speak one of the four known Yanomami languages. Together with the Yanomam, the Yanomami and the Yanam, they constitute the largest indigenous people in the

19

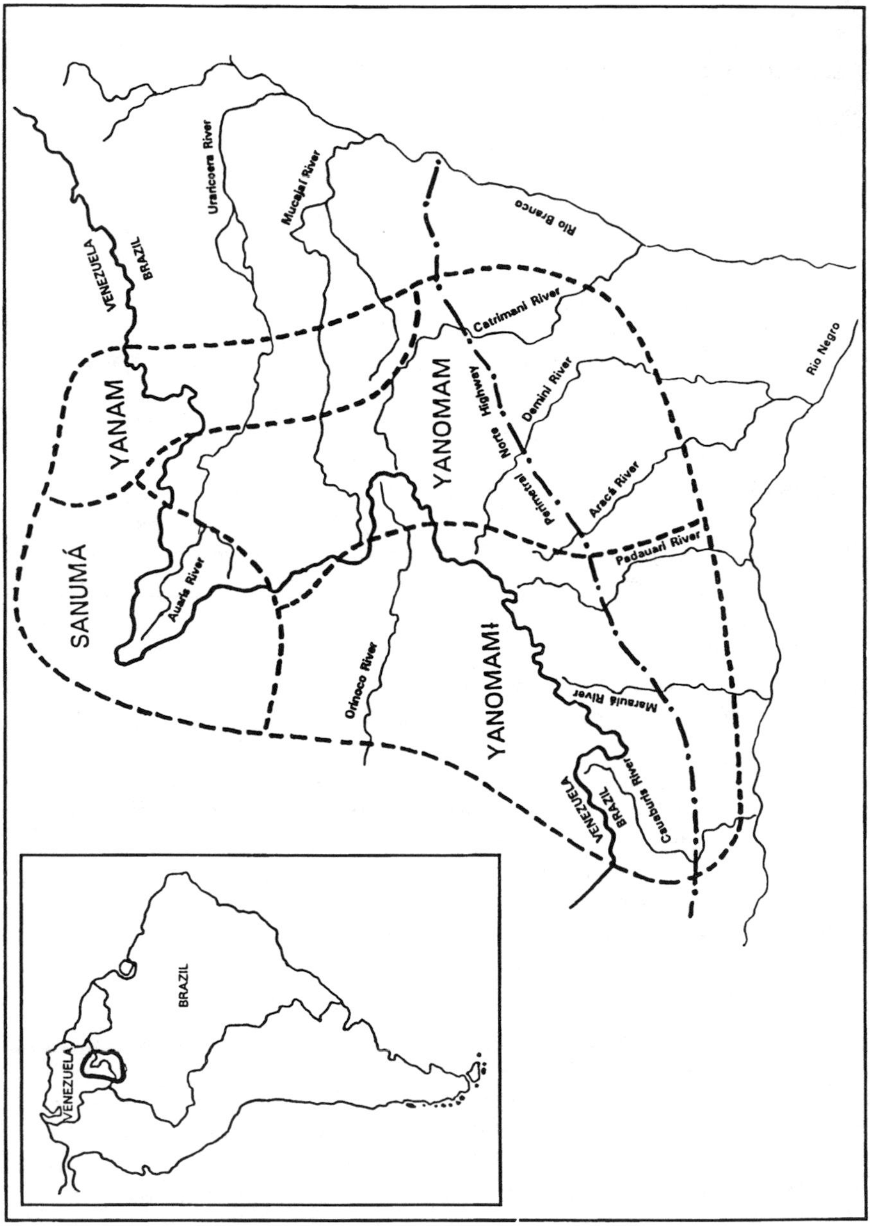

Map 1. Distribution of Yanomami

Americas who still preserve much of their traditions, despite the over-whelming pressures that many of them have suffered from massive invasions since the 1970s, as will be seen in Chapter 11. Mutual intel-ligibility among the four Yanomami languages varies with the dis-tance between them (Migliazza 1972). The closest are Yanomam and Yanomami, the farthest, Sanumá and Yanam. Substantial sociocul-tural variations are by and large associated with language differences. But behind subgroup diversity there is an undeniable family resem-blance that permits their identification as one single ethnic group which we, whites, have agreed to call Yanomami. A linguistic hybrid, the word Yanomami is a blanket term we use to refer to the language family as a whole.

The total Sanumá population is estimated to be 3,200 people lo-cated in the northernmost portion of the Yanomami territory. In Brazil they count between 900 and 1,000 people living in some twenty widely scattered communities, about a quarter of the eighty-eight communities reported for Venezuela (Colchester 1985:7). As the ma-jority of the Yanomami, most Sanumá choose their residence sites on high ground, away from large rivers, which makes travel on foot be-tween communities an exhausting exercise in ups and downs some-times as steep as forty-five degrees or more. Most communities get their water supply from small streams and springs often some dis-tance away from the villages, and it also requires quite a bit of daily effort to carry uphill containers full of water.

In the watershed region of the Parima-Pacaraima ranges, the up-per Auaris River begins its turbulent course strewn with waterfalls and rapids. I did my fieldwork on its banks and tributaries. The alti-tude is about 700 to 800 meters above sea level. The climate is humid, but the temperature is softened by the effect of altitude; during the day it is seldom unbearably hot, not exceeding 86 degrees F, and at night one needs blankets and often a fire in order to sleep comfortably while outside the thermometer can reach 50 to 60 degrees. Variable as it is during the twenty-four hours of the day, the temperature is very stable throughout the year whether in the rainy season (from June to November), or in the dry season (from December to May). Even in the dry season there is hardly a week without a rainstorm, albeit short and mild. It is in the peak of the rainy season, however, that the land-scape changes its face: small crystalline streams turn into vast muddy torrents; the groves where summer camps are set up in the dry season are transformed into immense flood areas impossible to negotiate on foot; unbelievable tangles of vegetation, sheltering wasps, thorns, and beautiful flowers which in the dry season one pierces one's way through in search of frogs, lianas, tiny fish, crabs or grubs become completely submerged. The wide lagoons that result chase away both animals and people. As a consequence of this seasonal variation, natural resources vary a great deal through the year. Certain fruits, nuts, larvae, wasps, and caterpillars are available only during a few months. The *azumato* fruit, for instance, red and sweet, matures in the dry season, whereas the *kasa* caterpillar grows in the dry season through the first months of the rains. Game animals such as the large agouti and capibara rodents are easy prey in the dry season when the streams recede and they come closer to the banks, to the gardens and even to the villages for water. The dry season is the time of abundance, the time for visits, for collective hunting parties, for family camping in the forest, and for ceremonies in memory of the dead.

In joining the Parima River, the Auaris contributes to the birth of the Uraricoera which further down, swollen by a multitude of tributaries, turns into the Rio Branco which feeds into the Rio Negro which in turn flows spectacularly into the Amazon, just a few miles downriver from Manaus. The increasing magnitude of the rivers that follow their southern course toward the Amazon contrasts sharply with the nearly miniature scale of the streams in the headwaters. A profusion of brooks, rivulets, and creeks, often clogged with fallen trees, make up the minibasin of the Auaris River, *ashikamou* for the Sanumá. By Amazonian standards, it is a very modest river, but in Sanumá judgment, it is a magnificent mass of water, especially in the eyes of those who live further away in its headwaters and are accustomed to crossing little streams over fallen tree trunks as improvised bridges. The width of these streams, tributaries of the Auaris, usually does not exceed the span of a canoe's length. Their proportions are comfortable and familiar to the Sanumá way of life; their muddy banks display animal tracks, crab hideouts, signs of raiders, and a whole gamut of clues easily detected by them.

Inscribed in these streams is a geography that is also history. Throughout the months of fieldwork, these creeks appeared constantly during the collecting of genealogies, of people and village moves, or of stories about animals and spirits. It is as though the streams were blood vessels and capillaries which not only supply the Sanumá with water, but provide a mnemonic frame for the practical and symbolic realms of their society. Along these streams people cheerfully catch fish stunned with fish poison, send news from village to village, keep track of old gardens and former residence sites, and maintain a rich topographic history brimming with details and bonds that link the various communities in a common trajectory. Stream names such as Walobiu, Õkobiu, and Kakudu among many others are always present whenever conversations turn to hunting episodes, old gardens, mortuary rituals, or places where someone was born or died.

As important as the streams are the trails that fan out from each village. More direct than the streams, the trails are like conduits of information that the Sanumá discuss on short walks of just a few hours, or on long trips of several days. These are stories about memorable hunts, about encounters with spirits, or about spotting hidden enemies. The trails form a vast and intricate network of paths linking each village with old and new gardens, hunting grounds, gathering and fishing spots, summer camps, and neighboring villages as well as distant ones. They convey, like nerves, all the social pulses that keep the long chain of community relations alive, rendering the isolation and atomization of local groups virtually impossible. Through them social meaning cuts across villages, gardens, the forest, and the supernatural. Trails and streams constitute an elaborate historicized topography, a world of remarkable events as well as ordinary relationships in continuous flux. The resulting pattern reveals at once an underlying permanence and a constant movement played out by the shifting of villages and gardens as well as of friendships and enmities.

The garden, *higali*, is the space of subsistence, but not only that. It is also the outcome of joint work such as felling and burning gigantic trees, and a source of social interaction such as amorous trysts both legitimate and illicit, to mention just one noneconomic activity. The garden is essentially a domesticated space, and even when it lies away from the village, it is an extension of it. Not only is the garden the place where the most reliable, regular, and abundant food is planted, such as manioc, bananas, potatoes, as well as tobacco, it is also where well-defined work relations are most emphatically stated: the men's strength in cutting down the trees, the women's patience in harvesting, the children's fun in their apprenticeship, and the sons-in-law's duties in marriage. Each new garden is like a file one opens anew. In the history of a village the gardens are building stones that demarcate the most meaningful social coordinates of its past and present.

Cleared in a circle and always on slopes, the Sanumá gardens of the upper Auaris region allow for the zoning of crops according to the amount of moisture each plant needs. Cotton bushes are planted right around the houses in the village, on higher ground. Bitter manioc, taking up most of the cleared space in the garden, is planted on its upper levels, for it needs less moisture than banana trees which

Grating manioc. 1974. Photograph by A. G. Oliveira.

occupy the bottom of the field where water accumulates. Midway is an assortment of roots, sugar cane, and tobacco. The latter's leaves are dried in the heat of the domestic fire, then soaked in water, mixed with the fine and sterilized ashes from the center of the hearth, and then shaped into a wad, placed between the lower lip and teeth, and sucked by virtually all adults and older children.

Trees are felled toward the end of the rainy season. After the first weeks of dry weather, the tree trunks and underbrush that have been cut down are sufficiently dry to be burned. A few weeks later planting begins. The hard work of chopping down the trees is usually shared among a group of brothers with the occasional help of a brother-in-law. From then on the women's work is very intense during the burning, planting, weeding, and harvesting phases. Six to twelve months later the bitter manioc is ready to use. Huge conical baskets, *wɨ a*, overflowing with roots, are then carried suspended from the forehead by the women, two or three times a week. Early in the morning they go to the gardens usually in small groups and return hours later bent over by the absurdly heavy load, in an Indian file that fades away as each woman disappears into her home. Washing, peeling, grating, and squeezing the manioc into the wicker press can take a whole day, even when the woman is helped by somebody else, like a young daughter. The cassava bread that results from her labor has been the most regular and reliable staple of the Auaris Sanumá ever since, some five or six generations ago under the influence of their Maiongong neighbors, they began to plant bitter manioc. Also from the Maiongong comes the equipment that is necessary for processing cassava bread—baskets, sieves, grating boards, squeezers—although several Sanumá men have learned to make them, with the exception of grating boards that are still traded with the Maiongong. Manioc has taken over the prominent place that bananas used to have in the Sanumá diet, even though the many varieties of bananas they plant are still widely consumed raw or boiled when ripe, or roasted when green; they still preserve their importance, among cultivated crops, in the ritual meals at mortuary ceremonies. The bone ashes of the deceased are still mixed with banana soup and shared among the living during the funerary rites that take place months after cremation.

One always eats meat with a complement, *di*, which is invariably a garden product, be it cassava or banana. The tortillalike cassava bread, *īshaī*, made in various sizes, is the ever-present staple; children nibble on it at any time of the day, men take it along on their trips, women crumble it into *nushi kõi*, the soothing drink with which guests are welcomed—the jokers compare it to the full moon. Without *īshaī* the liveliest summer camp comes to an end, people gather their belongings and go back home, for lack of *īshaī* means that hunger is in sight.

Some communities also plant arrow canes when soil and terrain conditions permit; many people import them from those who can produce them. Some plants, *alawali*, are also cultivated in the fields for the purpose of making magic substances for a variety of purposes: to make children grow well, to gain a woman's sexual attention, to provoke barrenness in someone's wife, or to cause serious injury to a foe. Each variety of *alawali* has a specific effect. Most people freely admit to planting and using them, except for the most dangerous types, the fearful material that is used by the *õka dibi*, enemies who come from afar and, in the still of the night, surreptitiously hiding in the bush, blow *alawali* powder toward the house or hammock of their victims.

In a couple of years a garden loses much of its productivity. Weeds take over and it is time to open a new field. In a given period of time, a family can have two or three gardens at different stages; an old one, another in full vitality, and a third not yet ripe or even planted. The job of weeding becomes so consuming that it is better to start anew. But there are other advantages in abandoning an old field,

A mature garden. 1973. Photograph by the author.

since the weeds are, in fact, the first signs of forest rejuvenation. First come small thorny bushes; then medium-size trees typical of second-ary growth provide shade for new shoots of the large ones that have not been uprooted, a procedure typical of slash-and-burn horticul-ture. It has been said that in the region of the Guiana shield, the rain forest would take no less than one hundred years to grow back to its original vigor if not reused for gardens during that time, which is what usually happens among the Sanumá.

Strictly speaking, an old garden is not abandoned before a long lapse of time. There is always produce that remains, such as banana trees and peach palm, to which the owners go back year after year. Peach palm takes several years to mature; when it begins to yield fruit, the garden where it was planted has become unrecognizable, entirely choked in weeds and secondary vegetation. Each dry season the Sanumá return to their peach palms, and then, for weeks on end, the houses are filled with red bunches of the oily fruit that is relished by all for its taste and sustenance. Old gardens are also visited by some birds and mammals drawn to the food that is still there; in turn, these animals attract human hunters who have that additional reason to frequent their exhausted fields.

The forest, *uli*, of which the gardens are temporary transforma-tions, is the basis for circumscribing the territory of a village or a vil-lage cluster. The term *uli* carries, among other connotations, that of "home," the place where one belongs; *iba dibi uli a*, "my people's land," is a current expression that communicates the feeling of comfort and coziness proper to what is familiar. It is interesting to notice that the gardens can also be called *uli*, thus suggesting the possibility that the borderline between the wild and cultivated, or, if you will, between nature and culture, is rather porous.

Nevertheless, the familiarity with which the Sanumá regard the jungle, and the ease with which they steer through it, do not entirely conceal the air of mystery that the forest emanates, filled as it is with material and immaterial creatures over which one has precious little control. If even for the Sanumá the forest is a source of fascination, reverence, and awe, imagine what it can be for the ethnographer. A multitude of sensory stimuli confer a very special flavor to life lived so near the forest: the deep and rhythmic call of the *soso* frog as one falls asleep; the shriek songs of the *soloshama* bird or the cacophony of the *caracará* hawk (as it is called in Portuguese) as one wakes up; the melancholy cries of the toucan at sunset; the roaring crash of some giant dead tree that, as it falls, drags along a myriad of vegetation in a vertiginous sweep of branches and foliage; the sound wave that warns of the fast advance of an approaching rainstorm. Scenes, sounds, smells, palpable or imprecise sensations give body and soul to the daily routine of living submerged, as it were, by the forest, and make this living practically impossible to narrate. No matter how absorbed we may be with our routines or with our ethnographic concerns, it is impossible to disregard the jungle which is always there, engulfing our senses.

The forest shelters spirits but also provides food. Hunting, expressly a male domain, can be done individually or in groups, daily or on ritual occasions. Solitary routine hunts, *namo hu*, happen all year round, whereas collective hunting expeditions, *hinomo hu*, are more typically dry season events that involve either men from a single village, or guests and hosts of a mortuary ceremony, *sabonomo*; also frequent in the dry season are camping trips by one family or a group of families, occasions known to the Sanumá as *wazimi*. In the relaxed atmosphere of a summer camp, women and children fish and gather fruits and nuts, while men hunt tapir, wild boar, various kinds of rodents, monkeys, and armadillos, a multitude of birds, and some snakes.

During the normal village routine, a man goes hunting two or three times a week, depending on his success with the catch. If he kills a tapir, there will be no need to go back hunting while the meat lasts; since it is widely distributed through the community, it may last for four or five days. If, however, he kills a small animal, such as an agouti, the meat stays in the hunter's home and in less than two days it has been consumed by his family; soon he will go back for more.

There is a sort of decorum that inhibits the display of a successful hunt, a little like the uneasiness we feel in publicly revealing our income. The Sanumá hunter arrives in the village laden with his prey; if it is small, it comes in a leaf bundle, if large, it is carried bare on his back, exposed to everybody who watches his return home. He walks with a concentrated gait, looking down or straight ahead, enters his house, silently throws the catch on the ground with a look of indifference, and immediately lies down in his hammock. For a few minutes, the people around him also act as if nothing was happening, and then preparations begin for the cooking of the meat. Children, always ready to spread the news, come to tell you in whispers who has killed what. Meat distribution follows well-defined lines of age and kinship (Taylor 1974, 1981).

Garden produce is much more regular and certain than the outcome of hunting. But without meat, no matter how much cassava bread and bananas one may eat, there is hunger of a special kind, *nagi*, that is, "meat hunger," different from the other kind of hunger, *ohi*, a more general feeling of empty stomach. Apparently derived from the word *nag* (tooth), *nagi* reflects the anxiety of long days without meat that makes wives jab at their husbands to pick up weapons and go hunting. When the meat comes, the children exult, chewing morsels with cassava bread, first by the family hearth, and later around the village, exhibiting their bellies with contented remarks about how *piti* (full) they are.

The meat can be boiled and consumed immediately, or it can be smoked. If it is a large animal, such as wild boar, tapir, or several monkeys, the first meal is a portion boiled in plenty of water to provide a much prized broth; the rest is smoked for preservation. After two or three days of sitting over a constant low fire, the pieces of meat are uniformly dark and hardened, for the Sanumá would never tolerate anything resembling a rare steak. This is, by the way, one of the signs of humanity, for only animals eat raw meat; human beings should not consume exceptionally tender, rare, or bloody meat lest they fall ill.[3]

As early as the 1960s, there were already a few shotguns in some Sanumá villages, specially near the mission station. Traditionally, however, ground mammals are hunted with a wide and flat bamboo arrowhead, birds with a bone point, and monkeys with a fine wooden shaft with three deep notches so that it breaks on impact, leaving the tip inside the animal's body and liberating the arrow to be recovered. These tips are covered with the hallucinogen *sakona* which produces muscle relaxation, thus causing the animal to fall to the ground and be easily killed. Whenever there is *curare* poison it is used instead of *sakona*, but being imported through intertribal trading, it is rarely available. In turn, armadillos are driven out of their holes with smoke and hit in their flight.

Hunting dogs are highly desired even though their competence is usually much lower than their owners' expectations. A good dog is a valuable trading item and can be purchased for a precious beaded apron, or for a used shotgun. In ambushing ground animals or in chasing monkeys doped with a *sakona* shot, the dogs are a useful complement to a hunter's skills and weapons. Early in the morning one commonly finds a dog with its head painted with red pigment, for its owner, having spent the night in shamanism, extends to his dog the magic attention that a good hunt deserves. Although not trained for that purpose, each dog seems to specialize in a given game animal. If it turns out to be a good hunter, it is kept reasonably well fed; if not, food will be withdrawn and the dog will starve to death. When a good dog is killed in a hunt it is mourned and cremated like a human being; the bones of the game it killed are hung over the family hearth for some time in its honor. Most Sanumá villages have a considerable number of dogs that usually roam around freely; they are insufficiently trained, host enormous amounts of fleas, and attract bats that suck their blood during the night as they lie on the warm ashes by the fire. At the approach of a stranger, they raise such a noise that the owners themselves have to scream at the top of their voices, throwing anything at hand in the dogs' direction to keep them quiet. Sanumá dogs have the invariable appearance of suffering, scrawny creatures, playthings in the hands of children who use them as targets in their training at arrow shooting. A reluctant dog that refuses to follow its master on a hunt, returning home over and over again, has to be dragged on a vine leash either by the hunter who keeps coaxing it with a friendly voice, or by his wife or a child who pulls it along under its protest. One has the impression that hunting dogs, although an object of desire, are not part of Sanumá tradition, judging by the inefficiency of their training and by the quantity of animals that die of neglect.

Other factors that count for the greater or lesser abundance of game meat are the nature of the terrain and the variety of ecological niches in a given hunting territory; the size of the community; and the length of its residence in the same place. A large concentration of people in one single site for a long time inevitably leads to scarcity of game, and it is one of the reasons why villages are relocated.

The considerable importance of the gathering of forest products is not obvious at first sight. Less spectacular than a good hunt carried on a man's back, or an oversize basketful of manioc hanging from a woman's forehead, small delicacies such as *nabi*, a larva that grows in rotten palm tree trunks, honey combs, caterpillars, frogs, fruits of various kinds, nuts, and other edibles can be eaten right away in the forest, or taken home wrapped up in modest bundles. They are regular enough to make a significant contribution to the supply of vitamins, protein, and mineral salts, as well as to provide a welcome variety in the diet. Palm fruits—some five or six varieties—in season are brought home in vast quantities several days a week. Gathering can be combined with short fishing trips by groups of women, groups of men, or by married couples. They often leave the well-trodden paths to exploit some portion of the forest where even Sanumá can get temporarily lost. All the while they talk in a light conversational tone, stopping to pick materials such as vines for basket making.

The fact that the course of the Auaris River is interrupted in several places by high waterfalls means that its upper portion has no big or medium-size fish. That is why fishing is less important for the Sanumá of that region than for other communities downriver. The small fish that exist are caught with hook and line, and in the dry season with the stunning *shilo shilo toto* vine. This vine (*timbó* in Portuguese, *barbasco* in Spanish), the thickness of a medium-size tree, is cut up in chunks, tied up in bundles, and pounded with wooden mallets on a rock in the stream. The milky liquid that exudes from the mush trickles into the water and gets to the fish that become temporarily asphyxiated; the fish that are not caught will eventually recover. This type of fishing is done at the peak of the dry season in small streams and inlets. No traps or nets are used. When the fish are immobilized they are collected in improvised baskets made on the spot. The spectacle of an entire village, men, women, children of all ages, baskets in hand, wading about in a great torrent of shouts, exclamations, trippings, falls, and laughter is one of my most vivid memories of the field.[4]

It is no surprise that the Sanumá have a sexual division of labor according to which men do the hunting and garden clearing, and women grate manioc, spin cotton, and make the *wi a* baskets. What is surprising is the flexibility with which most activities we would call economic pass fluidly from male to female hands and vice versa. Both

Dry season fishing with stunning vine. 1973. Photograph by K. I. Taylor.

sexes work in the gardens, fish, gather, and make hammocks and baskets. Domestic chores, such as fetching water or firewood, are more women's than men's, but it is not uncommon to see men cooking, babysitting all day long, chopping wood, and, albeit rarely and reluctantly, baking cassava bread or getting water when their women cannot do it.

As for age, there is a smooth gradation in the things children can and must do. Just before puberty, boys and girls are totally free to play together. Although girls are required to take care of younger siblings more often than boys, this does not keep them away from the other children. Rather than unfinished human beings with segregated spaces and activities as in the world of most whites, Sanumá children are miniature adults who very early acquire basic skills, such as handling fire without getting burned, or knives without getting cut. It is common to see women arriving from the fields with their overflowing baskets followed by a little daughter carrying her mini-*wɨa* with a few bananas, some manioc roots, or a couple of sticks of firewood. In turn, fathers help their sons make toy bows and arrows with which they practice their aim. On occasion an eight-year-old boy shoots a little bird, cooks it in the family hearth, and can hardly disguise his pride in the feat. When they reach adulthood young people have few mysteries of daily life to unveil. Although the cultural learning goes on through old age, the efficiency that is necessary to survive is acquired in the first ten years of one's life.

The Communities

Of the entire valley of the Auaris River, I got to know the seven Sanumá communities that in the 1970s occupied its upper course. In the region of the lower Auaris there is a cluster of villages known as Shikoi. Based on reports from some of their relatives who lived in Auaris, we estimated that they lived in four communities.[5] Apart from the seven communities of the upper Auaris, I collected information from another village—known then as the Mamugula people—on the Metacuni River, in Venezuela. Although we never visited them for lack of visas to cross the border, they came to us, regular visitors to the Kadimani village where we spent half of our first stay in the field. On a specific occasion, the entire Mamugula community spent several weeks at Kadimani, which gave us the opportunity to interact with them as intensely as did our hosts.

I use *community* to mean the group of people who share the same residence site, and *village* the combination of residence site and dwellings occupied by those people. The communities for which I collected census and demographic data can be grouped into two blocks. The first consists of the Sanumá communities of Mosonawa, Kalioko, what is here called "Colony" (Ramos 1980), and Sabuli, as well as a Maiongong community of about sixty people in 1974. Except for Sabuli, all the others were located around the mission station of the Unevangelized Fields' Mission. The rather odd term Colony refers to the community comprising the offspring and aggregates of two inter-tribal couples, two Maiongong brothers and their Sanumá wives.

The second block contains villages located on three right-hand side tributaries of the Auaris River, known as Lalawa, Kadimani, and Sogosi; part of this block is the Venezuelan community of Mamugula (see Map 2).

In 1970, the Sanumá population of these communities was as given in Table 1.1. Add to these figures 12 Sanumá who lived in the Colony and the total goes up to 296. It should be made clear that the children of the Sanumá women married to Maiongong are considered to be Maiongong, according to Sanumá patrilineal reckoning (Ramos 1980).

The data refer to the period between 1968 and 1970. On later trips (February–March 1973, January–March 1974), the communities around the mission station were revisited. Changes in their demo-

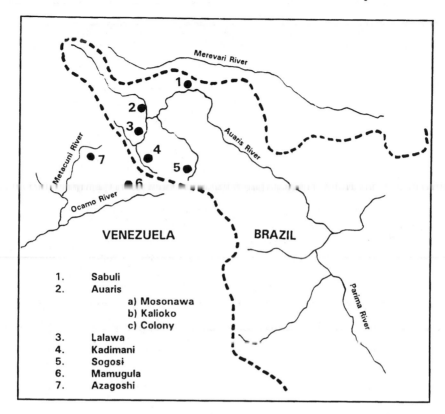

Map 2. Distribution of Sanumá villages studied

graphic composition in the intervening years were mainly due to births and to the incorporation of two young men in search of wives.

By 1974 the whole Kalioko community had moved to a site on the right bank of the Auaris River about four hours by canoe downriver from the mission station. While it was still in Auaris, it was housed in one single long building divided into family compartments; but at the new site the families were distributed through three separate houses, each headed by a mature couple. There were forty-three people in all, twenty-four men and nineteen women, just about the same as in 1970.

Two villages that had previously been on the Venezuelan side—Azagoshi and Mamugula—had crossed the border into Brazil. In 1974, Azagoshi, which had been several days' walk southwest of Auaris, was now about forty-five minutes upstream from the mission. Mamugula was now by the Walobiu stream, near the old site of the Kadimani village, which, in turn, was located on the bank of the

Table 1.1. Sanumá population of the upper Auaris River valley

Community	Men	Women	Total
Kadimani	27	25	52
Sogosi	26	15	41
Mamugula	14	19	33
Lalawa	28	20	48
Sabuli	23	19	42
Mosonawa	20	20	40
Kalioko	20	20	40
Total	151	133	284

Walobiu, closer to its mouth; in 1968–70, Kadimani was built on a magnificent hilltop from which we could see the mountains that divide the two countries. Finally, by 1974, Lalawa had moved from its location on the Kisinabiu stream to the region of the Kakudu stream near its mouth on the Auaris River, below the site of the Sabuli village.

In 1974, visitors from Kadimani told me that various people had died at Kadimani and Lalawa, among whom was a young man we had known as a teenager, recently married and with a baby. His father, a resident of Kadimani, was spending his mourning phase at the community of Mosonawa, busy with preparations for ceremonials in memory of his son.

The researcher who returns after years of absence is astonished each time, bombarded with the bustle of people's movements, changes of residence, deaths and births. They are the same Sanumá, yet different. One is left with a mixed feeling of dynamism and déjà vu.

None of the Sanumá villages of the upper Auaris has the shape of the well-known Yanomami communal houses shown in films and books. They lack the grandiosity of the huge closed conical Yanomam *yano*, or of the doughnutlike rings of the Yanomami *shabono*. Quite the opposite, Sanumá villages are usually made up of several modest rectangular constructions, scattered about in a casual arrangement with no apparent orientation. There is no central inner plaza like those of the Yanomam and Yanomami. Mortuary rites, heated arguments, great shamanistic sessions, interfamily and intercommunity debates, duels, and much of the children's games occur outdoors in a somewhat undefined space turned into a plaza by human activity rather than by physical markers.

When seen in the light of the splendid houses of other Yanomami groups, Sanumá villages give the impression of architectural poverty.

However, the concept of village can become quite complex if we pay attention to the language that reveals dimensions which are hidden in that material humbleness. While the Sanumá term for "house" is *sai a*, in Yanomam it is *yano*, and in Yanomami, *shabono*. A simple exercise in morphophonemics shows that the three words are closely related (the Sanumá initial *s* becomes *y* or *sh* in the other two languages). None of these words has its meaning restricted to the mere physical building; each one of them has a much denser semantic texture, rendering the Yanomami "houses" as true social and symbolic microcosms. Both the *yano* and the *shabono* are round, communal houses with hearths all around their inner walls, and a central plaza where *reahu*, the mortuary ceremonials, are performed (Albert 1985; Lizot 1975). For the Sanumá, who have no such houses, the term *sabonomo* (the suffix *-mo* turns a noun into a verb, hence "to make like *sabono*") corresponds to *reahu*, but its morphology is closely related to *shabono*. We can then see that even though the Sanumá term *sai a* does not in and of itself define a ritual space, such a space does exist conceptually. What is missing in terms of architecture is present in terms of concept: *sabonomo* is the Sanumá ritual activity equivalent to what takes place within the appropriate space indicated by the Yanomami word *shabono*, and the Yanomam *yano*.[6] With some variations, the ceremonies in memory of the dead have basically the same structure in all three Yanomami subgroups. We might say that, even without an inner plaza surrounded by round walls, the Sanumá conceive of their major ritual—the *sabonomo*—in terms of a spatial arrangement that, if no longer part of their lives, lets itself be envisioned in the symbolic realm of sacredness.

Regardless of what shape the houses may have, what matters is to point out that, above all, they are entities that are socially conceived and lived. Through the years the appearance, location, and composition of the houses change as the materials wear out, people come and go, and social relations flow along the life cycle of individuals and groups. During the twenty-seven months of my stay in the field, there were many transformations in the villages where I worked. From one trip to the next some houses had been moved, others abandoned, still others enlarged or newly built. A telltale clue, the soot that sticks to the thatched roofs, gives away the age of a house where family fires are always burning. In some villages the contrast between the green leaves of new roofs and the blackness of old ones testifies to the endless moving from one house to another. Sometimes the move is a shift of just a few yards, other times it means hours or days of walking or paddling when new gardens are opened very far

from the village, leading their owners to make new houses near the
new clearing. For instance, when we first visited the community of
Lalawa, in June 1969, there was an unusual five-walled house with a
pyramidlike roof, vaguely similar to the Yanomam conical houses and
already blackened with soot. Two months later, it had been torn
down and replaced with a rectangular construction like the others in
the village. In 1974, the Lalawa people had moved away to another
site, and were going through a realignment in their internal relations,
as one of their segments had broken off, at least temporarily.

Villages move for various reasons, the main one being the search
for a site with a greater yielding capacity. If a community stays in the
same place for too long, hunting becomes increasingly difficult, and
the growing distance between houses and gardens impractical. It is
better to erect a brand-new village somewhere else than subject
people to arduously long journeys just to get meat, raw materials, or
garden produce. But people also move for social and political reasons.
When the first signs of fissioning within a community begin to appear, normally one of the splinter groups moves away and creates its
own village not very far from its previous site. Social and ecological
dynamics thus guarantees that large tracts of land which at first sight
may seem untouched or empty are entirely occupied. There is virtually no stretch of forest in the Auaris valley that is unknown to most
Sanumá in Brazil.

House-building materials are wood for the frame and walls, and
thatch for the roof and, occasionally, also for the walls. There is a difference between the leaves used in village houses and those used in
temporary shelters. For the village houses the appropriate roof material comes from certain palm trees that can last for years, whereas for
camping shelters other kinds of less durable leaves are used, keeping
off the rain for no longer than two or three weeks. Many houses have
walls made of slats of a palm tree with aerial roots (*managa* in Sanumá,
paxiuba in Portuguese), a few have mud walls, and still others have no
walls at all.

The distribution of the families in a village house is basically the
same as in the summer camps. The shelters are put up according to a
plan that replicates the family dwelling arrangements. Once the site is
chosen, very often the same as in previous years, the shelters are
erected in less than an hour; first the triangular frame, extremely
simple and efficient, then the roofing leaves thrown over without
much care, secured with sticks and stones, and the shelters are ready
for occupancy. At these camps hunting, gathering, and fishing are
dramatically intensified; there is not a single day without meat, fish,

fruits, nuts, or honey. A strong reason to cut short a camping trip is shortage of cassava bread that is brought along from the village. For that reason, a summer camp may last some ten days, but not much longer.

Even in the dry season rainstorms are not unusual, flooding the shelters and making people crowd around the few dry spots that are left under the leaking roofs. Children in particular turn discomfort into amusement. With much shivering and teeth chattering they enjoy dramatizing the sensation of cold that seeps up from the soaked ground and down from the dripping trees. In contrast, those who are caught in the forest during a downpour are usually very stoic in braving the elements, putting up with the enveloping wetness without complaints. The same gestures of tightening the muscles in reaction to the cold air are made every morning in the village when people timidly begin their daily routine in the chilly mist that covers the upland communities.

The hearth is a family's physical and symbolic center. Arranged in a converging pattern like the spokes of a wheel, the family fires are voracious consumers of energy, requiring daily loads of firewood taken home in small pieces piled up in the women's baskets, or as logs carried on the men's shoulders. Everything indoors smells of smoke; whatever is hanging from the rafters or close to the center of the hearth for a period of time acquires a shiny dark veneer from the continuous billows. Over the fire hang animal bones from good hunts, tobacco leaves, small pieces of the magic *alawali* roots, and small bundles of red paint. Around the fire hammocks are tied from the house posts, usually in an array of sizes, levels, and angles, and soiled with a mixture of smoke and red paint that comes off people's bodies. Along the walls there are baskets, suitcases, sacks, clothes, bows and arrows, and other gear in a methodical jumble that confers on each family hearth an air of domesticity and coziness. This atmosphere is typical of the village households and is never developed in the forest camps owing to their improvised and temporary character.

The Family Spaces

Each house can have from one to six family compartments, indicated by the central hearth around which the hammocks are tied. If the family is large, the immediate space contained within the quadrangle around the fire is not enough for all the hammocks; in that case, extra hammocks are arranged in several layers to accommodate sons, sons-in-law, grandchildren, and, from time to time, guests. The position of

Childless couples usually sleep in the same hammock. 1973. Photograph by K. I. Taylor.

the hammocks is not random. In a very full compartment, the husband's hammock is above the wife's. Mothers sleep with infants, and other children hang their hammocks above their mother's, lengthwise or diagonally. A man's co-wives sleep on opposite sides of the fire; if they are neither mother and daughter nor sisters they tend to avoid each other. Low-hanging hammocks are usually women's who are charged with keeping the fire burning all night; the cadence of a sequence of fans moving to and fro at regular intervals is one of the most distinctive sounds of the Sanumá nights. At times, when the fire is low and the cold is biting, a man slides down from his hammock, perks up the fire, and squats for some minutes rubbing his limbs and chest before going back to the hammock for another bout of sleep.

Married daughters who are still childless usually sleep in the same hammock as their husbands, but after the birth of a baby, mother and child are left to sleep alone, and the husband moves up. If at all possible, a son-in-law ties his hammock across the fire from his mother-in-law; if both happen to be at home, he turns his back to her even if he has to face the wall for hours, for theirs is a strictly observed avoidance relationship. It is the man who moves out upon marriage to live with the wife's relatives. More often than not, he moves out of his village to find a wife. In this way, practically every

Sanumá man has experienced the discomfort of the silent and distanced cohabitation with his mother-in-law.

The hammock is the most versatile and essential piece of equipment a person owns. It works as bed, as table, and as a retreat for privacy; since only animals sleep on the ground, it is also a marker of humanity. If a hunter is caught in the forest after dark, he will look for vines for a makeshift hammock. In such circumstances it is much more critical to have a hammock than to have a fire. I do not think it is a mere coincidence that the verb *pili* designates both "to lie in the hammock" and "to live," to have a domicile.

Family groups, which we may call domestic groups, vary in size and composition, according to the stages of the family developmental cycle. If we pick one moment from this cycle, corresponding to the time of my fieldwork, for instance, we perceive an assortment of domestic groups ranging from conjugal families of husband, wife, and single children to large extended families of grandparents, parents, married children, single children, and grandchildren. Of the 47 Sanumá domestic groups that are part of the universe of my 1968–70 study, the majority (17) consisted of conjugal families, followed by extended families (14) and polygynous families (11). The remainder were couples without children and other unusual arrangements. In most extended families—that is, middle-aged couples with married children with or without grandchildren—the incoming spouses are men rather than women. Preference for uxorilocality is demonstrated by the high percentage (76 percent) of cases, as opposed to virilocality (24 percent).

The slice of time that reveals these "types" of families also discloses a dynamic process by which new domestic groups come to replace older ones as the generations go by.[7] Let us begin with the bride service duties, *suhamo*, that compel a man, often just after puberty, to live with his wife's parents. Child betrothal is common and may result in a long period of *suhamo*, depending on the bride's age and on the groom's patience to wait for the girl's maturation to consummate the marriage, that is, about six months after her puberty rite of seclusion. According to a son-in-law's version, bride service comes to an end with the birth of their second to fourth child, but in the eyes of a mother-in-law, bride service is forever. Actually, it may last as long as twenty years, even according to the male version, if the bride is a young child at the time the marriage was contracted, and considering that when she grows up and has children, the gap between births is about three years. During the *suhamo* period, the man has to provide goods and services to his parents-in-law and sometimes to his brothers-in-law as well. If he comes from a distant village, there is a tendency for his in-laws to exploit him. He must observe a rigorous avoidance toward his wife's parents and their siblings, and become familiarized with his new environment, particularly with regard to new hunting, gathering, and fishing grounds. While his wife is completely at ease among her own relatives, he comes in as a vulnerable outsider at the mercy of his in-laws' tempers, at least for the first years of his *suhamo* phase.

Once the expected number of children are born, theoretically and according to his own version, the husband is free to take his family wherever he wants. If he leaves his in-laws' house for a home of his own, he will become the head of a new conjugal family, or, if he acquires a second wife without a new period of bride service (in the cases of orphaned or divorced women), he will have a polygynous family. When his children grow up, the boys will leave to do their own *suhamo*, while at least one of his daughters will attract a son-in-law to do bride service for him. When his daughters have children, he will become the head of a new extended family until the younger couples move away, if at all, or the older generation dies out.

If the daughters and sons-in-law go away, and all there is left of the once extended family is a widow or widower (most often the former), this elderly parent will usually move to the house of one of his or her adult sons or daughters, who will then take care of him or her. Of the forty-seven domestic groups studied, three widows and one widower were living with their sons' families.

The general outline of the developmental cycle of the domestic group does not, of course, display unusual arrangements resulting from specific situations that induce a person to live in rather unorthodox ways, as, for instance, a divorced man who has not remarried and lives with a sister, a young mother without a husband who lives with a brother, or a child who lives with his mother's husband who is not his own father. In the communities I have known we find examples of all these situations in a wide range of possibilities that go beyond any attempt to confine them into rigid types.

Around the Communities

The farther away people are in physical space, the more distant their mutual relationships are. Such banality is no less true for the Sanumá. For example, their interaction with most of the other Yanomami subgroups is infinitely less intense than with the Carib-speaking Maiongong, in spite of the fact that the latter belong to a totally different cultural tradition and have had no historical ties with the Sanumá until about a century ago (Ramos 1980).

In the Sanumá subgroup itself, contacts are very regular within the community cluster of the upper Auaris River, especially between Mosonawa, Kalioko, Sabuli, and less so with Lalawa. Until 1973, the latter was in an intermediate position both geographically and socially between the mission communities and Kadimani, with habitual visits to all of them. In turn, the Kadimani villagers visited Auaris only sporadically, and vice versa, although news went constantly back and forth between them via Lalawa.

A geographic distinction in visiting patterns was easily perceived.[8] While Sabuli and the mission communities kept close contacts with the villages of the Merevari River in Venezuela north of the international border, the people of Lalawa and Kadimani frequented the Sanumá villages sprawled along the Ocamo and Cuntinamo Rivers to the south, southeast, and southwest, also in Venezuela (see Map 1). People who lived so far away from Auaris that they were not even mentioned were regular visitors to Kadimani. While in Auaris we often heard about the Kobali as wild people living to the south, including the Kadimani dwellers. But, as we reached Kadimani, the Kobali line had moved southward and no one admitted to being Kobali. There are thus indications that, at least in that region, Kobali may be a diffuse and slightly derogatory term used to refer to regional clusters of distant villages to the south rather than to specific villages. Smole (1976), who identifies as *cobari* seven communities on the upper Ocamo River in Venezuela just to the south of the Sanumá territory, does not, however, indicate which of the four Yanomami languages they speak.

Despite the large number of dialects that crop up from virtually every valley, there is a high degree of intelligibility among them and even among the four Yanomami languages. This results in a partial multilingualism in which it is possible to understand other languages and dialects and be understood without having to speak them. Such dialectal wealth injects alternative words and expressions into the lexicon of each community, with apparently identical meanings to those already existing. Among other things, this phenomenon created much confusion for the ethnographer. When I had incorporated kinship terms such as *nagai* (daughter, younger sister) and *pɨzai* (son, younger brother), suddenly I began to hear *notai* and *potai* which meant the same thing. I was told that these terms were used by the *oshigatali* people, an agnatic group originally from the Shikoi cluster to the south who were now at Auaris. The same occurred to *hiliwi*, apparently a synonym of *soli* (brother-in-law), and *pehekiamaba*, used by a young woman to refer to the son of her older half-brother; she added that she was *gili* (ashamed, afraid) of that youth, which makes *pehekiamaba* a probable equivalent of *sizo* (nephew), the term with which I had been familiar. Words such as *wazimi*, long family journeys, can also take different forms, such as *washimi*, which seems to be used in the Ventuari region, on the Venezuelan side of the border (Colchester 1982).

Dialectal variation can also serve as a topic in children's games. During the habitual evening gatherings of children around the ethnographers' hearth, one of their favorite games was to insert burning twigs in their own mouths so as to produce the sinister effect of a lit-up skull (like a Halloween pumpkin). Another game was to imitate the accent of Sanumá people such as the distant Hogomawa, or the Samatali, with infallible bursts of collective laughter.

Part of the Yanomami linguistic richness comes from the ceremonial dialogues. Intercommunity contexts par excellence, they are performed whenever agonistic relationships between villages come to the fore, sometimes dramatically expressed. They usually occur when visitors arrive.

The term *hama de* (visitor) is one of the most constant words in Sanumá conversations. Visits between villages are continuous, but the term *hama de* is hardly applicable to neighboring villagers with whom contact is very intense. They simply arrive, quietly settle down around a familiar hearth, and are virtually ignored for a few minutes, until a local woman brings them the much appreciated *nashi kōi* (water thickened with crumbled cassava bread).

In stark contrast to the ease shown at the arrival of nearby friends, visitors from villages that are distant both in geography and in social relations are received with varying degrees of commotion. A ritualized confrontation is acted out as soon as these visitors reach the village. Hosts express their disapproval through a spokesman chosen at the spur of the moment for his verbal skills and political experience. In the vocal duel that ensues, the hosts accuse the guests of perhaps conspiring to attack them; the guests, in turn, also through a representative, declare their peaceful intentions. All this is delivered in a style that is appropriate for the occasion, a sort of chanted harangue, one man at a time. Later, from sunset to dawn, the night is filled with the chants of pairs of men—always a host and a guest—who, in succession, perform their dialogues to a half-sleeping village. At first, the pairs stand up holding bow and arrows, taking turns to speak. A while later the pattern changes; the men squat facing each other, entwined as in an embrace, crisscrossing each other's speeches in the typical rhythms of the *wazamo*, the ceremonial dialogues that are a combination of exchange of news and plans for trading. The language of the *wazamo* is highly stylized, spoken in a series of interlocked staccatos: for every two syllables of a speaker, his opponent interjects two others, and so on until the end of the dialogue. It is a common Yanomami trait (Migliazza 1972; Albert 1985), although other types of ceremonial dialogues are practiced throughout Amazonia.[9]

Only men perform *wazamo*, but they do it almost invariably under the eyes and comments of the women, who often themselves engage in heated soliloquies inciting their men to get the best they can out of verbal battles. With an ear turned to his opponent and the other to the woman's diatribe, a *wazamo* actor puts his capacity for concentration and competition to the test. A successful political argument or a good economic deal may depend on a man's ability to defeat his adversary on the sheer strength of his theatrical skills at ceremonial dialogues. Training in *wazamo* begins in childhood, but full expertise is achieved only in maturity. A man of prestige is good in shamanism, in persuasive rhetoric, and in the arts of *wazamo*.

Exchange is of the utmost importance not only for the Sanumá but for the rest of the Yanomami and other Amazonian groups. Long journeys are taken through the forest with the main purpose of trading objects and news, two items that usually go together. Such visits seldom last longer than five days when done by individuals or groups of men. But when a whole family goes on a visit to another village, on *wazimi* trips, they stay much longer. *Wazimi* journeys are common when a family has an excess of garden produce and invites kith and kin from elsewhere to come and help consume the food. The Sanumá expression *iba nimi bi dibi*, which we might clumsily translate as "my co-eaters," exemplifies the importance of eating together to tighten intrafamily links. One is reminded of Weber's *communio* (1978:423), the "ceremony of eating together that serves to produce a brotherly community between the sacrificers and the god." Here we would have that same effect due not to the practice of sacrifice but to the conviviality and complicity generated by the act of eating together.

Ceremonies for the dead—*sabonomo*—attract great numbers of guests from nearby and from afar. Lasting about ten days to two weeks, they include group hunts of guests and hosts, a lot of dancing, shamanism, generalized weeping, and games of various kinds, some of which carry sexual undercurrents. The climax of the *sabonomo* is the drinking of ashes of the deceased's bones, which, following cremation, have been sealed in a calabash, waiting for the ceremony. The bone ashes are mixed with banana mush and drunk by close relatives, such as the deceased's mother, father, spouse, and all those to whom he or she was closely related. The moment of passing the bowl around is very solemn, and until the last drop of the ritual mixture is consumed, everyone's countenance remains grave and concentrated. Partaking of the bone ashes appeases the ghost and makes the living tough and fearless, *waithili.* Much worse than leaving a corpse abandoned to rot is to have the deceased's remains consumed by enemies, a possibility that induces horror in the dead person's relatives. The ashes are harbored with great zeal.

On the day of departure, guests and hosts engage in lively exchange. Indigenous objects and Western goods change hands in a succession of trading sessions; in a short time those goods will be channeled out of the villages from where they came into the vast network of Yanomami trading and beyond. Along with goods, many plans for future trading are exchanged, credits and debts are rearranged, and further transactions are guaranteed. After long hours of negotiations, the guests tie up their luggage in carrying baskets already filled with meat and cassava bread, and, with no gestures of farewell, they walk out of the village in segments that will be fused into one long file moving along the trails or, alternatively, filling up canoes to overflow capacity. The silence they leave behind, typical of a "party's over" atmosphere, is also a welcome change after days and nights of continuous agitation.

Amidst the images of violence and war attributed to Yanomami by some ethnographers (Chagnon 1968, 1988; Biocca 1971; Lizot 1976), the Sanumá never gave us reason to stress it over any other aspect of their lives. During all the months I spent with them, there was not a single case of raiding in the upper Auaris region. This does not mean that there are no armed conflicts. In October 1970, just after we had left the area, we learned from the missionary Donald Borgman that some Sanumá of the Mosonawa, Lalawa, and Azagoshi communities had attacked and killed four people of a Kobali group. That was done in retaliation for the death of an Azagoshi woman whose fate was diagnosed as the result of the killing of her animal spirit, *nonoshi,* by the Kobali group in question. We had no further news of counterattacks or of any other raids.[10]

Sanumá men, with a history of war against the Maiongong, as the Sanumá advanced into the latter's territory, maintain a lively rhetoric of courage and bravado. But, at least in their case, there is a long way from rhetoric to practice. Occasionally, a hunter returns home in a state of inpurity for advertently or inadvertently having killed someone's *nonoshi*. He will then be committed to a purifying confinement, *kanenemo*. As the *nonoshi* animals are always very far away from their human counterparts (Ramos 1986), retaliations for this sort of killing are very rare. When we collect genealogies we find a certain recurrence of deaths caused by raiding. Recounted many years after the fact, these cases cannot be empirically checked, but, at any rate, they signal the difficulties the Sanumá had in their gradual migrations from the south to their present territory. Running away from enemies in pursuit is one of the most common themes in the reports about the moving of entire villages fanning out from their original sites. Along the way, former co-villagers, now living in separate communities, became partners in political, economic, and marriage transactions. One result of this moving-and-splitting is that homicides and serious conflicts are very rare among the communities that make up the village clusters of the upper Auaris. They are, after all, former companions in premigration times.

Quarrels, fights, and misunderstandings are frequent, but they are usually resolved simply with a bout of heated argumentation; at the worst, they are settled with stick or machete duels that leave behind no more than a few cuts and bruises to testify to the Sanumá taste for public drama. Such episodes can happen both within a community and between neighboring communities. The reasons may be as varied as a quarrel between spouses, adultery or theft accusations, libel against a shaman, or a duel between a son-in-law and his mother-in-law, usually at the end of a marriage. One never accuses his immediate neighbors of sorcery, even if gossip attributes to dwellers in the same or a neighboring village the use of magic substances to cause minor misfortunes, such as the incapacity of a woman to have children of both sexes, or the tendency of a wife to indulge in extramarital affairs.

A closer look at village life may help one visualize what it is like to be around the Sanumá in their own element. I shall then describe the two places where I spent most of my research time: Auaris at the mission, and Kadimani. The twenty-three months of fieldwork between March 1968 and September 1970 were divided in roughly equal parts between them. Two months in 1973 and two further months in 1974 were spent around the mission.

Auaris

Since the mid-sixties Auaris has been the site of one of three mission stations of the Unevangelized Fields' Mission in Yanomami territory.[11] It is located on the right bank of the upper Auaris River, some 450 kilometers northwest of Boa Vista, Roraima's state capital; Venezuela lies about one day's walk both to the west and to the south. In 1968–70 the mission station was made up of three homes, a storehouse, and a fifth building that doubled as school and cult house, although both activities were more intentional than actual. Through the first two years of the research the missionary population was limited to a North American family of four and a Brazilian nurse. By 1974 its composition had changed around: the North American family was replaced by a Brazilian couple, and the Brazilian nurse by a North American woman. One more house had been built to accommodate the Brazilian family.

The mission's professional focus was the Sanumá population which, until 1973, was distributed into two communities, Mosonawa and Kalioko. But the missionaries extended their attention to the members of the Colony and to the Maiongong village. The 1974 outline of Auaris in Figure 1.1 shows the distribution of Indian and missionary houses.

The total Sanumá population in Auaris was nearly a hundred people in 1974. An equal number of Maiongong competed with the Sanumá for the same resources, that is, land plots appropriate for horticultural, hunting, and gathering grounds. By north Amazon standards, the Auaris population has a higher than usual density. The increasing scarcity of game and garden plots led the community of Kalioko to move away to a new location four hours of paddling downstream.

Some of the Auaris gardens are so distant from the village that it is impossible to go and come back on the same day. Overnight shelters are then built on new fields that frequently become a second home where the families spend long periods of time during planting and harvesting.

The concentration of Sanumá at Auaris is at least in part due to missionary presence. After 1964 when the mission was built, four Sanumá families moved to Auaris as well as an assortment of young men in search of wives. Most, if not all, were attracted by the prospect of acquiring trade goods from the missionaries as payment for services and food, besides health facilities such as medicines.

The Maiongong, original inhabitants of Auaris, represent another source of attraction for the Sanumá. Like most Carib speakers, the Maiongong are experts in the techniques of canoe building and river navigation, of planting and processing cassava, and of dealing with whites and their industrial paraphernalia. For all these reasons they

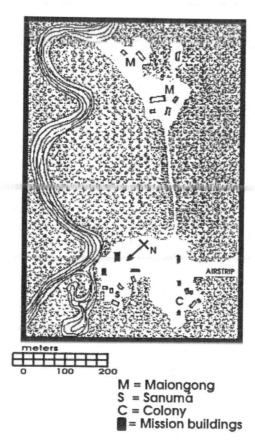

meters

0   100   200

M = Maiongong
S = Sanumá
C = Colony
■ = Mission buildings

Fig. 1.1. Auaris 1974

have become a precious source of goods for the Sanumá, albeit in a lesser degree than the whites themselves. As with the missionaries, the Sanumá trade services and goods with the Maiongong. Commerce between them has replaced decades of warfare for the occupation of a territory left half empty by the heavy mortality of other indigenous groups after white conquest (Migliazza 1972; Arvelo-Jiménez 1974; Koch-Grünberg 1979; Civrieux 1980; Ramos 1980).

In those days the impression one got of the physical appearance of the Auaris mission was that of a trim lawned ranch surrounded by the river, woods, and Indian houses, against a majestic background of mountains and ever-shifting cloud formations. In fact, the place is a vast patch of secondary growth, planted and replanted many times over by a succession of Maiongong and Sanumá families rotating their gardens. To give it a domesticated and tranquil look, the missionaries planted cashew and lime trees, kept the grounds clean, and mowed the lawn. The air of rural bliss was periodically broken by the arrival of the single-engine Cessna of the Missionary Aviation Fellowship that served the mission station.

Ethnically speaking, the Auaris population was thus quite diversified. Besides the Sanumá and Maiongong communities, and the North American and Brazilian residents, there is the Colony with its mixed composition. With regard specifically to the Sanumá, each one of the three communties—Mosonawa, Kalioko, and the Colony— enjoyed a relative autonomy, with its own cluster of communal houses and its own leadership and internal coherence that resulted from close kinship and marriage bonds. Linking these three communities together were affinal connections and distant blood ties, which were not enough to fuse them into one single unit under the same leadership. The convenience of being so close to each other was particularly felt in marriage choices, for a man who found a wife in any one of them could do his bride service without leaving his paternal village; all he had to do was move a few dozen yards away. Counteracting this comfortable proximity is the weight of population density that leads to economic problems, such as little game and distant gardens.

The Mosonawa community had a well-defined social background. Its head was the eldest son of the former leader, a very important man who died in the mid-sixties. Its cluster of three communal houses just a few yards apart was known as the *mosonawa dibi sai a* (house of the Mosonawa).

In the Kalioko community one found a greater diversity of origins, as most of its members had recently migrated to Auaris. A group of siblings—a man and four women—made up the core of the house, but the leadership was in the hands of a nephew, the son of another sister, an elderly woman who lived with her husband in the Sabuli village further downriver. The Kalioko group split up from Mosonawa as early as 1967. When I began fieldwork it was still getting organized. It was called *kalioko a sai a* (the house of Kalioko), in a direct reference to the headman, Kalioko.[12]

The third unit, the Colony, had at its center two Maiongong brothers married to Sanumá women, a sister and her family, and a distant brother-in-law. The elder sons and daughters of the two mixed marriages had Sanumá spouses. The elder of the Maiongong brothers was acknowledged by all Sanumá as the undisputed leader of the community they called *Lourenço a sai a*, or *Kadimani a sai a* (Kadi-

mani, apparently a Maiongong term, being one of Lourenço's personal names). He was fluent in the Sanumá language, and, in the
eventual absence of Sanumá leaders, he would play the role of
spokesman at the ceremonial dialogues performed at the arrival of
distant visitors. He had also been married to a Maiongong woman until her death around 1969. When she died, some Sanumá men, as a
sign of solidarity and common interests, tried to persuade him to
leave her children under Sanumá custody, but the Maiongong
claimed them back to their own village where they grew up as full
Maiongong. Lourenço was frowned upon by his Maiongong relatives
because of his intimate association with the Sanumá (Ramos 1980; see
Chapter 9 below).

Influenced by the Maiongong,[13] the Sanumá who live on the
banks of the Auaris are now expert canoeists. Various families own
canoes, and river traffic is relatively intense between the mission and
the gardens, hunting grounds, and the other riverside villages such
as Sabuli, and Kalioko after 1973. The importance of the Auaris River,
ashikamou, for these Sanumá may not be fully appreciated by the other
communities that do not know how to use canoes. As a means of lo-
comotion it is now as vital as the trails in the forest.

But the *ashikamou* is not just a convenient waterway. It is also a
source of drinking water for all its residents, a bathing place, and a
playground especially in the dry season when beaches crop up at
practically each curve. Public space par excellence, the river's edge
can become quite lively at the peak of the day's heat when crowds of
children bathe and play, and swarms of colorful butterflies feed on
the clay exposed by the receding water. In contrast with the little ones
who swim and have a lot of noisy fun, the adults are always very reserved when bathing or doing anything else by the river. They never
swim for pleasure, and bathe with an overstated modesty; men and
women who are not couples avoid each other at bathing time, usually
in the early evening.

Early evening is also the preferred time for drama. At the end of
the day's work and preferably after the main meal, one or more of the
following is bound to happen: signs of hidden enemies, *ōka dibɨ*, who
come to blow dangerous magic powder, *alawali*, and get everyone
worked up to chase them away with shouts and gun shots; quarrels
within a family or between families; confrontations with guests;
heated arguments that seem to arise out of thin air and attract practically everybody. It is also the time when a long-dead relative is remembered and mourned. The combination of dusk with the sound of
weeping creates an atmosphere of profound and woeful nostalgia not

In the dry season the Auris River turns into a playground. 1974. Photograph by A. G. Oliveira.

rarely accentuated by the melancholy call of the toucan in the background.[14] It is the transition between the shrill daytime sounds like birdsongs and children's laughter, and the grave tones of the night — the regular beat of the *soso* toad like an approaching outboard motor, the howling of nocturnal animals, the croaking of many frogs, or the soft hissing of a thousand crickets.

At night human silence may be, and often is, interrupted by one or more shamans performing their chants until dawn, or by a child who is *wakosɨbɨ*, "cry baby," a common condition that results from a feeling of, let us say, betrayal when its mother gets pregnant too soon after its birth, before some three years go by. The child can cry for hours on end, its eyes swollen red, its lungs exhausted, the grown-ups desperate for lack of sleep, the mother threatening to smear hot pepper in the child's mouth, and so a fraction of the night is filled with one more gloomy sound.

Our base in Auaris was at the Mosonawa community in a house built by the Maiongong with the help of some Sanumá. It was a building similar to the others, but divided in two parts, one public, the other "private," at least in intention, with a thatched roof, walls of palm slats, and a dirt floor to accommodate a hearth that doubled as a stove during the day and a fireplace during the night. The outer public part was designed to receive visitors and invariably attracted crowds of children and adults, especially at mealtime in the evening when they had finished their daily chores and main meal. The division of inner and outer halves was our attempt to preserve a minimum of privacy and of peace and quiet to carry out research tasks such as diary writing and data organizing. We were modestly successful in our strategy, for we managed to gain precious moments of solitude despite the almost permanent presence of Sanumá who observed us, required our attention, asked for objects, or simply engaged in absorbing conversations oblivious of our existence. Several subjects such as personal names, travel plans, or gossip about the Maiongong were recorded during those candid conversations in our "living room."

Unfailingly, after the arrival protocol, all visitors who appeared in the village would spend the next half hour in our house bargaining for trade goods, or making fun of us amidst the hearty laughter of their audience; sometimes they would bring wounds new and old for us to dress. In more serious cases, such as malaria, the local relatives would tie the patient's hammock in our outer room, not so much to supervise the supply of medicines, but to transform our house into a decidedly Sanumá dominion.

Being so close to the Sanumá and, at the same time, living apart from them had both benefits and drawbacks. On the one hand, we kept a certain amount of autonomy and privacy while missing very little of what went on in the village, such as quarrels, fights, arrivals and departures, children's games, and shamanistic sessions during the day or night. On the other hand, by not living under the same roof as the Sanumá, we did not have immediate access to certain intimate details of their domestic life. That we came to experience when we moved from Auaris to Kadimani.

Kadimani

While in Auaris, we made plans to find another place for fieldwork away from missionaries and the Maiongong. It would have to be on the Brazilian side of the border and with relatively easy access. We thought of the Shikoi region, southeast of Auaris, but it would have involved several days of canoe travel, as well as a large number of waterfalls and rapids. It being rainy season, no one would have risked the trip. We first postponed it and then gave it up altogether.[15] We headed southwest in the direction of the Kobali region, and settled down at Kadimani.

We had often heard that the Kadimani people were waiting for us, that they had even built us a house to lure us into staying with them. They were eager to host us because we meant a rare opportunity for them to get Western goods without going through the sometimes inconvenient chain of intercommunity trading. Thus, after a short reconnaissance trip, we moved to Kadimani in September 1969 for a first spell of four months.

The village site was about five to seven hours' walk from the mission, or ten to twelve hours' paddling down the Auaris River and then up the Walobiu stream, one of its right-side tributaries. The stretch of the Walobiu, from its mouth to the village harbor, seemed infinite to us with its interminable bends, fallen logs across the water, and impenetrable tangles of branches, limbs, and twigs hiding wasps nests, thorns, and other inhospitable surprises.

Travel in the rainy season can be very uncomfortable, as was the eight- or nine-hour journey up the Walobiu stream. Reading the diary entry for September 9, 1969, I still remember the discomfort of braving a two-hour rainstorm immersed in the chilly and damp air, with no recourse but to sit still in the canoe watching my fingernails go purple with cold. Both of us and our crew were soaked and immensely unhappy while the rain poured over the world as if forever.

At the village harbor, a good twenty-minute walk from the houses, we waited for the calls of our crew to be heard by the Kadimani villagers who were needed to help carry our luggage. The mini-safari that was formed followed the rather invisible path to the village, first through the forest, then along spaces left open by the recent slash-and-burn work for a new garden. The "trail" alternated between firm ground and suspended tree trunks that had fallen on top of each other at various heights and angles. It was only weeks later that I began to perceive some coherence in that route from the village to the stream, as I began to find my way around that open-air labyrinth of half-burnt wood. But only in part did I overcome the initial feeling of chaos left by the felling of trees and accentuated by the strong smell of charred vegetation.

That Kadimani site was the most beautiful spot I had seen in the Auaris valley. The houses had been built on a hilltop, and all around trees had been cut down to make room for new gardens. The open space thus created unveiled a spectacular view of morning and evening mists that highlighted the multiplaned succession of mountains reminiscent of a Chinese painting. White egrets flying as in slow motion added movement to the grand scenery. A huge log lying across the edge of the village clearing also fed our contemplation of landscape: serving as a bench where we sat talking to people, it allowed us to mix ethnography and aesthetics. Sitting on the log at sunset, we were equally precious objects of curiosity and observation for those Sanumá, most of whom had never seen a white person before.

The houses were new, as witnessed by the unsooted thatch. The clearing between the houses still had tree stumps on which chickens perched, adults squatted, and children played.

Apart from a narrow strip of forest along the ridge to the south, the rest of the trees around the village had been cut down to make room for new fields, awaiting the onset of the dry season to be burned. Two months after we arrived, on a windy day, two of the fields on opposite sides of the village were set on fire, producing enormous cascades of sparks. Predictably, one of the sparks caught the thatch of a house and the fire quickly spread to other buildings. Three of the four houses were reduced to ashes in less than an hour. A great commotion took hold of the villagers who, amidst cries and dramatic gestures, made repeated invocations to the skies. Shortly afterward, new houses were already being built on the rubble left by the others.

Our expectation of finding a house waiting for us was relativized on the spot when we were ushered into a compartment in a long house. Once and for all we learned to take into account the polysemic use of the Sanumá term *sai a* which we had simplistically translated as just "house." There are several levels of inclusiveness in the word *sai a*; it may mean anything from a family compartment to a building, a community, a village, or even a region. In our specific case, then, we were facing the least inclusive of them all, and let ourselves be ushered by our hosts to a rectangular building where three families lived. We were to occupy the fourth, empty, space between two others. Our *sai a* was separated from our neighbors' by a mixture of palm slats and pieces of bark that left convenient gaps for comfortable mutual peeping. We lived in it until the fire. We observed and absorbed the routine of family life on both sides of our domestic space as we were being intensely ethnographed by our neighbors, who would register everything we did and pass them on in endless reports among each other. This mutual observation continued, obviously with less intensity, throughout our entire stay at Kadimani, even after we moved to our interview shack, one of the few things that survived the fire.

Compared to the great expanse of the Auaris lawns, Kadimani village was small, compact, squeezed between houses, tree stumps, and steep slopes all around. Access to fresh water was painful, downhill through manioc plants, tobacco leaves, and banana trees to a tiny spring at the bottom of a field; in the dry season the volume of water was just enough to fill a bowl at a time, and in the rainy season it turned into a mud bath. The hill became a mountain whenever we had to haul potfuls of water back to the house. The fun of the bathing sessions at Auaris was now reduced to sporadic solitary bathing trips to the distant and shady Walobiu. What we gained in visual beauty we lost in physical comfort when we moved from Auaris to Kadimani.

Significantly more cohesive than Auaris, Kadimani presented itself to us as a community of affable, more spontaneous, and less aggressive people.[16] A simple but telling sign of this greater social cohesion was the habit the Kadimani people had of engaging in lively conversations held at night from their hammocks before sleeping time. Comments, jokes, witty remarks, and bursts of laughter coming from different houses crisscrossed the village as the chatter progressed and eventually involved everyone still awake. The full moon also contributed to create a special mood; it often inspired someone to do some manual work as if it were daylight. I would wake up late at night to the sound of a woman grating manioc or of a man weaving a basket for the sheer enjoyment of the bright moonlight.

The Kadimani people also had their *wakosɨbɨ* child, the daughter of one of our neighbors. With eyes that were permanently red, she would spend a great deal of her time simply crying away. Even so, Kadimani nights were much quieter than those at Auaris. Besides the crying girl, occasionally the insistent barking of some dog would excite the villagers who immediately interpreted the disturbance as evidence of the approach of night raiders, *õka dɨbɨ*, sneaking around with their deadly magic. Compared with Auaris, Kadimani had much less shamanism.

Kadimani's social composition was relatively simple: a group of eight brothers and sisters with the same father and two different mothers, a female parallel cousin, and the spouses and children of all these siblings, totaling fifty-two people (a 1970 figure). The community's outstanding feature was that, a few years back, it had hosted a group of refugees from another village far away to the south that had been attacked by enemies.[17] The immigrants consisted of two widowed sisters, their eight daughters, and two young sons. The six adult daughters married local men, establishing very close ties between the various couples.

Kadimani satisfied many of our research needs with the added thrill of our being the first whites in the lives of most of its members. Despite the sporadic contacts some of the men had with the missionaries and with the Maiongong, the latter's influence was much more diluted than at Auaris. It should be clear, however, that the Kadimani residents share the same historic process of warfare with the Maiongong that involved all the Sanumá of the Auaris region. In fact, the very appellation of the community is a Maiongong name that was given to one of its great men—*pada de*—who passed away a few years before our fieldwork.

2
Time as Space Organizer

Names and People

I set out to do research among the Sanumá convinced that I would
find a social system favoring cognatic relations. This expectation had
been raised by hints in the scanty literature that existed on the Yanomami at the time, and by the tone of kinship studies in the sixties.
I was thus surprised to find out that patrilineality was much more appropriate for making sense of the Sanumá at Auaris. Since I was not
prepared to find it, I did not look for it; in fact, I was rather slow to
recognize it. It came to me through a confusing repetition of the same
name given over and over to a large number of people of both sexes
and various ages who had a father in common.

Agnatic transmission came to my attention after I had collected a
certain amount of genealogical data for Auaris residents. In mentioning this, I do not want to give the false impression that the Sanumá
cultivate genealogies as important cultural artifacts, or that they are
concerned with pedigrees and obituaries. Quite the opposite. They
would rather not talk about their relatives' names. When I speak of
genealogies I am simply referring to the ethnographic technique by
means of which one can gather important material in a time sequence.
Genealogies are to temporal data as censuses are to spatial information. In the case of the Sanumá, time depth as preserved in the
memory of the adults rarely goes beyond the fifth generation.

In order to identify who was related to whom in the vast network
of intra- and intercommunity relationships, I would go up one, two,
or three ascending generations. For example, a man was referred to as
higadili. I was then given a whole string of other people with the same
name: his sons, his brothers, his sisters, in an interminable prolifera-
tion of *higadilis*. Instead of sorting people out, the name seemed to
fuse them together. Aware that all Yanomami treat personal names

56

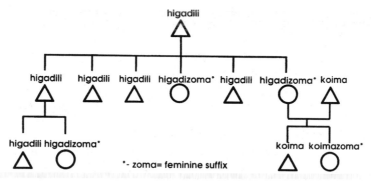

Fig. 2.1. Recurrence of names

with much reserve if not secrecy, I even thought that name repetition was just a trick of my interlocutors to avoid name dropping. But, if names are secret, why were names such as *higadili* so easily revealed and in such quantities? Diagrams such as Figure 2.1 began to appear in my notes. Like a compass, these names pointed in the direction of groupings of people who had at least two things in common: patrifiliation and a proper name. What I had to find out was the character and scope of such groupings and what they meant for the Sanumá. Very slowly the fog of my puzzlement began to lift as I made out the contours of social categories that spread out through several villages, to encompass the whole Auaris cluster and beyond, into Venezuela.

These social categories appeared as agnatic and dispersed entities. Every man and woman belongs necessarily to one and only one of them, which makes these units discrete and their membership universal. People belong to them by birth and leave them with death, if at all. Passage through them does not affect their continuity as units. Membership is transmitted through the father and conditioned by two important features: a common name and exogamy. Thus, a *higadili* man should marry a non*higadili* woman and pass on to his children the designation of *higadili/higadizoma* (-*zoma* indicates feminine gender).

Based on the ethnographic literature on similar cases, I chose to call these units sibs (or clans) with no intention of stifling their originality by forcing them into a prototype produced by some preestablished conceptual framework or fitting them into a rigid and culturally hollow typology. Sib or clan is rather a convenient label to refer to this particular Sanumá way of using names, space, and time to attain a social classification.

I refer to the sib names as patronyms which, rather like "surnames," persist over the generations. These patronyms outline categories of persons who are dispersed through various villages, but share a feeling of belonging to the same "people," as is commonly manifested in demonstrations of hospitality. It does not mean that people openly parade their sib membership wherever they go; to the contrary, they avoid disclosing their sib names as much as they can, and the best way to have access to them is to ask unrelated people. Sib identification is done at two levels: individual ("that man is a *higadili*") and collective ("those are *higadili dibi*"). The way in which individual identification is achieved amidst so much patronymic repetition is the subject of Chapter 7. Here I shall focus on the collective aspect of sib names.

The collective form of a patronym is given by adding *dibi*, the plural morpheme for both human and extrahuman beings such as spirits of various sorts, mythical ancestors, and so on, as opposed to objects and animals for which the plural *bi* is normally used.[1] When the Sanumá speak of *higadili dibi*, they refer to "*higadili* people," the dispersed but encompassing collectivity of agnatic relatives that contrasts with other collectivities, such as the *koima dibi*, the *saulagidili dibi*, or the *azatali dibi*, among many others. The plural *dibi* grants public recognition to something that is more than the mere sum of its parts. For a set of people to deserve such a collective name they have to display certain features that are common to all of them, at the same time as distinguishing them from other similar sets. These features entail much more than those related to mere family membership, and cannot be confused with it. Conjugal or extended families are not identified by proper names, nor are they defined by patriliny as a condition for membership. A person belongs to a family by virtue of being the child of a father as well as a mother, whereas sib membership can be acquired only through the father. A family necessarily includes both affinal and blood ties, whereas a sib excludes spouses and any other in-laws.

Proper names are instrumental to the definition of these socially meaningful units. In turn, the plural *dibi* attached to a proper name, when referring to a unit as a whole, is instrumental in setting the limits between what is public and what is private. What is private is not pluralized, as is the case of the great majority of personal names. It is, however, necessary to pluralize some names so that patrifiliation and naming can play the role of operators for extrafamily and extracommunity identities. This is done at the cost of certain people's losing the privacy of their names, for it is possible to have the "So-and-sos" only if the "So-and-so's" name can be disclosed (for further discussion see Chapter 6). It is not surprising, then, that families are not named collectivities, for otherwise each family head would have his name permanently unveiled; this would be intolerable due to the protection of adult names from public scrutiny (see Chapter 7).

Names in Time and Space

Sib names are like a magnifying lens. When we focus our attention on them, we can see some of the most puzzling complexities inherent in the Sanumá social system. In the first place, it is not possible to determine whether the sib names were once someone's personal names. They have been circulating for so long in the public domain that their origin is no longer known. In most cases their meaning is obscure and they are said to be "just names," *hilo bio* (*hilo*, "name"; *bio*, "merely"), as in the case of the *higadili dibi* sib, for instance; about the *koima dibi* sib, on the other hand, people comment that its name comes from the fact that its members are hairy, from *kōi* which means both body hair and bird's down; the members of the *hazatagidili dibi* sib are said to be as tall as deer, *haza*. Besides sporadic physical attributes such as these, no more is known about sib names.

Some sib names contain the *-dili* suffix, usually indicating some feature of a residence site; it is the equivalent of the Yanomam *teri* and the Yanomami *teli*. But the Sanumá suffix may also derive from someone's personal name, as when a man is named after the place where he was born. Some villages are known by more than one name. A natural feature of the environment can become a toponym; for instance, *kisinabidili dibi* refers to the community that lived by the Kisinabiu stream, although its more common name was *lalawa dibi* after Lalawa, its headman. Another situation is exemplified by the *wanabidili dibi*, after Wanabidili, a man whose name comes from his birthplace by the Wanabiu stream, unconnected to that community's location. When the sib names contain the *-dili* suffix, it is not always possible to know whether they come from a place name or a personal name, although we can safely presume that some of these patronyms derive from toponyms. Other sib names do not have the *-dili* suffix, such as *koima dibi*, *sadali dibi*, *nimtali dibi*, and many others. I shall return to these at the end of this chapter.

Passed on from generation to generation, sib names have lost their meaning and origin while apparently maintaining their form. Whether the first *koima* was a specific man covered in hair, or the first *hazatagidili* was as tall as his descendants claim, is not a very interesting question and quite beside the point. What matters is that by being applied to individuals, sib names protect the privacy of their members' personal names. With a single stroke a double operation is thus effected: the guarding of one of the most secluded zones of people's individualities, that is, their personal names, and the insertion of sib namesakes into a social network of homonyms that highlights relationships of interdependence and sociability.

Second, sib names evoke space. When asked the meaning of all those names—*higadili dɨbɨ, koima dɨbɨ, azatali dɨbɨ*, etc.—Zeca, an unusually bright man, himself a *higadili* who lives in Auaris, replied by comparing this Sanumá usage with that of Brazilians when these say they are from Boa Vista, from Manaus, or anywhere else. His immediate reference to place of origin is an important clue indicating how crucially the Sanumá category *space* works toward upholding the category *time*. With his comment, Zeca disclosed a feature that underlies much of the workings of Sanumá social organization, namely, the frequent transformation of space into time, and vice versa. In the case of the sibs, we have a social category that has time as its foundation and patriliny as its nexus, now associated with a place of origin, a specific space, and a point of departure. His analogy also provides one possible key to the emergence of the sibs, that is, through the transformation of certain residence sites into eponyms for residence groups. Co-residence is undoubtedly a crucial factor for the appearance of social entities, but the most striking aspect of Sanumá ethnography is the systematic transformation of space into time via patrilineality. As we shall see, this sort of metamorphosis appears over and over again in the social and political life of the upper Auaris region.

By the application of the simplest of rules, that of patrilineality, the sib sets the parameters for what is familiar thanks to a common patronym, to restrictions in the choice of spouse, and to the expectation of hospitality. The mere fact of being the child of a father puts in a person's hands his or her social map; with a minimum of ambiguity this father-oriented chart immediately tells one how to relate to anyone else. The entanglements that intrude in this originally simple network most often result from noncanonic marriages between people who are not expected to marry each other. But even the unraveling of such knots follows patterns provided by patrilineality, for it is usually the father rather than the mother of the offspring in these marriages that is considered in the reckoning of relationships. The sib is, thus, a device to bring together people with the same patronym, who avoid marrying their namesakes, and who share a tradition of belonging that is kept alive by the acknowledgment of their blood relations and the maintenance of mutual expectations. In the absence of an identi-

Table 2.1. Sib distribution per community

Sib	Community							Total
	Mosonawa	Kalioko	Sabuli	Lalawa	Kadimani	Sogosɨ	Mamugula	
higadili	8	10	13	28	27	2	9	97
koima	—	3	—	12	10	—	12	37
nimtali	—	—	—	—	1	23	—	24
waikasɨ	11	2	3	—	—	—	—	16
ōka	11	1	—	—	—	3	—	15
sadali	7	8	—	—	—	—	—	15
azatali	1	10	3	—	—	—	—	14
oladili	—	—	—	—	—	7	7	14
kazuma	2	—	—	4	—	4	3	12
magula	—	—	—	—	8	2	—	10
labadili	—	1	4	3	1	—	—	9
lobotali	—	2	4	—	—	—	—	6
oikoma	—	4	—	—	—	—	—	4
neadili	—	—	—	—	2	—	—	2
sakonadili	—	—	—	—	1	—	1	2
shilawa	—	—	—	—	—	—	1	1
Others	—	1	1	1	2	—	1	6
Total	40	42	28	48	52	41	33	284

fied common founder, it is these kin ties that blend people together. Although spread out in several villages, sometimes far apart, sib members tend to cluster in a given region which, in turn, is identified by its dominant sib.

Table 2.1 presents the distribution of members of the sixteen main sibs in the Auaris region, but it does not cover all extant sibs. It shows how they may concentrate in certain villages or disperse widely. Just as only a few *neadili dɨbɨ* or *sakonadili dɨbɨ* live in the upper Auaris village cluster, so also some scattered *higadili dɨbɨ* people, concentrated in Auaris, can be found in distant villages.

It is said that the region of the *koima dɨbɨ*, the *kazuma dɨbɨ*, and the *magula dɨbɨ* lies to the south and southwest of Auaris, whereas that of the *labadili dɨbɨ* is to the northwest, the *lobotali dɨbɨ* to the north, and the *waikasɨ dɨbɨ* and *neadili dɨbɨ* to the east and southeast, on the lower course of the Auaris River. This association of certain sibs with given areas might be seen as the historical outcome of their having belonged to the same residence groups before dispersing. Membership through patrilineal transmission would then become the means to preserve the memory and record of that past association. I will return to this point at the end of this chapter.

The distribution of sibs in the villages points to some remarkable concentrations of some of them. In the village cluster of the upper Auaris, the *higadili dɨbɨ* dominate. Together with the *koima dɨbɨ* and the *nimtali dɨbɨ*, they comprise more than half of the population of the seven villages in my research corpus. I shall focus on these in the following discussion of the sib as a social category.

The largest concentration of the *higadili dɨbɨ* is in five of the six northernmost Sanumá villages on the Brazilian side. The *nimtali dɨbɨ* are represented in just two of these villages, the majority living to the north and south of the international border. The *koima dɨbɨ*, in turn, are found in four of these seven villages, but their distribution is much wider, covering most of the northern portion of Sanumá territory in Venezuela.

Sib Relationships

Every Sanumá, as already stated, is necessarily a sib member. Both men and women belong to their father's sib, and there is no way to change that condition; married women never relinquish their sib patronym. When a woman accompanies her husband to his village, she never stops identifying herself with her father's sib. But then she acquires a double identity: in terms of residence she is identified with her husband, in terms of descent, with her father.

It is the man, however, who most often faces the need to leave his own village in order to find a wife; he then has to live with her parents. We find *higadili* men living with *sadali dɨbɨ*, or *sadali* people living with *azatali dɨbɨ*, or members of the latter living with *labadili dɨbɨ*, and so forth. If a person enters a community as a spouse where he or she has no kin relations, he or she is initially treated as a stranger, especially so in the case of women. As women are expected to stay where they are after marriage, when they follow their husbands they are out of their element. If a young girl is taken away to join her husband's polygynous family, she suffers a mild form of ostracism, as a result of the slight avoidance that exists between co-wives who are not sisters, or closely related. That was the case of a woman at the Kalioko village and another at Kadimani.[2] Both were identified by their respective sib patronyms, and nobody, except their children, used kinship terms to refer to them, in sharp contrast to the usual procedure. The woman at Kalioko was beginning to be called by a teknonym some six months after the birth of her first child, a boy named Koli. Her new name, Koli a pɨbɨna, "Mother of Koli," was the first sign that she was being incorporated into her husband's community.

Members of the same sib acknowledge each other by means of its distinctive features, that is, an exclusive name, and a kinship term that denotes a blood relationship which varies with age, sex, and generation. It is common to hear a man refer to a fellow sib member as *iba hebala*, "my older brother," or *iba hoosa*, "my younger brother," even when there is no apparent genealogical connection between them. Within the same sib, affinity terms are never used, unless someone marries a co-member, in which case in-law terms replace the kin nomenclature previously used.

As far as I know, there is no specific word for sib, as there is none to define family, for instance. One may refer to all members of one's sib as *iba dibi*, "my people," in a context where two or more sibs are being contrasted. At any rate, *iba dibi* tends to be used for close blood relatives, whereas *iba ai dibi*, "my other people," includes both affines and distant consanguines. In this way, descent seems to preclude the full incorporation of in-married residents of the same community. When the Sanumá want to stress their inner blood group, they say *iba dibi sai*, "my real ones."

Along this gradation of relatives there is a whole series of different rights and duties. The nearly constant flow of visitors who go around Sanumá villages gives plenty of occasion to observe the importance sib bonds can have for a traveler, for he will invariably tie up his hammock at the hearth of a sib companion, unless he has a very intimate relationship with another local resident. Given that sib members can be widely dispersed, hospitality, a trademark of patrilineality in general, provides considerable support in the specific case of a person who, moving through a wide area, can be confident of finding shelter practically wherever he goes.

By virtue of the automatic and exclusive patrilineal transmission of sib membership, the sibs are discrete units, that is, there is no overlapping membership. Sibs never lose their mutual differentiation, even when the rule of exogamy is broken, which is not infrequent. Marriages within the same sib are frowned upon, but censure is usually limited to the verbal reproaches that inevitably occur with varying degrees of malice. There is, for example, the case of a man from the Mamugula community who took as his third wife the daughter of a parallel cousin (his father's brother's son), which by Sanumá reckoning made her his classificatory daughter and sib co-member. His mother's reaction was so strong that the couple had to leave the village and spend a month camping alone in the forest. They returned and were accepted, but the episode was recorded in the form of a personal name given to the wife, Saulisisoma, after *saulisi*, a mythical sloth that symbolizes incest. The man was already married to the girl's mother, who had always been an affine of his (the daughter of a

Table 2.2. A model of marriage exchanges

Men		Women
koima		higadili
higadili		koima
labadili		higadili
oladili	MARRY	shilawa
nimtali		oladili
magula		neadili
neadili		magula

classificatory brother of his mother). Had he married the girl first and transformed her mother into his own mother-in-law, his marriage to the latter would have been impossible, because of the very strict avoidance that surrounds a man and his mother-in-law.

People tend to attribute cases of *saulisimo* (acting like a *saulisi*) to sibs that are remote or unrelated to one's own. For instance, a woman from Kadimani asserted that the *koima dibi* keep marrying their own daughters. She was referring to the case just mentioned. She added that the *higadili dibi*, her husband's sib, never do that, although the Sabuli community comprised *higadili* people who had been intermarrying for two generations!

Be that as it may, there is the expectation that each sib should have one or more marriage partners. Some of the ideal combinations were put to me by that same Kadimani woman (see Table 2.2). But the woman also affirmed that *higadili* men do not marry *labadili* women, and that *oladili* men do not choose *nimtali* wives, which raises the question of reciprocity in the marriage exchanges. If it occurs between *koima dibi* and *higadili dibi*, *magula dibi* and *neadili dibi*, why would it not happen with the other sib pairs? In fact, there are concrete cases of such combinations in several villages. At Lalawa, a *higadili* man was married to two *labadili* women; at Kadimani, the old headman, a *higadili*, had been married to a *labadili* woman; at Sogosi, an *oladili* youth was married to a *nimtali* girl.

We are left with two alternatives: either these latter cases are exceptions to a fixed model of sib marriage rules, or the combinations provided by the Kadimani woman reflect her personal interpretation of what those rules should be. The second alternative seems more likely, as I never heard it from anyone else. The common assertion was that members of the same sib should not marry each other, but whom they should marry was an open question. Rather than an enigmatic contradiction, what my informant's version seemed to reveal was that proximity between sibs is an important factor in the

Table 2.3. Relations between sib clusters

	Cluster I		Cluster II	
B L O O D	*higadili* *sadali* *azatali* *oladili*	A F F I N A L	*koima* *nimtali* *magula* *labadili*	B L O O D

maintenance of marriage reciprocity. The statement that no mutual exchange exists between *higadili dɨbɨ* and *labadili dɨbɨ*, or between *oladili dɨbɨ* and *nimtali dɨbɨ* may not fit the actual practice, but the marriage combinations which the Kadimani woman spelled out account for the most common marriage exchanges between clusters of people who see themselves as affines to each other. Everything seems to point to a framework of sib relations where some are in the position of fathers, *pɨ*, older brothers, *pebala*, or brothers-in-law, *soli*, vis-à-vis their counterparts. Let us see some examples of sib relationships:

higadili dɨbɨ are *pɨ* (father) to *azatali dɨbɨ* and *sadali dɨbɨ*;
magula dɨbɨ are *pebala* (older brother) to *nimtali dɨbɨ*;
nimtali dɨbɨ are *pebala* to *koima dɨbɨ*;
higadili dɨbɨ are *soli* (brother-in-law) to *koima dɨbɨ*, *nimtali dɨbɨ*, and *labadili dɨbɨ*.

On the basis of statements such as these, we might conceive of a pair of clusters constituted by blood and affinal relations between sibs, as in Table 2.3. Within each cluster we would have blood relations, and across the clusters, affinal relations. Such a division, of course, is only my attempt to organize the data gathered from the Sanumá; it is not a literal transcription of what they said to me. Any sib is related to any other in the same cluster as a consanguine, and any sib is related to any other in the opposite cluster as an affine. This does not mean that there are no marriages within the same cluster, or, inversely, that there are marriage alliances between all sibs in opposite clusters. What it means is that sib relations are expressed through the idiom of kinship, as if they were always in a kin or affine position regarding each other. To give an idea of the extent to which this kinship analogy is put into practice, Table 2.4 presents a summary statement of marriages involving sibs from the two clusters defined above as they occur in five communities. Only living spouses are included. At Kadimani, Sogosi, and Lalawa the expectation is confirmed. At Kadimani, of a total of fourteen marriages, six involve sibs that stand to each other as expected; at Sogosi, of a total of eleven marriages, also six follow the pattern of exchange between affinal sibs; at Lalawa, of seventeen marriages, fourteen comprise three of the above-

Table 2.4. Marriages between sibs related as kin or affines

Community	Marriages			Frequency
Sogosɨ	*oladili*	=	*nimtali*	4
	nimtali	=	*higadili*	2
Kadimani	*higadili*	=	*koima*	5
	higadili	=	*labadili*	1
Lalawa	*higadili*	=	*koima*	12
	higadili	=	*labadili*	2
Kalioko	*higadili*	=	*azatali*	4
	higadili	=	*sadali*	1
	sadali	=	*azatali*	1

mentioned sibs, according to the expected model. But at Kalioko, out of eight marriages, four occur between *higadili dɨbɨ* and *azatali dɨbɨ* that are supposedly in a "father-son" relationship, one between *higadili dɨbɨ* and *sadali dɨbɨ*, also "father" and "son," and another between *sadali dɨbɨ* and *azatali dɨbɨ*, considered to be "brothers." Most of the Kalioko marriages are, therefore, between "kin" sibs, which seems to indicate that over and above the alignment of the sibs along the kin-affine axis, there is a bigger consideration—sib exogamy. Even if the future spouse is called by a kin term, what matters is that he or she belong to a different sib.

Several sibs that do not appear on the above list comprise different clusters of affinity and consanguinity, and beyond these are yet others so remote as to be totally unrelated to the Auaris people. Of those sibs it is said they are *tiko dɨbɨ*, "others," "different," falling outside the bounds of what is known or familiar. Some Auaris women cringed at the thought of marrying men from those sibs, saying they would be *gili*, a mixture of fear and shame.

As on a chess board, in the sib system the pieces are arranged and rearranged according to the players' moves, but are never merged into one undifferentiated whole. For some people *higadili dɨbɨ* and *sadali dɨbɨ* are related as father-son, for others, as brothers-in-law, depending on the focus they select from concrete marriages. This flexibility of interaction accompanies the flow of a person's moves in the sib game, steered by specific interests, be they physical proximity or convenient political alliances. But—and here there is consensus—those born *higadili* never change into *sadali*, or vice versa.

In the Name of the Founder

When I began my research among the Sanumá, I knew it would be difficult to learn about personal names. The literature, such as it existed on the Yanomami, referred to name secrecy and the problems of eliciting names. What I did not expect was to find that village names were also confidential. When my scanty knowledge of the Sanumá language allowed me to pose my first questions, I naively began by asking where all those visitors who showed up at Auaris lived or came from. My questions were met with prolonged silences, embarrassed looks, or a reticent . . . *"kuue!"* ("I don't know") that pointed toward an area of turbulence in the path to intercultural understanding.

Several months went by before I grasped the extent of that resistance. Village names, I found out, were almost invariably names of persons either living or dead. These names are instrumental in the process by which certain agnatic groups obtain political hegemony in their village of residence, a process that very gradually was revealed to me over many hours of interviews with patient women and men; with impressive ability, they tried to educate me in things Sanumá at the same time as coping with two major obstacles—keeping the personal names undisclosed, and overcoming my linguistic ineptitude. Months later, when I asked one of the women why, earlier on, she had told me only half of the story of some particular case, she had no hesitation in replying, "If I had told you everything, you would have understood nothing"!

As the Sanumá grew more familiar with me, the initial reluctance to spell out people's names eventually faded away. Communities were first freely named, then the personal names of most people. Nevertheless, some remained buried in secret to the last day of my research.

Names paved the way that led me to the Sanumá lineages. I use the term "lineage" to refer to a well-defined agnatic group, identified by a common founder, a common name, and a strong intermarriage prohibition. As with the sibs, I would like to emphasize that the term "lineage" is applied here as a matter of convenience rather than as a statement on the univocality of the concept. The reader should not expect to see in this analysis of Sanumá lineages the same thing that is described elsewhere, such as in Africa, in New Guinea, or in China. My concern is not to fit the Sanumá agnatic groups into a preexisting typology, for no other reason than that "lineage" is not a signifier with a universally agreed upon signified, as the concepts of "gravity" or "atom" would be. Since every empirical case corresponds to a unique configuration, the term "lineage" is but a mere label that comes in handy to help us speak with an economy of words about certain social phenomena. What all these social things have in common is at most what Wittgenstein, endorsed by Needham (1972), called a "family resemblance." As Geertz said, "If . . . we use a concept like "mysticism"—or "mystic" or "mystical"—not to formulate an underlying uniformity behind superficially diverse phenomena, but to analyze the nature of that diversity as we find it, then pursuing the different meanings the concept takes in different contexts does not dissolve its value as an ordering idea but enriches it" (1968:24). This being said, let us begin the analysis of Sanumá lineages in their ethnographic specificity.

As with the sibs, personal names are my point of departure to get to the lineages. Springing out of the sibs and following a patrilineal route, the lineages are grouped by village, their membership is smaller, and their genealogical definition is clearer than those of the sibs. They are easily identified by a proper name, a well-known founder, a strong exogamy, and a marked political role.

Even more so than with the sibs, the normal privacy of personal names is suspended when they become lineage eponyms. This signals the passage of certain men—their founders—from the private to the public domain. All lineages are named after their founders, or sometimes one of their founder's sons. A lineage eponym is, therefore, a personal name that has been definitely cast into the public sphere and remains there even after its owner's death. One of the striking differences between the Sanumá and the other Yanomami is that the latter's extreme zeal to guard the names of the deceased is much attenuated among the Sanumá.[3] This is no mere detail, for if the Sanumá guarded their deceased's names as much as the other subgroups do, there would be no lineages, as there are none, at least readily identifiable, among the Yanomam and the Yanomami.[4] It is by means of their human eponym that Sanumá lineages come to the fore and become highly visible not only to the ethnographer but to the Sanumá themselves. On various occasions, I found myself eavesdropping on or participating in conversations in which someone was making a mental calculation to locate a stranger by referring to his group name, that is, to the public name of its founder, as if a code was being deciphered.

The emergence of new lineages is closely associated with a wide-range teknonymy which means the use of a person's name combined with kinship terms that include not only father and mother, but also other blood (older brother, younger brother, sister, son, and daughter) as well as affinal relatives (husband, wife). As teknonymy and its ramifications will be treated in Chapter 6, I shall limit myself to what is essential for the present discussion of the lineages.

Among a group of siblings, it is common for one name to be selected, usually the eldest brother's, to serve as referent for the whole group. At first the closest relatives are individually identified as "Mother of So-and-so," "Father of So-and-so," "Older brother of So-and-so," "Sister of So-and-so," etc. As time goes by, his name becomes pluralized when the *dibi* suffix is added to it, and is then applied to his relatives as a whole who become known as "the So-and-sos." Nevertheless, individual teknonymy will persist. As the group becomes established as an acknowledged collectivity, his name stops being used in teknonyms (other children born in the family will provide new referents) and passes definitively to the public domain.

A personal name thus transformed into a collective name is one of the first signs of the conceptual differentiation of an agnatic group, the name being its most outstanding diacritic. All the questions I put to the Sanumá about the origin and meaning of lineage names met with a unanimous reply — the founder's or his son's personal name. Kadimani, Sogosi, Mosonawa, Lalawa were all prominent village headmen already dead or still alive. These are not, therefore, *hilo bio*, "mere names," as are many sib names. Rather, they are personalized hallmarks that were transformed into sociocentric insignia that, by means of homonymy, encompass all members of the agnatic group in question. "The *kadimani dibi*," for instance, exemplify the consolidation of a process that is both complex and fleeting. Unlike the sibs that are dispersed, permanent, and universal categories, lineages are localized social groups that come and go according to a number of factors that directly affect their destiny.

Localized Patrilineality

As with the sibs, lineage membership is acquired exclusively through one's father. Lineages cannot, therefore, be confused with extended families, for these necessarily include people related as affines. Again, membership is for life, and women preserve theirs after marriage. As most men live with their wife's parents, there are many three-generation families where grandparents and grandchildren belong to different lineages. Furthermore, whereas an extended family always occupies one single domestic space, lineage members are spread out through two, three, or more residences in the same village, or in different villages. A lineage may be entirely contained in one single village, but the need for men to marry elsewhere, and the natural growth of the lineage, are constant factors for the scattering of lineage members. Before going into the ramifications of lineage dis-

Table 2.5. Lineage distribution per community

Lineage	Community							
	Mosonawa	Kalioko	Sabuli	Lalawa	Kadimani	Sogosɨ	Mamugula	Total
kadimani	4	1	—	—	26	2	9	42
sogosɨ	—	—	—	—	1	23	—	24
lalawa	—	—	—	20	—	—	—	20
mamugula	—	—	—	—	3	—	10	13
oshigatali	12	—	—	—	—	—	—	12
mosonawa	6	—	—	—	—	—	—	6
sabuli	—	—	4	—	—	—	—	4
azagoshi	—	2	—	—	—	—	—	2
soboshidili	1	—	—	1	—	—	—	2
Others	—	1	2	—	—	—	—	3
Total	23	4	6	21	30	25	19	128

persal, it is necessary to identify them with regard to the villages where they are located, as shown in Table 2.5. It should be noted that the total number of members of each lineage per village is smaller than the total village population. This is due to a very specific and relevant feature of the development process of Sanumá lineages. At any given period of time, they may include only half of the population. In the case of the upper Auaris village cluster, in the six-year span between 1968 and 1974, about fifty percent of its inhabitants were affiliated with a lineage.

Odd as it may seem, this feature is not unique to the Sanumá. I have not done an exhaustive search for ethnographic examples on the subject, but by chance I easily located two other cases of this type of process, among the Balinese, and in rural Turkey.

In the Sanumá case, this aspect results from the collision of two principles, uxorilocal residence and patrilineal descent, which turns the lineage into a highly vulnerable group at its outset, particularly in its capacity to survive through generations. I must emphasize that uxorilocal residence in and of itself does not necessarily lead to the dispersal of men. If they marry within their own village, all they have to do to satisfy the requirement of uxorilocality is move to their in-laws' house a few yards away (Ramos 1982). The centrifugal effect of uxorilocality is felt when agnatically related men are sent off in different directions, and thus become incapable of keeping alive the close daily interaction that is needed to actualize lineage affairs. It should be made clear, however, that even those who have no lineage to belong to are necessarily affiliated to a sib.

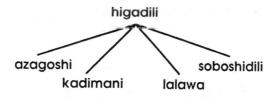

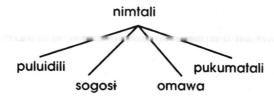

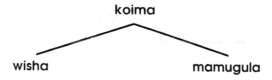

Fig. 2.2. The internal divisions of the sibs

To better account for this complicated process, I shall focus on some of the lineages that are associated with the three sibs mentioned above. The relations of these lineages to their respective sibs are shown in Figure 2.2.

It is interesting to show a graphic alternative to the figure above so as to better visualize the arrangement of lineage members and non-lineage members within the same sib (Figure 2.3). As can be seen, lineages appear as islands of agnatic concentration, as differentiated groups amidst the anonymity of the other, nonlineage members of the sib.[5]

Although the lineages are encompassed by the sibs, they have their own dynamics and play a very different role from that of the sibs. While the latter are long-standing categories the main purpose of which is identification and social mapping, the former are groups with a much narrower space and faster timing. Under the stable umbrella of the sib, the lineages are in constant movement, which makes

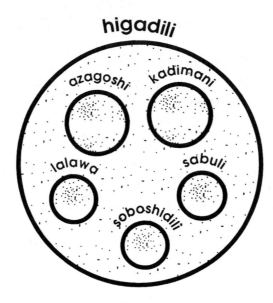

Fig. 2.3. Inside the *higadili* sib

them highly elastic and impermanent. Their greatest contribution is to provide a vantage point for the political action of village leaders.[6] The details of this contribution are the subject of Chapter 3.

Each one of these lineages is the outcome of a combination of various factors, one of the most important being common residence. If several men related through a common father live far apart, there is hardly any possibility that they will start a lineage of their own; for this to happen it is essential that they live in the same village. If, on the contrary, a core of father and sons or of brothers succeed in holding themselves together, it is likely that they will establish the beginnings of a new lineage, if they beget male children, and if the latter, in turn, stay in their father's village after marriage. The continuity of a Sanumá lineage thus depends on the spatial coherence of a minimum group of agnatically related men with male offspring. Only then will it be possible to generate a critical mass of members and a critical time span, without which a lineage will not materialize. A random assemblage of fathers and sons or of brothers living in separate villages is just that, a mere assortment of males. Each one of these men may become the founder of a new group, but the sheer sum of dispersed agnates does not make up a lineage.

As I have mentioned, the rising of a new lineage is announced by the depersonalization of someone's personal name, that is, when a core of blood relatives is collectively identified by the name of one of its members, usually a still unmarried youth. The importance of a name for an emerging lineage cannot be overemphasized, for it is the name that distinguishes it from the rest of the sib; it gives the new group a distinct identity that is accompanied by a number of expectations and attitudes in the rest of the community. The close association between lineage and community is expressed in the fact that the community gets to be known by the name of the lineage that provides its headman.[7] With the exception of Kalioko and the Colony, all other communities of the upper Auaris are named after a lineage.

In the same way as we looked at the development of families through time, I shall assess the dynamics of lineage formation as a long-term operation in a continuous process of reconfiguring. The advantage of the diachronic approach over a synchronic outlook is that it avoids the tendency to freeze coeval phases of the same process as if they were a patchwork of disparate components. If taken in isolation, the various phases may seem incomprehensible, but if put into a developmental sequence, they turn out to be both coherent in themselves and meaningful vis-à-vis the whole system.

First of all, we must know what goes into the lineage developmental cycle. To this end, and also in the hope of making my point more effectively, I shall begin with some synchronic manifestations of agnatic groups in all their diversity and apparent incongruity. In the next chapter the patchwork will be undone and rearranged in a time sequence.

Synchronic Faces of a Diachronic Process

Mamugula dɨbɨ, *sabuli dɨbɨ*, and *lalawa dɨbɨ* are agnatic groups with three generations and founders who, in 1970, were still alive. In turn, the *mosonawa dɨbɨ* lost their third generation when the founder died in the mid-sixties, and the group was reduced to two adult males with small children, a married sister, and a little brother. The group leadership went to the eldest brother, who did not have enough of his father's political talent and was a disappointment to the community.

In fact, his position was being threatened by the rise of a man of the *oshigatali dɨbɨ* lineage. Now permanent residents at the Mosonawa village, the *oshigatali dɨbɨ* left their original territory in the Shikoi region, after an enemy attack. The group's father and eponym was killed, and his widow and children took refuge with a group of siblings of the *ōka dɨbɨ* sib who lived to the east of the Oshigatali community; the *ōka dɨbɨ* brothers married the daughters of the deceased

Oshigatali leader. Years later, they all moved to Auaris. Among the *oshigatali dɨbɨ* there were two brothers who, in the seventies, were competing for the headmanship at Mosonawa. When the older of the two brothers moved to Venezuela, the younger grew in political stature. Moreover, there was a considerable demographic increase in the *oshigatali dɨbɨ* group as compared to the *mosonawa dɨbɨ*, a strong factor for a successful headmanship.

At Mosonawa there was also a group of unmarried siblings who belonged to the *higadili dɨbɨ* sib and the *kadimani dɨbɨ* lineage, but who were beginning to be known as the *sopai dɨbɨ*, after the name of the second brother, a young man who had gone through puberty in the early seventies. Their deceased father was the brother of the *kadimani dɨbɨ*'s eponym. Sopai's elder brother was betrothed to a young girl and Sopai himself to a toddler, while his younger brother was still a child. In spite of their young age, these people were already being differentiated as a group by the Mosonawa residents who selected Sopai's name as a mark of their distinctiveness.

At the Lalawa village, a group of agnates of the *koima dɨbɨ* sib was known as the *hanisho dɨbɨ* after the name of their eldest brother. The group was made up of three brothers and two sisters, all married with children, except for Hanisho whose wife was said to be barren. Regarded as a diplomatic type, Hanisho was respected in and out of his community. It was by his initiative that the Lalawa village changed site in the early seventies.[8]

At the Sogosɨ village, the father of the four brothers and two sisters composing the *sogosɨ dɨbɨ* died before he had grandchildren. The group's eponym and village headman had children who were still unmarried. All of Sogosɨ's brothers and paternal nephews were identified as *sogosɨ dɨbɨ*. They were a harmonious group of agnates, but their community did not provide a sufficiently large number of prospective wives for the younger generation; at least two of its boys had already left for other villages to get married.[9]

Kadimani dɨbɨ is the oldest and largest lineage I have known. It had at least four generations between the living and the dead. With a strong nucleus at the Kadimani village, in 1970 they were more than forty (twenty-two of whom were adult men) in a community of fifty-two people. Besides their concentration at Kadimani, they had branches in other villages, such as Mosonawa, Mamugula, and in the remote Samatali country in Venezuela. One of their young men was doing bride service at Kalioko's, and two women were married at Sogosɨ's. Figure 2.4 shows the *kadimani dɨbɨ* and their various branches. The *kadimani dɨbɨ* residents at Mamugula were clearly iden-

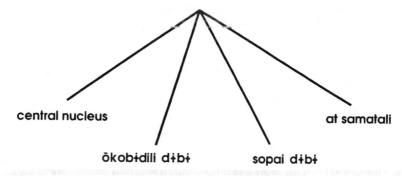

Fig. 2.4. The *kadimani dɨbɨ* subdivisions

tified as such, even though they were under the leadership of the *ma-mugula dɨbɨ*. They consisted of Gastão, the only surviving brother of the lineage founder, his three wives, and his many children. When the founder was still alive, all the brothers lived together by the Õko-biu stream. Right after his death, the various families separated and scattered in the forest, a common procedure in moments of crisis such as the succession of village leadership. The dispute between Gastão and Manoel, the eldest son of his deceased brother, was resolved in favor of the latter, and Gastão moved away to the Mamugula commu-nity where a sister of his was an in-married spouse.

Gastão's segment is also known as *õkobɨdili dɨbɨ*, not only after the Õkobiu stream, the site of their former residence, but also because Gastão's eldest son is called Õkobɨdili for having been born by the Õkobiu. In 1970, young Õkobɨdili was approaching puberty and his name was widely used as a teknonym for his relatives: Õkobɨdili a pɨ a (Father of Õkobɨdili), Õkobɨdili a pezea (Sister of Õkobɨdili), and so forth. Gastão and his offspring thus represent the *õkobɨdili dɨbɨ* branch of the *kadimani dɨbɨ*.[10]

The *kadimani* branch at the Mosonawa village consists of the sib-ling group already identified as the *sopai dɨbɨ*. They are the children of the youngest brother of the old Kadimani leader; he was killed in a raid while his elder brother was still alive. His widow fled with the children and took refuge at Mosonawa, whose leader was a classifi-catory brother of her deceased husband's. In 1974, the *sopai* siblings were still very young; they lived with their mother and maternal grandfather in a compartment of the local headman's house.

Spread out as it is, the *kadimani dɨbɨ* lineage shows some signs of imminent fissioning. Perhaps the *õkobɨdili dɨbɨ* and the *sopai dɨbɨ* will become autonomous agnatic groups, but as long as the main core continues to reproduce itself in new generations, the *kadimani dɨbɨ* as such will persist.[11]

The constant partition of a lineage into breakaway segments may eventually crumble an expanding agnatic group, perhaps giving rise to a sib or resulting in its total dissolution and social oblivion. Unfortunately, for this process to be properly studied, we would need a very long time, generations perhaps. All I can do is make an informed guess on the basis of the clues that the operation of the system leaves behind in its wake. For example, it is possible for a certain group to accumulate a number of names for some time. The *sopai dɨbɨ* are also *kadimani dɨbɨ* (their lineage) and *higadili dɨbɨ* (their sib), not to mention *saulagɨdili dɨbɨ* (a historical category to which I will return later). If the *sopai dɨbɨ* establish themselves as a full-fledged lineage, it is unlikely that its members will keep all those names in current usage and memory. In the words of Zeca, if people split up, they will no longer use the same name. His example was precisely the *sopai dɨbɨ* who had separated from the *kadimani dɨbɨ*. Zeca also said that when the *pada dɨbɨ* (old, important men) die, people move away and get another name derived from the new village site. But his statement is not always confirmed. Expressions such as *hilo tolea* (the name beyond) and *pɨ dɨbɨ tolea* (the fathers beyond) indicate that names and memories are retained after the death and separation of agnates, at least for a certain period of time.

Among the various statements I heard about what happens when an important man dies, the most complete was that of Jorge, a man in his early twenties in 1970, the son of an *oshigatali* woman and an *ōka* man. His talent for linguistic work made him one of the missionaries' best informants. According to him, when a father with many children dies, the sons split up (*pɨ a nomazoma, pilubi dɨbɨ selegɨbazoma*).[12] If all the brothers are already married and live together, they will stay where they are; but if only one of them has a wife and children, he alone will remain, while one by one the others, younger, will move elsewhere because they are "grieved" (*pii honio*); unmarried, they will not stay where their father lived (*pizɨba mi, kudio maigite*).[13] If, as Jorge affirmed, most sons disband after their father's death, the frail bond of co-residence of father and sons will snap. Set apart, these men become diluted in the various communities where they go to find wives and where they have to face the uncomfortable position of outsiders. "When one is alone one has no name," was the spirit of one of Jorge's remarks. He was referring to two pairs of brothers of the *higadili dɨbɨ* sib. One of the pairs includes his sister's husband; the other pair are Zeca and his elder brother. In contrast to the *kadi-*

mani dibi who are many, Jorge continued, these men, being alone (*sami kuloni*),[14] have no further name. What this lack of a further name actually means is the absence of lineage membership.

There are many other examples of people with no recognized lineage affiliation. It is interesting to note that Jorge made his comments while in the position of a nonlineage member. But, having married an Auaris girl, he was comfortably surrounded by his blood relatives, agnatic and nonagnatic. A resident at the Mosonawa community, he was doing bride service at the Colony, just a few yards from his parents' house. In turn, his younger brother and his eldest sister were both married and lived at Mosonawa. As will be seen in Chapters 3 and 9, Jorge has always shown a great ambition to become a political leader in Auaris.[15]

If we take all these assorted cases of named agnatic groups—some large, some small, some recent, some old, some politically prominent, some not—plus all the people who do not belong to any of them, and observe their behavior through time, we will see, one, that each of these groups represents a different phase in the developmental cycle of the lineages, and two, that all Sanumá, lineage members or not, participate in this complex trajectory. The cycle is directly related to the circulation of political power in a given community, as will be seen in the next chapter.

Part and parcel of the development process of the lineages is the possiblity of their rise, expansion, retraction, dissolution, and rejuvenation, as important factors such as male births and prolonged co-residence of agnates are present or absent through the generations. The absence of one or the other of these factors may throw an established lineage back to stage one, or cut short a potential one just on the verge of coming into being.

Androcentric Genetics

Male babies carry with them the destiny of their agnatic group. Thus, they are often claimed by their father's agnates when their parents separate, even if that means depriving the child of its mother and her milk. At Kadimani, a man I will call Homero had married a girl from Venezuela. Because she did not have a father, he felt free to interrupt his short bride service and bring her and their baby son to his village where he already had two wives. A while later, some of her relatives came down to rescue her, taking advantage of the festive climate of a mortuary ceremony at the Lalawa village where most Kadimani people had congregated. In the skirmish that ensued between the husband and the wife's relatives, each pulling away at the woman as in a tug-of-war, it was the husband's people who kept the child. "It's my son," said Manoel, Homero's elder brother and Kadimani's headman, speaking in the name of his agnatic group. "He won't be taken away from us." While the desolate husband expressed his sorrow in interminable soliloquies, his mother painstakingly tried to find a milk donor for her grandson. For a while some women, especially Homero's sister, took turns nursing the infant, until she decided her own baby needed all her milk and stopped nursing the boy. Her mother objected, and she got annoyed and left Kadimani for a few weeks, taking refuge with her sisters at the Sogosi village. One way or another the boy survived, thanks to the prematurely solid food his father's mother diligently provided for him.[16]

The trauma of the parents' separation is not always as great as in the case just described. At Mosonawa, an eight-year-old boy whose mother had separated from his father, the headman of the Kalioko village, lived with his mother while dependent on her for nourishment; once self-sufficient, he began to alternate his residence between Mosonawa, his mother's village, and Kalioko at its downriver location. His mother, a practical woman with a very strong personality and deeply in love with her new husband, made no objection to her son's moves. Her relationship with Kalioko was friendly, and the boy continued to visit her regularly for short periods of time.

Associated with all this is a Sanumá genetic theory which, in slightly different versions, was explained to me by various people, both men and women. The sperm, *moshilibi*, is the substance that makes the embryo (*ulu de thawi*).[17] In the male version rendered by Zeca, the child's sex depends on the testicle that provided the semen; the left testicle produces males, the right one, females. A pregnant woman, *shibinabi*,[18] merely carries the foetus, and it is only after the birth that the child is "really" hers. Close contact with his father makes the boy look like him, and the girl like her mother. Just as the semen is indispensable for the formation of the foetus's physical components, so the mother's milk is essential for the life of the child after birth. That is why nursing is so long, from two to four years, the period of time when the child is most vulnerable and should not share its mother's milk with another baby, for the life of both children would be put at risk. A child can easily die for lack of milk; in such cases it is said to have died *amishi*, "thirsty."

The different roles men and women play in reproduction can also be detected in the collecting of genealogies. Amidst the generalized use of the term for father, to cover all of his brothers and parallel cousins, and mother, to cover all of her sisters and parallel cousins, the least ambiguous way to define paternity and maternity is to refer to the father as the one who "made" (*thabalima* or *thagɨma*) the child, and to the mother as the one who "hugged in the hammock" (*hãkoboma*) or who "nursed" (*sakaboma*) the child. This is the most explicit way for an outsider to know whose child is whose. In its outline, Sanumá genetic theory finds echo in other Yanomami groups as well as in other Amazonian societies with cognatic reckoning.[19] But in the specific case of the Sanumá, this paternal bias seems rather strong, to the point of jeopardizing the child's life by having it separated from its mother in cases of disputes with her and her relatives. It goes hand in hand with name and membership transmission of both sibs and lineages. If a baby's biological father is not its mother's husband, the child will tend to be identified by the former's patronym, regardless of his not having been actually married to the mother. In this way sexual affairs that result in offspring tend to documented in the form of the children's names.

Ideally a woman should have children of both sexes. If she conceives only males she becomes apprehensive that when they grow up they will all go away; on the other hand, when she has exclusively female children, she is equally dissatisfied because, as some mothers said, women do not hunt.[20] In an attempt to correct the imbalance in a family's sex ratio, a woman may seek the services of a shaman who, with the help of his *hekula dɨbɨ*, "assistant spirits," prepares a special baby sling, *tãintata*, or a belt, *shida*, that the woman wears before sexual intercourse. The sling induces the birth of male children, and the belt the birth of female babies. As will be seen in Chapter 4, the balance of the sexes is crucial for group reproduction, as it provides cross-cousins, the preferred spouses, for the next generation.

Whereas certain sibs are said to have specific physical characteristics that identify them, lineages and other agnatic groups have features that are symbolic rather than physical. Each lineage has its own catalogue of food taboos, of dueling and raiding practices, of ceremonial dialogues (Taylor 1977), and of names that are appropriate for its children (see Chapter 8). The array of activities that differ according to lineage affiliation is so vast that we are led to ponder whether the Sanumá complicate their social game in order to make an implicit statement about their own way of conceptualizing themselves. If, on the one hand, there are no specific terms for *lineage*, for *sib*, or for *family*, on the other, there are several layers of references, allusions, proper names, activities, and practices within other practices, all implicating those units. Unlike the "explicit structures" of the Ge societies in Central Brazil, the Sanumá social organization tantalizes the ethnographer by appearing as a huge jigsaw puzzle constantly challenging her interpretive skills.

There are, however, some hints in this Sanumá conceptual teasing that help us dispose the pieces into an intelligible contour. These hints are some relationship terms that are used in a polysemic manner and seem to cover wide regions of the social space like an elastic band binding together various agnatic groups. Let us see what these terms are.

The Inner Circle, the Outer Circle, and the Others

There are terms in the Sanumá language that refer to a close relationship between both people and agnatic groups. Two of these terms are not very common; *awai dɨbɨ* was mentioned only once when two agnatic groups were described as kin; *hanuwɨ de* appeared twice to indicate the distant sibling relationship between two men whose fathers were distant parallel cousins. A third term, *hedu*, is much more common and is used to designate a complementary relationship between peers. Its usage is also polysemic. For instance, it can refer to animal species of the same genus, to a pair of brothers, to members of the same lineage, to lineages that are in a blood relationship to each other, or to persons of the same sib. As far as I know, *hedu* is never applied to affinal relationships.

But the prevailing terms to denote social proximity or distance are *iba dɨbɨ* (my people), *iba ai dɨbɨ* (my other people), and *tiko dɨbɨ* (other people). According to Jorge, *iba dɨbɨ* includes father (*pɨ a*), mother (*pɨbɨna*), siblings of opposite sex (*peze dɨbɨ*), and younger brothers (*poose dɨbɨ*). Although the list is incomplete, it gives an idea of what terms are used within the same family. In Jorge's description, older brothers, *pebala dɨbɨ*, fall into the *iba ai dɨbɨ* category if they have different mothers.[21] *Iba ai dɨbɨ* also refers to distant paternal or maternal kin as well as to affinal relations, such as cross-cousins. As for *tiko dɨbɨ,* Jorge affirmed that they are not relatives at all, but that the expression can be applied to fathers-in-law, *pɨshi dɨbɨ*.

Looking at different situations in which these terms are used, I realized that their application is much more complex than that which Jorge described. Depending on the context and level of contrast one wants to stress, *iba dɨbɨ* may include distant relatives, and *tiko dɨbɨ* may include closely related people (see Chapter 10). If the intention is to reinforce the priority of immediate relatives, one often says *iba dɨbɨ sai,* "my real ones," so as to set them apart from the rest. But if one wants to oppose, for example, his own community to another, he will declare that all his co-residents are his *iba dibi* regardless of kin-affine distinctions. On the other hand, *tiko dibi* can be applied to full brothers as a rhetorical device to mark internal differences within a given agnatic group.

All these terms reveal the great flexibility in the definition of relationships between persons and between agnatic or residence groups. This Sanumá way of applying relationship terms can like a telescope modify the distance between people depending on specific situations and different interests. This flexibility is forged by conjunctures that change both in time and in space. If it is convenient for someone to widen the gap between him and someone else in a given moment, he can simply transform that person from *iba de* to *tiko de*, but the place each of them occupies in the social network will not be affected by this change of treatment. Half brothers do not stop being half brothers just because they referred to each other as *tiko dibi*; in such cases the relationship terms are used as tropes rather than as categorically established concepts.

What emerges from these rhetorical exercises is not only the volatile affect that permeates concrete interaction between real people, but also the intricate meanderings of social conceptualization. We can learn a great deal about the twists and turns of the complicated kinship game at the interpersonal level, but, in order to understand how new agnatic groups come into existence, and how new dialectic relations are established, we have to look elsewhere for clues.

Increase and Divide

In examining genealogical charts we can detect the appearance of agnatic groups within a sib when a new *hedu* relationship is established. Most lineages have less than five generations, for the Sanumá are not concerned with keeping a record of genealogical ties between closely related groups. Even so, I was able to connect two or three of these groups through a single forefather, as follows.

The *lalawa dibi* and *soboshidili dibi* split apart around 1930. Their respective founders were brothers with the same father; some say they had the same mother, others say their mothers were different women. The younger of the two, Lalawa, separated from his brother and joined a distant village; with his offspring he founded the *lalawa dibi* lineage. Meanwhile, his elder brother, known as Lalawa pebala, "Older brother of Lalawa," left his son Soboshidili to play the part of eponym for the group that remained in the original village. *Soboshidili dibi* and *lalawa dibi* were then identified as distinct units within the

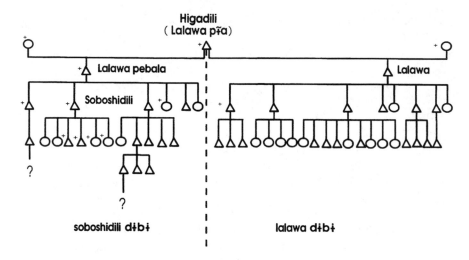

Fig. 2.5. Genealogic connections between *lalawa dɨbɨ* and *soboshidili dɨbɨ* lineages

higadili dɨbɨ sib. Soboshidili died with no progeny, but that does not seem to have altered the consistency of the group. His brothers and their children went on being identified as *soboshidili dɨbɨ*. The diagram in Figure 2.5 illustrates the *lalawa dɨbɨ–soboshidili dɨbɨ* segmentation.

The *nimtali dɨbɨ* sib is divided into at least four lineages. I was able to trace the outline of the fissioning process of three of them, *sogosɨ dɨbɨ*, *omawa dɨbɨ*, and *puluidili dɨbɨ*; of the fourth lineage, *pukumatali dɨbɨ*, located in Venezuela, I know very little. The eponyms of the first three are all sons or grandsons of the same man, already dead. Each son has a different mother. The circumstances that led to the separation of the three brothers and their respective branches are only dimly known, but there is evidence that attacks by the Kobali might be responsible for the dispersal of most of the *nimtali dɨbɨ*. When they separated, each group was already distinguished from the others by virtue of their different mothers. This is one of the most revealing cases of the importance of the mothers for the internal differentiation of a set of half brothers within a sib. Distinct mothers signal important cleavage points, as they herald the particularities generated within polygynous families. This is where the articulation between families and lineages is most prominent. The configuration of the *nimtali dɨbɨ* sib and its lineages is shown in Figure 2.6.

At the community of Mosonawa, the *mosonawa dɨbɨ* lineage, while the founder was alive, consisted of the offspring of his two wives: two sons and one daughter by his senior wife, and one son

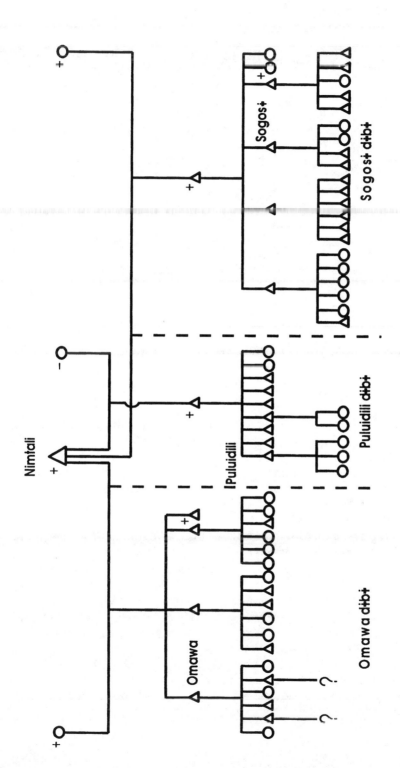

Fig. 2.6. The *nimtali dɨbɨ*

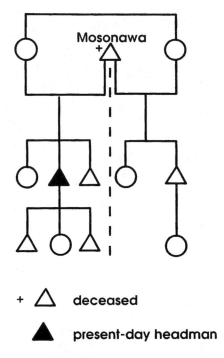

+ △   deceased

▲   present-day headman

Fig. 2.7. The *mosonawa dɨbɨ*

and one daughter by his junior wife. After Mosonawa's death, the two uterine groups of siblings separated; the older branch stayed at Mosonawa, while the younger oscillated between the Kalioko village and the Colony for some time before settling down at the latter, where the daughter was married to a Maiongong man. They are represented in Figure 2.7.

But it is the *kadimani dɨbɨ* lineage, described above, that best illustrates the set of factors that influence the fate of a lineage. For more than thirty years, it has been expanding and fragmenting after an initial phase of concentration in one single village. As we have seen, its satellites are now spread out in various villages, particularly at Mamugula, Mosonawa, and in Samatali country in Venezuela. At Kadimani, its main base, there were, in 1970, some signs of further segmentation. Again, the cleavage point seems to be the line between groups of uterine siblings, that is, half siblings with the same father and different mothers. The sons of the founder's senior and junior wives are considered to be distinct from each other. When the entire agnatic group dispersed following the founder's death, the two sets of siblings went their separate ways along with their respective mothers. It was a temporary division, and they got together again as soon as it was decided who the new headman would be. As it turned out, it was the senior wife's eldest son. I was told by the new headman's sister that they separated from their half siblings because these were *tiko dibi*, "different people." As mentioned earlier, the hyperbolic use of *tiko dibi* when referring to such close relatives as half siblings is a rhetorical way to call attention to the differences that can exist within the same agnatic group. In fact, the junior wife and her children — two young married men, their married sister, and a little girl — carried out most of their daily activities separately from the others and acted as a quasi-independent unit with regard to their half-siblings. Until 1970, they occupied three adjacent compartments in the same long house, and their gardens were contiguous, across the village from those of the other uterine group. They often went camping in the forest by themselves, and when the whole community traveled together, they would erect their shelters near each other, apart from the rest. Nevertheless, they were considered to be full members of the *kadimani dibi* lineage.

The extraordinary growth of the *kadimani dibi* was due to a series of very favorable, even exceptional, circumstances. One of these was the large amount of male births in at least two consecutive generations. Another, perhaps as important, was the opportunity they had to shelter several Magula refugees from an attack by the distant Shikoi. Leading the group of refugees were two elderly sisters who had lost their common husband in the attack. They lived in the mountainous region known as Pasotagi (Mountain of the spider monkey), southeast of Kadimani. The two women and their families were then adopted as co-residents by the Kadimani villagers. Between the two widows they had nine children, seven girls and two boys, plus a pair of grandchildren. With eight marriageable women at home, the *kadimani dibi* men not only found themselves wives with no effort, but even could afford the luxury of contracting polygynous marriages. Even their bride service was light, for their refugee mothers-in-law were in no position to demand much of them. Of all the *kadimani dibi* brothers only one was away, doing bride service at the Kalioko village. Such unusual convergence of lucky factors strengthened the main core of the lineage and guaranteed a whole generation of its men the desired possibility of living together as a coordinated group. Figure 2.8 represents the *kadimani dibi* lineage.

The *kadimani dibi* also evidence two important aspects that may cross a lineage's path. One is the issue of succession to headmanship.

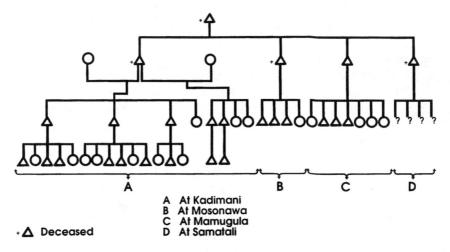

A At Kadimani
B At Mosonawa
C At Mamugula
D At Samatali

+△ Deceased

Fig. 2.8. The *kadimani dɨbɨ*

If the dead leader has no brothers, one of his sons, usually the eldest, will easily take over. But if there are living brothers who are candidates to leadership, then the decision process may result in the dispersal of the entire group. In the case of the *kadimani dɨbɨ*, Gastão, the deceased headman's young brother, lost the position to his nephew, and moved away to live under the leadership of the Mamugula headman.

The other aspect the *kadimani dɨbɨ* exemplify is the solidarity that binds together groups of uterine brothers. By marrying different women, a polygynous man creates cleavage points in his children's generation that may result in distinct agnatic segments epitomized by the figures of their respective mothers. Besides the *kadimani dɨbɨ* and the lineages within the *nimtali* sib, this is likely to occur to the *mosonawa dɨbɨ*, and seems also to have happened to the *lalawa dɨbɨ* and *soboshidili dɨbɨ*. It is a rather predictable fissioning point and becomes publicly recognized when dissident branches acquire a collective name of their own.

Connections between different branches of the same sib are expressed by terms such as *hilo tolea* (the name beyond), and *pɨ a tolea* (the father beyond). It is said, for instance, that the "father beyond" of the *kadimani dɨbɨ*, a member of the *higadili dɨbɨ* sib, "made" the *lalawa dɨbɨ* and, therefore, the *lalawa dɨbɨ* are *hedu* (counterpart) to the *kadimani dɨbɨ*; or that the "name beyond" of the *kadimani dɨbɨ* is *higadili dɨbɨ*. These concepts at one and the same time designate horizontal relationships between agnatic groups and indicate their common

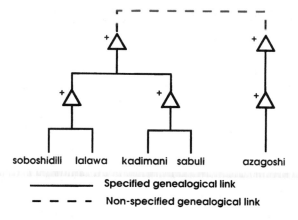

soboshidili lalawa kadimani sabuli   azagoshi

———————— Specified genealogical link

– – – – Non-specified genealogical link

Fig. 2.9. The "fathers beyond" of the *higadili dibi* sib

origin. Within the *higadili dibi* sib we have the connections shown in Figure 2.9. These links refer to forefathers who are supposed to have been elder and younger brother to each other. Genealogical connections are known only in the case of the founders of the *soboshidili dibi*, *lalawa dibi*, *kadimani dibi*, and *sabuli dibi*. Once we reach two generations above the living adults, precision is lost, and the criterion of classificatory relations takes over, either with kinship terms such as *pebala* (older brother) and *poosa* (younger brother), or with sib patronyms.

Encounters and Confrontations

The bonds between people within an agnatic group are very strong. Tense situations among them are rare as compared with the interaction between brothers-in-law, or distant parallel cousins. Full brothers are seldom involved in disputes leading to physical aggression, but when they are, they display as much drama as in any other kind of confrontation. I witnessed only two such occasions. One, at Mosonawa, involved two young brothers, Jorge and Angelo. Their fight was triggered off by the former's irritation with the fact that the latter had denied their little sister a piece of meat, making her cry. The squabble was limited to a bitter argument and some shoving around.

The other case was more dramatic and happened at Kadimani between the two senior brothers of the *kadimani dibi* lineage. It was on an October evening in 1969, at Homero's hearth. Homero, the second son of the deceased founder, is regarded as a difficult character with a volatile temperament. Gossip had it that his real father was a man from a faraway village of the Hogomawa cluster in Venezuela, and that he had been conceived during a *sabonomo* ceremony for the dead. The fight at his house began when he hit his senior wife and one of her sisters, of the refugee family. As the women screamed, he just stood very erect by his wife's hearth, waiting for retaliation. The wife hit him back a few times with a piece of firewood, while his favorite wife, the girl from Venezuela who was later retrieved by her family, simply watched, aloof, from her hammock. All of a sudden, Manoel, Homero's elder brother and village headman, leapt in from the eastern entrance and, brandishing his cutlass, made two or three blows on Homero's back. The entire long house was carried away in a sudden and mighty commotion with people running around between the maze of hammocks and household fires, arming themselves with sticks or whatever they could find. Center stage, the two brothers went on challenging each other amidst a portentous clamor in the best Sanumá style. Manoel burst out saying something about *iba hiziba*, "my wife," referring to the generic term for wife, as his junior wife was a sister of Homero's victims. Once recovered from the surprise attack, Homero demanded *iba boo a, iba boo a* (my cutlass, my cutlass), while his bodily posture was ready for duel. As no *boo a* materialized, he simply borrowed Manoel's and, taking position, struck his elder brother on the back with a blast that resounded through the entire house. Still standing, Manoel shook his head and said, *ma, ma, ma* (no, no, no), as if criticizing his brother's hitting technique. They had moved to the extreme west of the house; Homero's Venezuelan wife had abandoned her hammock and stood about with a stick in her hand. The brothers returned to the center, Manoel was hit again, uttered some more *ma, ma, ma* as he shook his head, shouted *iba boo a* and someone handed him one, but then their mother intervened and no more blows were hurled. Still fuming, Homero left the house muttering something about *sui* (woman) as if to go after his wife, but returned shortly afterward. He kept swaying his body in the typical dueling posture, cutlass in hand, repeating the same phrase over and over again, apparently oblivious to the frenzied crowd around him. Manoel gave up fighting as his mother held his arm (at one point Homero pushed her as if to say contemptuously, "You who gave birth to this man!" or "Get out of my way"). Meanwhile, the issue was being amply discussed. Manoel was still standing with his arms around his shoulders when Homero walked to his hammock, lay down, and the case was closed. Slowly people returned to their hearths. The next day I heard hints that Homero's rage was due to his wife's unfaithfulness; the comments were that she was pregnant by someone else. At any rate, the general criticism aimed at Homero was that one should never hit a pregnant woman, no matter what the reason.

Much more frequent and equally dramatic are the fights between classificatory brothers who belong to different agnatic groups. While we lived at Kadimani we witnessed another confrontation, this time in bright daylight, with long sticks as dueling weapons. One of the men, of the *koima dibi* sib, had made some slanderous remarks about the quality of another man's shamanism. The victim, the leader and oponym of the *sogosi dibi* lineage, interpreted these remarks as an accusation of charlatanism and threatened to beat up the accuser. Sogosi gathered his supporters and they all marched on Kadimani, with black paint on their faces, while local women ran around in panic alerting the others of the approach of *wazu dibi* ("Raiders!" "Enemies!"). The men picked up their weapons, the women yelled apprehensive omens, the children screamed in fright, the dogs barked in excitement, and even the hens ran around in disorientation. The main event was the duel between the two men who called themselves brothers, for they were related as distant parallel cousins. Under the watchful eyes of the large and nervous audience, the victim sent his dueling pole flying in an arc to land with force on his opponent's head; a second blow nearly knocked the opponent over, while blood slowly trickled down his face and body, all the way to his toes. There was an intensification of the screams and shouts from the audience, and when the offender recovered a little, he took his turn to also hit the victim's head twice. Both men were bleeding profusely, and the audience's agitation reached a climax. The duel was over, but tension was still very high. Men from both villages began to hit each other, taking advantage of the occasion to settle old grudges. A generalized melee ensued and lasted for some minutes before the air began to clear. The whole event took no more than one hour. At the end of the catharsis exhaustion took over and remarks began to be heard about how the whole thing had been an unfortunate misunderstanding. The offender declared that his remarks about the other's shamanism had been meant as a joke (*shiwashimo bio*), and the world resumed its normal course. Among people who stand as *iba ai dibi* to each other, as do the actors of this drama, relationships are intense, friendly, but potentially explosive.

Quarrels between brothers-in-law are more frequent, particularly when a brother protects his sister from the beatings of a husband. Women, who usually stay with their blood relatives after marriage, count on their brothers for support and security whenever their husbands attempt to beat them. In this sense, bride service represents protection for the woman and an opportunity for her brothers to show the husband their strength, especially if he is an outsider. In Auaris, with its three communities in proximity, the effects of village exogamy are much reduced. For a Mosonawa man to marry a Colony woman all he needed to do was to cross the mission's lawn. That meant that the least sign of a husband-wife skirmish attracted the attention of the entire set of communities, the members of which always acted as both audience and referees.

Conflicts are reduced to a minimum within a lineage or a co-resident group of agnates who stand, after all, as a virtual lineage. As we have seen, fights do occur, but they are few and far between. A high degree of solidarity and cooperation is expected of lineage companions. The phrase *iba dɨbɨ sai* (my real people) is an expression of this solidarity, as is the sharing of food and services, and the proximity of their dwellings and garden plots.

The closeness and cooperation between co-resident agnates, made evident with a simple glance at a village's "economic map," are even more apparent when compared with the situation of people who have no agnates nearby. Agnatically isolated men may not be economically deprived, but they lack the comfort and security of counting on their own relatives for whatever needs arise. Men who have no close agnates or live apart from them are more likely to be exploited by their in-laws and more prone to accusations of theft, adultery, and other abusive acts. The phrase *iba ai dɨbɨ* (my others) denotes the ambivalence that exists in the relationship between affines and distant kin. They are both "my people" (*iba dɨbɨ*) and "other people" (*ai dɨbɨ*). The discomfort that accompanies much of their interaction can be observed in certain situations (see Chapter 8). Children, for instance, react with whispers and facial expressions of slight annoyance at the approach of one of their *iba ai dɨbɨ*. With their ever candid and disarmed reactions, children are the best conveyors of information that adults are often reluctant to disclose but end up confirming.

The development of agnatic groups into lineages is a manifestation of one of the most striking features in Sanumá social life. The passage from a mere group of father and sons to a full-fledged long-term collectivity represents a triumph over the centrifugal effect of village exogamy; that can happen when this effect is neutralized by the continued co-residence of agnatically related men after marriage. A lineage is, therefore, the time-honored expression of men's success in conquering their own space against all odds. To live in the parental community, which women take for granted as their place from birth to death, is, from a man's point of view, a privilege that can be gained or lost with marriage. The male success in winning this space is attested by the achievement by certain men of the status of founders, *pɨ dɨbɨ tolea* (fathers beyond). These were politically skilled men who secured for their heirs an abode of their own, wise men who transcended space and transformed it into a time sequence embodied in lineages that have lasted for generations.

From Historical Communities to Patrilineal Categories

Lineages are not the only way in which residence coalesces into patrilineality. In the history of the upper Auaris communities there are certain social categories associated with old residence clusters. Their size and social importance for the present-day Sanumá were evident in virtually every narrative I heard about their past. For a number of reasons, among which were enemy attacks, about two or three generations ago, the residents of those former villages had to abandon their houses and gardens and scatter northward. The most intriguing aspect of these communities is that, in the process of dispersing, they were transformed into patrilineal units. A brief outline of these categories and of their spatial trajectory is necessary for the understanding of the whole process. In order to simplify the reading, I omit most details related to their moves, as they are laden with names of rivers, streams, gardens, and peoples that do little more than clutter the text.

Around 1940, the parents and grandparents of today's adult residents of the upper Auaris communities used to live in the region of the Ocamo River, a right-side tributary of the Orinoco in Venezuela, several days' walk from Auaris (see Map 1). The Sanumá name for the Ocamo is Sauladu, and that is why the Auaris people regard themselves as *saulagɨdili dɨbɨ*, the "people of the Sauladu." The Saulagɨdili category encompasses the Kadimani, Mosonawa, Sabuli, and Azagoshi communities. As a historical site, the Sauladu has a very prominent position in people's memory, judging by the constant references they make to the huge village or cluster of villages (a woman described it as a big round house) by the edge of the Ocamo River. People mention enormous gardens to indicate how large the Saulagɨdili population used to be.

The term Saulagɨdili is always employed in contrast to place names, such as villages, rivers, or mountains already occupied and historicized by the Sanumá. When I asked if someone was a Saulagɨdili and the answer was no, they said that the person used to live in another place, *tiko ham*, named X. Membership in the Saulagɨdili is never contrasted or compared to sib or lineage membership. But nowadays *saulagɨdili dɨbɨ* has become a patronym, and even the young generation who were born at Auaris are *saulagɨdili dɨbɨ*, following their paternal identification. It is said that they should not intermarry, but it happens with some frequency, as between the *azatali dɨbɨ* and the *sadali dɨbɨ*, both *saulagɨdili* sibs.

The *higadili* sib has the particularity of having some members who are *saulagɨdili dɨbɨ* and others who are not. At a phase before the settlement at the Sauladu, the *lalawa dɨbɨ* and *soboshidili dɨbɨ* lineages were together with other *higadili* members. When they separated, they took different routes and never lived at the Sauladu; as a consequence, they are not regarded as *saulagɨdili dɨbɨ*. This Saulagɨdili category thus cuts across sibs and bisects lineages within the same sib, depending on the course of people's migrations. The sharing of the same site for an extended period of time is then imprinted in the history of the agnatic groups as yet another diacritic for their identity. This may be why the *lalawa dɨbɨ* displayed a marked social distance with regard to the other *higadili* lineages.

In a previous phase, the Totobɨdili were another residence cluster located on the Totobiu stream southeast of Auaris. I know very little about it, young people know practically nothing, and only the elderly still retain a dim memory of their experience of it. It was an old woman who told me that the *higadili dɨbɨ*, the *azatali dɨbɨ*, and the *hazatagɨdili dɨbɨ* sibs were all part of the Totobɨdili cluster. From her report I could gather that this cluster once included these groups that were to constitute the *saulagɨdili dɨbɨ* and a few others that did not join in the Sauladu phase. We could attempt a graphic representation of the relationship between the *saulagɨdili dɨbɨ* and the *totobɨdili dɨbɨ* as in Figure 2.10.

The Saulagɨdili disbanded because of attacks by the Samatali who lived downriver on the Sauladu. Their northward exodus was done in stages with several relocations. At each move, one or more agnatic groups broke away from the others. Gardens that were opened along the way have become historical landmarks of their migrations and subsequent occupation of a new territory. Some sites were held for longer than others, making a stronger mark in people's memories, as, for instance, the place known as Pɨlɨsɨbɨ-dulia (Clean land, Savanna), where many of the present-day adults were born. Like beacons in the trajectory of these communities, births and gardens allow us to retrace, albeit rather imprecisely, some of the steps of that long journey northward.

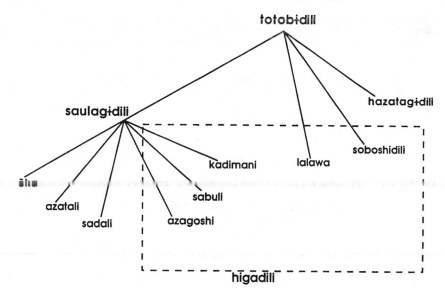

Fig. 2.10. The *totobɨdili dɨbɨ* and the *saulagɨdili dɨbɨ*

In their dispersal, the Saulagɨdili subdivided into at least six large groupings that include three communities in Brazil and three in Venezuela. The Venezuelan branch comprises the brothers of the deceased Mosonawa headman. From a report by Mosonawa's senior widow, his father was killed by the Maiongong (*nabɨ dɨbɨ*), while they lived in a place known as Holemabɨ-dulia (The place full of worms). They were on a family visit, *wazɨmɨ,* at Sauladu when the Maiongong killed him. Mosonawa was already married and living on the Sauladu with several brothers, when they suffered an attack by the Samatali and moved away again (*dɨbɨ selegɨbazoma,* "people dispersed"). Mosonawa headed for the Auaris region; his elder brother stayed with the *azagoshi dɨbɨ* to the south; a younger brother went to the Merevari River looking for a wife; and another younger brother went north, also into Venezuela, made a garden, and settled there.

The Sauladu residence group seems to have lasted about two generations, for none of the parents of the Auaris adults seems to have been born there. The village, or village cluster, was established during the lifetime of the older generation, and abandoned when their children were still young. To this day, their children and grandchildren are identified as *saulagɨdili dɨbɨ,* even though their birthplace and residence are nowhere near the Sauladu.

With regard to the Sogosɨ, Mamugula, and other communities

that are now located south of Auaris, most come from a residence cluster named Pasotagɨdili, after the Pasotagɨ Mountain, several days' walk southeast of Auaris. Sib members of this cluster are *nimtali dɨbɨ, kazuma dɨbɨ, magula dɨbɨ, oladili dɨbɨ, neadili dɨbɨ,* and *shilawa dɨbɨ.* Their dispersal seems to have been more limited and recent than that of the Saulagɨdili. It is said that only the Magula still live in the original site, but my genealogical survey indicates that various members of other sibs are also there.

As in the case of some lineages, these historical residence categories have a well-defined local base, have gone through a process of geographic dispersal, and are a way of fighting oblivion by transforming space into time. The collective memory of these residence clusters is preserved by the tactic of recourse to patrilineal transmission. What was a grounded reality, that is, the experience of village co-residence, has become a temporal entity embodied in the members of a rather blurry category. It is as if the Sanumá painstakingly hold onto a past that not only belongs to the elderly who lived it but must be carried on indefinitely by their offspring.

We may ask what these historical categories have to do with the sibs. In what way might they help us uncover the riddle of sib formation? The fact that these categories persist through time, well after they have lost their spatial locus, evokes again the comparison made by Zeca between the Sanumá sibs and the whites' hometowns. Can we assume that groupings such as the Saulagɨdili might be the forerunners of future sibs? Although manifestly speculative, such a hypothesis has at least the merit of making sense of the fact that some sib names take the *-dili* suffix, thus denoting "dwellers in a given place," such as Saulagɨdili, Pasotagɨdili, and so forth.

On the other hand, I have already raised the possibility that oversized lineages, by a continuous process of expansion and subdivision, may be transformed into sibs, which would make sense of those sib names that have no *-dili* suffix. Sib names such as *nimtali* or *koima* might be traces of the personal names of the founders of extinct megalineages. It would not be too hard to imagine the present-day *kadimani dɨbɨ* lineage having grown to such proportions as to erupt into a myriad of dispersed agnates, as was the case with today's *higadili dɨbɨ* sib. A lineage that expanded into a sib would no doubt be related to its parent sib as a son to a father, a possibility that is signaled in a number of empirical examples. Memory of their former relation of inclusiveness—a lineage within a sib—would be kept in the form of a kinship father-son relation.

Taking this conjectural exercise to its logical conclusions, it is possible to envision two separate roads converging into one single solution, the sibs. One of these roads would be that of lineages that outgrow the limits of their expansion; the other would be that of historical residence clusters that lose their roots in space and are transposed to a time dimension via patrilineal descent. Either way, the focus on descent stems from a group's previous experience of prolonged co-residence. That which begins as a space referent resolves itself as the cornerstone for a descent construction. And so events become names, names become patronyms. In this way they enter the group's memory and are passed on to posterity. It is as if the Sanumá were intent on testing how far they can push their luck with transmuting space into time.

The historical residence clusters are perhaps the most finished products of such experiments in space diachronization. They are the nodes of a historical interest that is preserved in the social memory, so as to resist the hazards of the migrations the Sanumá underwent in the last one hundred years.[22] Once the hub of Sanumá society, these residential spaces have won the status of topographic ancestors for many of the upper Auaris people. Who knows if, together with some exceptional lineages, they will not become the sibs of future generations.

3
Diachrony and Leadership

A Diachronic Structure

In Chapter 2 we saw the plethora of agnatic groups large and small that constitute the social core of Sanumá communities. Related to each other in the fashion of Chinese boxes, these agnatic groups reveal an ongoing trend of fissioning all the way from well-established lineages to simple father-son arrangements. The result is that, in the span of a field research—six years in my case—what the ethnographer perceives at first sight is an assorted collection of social specimens with no apparent nexus to hold them together in a coherent whole. The underlying meaning of it all came to me only after a considerable effort to analyze the material I had gathered in the field. What follows is the result of my retrospective venture.

In my search for a way to render intelligible the array of agnatic groups that come in different shapes like loose pieces of a jigsaw puzzle, I resorted to the classic developmental cycle, as I had done with the families in Chapter 1. This analytic recourse, initiated by Meyer Fortes in 1958, was also used by Hildred and Clifford Geertz in 1975 in their attempt to make sense of the *dadia* phenomenon they found in Bali,[1] and implicitly applied by Stirling (1965) for rural Turkey.[2] In order to carry out this exercise, it is necessary to introduce a series of variables that play an important role in the developmental cycle of Sanumá agnatic groups. These variables are as follows: the birth of male children; the demographic balance of the sexes within a village; the deflecting impact of marrying out, or its reverse, the consolidating effect of marrying within one's own community; and the process of village fissioning with its fairly predictable cleavage lines.

Theoretically, any man can become a lineage founder, but for this to happen two conditions are necessary, albeit not always sufficient. He must have sons and keep them together as his co-residents for the amount of time it takes to consolidate them as an agnatic group. A number of factors, however, can and often do conspire against such a plan, and at any moment may halt the growth of an agnatic group. One of these factors is the dispersal that uxorilocality can bring to a group of brothers. Although the preference is to marry within one's own village, there may not be sufficient marriageable women available to all brothers, which means that at least some of them will have to leave in search of wives. In fact, during the six years of my field research, less than 40 percent of the men succeeded in getting married and remaining in the company of their fathers. The long period of bride service may render a man's departure irreversible as he becomes increasingly integrated into his wife's community. Unless he separates, the odds are that he will stay with his in-laws. Therefore, a man's chances of founding a distinct agnatic group will dwindle considerably if most or all of his sons go away to marry. In such situations, there will be no nucleus of co-resident agnates capable of sustaining the minimum of continuity in time and in space for a lineage to develop.

But even under auspicious circumstances, at any moment an agnatic group may have its existence threatened by the vicissitudes of the marriage market and random birthrates. Recognizing these hazards, women affirm their dislike for having children of just one sex. In the long run, an ideal sex ratio is an equal number of sons and daughters. If, on the one hand, a large number of male children increases the chances of perpetuating the membership of an agnatic group, on the other hand, it is the combination of co-resident brothers and sisters that provides the next generations with the desirable spouses, that is, cross-cousins.

When a lineage grows and takes over the village headmanship, the probability of its splitting also increases; some branches move away, leaving behind the main core around the village headman. For an indeterminate period of time, the splinter branches retain the name of the parent lineage while their social ties are still strong. Slowly, these collateral offshoots become more independent, and eventually they will either develop into full-fledged lineages of their own, or will fragment still further, leaving in their wake a number of scattered individuals residing in different villages. Having lost their old lineage identity, these expatriates, as it were, are left with their sib affiliation and nothing more specific.[3] These are men usually found as incoming husbands in villages that are dominated by one or two lineages to which they can never belong. But, at least in theory, there is always the possibility that they may initiate a lineage of their own.

Sanumá lineages are an example of how space can be translated

into time, but this is an unpredictable time that may range all the way
from a short interlude to a period of several generations. At any rate,
even in the case of well-established lineages, they might be better pic-
tured as a normal curve that rises and falls than as a pyramid, a tree,
or any other figure that insinuates stability. We can follow the twists
and turns of their fate by accompanying some moments in the trajectory of a hypothetical lineage. The concrete agnatic groups that I observed in the field are the pieces of the jigsaw puzzle I now attempt to
put together.

We can begin the cycle with the members of a family—father,
mother, sons and daughters. Each one of them begins to be identified
by a teknonym that takes as its referent the personal name of one of
the children, preferably a boy; for example, Father of Koli, Mother of
Koli, Sister of Koli, Younger brother of Koli. The whole family group
may become known as "The Koli people." In this phase it is fundamental that all these close relatives live together. With luck all the
sons will marry neighboring women so that they will have only to
change houses to perform their bride service duties, while the daughters will attract husbands to their parents' house. In that way, in the
next generation there should be a reasonable proportion of cross-
cousins who can intermarry.

In the third generation, the sons' children will also remain together, boys and girls marrying into the community. Several male
children are born to the men, thus increasing the number of agnatically related males. By now a collective name is applied to all of them.
Demographic factors such as sex and number of children continue to
be decisive for the group's development. It may reach a considerable
size, especially if the men have polygynous marriages. Thus strengthened, the group is bound to take over village headmanship. From
then on there is a tendency for the community to fission.

The reason for fissioning may be the disproportionate growth of
the lineage for the ideal village size. A population well above fifty
people begins to be a strain on the accessible natural resources, on its
political consistency, or both. Conflicting interests arise due either to
the quest for autonomy on the part of some segments, or to the intensity of strife within the community. The occasion for fissioning
may come at the time of dispersal following the death of the village
headman.[4] The dispersed segments may reunite after the issue of succession is resolved, or they may not. The shattering of the original agnatic group may then be inevitable.

The segments that are thus separated may disperse even further
until they become reduced to small fragments of agnatic relatives or

even isolated individuals under someone else's leadership. The central core of the original lineage may linger, holding onto the village headmanship by sheer political inertia. There will be a time, however, when another group in the village will become demographically and politically more important, and then headmanship will certainly change hands. In these cases, the shift of headmanship seems also to be preceded by the temporary dispersal of the community.[5]

Dispersal at moments of crisis thus seems to soothe the social strain that comes before an important collective decision, such as the change of political leadership *inter vivos*. It is as though dispersal were a sort of rite of passage that suspends normal time and space so as to create a shield against direct and immediate confrontation between the possible candidates to village leadership. Physical separation would have the effect of cooling down the tempers at the same time as paving the way to a smooth headmanship transmission.[6]

But if, on the one hand, dispersal can ease the way to the resolution of a community's political problems, on the other hand it may condemn to social solitude people who are severed from their forefathers' lineages. Those who are unable to create their own agnatic group will be reduced to the condition of appendages to other groups in other villages, while their offspring will probably lose the identity of their original lineage.

In another scenario, we may consider the lineage that overcomes all the obstacles against its growth, reaches maturity, and disperses its segments in different directions. This lineage may very well be on its way to becoming a sib. If it keeps its collective name and the concept of blood relations among its members, and if its founder is forgotten, the lineage may acquire the characteristics of a sib, that is, a long-standing social category comprising people loosely interconnected and without a common residence.

This brief summary of the hypothetical cycle of development of a Sanumá lineage reaching maximum expansion presumes the convergence of all favorable circumstances (recurring male births, intravillage marriages in successive generations, and the holding of political leadership). The *kadimani dibɨ* lineage, as described in Chapter 2, is the closest living example I know of this ideal trajectory. It has several collateral branches, some already separated, others about to break off; its men benefited from the arrival and subsequent settlement in their village of a number of refugee women who greatly contributed to its growth. Most lineages, however, never reach these dimensions, dissolving before they have the opportunity to grow and propagate themselves in various communities. There are also lineages that do

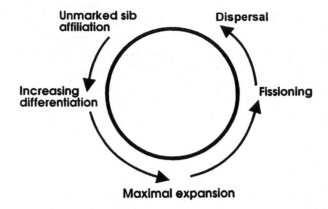

Fig. 3.1. The developmental cycle of Sanumá lineages

not obtain headmanship, and probably never will. Attempts by groups of kinsmen to hold together and construct a joint future are constantly aborted by setbacks that return them to step one. Considering all the circumstances that conspire against the expansion of agnatic groups, it is no wonder that so few of them get to be mature lineages. The fact that only half of the people in my data were lineage members shows how strongly inhibiting those circumstances can be. The traces left by collapsed lineages attest to this continual disintegration.

The path agnatic groups tread is so fluid as to blur the different phases in the developmental cycle, especially since there is a great deal of overlap between these phases. It is difficult, for instance, to decide whether a certain group of kinsmen is a swollen agnatic nucleus, an incipient lineage, or a dying lineage. A similar problem was confronted by the Geertzes (1975) in their analysis of the Balinese *dadias*.

Perhaps the graphic image most appropriate to depict the Sanumá lineage cycle is an arc or open circle, as in Figure 3.1. It should be noted that the direction of the arrows can be inverted at any point in the circle. Like a pendulum that swings into a near circle when given a hard push, the momentum of a developing lineage may take it all the way to a full arc, or may halt its course if the initial impetus is removed. The developmental cycle of the Sanumá lineages may lead them to a climax, or may reduce them to inertia and oblivion.

The Sanumá, Balinese, and Turkish cases indicate the importance of considering time as an essential component in the workings of at least certain types of social organization. An integral part of "diach-ronic structures," as these three seem to be, is the disclosure of their intelligibility through time. If time is omitted, we get a distorted pic-ture of either an excessively "fluid" organization, or a disparate as-sortment of fragments of a structure that appears to be unfinished. Structures such as these make sense only when viewed as a process that unfolds through time and is part and parcel of their internal logic.

The theoretical implications of all of this cannot be overlooked, as they lead to the inevitable conclusion that time is a necessary feature of social structures and that anthropological analysis must take it into account as a matter of course. I am not referring to change in struc-tures, be it internally or externally induced. What I am saying is that "structural diachrony" or, alternatively, "diachronic structures" are themselves in a permanent state of flux. They are exemplified in Leach's famous analysis of the oscillation between the *gumsa* and *gum-lao* categories in Highland Burma. Pareto's model of "moving equilib-rium," says Leach (1954:xi), "presupposes that the total phenomenon which is in equilibrium is a social system which has extension in time as well as in space."

It is therefore possible that all social structures have a built-in time component that goes unnoticed because of the consistency and regu-larity of their concrete manifestations at a given moment. For in-stance, could the village plans of the Ge societies of Central Brazil, with their exemplary symmetry and coherence, conceal another di-mension, more complex and revealed only when examined diachro-nically? Not only is it possible, but there are strong signs that it might be so, at least in some Ge groups.[7]

But in such cases as in the Sanumá lineages, the time element comes to the fore precisely because it renders chaotic the synchronic manifestations of a process that lasts much longer than the life of any specific lineage.

Two issues can then be raised. One has to do with the limitations of the synchronic approach as the only lens for observing social struc-tures or, for that matter, anything else. The other issue is the temp-tation to attribute unresolved problems of analysis to the conse-quences of change in the society in question. In the Sanumá, Balinese, and Turkish cases, it is essential to resort to diachrony. But how many other cases are there which, because they did not pose these same problems to the researcher, leave us with a false synchronous façade, and therefore an only partial understanding of that society? It would seem reasonable to propose that, before attributing apparent anoma-lies to social change or to research distortions, we consider the possibility that such "anomalies" may well be part of the normal dynamics of the society under study.

My point here is different from that raised by Sahlins (1981, 1985) about Polynesia. In his case, both native and Western cultural elements combine to make a "structural history" and show ways in which "history is organized by structures of meaning" (Sahlins 1981:8). In the Sanumá case, I find heterogenous elements that are apparently coming from the same tradition and arranged in juxtapositions that are keyed to a diachronic rather than historical order. My purpose is not to show that the seemingly chaotic course of history is, after all, structured, but to emphasize that structure itself, even at its most formal, is embedded in a time dimension. Lineages enter and exit the system without substantially altering the essence of that system, just as individuals enter and exit sibs without transforming them. It is a matter of processuality rather than historicity. My problem seems closer to that analyzed by Terence Turner for the Ge, if I understand the following passage to point toward structural diachrony:

> This set of coordinated transformations leading from stage to stage of the reproduction of the entity *is* the structure of its process of reproduction. The invariant principle of coordination regulating all of the stages of the reproductive or developmental cycle of an entity must obviously be of a higher order of abstraction and generality than the structure of the particular phases considered separately. . . . It can only be defined analytically by analyzing structures as developmental . . . processes rather than as static finished products. (T. Turner 1979b:171)

The most striking feature of the Sanumá lineages is their immense plasticity. Just as they can die out at each generation, they can also emerge out of nothing from one generation to the next. Their fragility results directly from incidents which are always lurking around the corner ready to halt their course, and which are in turn responsible for a very dynamic flow of agnatic groups. It is this dynamism of the groups, most of them ephemeral, that leads to the circulation of men from village to village, and of political power from hand to hand. A lineage reaches its peak when it retains the village headmanship, yet one lineage's decline is another lineage's ascent. And so this continues through the generations, in the trail of chance events over which people have little or no control, no matter how predictable these events may be.

Before moving on to the consequences of this process for the political life of the villages, I would like to draw a few profiles of men who are outside the lineage system and who circulate around Sanumá society as if they were actors without a well-defined role, or characters without an author. The notion of character or personage relates to the fulfillment of the social persona, and that of author evokes the quasi demiurge who opens the channels for that fulfillment, to wit, a lineage founder.

Two Characters in Search of an Author

After two years of intense interaction with the Sanumá of the upper Auaris River, especially in the communities at the mission and Kadimani, I was left with the impression that the most complex and controversial characters are men without lineage affiliation. If my impression has any basis, this phenomenon might be attributed to reasons associated with these men's socialization and life experience. Although I have no thorough knowledge of their life histories, I can indicate some aspects that seem to me too salient to be simply a figment of my imagination or mere coincidence.

Let us take Zeca, a witty man who in 1974 was still young and living at the mission. Like many other people I met at Auaris, Zeca was sumi, "alone," that is, he belonged to no agnatic group. He and his elder brother, orphaned of both mother and father since childhood, are two of the many members of the higadili dɨbɨ sib without lineage affiliation. The two brothers are very different in temperament. While Zeca is shrewd and extroverted, his brother is shy to the point of being nearly invisible.

In the two years I lived at Auaris, the vivacious and sardonic Zeca had plenty of opportunity to demonstrate both humor and pain. Capable of making his companions roar with laughter, of exasperating his ethnographers with constant jokes and mocking allusions, he had also lived the trauma of the loss of a five-year-old son. For nights on end he roamed around the mission trails, all alone with the echo of his own wailing, piercing the darkness with his cries of piza wai, piza wai (my little son, my little son). He was consumed with regrets for the harm he felt he had done to the child and for the good he had failed to do him. He refused to have a sabonomo ceremonial for the boy because he was too sad and too enraged with the death (both feelings are expressed by the term hɨsho). It was the azagoshi dɨbɨ and the sadali dɨbɨ, neighboring people, who drank the deceased's bone ashes well after Zeca's friend, Kalioko, had cremated the body.

Zeca affirmed that ever since long ago he had not danced at sabonomos and that he never drank bone ashes, tutu ɨshi. Way back he

had drunk the ashes of a sib companion and was very sick. From then
on he decided not to take them again, and he even had the approval
of the elders, *pada dɨbɨ*, who recognized that he was an exception to
the Sanumá norm. He does not suck tobacco, *pini*, in Yanomami fashion (a wet bundle of tobacco leaves wrapped up in ashes and pressed
against the lower lip and teeth), which is very unusual for a Sanumá.
Since he was a child he has rejected it, saying that tobacco is dirty,
and even the Maiongong ask him why he does not like it. He engages
in no ceremonial dialogues, *wazamo*, because, he says, he can only
speak slowly; in order to do *wazamo* a man has to be skilled in the
strong and fast speech that is fired at his opponent. He is not a shaman because he never learned how to shamanize, although his father
was a great shaman and would have taught him were he alive. But his
father died, and Zeca, *hɨsho*, refused to acquire any *hekula* spirits. Neither he nor his brother does shamanism or knows how to use the shaman's *sakona* hallucinogen. Several times I saw his brother get completely giddy, oblivious of his surroundings, lost in the drug's effects,
showing no sign of shamanic competence, but I never saw Zeca take
sakona.

In short, Zeca rejects the use of *pini*, does not perform *wazamo*,
does not drink *tutu ɨshi*, does not perform shamanism, and does not
take *sakona*. Taken together these denials and abstinences amount to a
resounding divorce from Sanumá life.

Zeca was born west of Auaris at a site know as Totobɨ-dulia, in
Venezuela. He was a toddler when first his father, and then his
mother, died. He and his elder brother were raised by their maternal
grandmother, an almost legendary female character who came to the
fore again and again during the collection of genealogies. Zeca lived
with people of the *sadali dɨbɨ* and *ōka dɨbɨ* sibs, and with the *azagoshi
dɨbɨ* lineage, a member of his own *higadili dɨbɨ* sib. He spent his adolescence at the Sabuli village where he accompanied his brother who
was doing bride service to the local headman. From Sabuli they
moved to Venezuela. He was still very young when he married a prepubescent girl of the *sadali dɨbɨ* sib, but he loathed how she cried for
her mother whenever they traveled. He visited other villages regularly, and, at last, he left the girl for good. He was single for a long
while until, in his version, he was attracted by an older woman who
was about to divorce her husband and had a prepubescent son. She is
one of a group of eight sisters who live in various villages of the region. Before marrying her, Zeca used to call her *nawa*, "mother,"
a fact that he did not admit to me, but that was confirmed by several other people. For him she was *tiko de*, "other," from the *azatali*

dibɨ sib, and, therefore, perfectly marriageable. Her ex-husband, a man from the *koima dibɨ* sib, was not very upset and remarried soon afterward.[8]

Zeca's profile is that of an agnatically lonely man. He lost one son, but his other male children may still come to initiate a lineage. His brother, on the other hand, has a lesser chance of becoming the founder of an agnatic group, as he is sexually impotent, a fact that became known when his ex-wife got pregnant by another husband. This piece of information was given to me by a Mosonawa woman with great dismay and after much reluctance. I was doubly surprised by the fact in itself, and by the woman's reaction to it. Her tone denoted a tragedy, a misfortune that could be caused only by someone's evil magic with *alawali* magic plants.

The future for Zeca and his brother seems to be the life of an in-marrying spouse amongst affines and distant kin. Zeca's extroverted character makes him the target of much village gossip; people accuse him of various sorts of tricks, such as small thefts and other misdemeanors. His exuberance conceals a life of hurdles and contradictions; he is a Sanumá like anyone else, but he dislikes or avoids things and actions that are ostensibly Sanumá; he is smart and gifted, but he cannot or does not want to channel his talents to a career as a Sanumá great man.

In contrast to Zeca's vivacity, another Auaris man, Lucio, has a reputation for being gloomy, bad-tempered, and violent. People criticize him for his bitter, even cruel disposition, and for his eccentric behavior as manifested, for instance, in his phases of isolation when he leaves the community and goes to the forest to live alone with his wife of the moment. He was once accused of having caused the death of his stepdaughter and niece (daughter of his deceased elder brother). When the nine-year-old girl died, her belly swelled abnormally, and Lucio was then blamed for having raped her, thus perpetrating two offenses at once: molesting a child, and committing incest. His marriage to the girl's mother was a succession of bitter fights and difficult reconciliations. Easily incensed, Lucio is a source of anxiety and censure in whichever community he happens to live. When tension around him grows too high, he takes refuge in the forest.

The only surviving male of a group of nine siblings, Lucio belongs to the *azatali dibɨ* sib, the son of a man regarded as important, but who did not found any significant agnatic group. Lucio's elder brother, also highly respected, died a mature man, leaving two widows and five children. Kalioko married one of the widows, and Lucio married the other. Judging by his hostility toward his wife, it is as though Lucio never forgave her for reminding him of how much greater his brother was than he, and how he went on to become even greater after death.

A very warm, congenial and quick-witted woman, Lucio's wife had various intense conversations with me when she revealed how miserable life with Lucio was for her. One of the babies she had after marrying Lucio was supposedly illegitimate. The baby died of apparent neglect on her part; she insisted that the infant "didn't know" how to suckle. Yet another had died earlier in one of the most terrifying episodes I ever heard of in the field. One night, she was holding the baby and fell asleep by the fire. The infant slipped from her lap and fell into the flames. Awakened by the screams of a co-resident, she watched as the child burned to death before her astonished and paralyzed eyes. It was the sixth child of her twelve pregnancies, and the last one she had by Lucio's elder brother. In 1974, only three children remained; the older of the two boys had been living in the outskirts of the town of Boa Vista for a number of years.[9]

The story of her marriage to Lucio is saturated with resentments caused mainly by Lucio's constant womanizing. When I looked at the data I collected on her reproductive life, I noticed that whenever she spoke of the loss of her babies she also expressed bitterness about her husband's infidelities. One wonders whether this is a coincidence.

Lucio seemed to use polygyny not only as a weapon against his wife, but also as a possible source of prestige which in his case did not work. Once he brought a young orphan from Venezuela to Auaris. She was extremely shy and appeared frightened among the strangers who were now her neighbors and in-laws. She bore him a son and a little later he abandoned her. The baby stayed with him. A while later, he kidnapped the beautiful young wife of old Armando, a respected man at Sabuli village. Rather than accruing prestige, Lucio was stalked in the forest by two sons of the old man. Because they rescued not the woman but her infant girl, the child was separated from her mother and died *amishi*, "thirsty [for mother's milk]." I found Lucio at the mission in 1973, proud of his latest woman. For a change, his senior wife did not object for the simple reason that her new co-wife was her sister's daughter, a close kin, and, therefore, an ally rather than a rival.

In his adolescence Lucio accompanied one of his half sisters who was married to Lourenço, the Maiongong who later founded the Colony. He lived among the Maiongong for several years, learned their language, and became an interpreter whenever there was a confrontation between Sanumá and Maiongong (Ramos 1980:36–37). It

Lucio and one of his young wives. 1973. Photograph by K. I. Taylor.

was a very remarkable experience for him and makes one think that perhaps he never got over it, this being the reason why he is so clearly uncomfortable among the Sanumá. He is a shaman, but not an exceptional one. He does *wazamo*, but his performances are modest.

Cruel, out of control, bad husband, worse father, a runaway from the company of his peers — these are not the attributes that go into the making of the founder of a lineage or of anything. People put up with Lucio rather than accept him.

With these vignettes I would like to raise a question that may be unorthodox but that is deserving of attention all the same. I am not implying that every man who has no lineage affiliation is psychotic, maladjusted, or the living image of the antihero. I have known many others in situations similar to those of Zeca and Lucio who do not stand out for anything more spectacular than quietly performing their bride service duties. I have also known a few who, even as lineage members, attract people's attention because of a random peculiarity, such as a *lalawa dɨbɨ* man who was the target of constant jokes and exploitation by other men who had him do women's work (such as fetching water). What is distinctive about Zeca and Lucio is the wide range of ways in which they disregard the Sanumá canons of propriety. It is not common to see such a display of willful rebelliousness toward things Sanumá as that demonstrated by Zeca, nor is it every day that the same person can annoy so many people as Lucio does. Irresponsible conduct is always around, but seldom so regularly and predictably. The little I know of Zeca's and Lucio's life histories shows the uprooting of their family and community ties as perhaps the deepest scar in their lives. Those who are born, grow up, and live their lives surrounded by close kinsmen, as is the case with lineage members, uplifted by the comfortable assurance that they can count on them for whatever comes their way, rarely experience the isolation that can be detected in the actions and words of those two men.

Extreme cases such as theirs seem to be exceptions that confirm the rule. Although the majority of nonaffiliated men lead a much more tranquil existence according to their social canons, trajectories such as Zeca's and Lucio's demonstrate in sharp relief what a "solitary" man (*sami* or *shino*) goes through in a world that treasures gregariousness. They also differ widely from the other extreme, that of the self-made leader who even in the absence of supporting kinsmen successfully amasses prestige and builds a following on the basis of personal talent and socially valued qualities. This is the case of Kalioko, a nonaligned leader to whom I will come back later.

The Political Tissue

Even though at the time of my research roughly only half of the population belonged to some sort of descent unit other than the sib, it does not mean that lineages are unimportant or that belonging to them is irrevelant. I have already mentioned that lineage membership shapes

the performance of certain activities such as shamanism, food avoidance, and the choice of personal names. However, it is in the political
domain that their influence is the greatest.

Nonlineage members are usually in a weak political position.
Without close agnates around them, these men are virtually alone in
disputes and claims. If in economic terms it makes little difference if
one is not a lineage member, in political terms it transforms one into
a second-class citizen. Socially speaking, decisions that affect the
community are made and channeled through the groups of agnates
that are larger and better represented. As individuals, nonaffiliated
men are rarely backed in disputes with local people who have a strong
agnatic support. They are always on the weaker side of the rope.[10] In
the position of in-married outsiders, as they usually are, they are often harassed by their in-laws, have their belongings confiscated by
their wives' brothers, and can even play the role of scapegoats until,
as they mature and become family heads, they prove themselves to be
reliable.[11] It is possible, however, for a collection of nonaffiliated
people to organize themselves around a leader and construct their
own community. For this to happen there must be a series of favorable circumstances and someone with enough talent to achieve political autonomy.

The community is the most meaningful political unit, with the village as its territorial base. All adult members of a community to a
large extent have the right to voice their opinions and claims in matters that concern them. But there are proper channels to convey collective decisions, and these channels are the lineages. Unpredictable
as they are, Sanumá lineages, like their Balinese and Turkish counterparts, are the catalysts in the political process in most communities.
But they do it in such a way as to cut short any intent on the part of
any single group to have long-term hegemony.

The specific ethnographic flavor of Sanumá lineages is precisely
their susceptibility to the effects of often random factors. Just as the
Geertzes (1975:5) declared their "puzzlement during the initial phases
of fieldwork" regarding the "sometimes/sometimes not" aspect of the
dadia, so, four years before the publication of their Kinship in Bali, did
I face a similar theoretical and methodological bewilderment. I first
brooded over how to interpret the data, and then confronted the
problem of how to communicate this apparently incongruous feature
that might even be the result of an ethnographic faux pas. I had to
exorcise the old habit of favoring synchrony over diachrony, the main
source of my confusion, in order to transform imagined incongruities
and blunders into material of some anthropological interest. It was

also an opportunity for me to venture into analytic fields that had been left fallow by the methodological inertia which had seized kinship studies in the 1970s.

Particularly prone to mishaps, Sanumá lineages are doomed to be forever temporary affairs. It is very unlikely that the same lineage will retain a community's leadership for more than three generations in a row. As an institution, the phenomenon "lineage" persists through time, playing the role of political catalyst, and dispensing positions and identities around the villages. As a concrete group, however, each lineage is subject to drastic revisions at practically every generation. Walking a tightrope, their leaders face the constant prospect of having their power, slight as it is, drop out of their hands. A very significant outcome of the uncertain fate of the lineages is precisely the mobile character of political authority. It is this mobility that precludes the advent of hegemonic lineages. It also discourages any politically ambitious project that may opportunistically insinuate itself when there is a conjunction of favorable circumstances in the life of a particular lineage. The death of a leader, for instance, may bring definitive ruin to the privileged position of a successful lineage. On the other hand, men who are now outside the lineage system may live long enough to see their descendants create agnatic groups and gain political positions that they themselves never had. The endless carousel of the births and deaths of lineages results in the continuous circulation of political power and social prestige, leaving no room for their prolonged concentration in just a few hands.[12]

Let us now see how village leadership is constituted and exercised, both via lineage succession, and by the strength of individual talents to conquer new political spaces.

Inherited Leadership

The Sanumá remember their great leaders: Mosonawa, Kadimani, and Lalawa among others. Elderly or deceased, they are revered for their wisdom, their ability to speak surely and persuasively, and for being good shamans. In short, they represent all that is *waithili* — to be brave, daring, and magnetic. Though they are referred to as *pada dɨbɨ*, or "old ones," they are old people who enjoy the kinds of benefits that only the experience of a long and well-lived life can bring. They are reservoirs of knowledge that is beyond the pale of the young, no matter how skilled the latter show themselves to be at shamanism, oratory, technical matters, and everything else that yields prestige and respect. The *pada dɨbɨ* are those people to whom one appeals for justification. "So the old people say," *ina pada dɨbɨ kuu shinomo*,[13] is more than enough reason to convince someone of the legitimacy of what is being said or done.

Death only increases the reverence people have for important elders. In four of the seven villages I studied, political authority was in the hands of relatively young men, yet there were frequent comments, even complaints, that those villages had no real headmen. The "real" leaders were dead and their successors still a long way from becoming *pada dɨbɨ*. If we are to take these complaints at face value, those four villages were flung in a leadership crisis. However, after observing the daily routine of three of these communities, I concluded that the criticisms aimed at the young leaders spoke more nostalgia for a romanticized past, or careerist ambitions on the part of the critics.

Pada is a Sanumá term with very close cognates in the other Yanomami languages where *pata* is most often heard. But the Sanumá who have had prolonged contact with the Maiongong have adopted the term *kaikana* from their Carib-speaking neighbors to mean specifically village headman.[14] The Sanumá can thus make a distinction that may not be possible for the other Yanomami, that is, between *pada dɨbɨ*, old people in general who are respected for their wisdom, and the village leader, *kaikana*. Although *kaikana* are expected to be *pada dɨbɨ*, not all *pada dɨbɨ* are *kaikana*, if we grant that a *kaikana* is recognized as such only when he acquires the wisdom that comes with age. In fact, they represent two kinds of leadership; while the *pada dɨbɨ* are cultural leaders, the *kaikana* are political leaders. When both coincide in one person we have the memorable men whose prestige does not fade away with death but, quite the contrary, seems enhanced by it.

"What does *kaikana* mean for the Sanumá?" I asked Zeca.

"It is like the *ishalo* bird: fast, strong speech; he does shamanism, is not afraid of *sakona* [the hallucinogen]. There is no *kaikana* around here, they're all young. Later, when they grow old, they'll know how to speak strongly [*hɨla lotete*],[15] and then they'll become *kaikana* all right."

Later, back to the subject, he added:

"The son of a *kaikana* becomes a *kaikana* if he knows how to argue vehemently, with no fear of visitors."

He was referring to the verbal contests that are held whenever geographically as well as socially distant visitors arrive in the village, with whom relations are always tense and potentially dangerous. In these verbal duels, *wazamo*, the village headman, as the major host, puts to the test his rhetorical skills in ceremonial dialogues that are

Taking *sakona*. 1973. Photograph by K. I. Taylor.

laden with mutual accusations of hostility and promises of peace. The
narrow gap that divides a friendly welcome from a hostile reaction is
always a source of collective anxiety, no matter how much ritualization surrounds it. This is a stage where a leader can display his gran-
deur.

If oratory is one of the most treasured qualities of a leader,[16] the
ability to speak well must be accompanied by the ability to hear well.
If you cannot hear you cannot understand, which for the Sanumá
means lack of intelligence. It is, therefore, inconceivable for a village
leader to be intellectually poor. A good speech and a keen, convincing
argument rest on the capacity to hear well, that is, to understand.
Apart from references to a strictly physical hearing impediment, to
say that someone has clogged up ears, *simiga komi*, is to say that he or
she is stupid, which amounts to a serious offense. The verb *hini*
means both "to hear" and "to understand," and should not be confused with *tai*, "to see" and "to know." The worst thing one can say
about a man who is a leader or who intends to be one is that his ears
are clogged. He who hears well must, necessarily, be capable of understanding and acting sensibly without haste or foolishness. A living
example of the value of good hearing came from the Mosonawa com-

munity in 1973 during a dispute between the *azagoshi dɨbɨ* and the *oshigatali dɨbɨ* lineages. A year or so earlier, the *oshigatali* wife of the *azagoshi* leader died, and her death was attributed to the killing of her spirit animal (*nonoshi*) by the Kobali of the Metacuni River in Venezuela. On account of this incident, the *azagoshi dɨbɨ* moved to the upper Auaris River near the mission where most *oshigatali dɨbɨ* lived. The proximity between the two groups, however, turned out to be a source of conflicts, the *azagoshi dɨbɨ* being charged with theft and bad manners. A point was reached when the *azagoshi dɨbɨ* accused a young man doing bride service for the *oshigatali dɨbɨ* of having made *alawali* sorcery to kill some of their people. Bad feelings which had been veiled until then became quite open. The *oshigatali* leader took offense and responded by saying to the *azagoshi* headman and his own sister's widower: "Your ears are clogged up, go back, go back where you came from!" ("*wa simiga komi, ki ha konini, ki ha konini!*").[17] The event was reported to me with much indignation by the daughter of old Mosonawa. Her opinion of the *azagoshi dɨbɨ* was plain and clear: they don't know how to behave. They are obtuse and unwelcome in the neighborhood, so they might as well go away, back to the place they should never have left.

To be deaf to good sense is equivalent to having your senses dulled, to being like children before they acquire their full capacity for perception. The term *pii moodi*, "to be unaware, to forget," indicates the state or condition of dullness of the senses, and hearing is the most appropriate sensorial channel from being ignorant, *pii moodi*, to being aware, *pii hadugu*, or alert, *mosawi*. In matters of political leadership, hearing is fundamental for taking decisions that depend on being well informed about what happens in the community and beyond it. We might say that for the Sanumá the all-pervasive control mechanism would be something like a "panaudio" rather than a panoptic.

Although good hearing and good speaking are not inherited from one's father, it is presumed that these leadership qualities will be repeated in the leader's sons, especially in his possible successor. Let us take the example of the *mosonawa dɨbɨ* leader. Even though he did not have the talents of a true *kaikana*, he was expected to become a strong leader. According to Zeca, he would be a real *kaikana* when he grew older, and when he died, his son or younger brother[18] would take over the leadership. Zeca's comment evidences that, in spite of his own life history, he promotes agnatic succession as the canonic route to headmanship.

The institutional road opened by patrilineal succession to community headmanship is thus a necessary but not sufficient condition for a man to have full legitimacy vis-à-vis his co-residents and members of other communities. In the daily life of the Mosonawa village I had many occasions to notice how little respected the son of the old leader was. He was criticized for a variety of reasons: for a certain childishness, for being easily drawn into fighting, for being too young, for beating his wife, for being a bad hunter, and for not living up to his father's stately personality. The weight of the memory left by old Mosonawa imposed on him expectations that went far beyond his capacity or will. Perhaps that is the reason why he attracted so few followers. His younger half brother moved away to the outskirts of the Colony, while Heitor, his sister's husband, a strong *oshigatali* man, went to Venezuela to start bride service for two sisters, the daughters of Labadili, a very respected *kaikana*. Even so, Heitor's *oshigatali* lineage was visibly growing both in numbers and in political prestige. In 1974, we could hear comments to the effect that they were more important in local politics than the man who had inherited the headmanship. Nonetheless, in his three-compartment house, the leader sheltered the *sopai dɨbɨ*, the Kadimani branch who immigrated to Auaris after their father's death. The witticisms and jokes that animated the interaction between the leader and the young eponym of the *sopai dɨbɨ*, as well as allusions to a liaison between the young man and the leader's junior wife, betrayed a degree of frivolity and lightheartedness that impressed nobody as the way for a *kaikana* to behave.

At the Kadimani village, the eldest son of the deceased headman is an unquestionable leader. Even as a young man, he was much closer to the ideal *pada* than the oldest male in the village, one of his brothers-in-law. With sober manners, he dispenses his verbal skills always in the right measure. I saw him several times act as a judge in matters that affected members of his lineage and the community as a whole, at the same time as successfully cultivating relationships with other villages so as to make him one of the most respected headmen in the region. At the mission, he is seen as an important man, but in the 1970s he was still too young to deserve the title of *kaikana*. Several times I heard people refer to him admiringly as Sabuli, "shaman," his prestige and solid reputation in that field giving him a personal name. His eldest son reached puberty at the end of the sixties, and his daughter, also a teenager, had not yet attracted a permanent husband. This man's role seems to be, above all, to conduct the flow of his enlarged and expanding lineage with its departing branches, for its continuity depends on keeping together the central core under a strong leadership. His task is to maintain his agnatic group united at the same time as articulated with the political interests of the community as a whole. There are no signs of rival groups rising up and threatening his legitimacy.

To be a first-born son of a headman does not automatically entitle a man to political succession. In the case of the Sogosi community, not only was the old leader, Nimtali, replaced by his third-born son, but he had his descendants named after that son. *Sogosi* is a contraction of *sogo ose* (*sogo*, a small anteater; *ose*, young) and refers to Sogosi's elder brother, Sogo, whose name is rarely pronounced. Sogosi is married to a sister of Sahuli, the Kadimani headman, and is acclaimed for his hunting skills. Proud of his shamanic reputation, he did not hesitate to fight for it when he was accused of charlatanism, as described in Chapter 2.[19]

To be both a lineage member and the leader's son opens the institutional way for village headmanship. But the examples given above are meant to show that this is not always the whole story. Personal disposition and character are important factors in determining whether or not the potential to patrilineal succession is actualized. Also important is a growing, or at least stable, number of people who support and legitimize the leader. When a political heir sees his support group wane for lack of births or the emigration of relatives to other villages, he anticipates rivals ready to depose him and take over the village leadership. This is the case of the Mosonawa leader, who has been facing the increasing influence of his in-laws, the *oshigatali dibi*.

If patrilineal succession is not a sure path to stable and permanent leadership, it certainly is the most regular and dependable mechanism to maintain political authority in a village. Another path, much rarer and unpredictable, is the attainment of headmanship by sheer personal drive and talent.

Conquered Leadership

If, on the one hand, we find problematic trajectories for lineageless men, such as Zeca and Lucio, on the other hand, there are also success stories bred by aptitude, temperament, and opportunity. To be without a lineage does not eliminate the prospects for headmanship, but the way to it is certainly harder; without adult brothers and sons nearby, one has to overcome the agnatic void of guaranteed supporters. Lacking a critical mass of automatic followers, a man with political ambition but no lineage membership counts on other factors to build his career. What follows is a summary description of the way in which one aspiring leader constructed his prestige on grounds other than agnatic affiliation.

Kalioko: A Nonaligned Leader

We might say that the privacy which protects the personal names of Sanumá adults stands in inverse order to a man's political prestige. The more public a man is, the less secret his name will be. Kalioko was one of the first personal names I learned in the field. It was the name of an eight-year-old boy and of his father, whose political stature grew prodigiously between 1968 and 1974. It was at this time that the father organized an entire village out of what were more or less lineage scraps. For some he was not a *kaikana*, again, because he was too young. But young or not, Kalioko was one of the most respected political figures in the area, with a reputation as a peacemaker, a competent shaman, and someone capable of leading his followers to decisions that were as bold as they were right.

When we first arrived at Auaris, in March of 1968, Kalioko's residence group was camping in temporary shelters just outside the old Maiongong round house, some three hundred yards from the mission houses. They were part of the Colony, having as links to it five of Lucio's eight sisters with their respective spouses and children. Kalioko, the son of the eldest of these sisters, was married to the junior widow of Lucio's deceased brother. A little later, he also married his wife's daughter from her previous marriage.

A few months later, two long houses were built, one for the Colony, the other for Kalioko and his followers. In the next five years, the Kalioko households moved two or three times, and were joined by thirteen new residents. These were the family of Kalioko's senior wife's sister who migrated from their Venezuelan village after a fight that involved that sister's husband. In 1973, Kalioko and his group left the mission and set up a new village four hours downriver by canoe, on the right-hand bank of the Auaris River, halfway between the mission and the Sabuli village. In this move, two families were left out, Zeca's and Lucio's. Zeca was married to a sister of Kalioko's mother and remained at Auaris in a little house of his own. Lucio, Kalioko's maternal uncle, spent most of his time between a field house, the mission, and forest camps. In turn, a young man from Sabuli village moved to Kalioko's for bride service, while one baby had been born to a couple who had married right there, at Kalioko's.

In its new location, Kalioko's community had a group of four women acting as a sort of thread running through and stitching to-

gether all the relationships in the village. These women were Kalioko's three "mothers" and senior wife; two of these "mothers" were
separated from their husbands, and only one was still married to an
elderly man whom Kalioko called *hawa*, "father." Kalioko's real
mother was married to old Armando and lived downriver at Sabuli's.

Of all the residents at Kalioko's, only three were lineage members: his *azagoshi* senior wife and her sister, and a young *kadimani*
man married to the young daughter of Kalioko's senior wife. All the
others had only sib affiliation: *azatali dibi, higadili dibi, sadali dibi,* and
Kalioko's own sib, *oikomi dibi,* concentrated in a distant region in
Venezuela.

Kalioko's leadership was then defined and established. However,
it is worth noticing that, although his village was known as "Kalioko's
house," *kalioko a sai a,* his community was never referred to as *kalioko
dibi,* "the kalioko people." Unlike many other cases of the appearance of new agnatic groups acknowledged by a collective name (*sopai
dibi, ōkobidili dibi,* or *hanisho dibi*), the Sanumá never used *dibi* and
actually denied that it was appropriate in the case of Kalioko and his
co-residents.

Kalioko's father belonged to a large cluster of villages known as
the Samatali, the epitome of distant and hostile people. As a small
child, upon his father's death, he followed his mother northward,
joining the villages that today are part of the upper Auaris cluster.
Kalioko grew up amidst nonagnates, with no patrilinear support to
yield prestige and promote a headman's career.

Of the villages included in my sample, apart from the Colony,
Kalioko's was the only one led by a man who conquered his leadership entirely on the basis of talent and personal strength. His trajectory is somewhat similar to that of the Melanesian Big Man, but without the exacerbated feature of converting social favors into economic
advantage (Sahlins 1963). His strength was in knowing how to attract
both mature couples and young husbands for local bride service. Figure 3.2 gives an idea of Kalioko's ability to draw followers, by showing four men who became Kalioko's co-residents because of their marriage to women related to his mother, or to his senior wife. In this
case the role of women, rather than establishing cleavage points as in
the case of lineage segments, is to unite people with no agnatic connections into an entity that is recognizably greater than the mere sum
of its parts. Figure 3.2 presents the genealogical links between the
adult residents at the Kalioko village, as well as their relationship
terms.

Of all the qualities of a leader, generosity is one of the most ap-

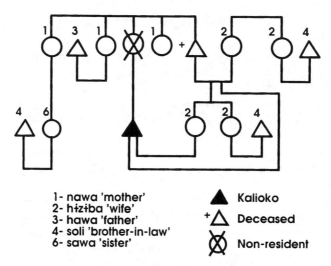

1- nawa 'mother'
2- hɨzɨba 'wife'
3- hawa 'father'
4- soli 'brother-in-law'
6- sawa 'sister'

▲ Kalioko
⁺△ Deceased
Ⓧ Non-resident

Fig. 3.2. Relationships at Kalioko's community

preciated, and Kalioko knew how to employ it effectively when he allowed the family of his senior wife to use his garden for planting and harvesting before they had a garden of their own. While at Auaris, this family exhausted the patience of their hosts at Mosonawa for having overstepped their rights to hospitality and generosity. What Kalioko did was welcome this family that had a number of boys and girls approaching marriageable age who might provide his community with economic, social, and political dividends in the near future.

Kalioko is a political *bricoleur*. Exceptionally cunning in making the right decisions at the right time with the right people, he succeeded in picking up the shreds of old lineages, joining them together via his female relatives, and creating an organized and respected community. Surrounded by "mothers," "wives," and their respective connections, he was the catalyst for bringing together an auspicious mixture of unaffiliated people into a working residential solution. It was as if all those widows, divorcées, and wives had been waiting for a genius at *bricolage* such as Kalioko to do what they, as women, could not do themselves—found a village of their own. Kalioko, the gifted "son" and "husband," came in handy, providing them with a politically and economically autonomous home and turning its rather unorthodox social arrangement into a coherent whole.

Kalioko's type of leadership, mainly grounded in the force of his personality, has, however, an uncertain future. Depending on one single individual as the connecting agent of people who otherwise

might not be together, a residence group of this sort is totally susceptible to the hazards that may come its leader's way. On the one hand,
his premature death would certainly lead to the breakup of several
families in search of other headmen. On the other hand, the fact that
freelance leaders such as Kalioko lack the status of an elder, of a real
pada, deprives them of a more stable basis for being fully recognized
as strong leaders by other communities. The full exercise of authority,
legitimacy, and power—the political triad par excellence—is a prerogative of the *pada dibi*, and its effects reach out well beyond the limits of a single community.

A venerable *pada* builds his reputation on many years of inter
action with other *pada dibi*. It is a constant learning process within a
tradition that, paradoxically, seems to favor predictability and continuity, perhaps because one's social life depends so much on circumstances that forever threaten permanence and stability. Cases such as
Kalioko's are like occasional oases on a road strewn with political un-
certainties for those without agnatic support. Precisely because they
are sporadic and random, such cases seem to highlight all the more
the ghost of dispersal. Kalioko has several sons; the eldest was about
ten years old in 1974. It would take but the spread of some white
man's epidemic disease to knock down the fruits of his immense organizing effort.[20]

Jorge: Interethnic Opportunism

While Kalioko built a traditional profile to establish himself as a nonaligned leader—good hunter, good shaman, good listener, good
speaker, fearless and daring—yet another play on leadership was being rehearsed in 1974 by a young Auaris man, only now the emphasis
was on the emulation of white men's values. Whereas Zeca, with his
humor and irony, heralded the "Dionysian" qualities of Sanumá leaders, Jorge, a young, bright, ambitious, but rather confused linguistic
informant of the missionaries would say: "*Kaikana* is the man who
tells people to stop fighting: Stop, don't quarrel!" ("*dibi hila ha, hila
die, kuu*").[21] For him, the great *kaikana* at the *shimatayam* community
on the Merevari River in Venezuela owed his prominence to having
traveled several times to the white man's land. When he speaks,
people listen: he tells them not to fight, not to covet other men's
wives, and to do their garden work with the diligence advocated by
the missionaries. "Later," Jorge said, "I shall become a *kaikana* myself,
that is why I want to go to Boa Vista to learn the language [of the
whites]. Albertino, Chico, and João [all Maiongong men] tell me to go
and become a *kaikana* here, because people fight too much. A long

Jorge and Zeca visit the Maiongong village during a feast. 1974. Photograph by A. G. Oliveira.

time ago, Mosonawa was the *kaikana*. He used to visit the whites in Venezuela. He died and now his son doesn't go to the whites, he is no *kaikana;* he keeps beating up his women."

Jorge's Western and rather moralistic discourse conceals, however, his quest for legitimacy according to the traditional standards of Sanumá culture. One night in March of 1973, he became the center of attention at Auaris during a dramatic episode much in Sanumá style. As he participated in a shamanism session with several local men, he detected the approach of enemy spirits armed with burning torches. In a performance verging on hysteria, the group of shamans with Jorge in the foreground struggled to defend themselves from the attacking spirits, using desperate gestures and screams of pain to act out the horror of the burning, while bewildered women frantically threshed wet branches over them. At last, the shamans succeeded in chasing away the spirits (Ramos 1986). Jorge, who later declared that he had never shamanized before—an amazing feat in itself, considering the long and painstaking shamanic training— gained precious points with the community for having given the warning call just in time. Something similar would happen a year later, when he put his shamanic abilities at the community's service by sending his *hekula* spirits to check the fate of Maiongong and

Sanumá travelers said to have been killed on their way back from Boa Vista (see Chapter 9).

Caught between a tradition that values shamanic skills, the control of hallucinogens, and other practices censured by the missionaries, and his own desire to emulate whites, Jorge lived a dilemma that deepened as interethnic contact intensified. Out of the two or three trips he took to Boa Vista as the missionaries' preferred language assistant, he attempted to build social and political prestige among his fellow villagers by exploiting a line of knowledge which at the time was almost exclusive to him—the white man's way of life. But, precisely because it was inaccessible to his companions, this source of knowledge was also unintelligible to them, which tended to diminish his political returns. So as not to risk being alienated by his own people, he disregarded the missionaries' pressure against shamanism, and invested in a display of traditional and widely approved aptitudes. He was then caught in a sort of double bind: his rhetoric praised white values, while his actions followed Sanumá conventions. For all his efforts in the political arena, his legitimacy was far from being a social reality.

Right after puberty Jorge married the daughter of a Maiongong-Sanumá couple. Although he insisted that the girl's father was actually his mother's brother, Heitor, he lived under the weight of a Maiongong father-in-law, with the typical demands and resentments that characterize intertribal relations at the Colony (Ramos 1980). His trump card in that uncomfortable situation was the contact he labored to keep open with the white world by means of a number of signs, actions, and words used for effect, all the way from wearing blue jeans and hair gel, to criticisms of the unruly ethos of his companions and appreciation for the achievements and good behavior of the whites.

Meanwhile, his younger brother, Angelo, was quietly building up a reputation as a good, intelligent, and competent family provider. I first met Angelo in 1968 during his boisterous adolescence, as Sanumá male adolescence usually is. He made a point of exasperating as many people as he could with practical jokes, such as the noisy homosexual games he promoted on the rickety veranda of the nurse's house. But in 1974, he had grown out of his carefree puberty phase, and was my host at Mosonawa. He had rejected the prospect of a long bride service for a little girl, the daughter of one of the sisters at Kalioko's, and married a divorced woman with a baby, the daughter of yet another of the Kalioko sisters. Her parents were separated, and this fact made it easier for Angelo to stop his bride service after a very short stay with his father-in-law in Venezuela. His mother-in-law had another young man doing bride service for a prepubescent daughter. Angelo built a separate house beside his father's at Mosonawa, and soon his good sense and competence made him a serious candidate for future headmanship in Auaris where political vocations and ambitions are not lacking.

Parenthetically, I would like to make some remarks about the political weight of bride service. A Sanumá man does not acquire any special power from having one or more sons-in-law working for him and his wife. Most family heads have at least one of them as co-resident, in some cases, two or three, and they are no more nor less powerful or prestigious for it.[22] Whereas in other Yanomami societies political power at the community level and even beyond it is built on a man's ability to control as many sons-in-law as possible (Albert 1985; Chagnon 1968), for the Sanumá the power that comes from bride service is strictly domestic, and does not propel the recipient father-in-law into any distinguished political career. On the other hand, from the son-in-law's point of view, to evade bride service is to demonstrate strength, a strength which can help him establish a reputation for autonomy and leadership.

That is Angelo's case. While Jorge manipulated unorthodox channels to conspicuously project himself as a leader, his brother was slowly accumulating authority without any display of overt ambition. His shrewd decisions allowed him to admirably elude bride service, settle down near his agnates, and successfully support the family he acquired and expanded. The styles of these two brothers are very different: one wagers on new, external influences coming into Sanumá traditions, while steering them through traditional courses; the other plays on the limits of legitimacy and propriety in his own culture. Unlike Jorge, Angelo bets on tradition and especially on its loopholes for a certain amount of audacity which can be rewarding if put at the service of other values, such as agnatic loyalty, technical expertise, and discernment in domestic and political matters. In the long run, Angelo's tactics seem to be more fruitful.[23]

The Authority of Persuasion

To be a village leader does not translate into the power to make people do what they do not want to do. His power, diluted through the whole community, is based on his ability to persuade rather than coerce. Hence the importance of the art of speech that is attributed to a true *kaikana*. A leader's authority emanates mainly from the political talent for putting his knowledge and experience at the service of his community. The competent hunter, the expert on detailed knowledge of the environment, the shaman with a vast esoteric erudition, has more means at his disposal than his companions to advise them as to the best choice for a new village site, for a new trail in the forest, and for the protection of the community by means of shamanism. He suggests and can ultimately decide when and where a hunting or fishing expedition will be carried out, or when a collective visit to another village will be paid. But his decision always comes after the subject matter has been widely discussed by most of the adults. A general assembly is not necessary to draw consensus or a majority vote; chats, conversations, much talk in small gatherings around someone's hearth are the usual forums in these persuasion campaigns. The leader, as such, does not control anyone's activities, unless he is himself involved. People come and go, circulate about the village and between villages, engage in trade, in marriage arrangements, and in personal disputes without the supervision or interference of their headman. It is with regard to collective affairs that he has his say. When he speaks, people listen. When he goes, people follow. If, however, he pushes the limits of his power, demanding blind obedience, people will turn their backs to him. His authority evokes very well the humanist ideal as proclaimed by Gadamer (1975:248):

> [T]he authority of persons is based ultimately, not on the subjection and abdication of reason, but on recognition and knowledge—knowledge, namely, that the other is superior to oneself in judgment and insight and that for this reason his judgment takes precedence, i.e., it has priority over one's own. This is connected with the fact that authority cannot actually be bestowed, but is acquired and must be acquired, if someone is to lay claim to it. It rests on recognition and hence on an act of reason itself which, aware of its own limitations, accepts that others have better understanding. Authority in this sense, properly understood, has nothing to do with blind obedience to a command. Indeed, authority has nothing to do with obedience, but rather with knowledge.

This idea of authority, dreamt but rarely experienced in the political arenas of the West, is the norm in the internal politics of a Sanumá village. Authority—this publicly honored capacity to lead—is the principal substance that makes for power amongst the Sanumá or, for that matter, virtually any indigenous society in the South American lowlands. Quietly, with no pomp or circumstance, the Sanumá headman exercises his political skills with an apparent anonymity that can exist only when there is a strong sense of self-confidence. He is a coordinator of activities rather than a politically conspicuous chief. This feature of indigenous politics baffles many a white man who, mimicking the old English colonial administrator in search of his prize native ("Take me to your leader!"), goes around asking to be shown to the omnipresent *tushawa*, the vulgarized and generic figure of the Amazonian Indian chief. Not finding it, whites declare the society to be in a disorganized stage of savagery and proceed to invent a chief that will conveniently obey their orders. The subtlety of Sanumá political authority—and not just Sanumá—easily escapes the truculent habits of those who are accustomed to take the imposition of blind obedience as the only means to guarantee law and order.

For this reason, it is important to stress the need for understanding the raw material that goes into the making of Sanumá authority. Without the ingredients that are combined to produce the political alloy that is called authority, there is no leadership, even if the formal mechanism of patrilineal succession is available. On the other hand, if those ingredients exist to consolidate the alloy, the resulting authority, like a magnet, will attract people left out of living agnatic groups by the vicissitudes of the erratic process of lineage formation. One way or another, no Sanumá community lacks an authority figure; in fact, there may be several competing leaders at the same time. Despite the frequent remarks the Auaris Sanumá make about the political void they live in, it is not actually very difficult to detect who has the strong speech, who is respected, and who is followed in the daily affairs of a community. This situation is only somewhat blurred when leadership is about to change hands, due not so much to succession as to competition. Whoever proves to have such authority wins the political contest. This victory does not distinguish the leader from the others in terms of material privileges, or of exclusive rights to polygyny, as Lévi-Strauss (1948) described for the Nambiquara, and as Clastres (1974) proposed for indigenous South America. Both these authors regard the prerogative of having many wives as the main asset of a South American chief for amassing political power. But the Sanumá case belies their claim. Though many Sanumá men have more than one wife, it is not polygyny that sorts out who is who in the political scene. The benefits of Sanumá leadership are elsewhere, in the respect and prestige conferred on its holder, forged by a reputation for seriousness and bravery that extends well beyond the limits of one village.

But respect and prestige can be granted to one man precisely and only because he is neither the sole nor the principal retainer of power. It is exactly because power exists in a rather Foucauldian capillary fashion throughout the whole community that it is possible to delegate a priority position to one of its members. It is a choice among peers rather than an imposition of a few upon inferiors. When all agree on their assessment of the leader and accept his authority, the leader is safe. It is up to him to comply with and to the villagers to maintain their judgment and acceptance. The Sanumá would have no difficulty in grasping both the letter and the spirit of Western famous phrases such as "We the people."

In brief, within the limits of operation of Sanumá headmanship, we can see three different paths that lead to it, although they are all part of the same basic ongoing process, that is, the developmental cycle of the lineages. What divides these paths is what separates all members of full-fledged lineages from members of ascending agnatic groups and these from nonaffiliated people. The first path leads to patrilineal succession, the second to the change of headmanship by means of political competition between rival lineages, and the third is opened by the effort of nonaligned individuals. The combination of elements that results in either the advent or the downfall of a lineage is also responsible for the contours political leadership can take.

Nevertheless, the force of a specific leader is not dictated by the fate of agnatic groups alone. A man's capacity to attract people to his community is, in and of itself, a decisive factor for the outcome of these groups. "When there is a kaikana, people come," Zeca told me. It was the case of the old Kadimani leader, who aptly drew together a number of refugees and thoroughly integrated them into the fabric of his community by a series of successful and productive marriages. It was also the case of Kalioko, who knew how to attract entire families linked to his immediate female relatives and created for them a locus as well as a sense of community.

In the internal affairs of a village, people delegate the political management of activities to a leader, but in terms of intervillage relations, his role is rather modest. He does little more than play host to his visitors. It is precisely in the field of its external relations that a community's capillary power becomes more apparent, particularly regarding the exchange of goods, services, and spouses. In the scenario that results from these exchanges, the village headman is no longer in the foreground. Center stage now is a vast chain of favors and counterfavors, gifts and countergifts, debts and counterdebts that initiate, reinforce, shake, revoke, or interrupt relationships between villages. Here the success or failure of a transaction, and as a result the gain or loss of prestige, no longer depend on the local headman, but on a whole set of ongoing associations between a vast array of people. In the long run, it is the sum of these individual connections that molds the interaction between villages. When a family exports a son to marry in another community, it is also extending its bonds and expectations to that community. The quality of the interaction between these two families will, to a large extent, depend on the fate of that son's marriage. If he evades bride service, it will no doubt affect their relationships. In turn, their experience will be incorporated into the pool of collective experiences shared by the two communities in question. It is the accumulation of lived routines such as this that shapes the way communities interact with each other. In the next chapter I shall describe, from the point of view of intermarriages, how this intercommunity chain is built and maintained to create a vast social network both in time and in space.

4

The Marriage-Go-Round

Married Life

In matters of descent, a Sanumá person has no choice but to belong to his or her father's category or group, but things are very different when it comes to marriage. Few Sanumá stay married to the same spouse all their lives. Divorces are frequent, serial marriages are very common, and polygyny is widespread. Besides, as in any other society, there are couples who get along very well in lasting marriages full of mutual affection, and there are others who live a routine of emotional outbursts interrupted by a few moments of peaceful coexistence. There are passionate and jealous spouses, others who are indifferent; some are courteous, others are selfish, some are faithful, others are monuments to infidelity. Some mature couples, such as the *oshigatali dɨbɨ* twin sisters married to two *õka dɨbɨ* brothers, Jorge's "parents," are examples of conjugal harmony and epitomize what is solid in Mosonawa. I never noticed any signs of quarrel or bad temper among them, and my impression was that their marriages would last forever. The eldest daughter of one of these couples, Kalioko's ex-wife, married an outsider; he was a very quiet, good-looking man who prompted the jealousy and resentment of the village headman, the woman's eternal admirer. He was actually beaten more than once by the leader and by his own in-laws. Even so, the young couple did not conceal their mutual affection. At Kadimani, there was the desolate love of Homero for his lost Venezuelan wife; for a while he even went berserk when her relatives took her away from him. There was also the chronic warfare between Lucio and his senior wife who, amidst blood and tears, provided the residents of Auaris with periodic exhibitions of mighty mutual beatings.

But beyond this wide range of conjugal styles, there are certain expectations and norms of conduct that turn marriage into a special focus of attention both for the Sanumá and for the anthropologist. Its

127

importance to social dynamics is revealed, among other things, in the many plans and discussions about who will marry whom. For instance, we can often see groups of women engaged in animated conversations telling each other whom their little children will marry; they invariably choose a prospective "correct" spouse, that is, someone in the category of cross-cousin to the child, or, more specifically, the child of one of the speaker's brothers. Their reckoning follows the general wish of having their children marry within the village. This is one more reason why groups of brothers and sisters prefer to live in the same village, for their children will be potential spouses to each other. Whether these children meet their parents' expectations when they grow up and reach the point of choosing their mates is another matter. In fact, it seems to be the exception rather than the rule.

Child betrothal, a very common practice, rarely results in a lasting marriage. As it involves a long period of bride service that may last for decades, the boys usually give up and go looking for another wife, preferably an adult woman, divorced, or, better still, an orphan. As a consequence, we find couples where the husband is much younger than the wife, a circumstance to which no prejudice or embarrassment is attached. Between an immature little girl and a grown-up woman, men do not necessarily prefer the former. The appeal of an older woman resides not only in her sexual availability but in economic considerations, not to be neglected by a young man who dreams of domestic autonomy. Obviously, an adult woman works and produces much more than a child. It seems, however, that the decisive factor in this kind of choice is the man's exemption, partially or completely, from the bride service obligations toward his parents-in-law, even when they all live in the same village.

A woman does not "take" a husband, she is "taken" by him. That is how the Sanumá express the marriage transaction, with the verb po, "to take," or te, "to secure." But a woman can "throw away," hozali, her husband in the same way as he can separate from her. These expressions insinuate a relation of unequal rights of possession in favor of the man, but they conceal the fragility of the husband's position when he lives with her parents. "To take" a woman involves abdicating a portion of autonomy which men yield with uneasiness. The ambivalence inherent in a man's position during bride service is reflected in various ways. The main focus of this ambivalence is centered in his mother-in-law, pizisa. While stating their dissatisfaction with their in-laws' unreasonable demands, men submit to the profound abyss that the rule of avoidance creates between them and their mothers-in-law. Proverbial as it is in ethnographic circles, in its Sanumá manifestation mother-in-law avoidance is a tangible reality. If a young man has so much as a glimpse of his mother-in-law's approach, he shifts his course, turns around, or hides so as not to meet her face-to-face. Comic situations are easily created by such maneuvers. In a split second, a man stops a conversation in mid-sentence and runs away, jumping over whatever obstacles are in his path, crawling into improvised hideouts and diving into the next hammock to cover up his face. With these gimmicks he tries to make himself invisible to his wife's mother until she takes pity on him and goes away. Paternal aunts, a man's potential mothers-in-law, are also avoided, but not so dramatically and conspicuously; he never speaks directly to them and keeps a respectful distance from them. As for the wives, very much at ease in their family milieu, they take no special precautions toward their affines, older or younger, unless, of course, they are themselves someone's mother-in-law.

The ambivalence that is inherent in the son-in-law/mother-in-law relationship is sometimes overtly manifested in duels when the young couple are about to end their marriage. Having the whole community as both spectator and referee, young man and mature woman engage in a ritualized fight where each strikes one or more blows on the other's head. These are usually situations where the wife is still immature, before or immediately after her first menstruation, and still very attached to her mother. The separation is then sealed, but it does not preclude a future reconciliation. I know of one case in which the couple was reunited, and two or three cases of definitive breakup, followed by the subsequent marriage of the spouses to others.

Mothers-in-law can be regarded in a double light: as objects of avoidance in an individual's daily life, and as magnets at the sociological level. They epitomize the focal point of uxorilocal residence. A *mosonawa dɨbɨ* woman told me that her little brother would not marry in their own village because there was no *pizisa*, "mother-in-law," for him and therefore he would have to go away to look for one.[1] Obviously, before a *pizisa* there is always a *piziba*, "wife," but it is intriguing the way she put it, giving priority to the mother-in-law. In turn, her mother had once declared that the right type of marriage is that between the children of *peze dɨbɨ*, "siblings of opposite sex."

If the confrontation of a man with his mother-in-law can be seen as a sort of ritual of separation, marriage itself is not celebrated by anything more spectacular than the act of the husband in tying his hammock in his wife's compartment. It is as though the sliding knots that hold the hammock, facilitating its adjustment and removal with occasional resounding tumbles, were a metaphor for the marriage tie itself: it unites, but is potentially unstable and always on the verge of snapping.

The reserve with which husband and wife treat each other is evident in a number of situations: when they sit side by side at informal gatherings around a fire and rarely caress each other; when they walk in the forest, husband ahead, wife behind, each one in deep concentration; and in the habit, especially among women, of referring to the spouse, not by name or kinship term, but indirectly through a child. When a woman wants to mention her husband, she often touches her child's head and says, "*ĩ pĩ a,*" "this one's father." In short, there is a whole gamut of gestures and words that make the public presentation of couplehood a display of restrained cordiality. This does not mean moralism or denial of sexuality, for the frequent appeal to eroticism in conversations, jokes, and games between same- and opposite-sex cross-cousins, as well as in the socialization of children, attests to the contrary. It is rather the appropriate behavior of people whose bond, being less binding than that between close blood relatives, is nevertheless charged with the not negligible responsibility of social reproduction. They are the affinal dyad par excellence, and, as such, husband and wife epitomize the double bind of affinity — opposition and interdependence.

Behind the restraint shown by married couples there may be either a deep affection or a disguised hostility, depending on the personalities, their emotional involvement, and all the other imponderables that constitute a couple's life. At any rate, living happily or not, married people are regarded as a unit of complementary parts. People often use the *penoba/piziba* (husband/wife) pair as a metaphor to emphasize a complementary relationship between things or animals. Whereas the image of "mother/son" (*pibina/piluba*) is invoked to stress a contrast in size as, for example, a big basket beside a small one, the pair *penoba/piziba* lends metaphoric color to things and beings that are distinct but matched in a twosome, such as two different arrow points side by side.

One of the most uncommon and bizarre human conditions for the Sanumá is celibacy, especially for men. I knew only one unmarried man, at the Lalawa village. He was the center of constant jokes and malicious remarks. When he visited Kadimani, the local men sent him on women's chores, such as fetching potfuls of water, amidst bursts of laughter. I was told that he was not married because women found him too ugly (to which I had to agree, making me wonder about the universality of aesthetic preferences). As far as I know, it seems less painful to be an adult woman without a spouse. Between one marriage and another, we still find young women, usually with children, who live with close kinsmen and who suffer no stigma for being un married. At the Kalioko village, however, there was a mature mother of two children whose latest husband had run away years earlier after having murdered another man at Auaris. A hypochondriac, she had a permanent look of malaise and self-pity. She lived with two sisters and, according to the missionaries, traded sexual favors for food. In their eyes, this behavior made her into a prostitute, a concept totally alien to the Sanumá, for behavior such as hers could never become a way of life, a profession.

In crises, husband and wife quarrel and fight just like any other pair of opponents engaged in a duel. Extramarital liaisons are frequent and can trigger off conjugal traumas that affect husband and wife equally. In the case of female adultery, she is punished, but so is her lover who has to confront the enraged husband in a duel. If the man admits having had the affair, he will let himself be beaten without reacting. Men's infidelities are much more common, or perhaps less conspicuous, but they can also be made accountable. In 1974, I witnessed a marriage crisis between my neighbors at Mosonawa because Lilia, Jorge's sister, jealous of the looks her husband cast at Cici, a beautiful and single teenager of the Colony, challenged him to a fight. She hit and was hit, attracting everyone around, until Jorge jumped in to defend her in case the husband insisted on beating her, which did not happen. The couple were estranged for weeks, and she threatened to leave him and go away to stay with the *azagoshi dibɨ* nearby, even though her close relatives were all at Mosonawa. She would come to my hearth to tell me between sobs how unhappy she was. Both of them walked about looking miserable, without the usual playing and laughter; the husband, an outsider, seemed to have lost his bearings until, one day, they were reconciled.[2]

Quarrels between couples are never private. They occur in open view of the entire community and are watched by whoever happens to be around. Amidst the husband's dramatic screams of indignation, the wife's dismal sobs, and the ruckus raised by so many remarks all being yelled at the same time, some curious and even comical things can happen. Orlando, of the *mosonawa dibɨ*, found out that his beautiful wife was having an affair with a young outsider who was doing bride service for Jorge's parents. When Orlando challenged the other to a duel, everyone rushed to the Colony where Orlando lived. The boy, with his head bent down, his body tense and still, let himself be hit on the head with the flat of a brand new machete recently acquired from the missionaries. On impact, the blade broke in two, one half of it, shining in the sun, going spinning up in the air. I remember vividly the end of the scene. An ancient woman from the *azagoshi dɨbɨ*, all skin and bones, crawled over to the broken blade, laboriously bent over to pick it up, and proceeded to examine it with fascination, oblivious of the commotion around her.

Marriage is the most immediately available channel for the regulation of sexuality, but perhaps not the most efficient. There are also certain norms related to the process of procreation that set limits to women's sexual availability. Particularly in the nursing period, they are as if in a sexual limbo, as a way of protecting the baby from another pregnancy too soon after the previous birth. Since the infant needs all the reserves of its mother's milk, another baby would jeopardize the health of both. To avoid having an undernourished child or a crybaby, *wakosɨbɨ*, who resents being weaned prematurely, it is necessary that the parents abstain from sexual intercourse. This aspect of Sanumá sexuality could not be better demonstrated than in an episode where an enraged woman from the Kalioko village repelled Lucio's sexual advances. She cried out for everyone to hear how appalled she was, not so much for his invitation to adultery, but for his nerve to make a proposition while she was nursing an infant. The scandal resounded through the communities at the mission as an emphatic lesson on decorum.

In regulating sexuality, the Sanumá map out three fields; the first consists of people who are from the ideal spouse pool; the second consists of people one can marry but are not the best choice; and the third consists of people one should not marry. This plotting of marriageable regions presupposes the conceptual separation of affinal and blood relatives, and the inclusion of a third category, that of unrelated people, *tiko dɨbɨ*.

Once an Affine Always an Affine, or Almost . . .

As Louis Dumont insisted for three decades (1953,1957,1983), in the Dravidian kinship system of which the Sanumá make up a variant, people are born to an already established set of affines. It is the result not of specific marriages, but of specific births. In order to clarify this central point on affinity, it is necessary to see how the kinship nomenclature is organized, starting with reference and address terms Sanumá men and women use for their peers. Once we overcome the sense of unfamiliarity, we realize that the system is very simple. In each of the three medial generations—one's own, that of one's parents, and that of one's children—there is one distinction by sex and another by affinity or consanguinity. We thus have, by consanguinity,

"father" = *hawa*
"mother" = *nawa*
"older sibling of same sex" = *hebala*
"younger sibling of same sex" = *hoosa*
"sibling of opposite sex" = *sawa*
"son" = *ulu*
"daughter" = *thewi*

by affinity,

"uncle," "father-in-law" = *soaze a, pichi a*
"aunt," "mother-in-law" = *saaze a, pizisa*
"brother-in-law" = *soli*
"wife" = *hiziba*
"husband" = *heano a*
"nephew," "niece," "daughter-in-law" = *hizagiba*
   (men speaking)
"son-in-law" = *suha*
"nephew" = *sizo* (women speaking)
"niece" = *sizomi* (women speaking)

The terms in English are not meant to be literal translations, but mere devices to help the reader understand the system. The emotional charge that goes into each of these English terms is not equivalent to their Sanumá counterpart. All we can do is to find descriptions and images from whatever sources that arouse in us similar reactions to what the Sanumá may feel in the context of kinship. One of the masters of cultural translation, Maurice Leenhardt, showed us in *Do Kamo* (1979) how far one sometimes has to go in search of semantic fields that have some cultural equivalence. For instance, the fact that the Sanumá call several woman *nawa*, "mother," alerts us to possible differences between their mothers and ours. It seems quite obvious that the symbolic load that our mothers carry does not entirely apply to their *nawas*; a Sanumá *nawa* does not inspire the image of a woman who suffers in heaven, nor does it trigger off an orgy of gifts on a certain date of the year; nor is their *saaze a* the sweet "Auntie" that we construct in our ideal cast of family characters. The avoidance that surrounds their *pizisa* can vaguely resemble our own idea of mother-in-law, especially from a man's point of view, but even here the feelings that these concepts evoke among native speakers of English and Sanumá are not comparable. That became clear when a North American missionary at Auaris had his mother-in-law visit his family in the field. To the horror of his Sanumá audience, he hugged his wife's mother, an act which for the Sanumá is the epitome of incest. Perhaps it would be akin to watching a mother and her son publicly engaged in a sensual kiss.

Enough warnings about the danger of misstepping distinct semantic threshholds. Let us now look at kinship terms and relationships. We have seen in Chapter 2 that the phrases *iba dibi* (my people), *iba dibi sai* (my real people), *iba ai dibi* (my other people), and *tiko dibi* (other people) are applied to both close and distant relatives and even to nonrelatives in a sort of *continuum*. Depending on the level of contrast one is at, one can call one's own brothers *tiko dibi*, or classificatory uncles *iba dibi*. Only context can reveal at what level one is operating at any given time. In any case, there is no symmetry between the terms *iba dibi/iba ai dibi* and the categories kin/affine. While *iba dibi* is usually applied to close kin (father, mother, siblings, children), *iba ai dibi* normally includes both kin and affines.

In contrast to these relational phrases that can be defined only by context, kinship terminology divides the social universe into set positions. Although these positions can be manipulated, they are nevertheless landmarks for categorical relationships. A brother may today be part of someone's *iba dibi*, and tomorrow turn into a *tiko*, but he does not stop being a brother. Manipulations, when they occur, are due to rearrangements that result from noncanonic marriages. The Sanumá kinship terms are shown in Figures 4.1 and 4.2, the first for reference terms, the second for terms of address, both from a male speaker's point of view. The female equivalent follows in Figures 4.3 and 4.4.

Notice that the siblings of the same sex as the referent are always differentiated by relative age, which is not the case with siblings of opposite sex. I should point out that, in the case of parallel cousins, this age difference is marked not by the actual age of the cousins, but by that of their respective fathers. For example, a young man used *hoosa* (younger brother) to refer to another man who was obviously older than he was, because the latter's father was younger than his own.

In these figures, the affines appear surrounded by kin on all sides. They are like enclaves in a system that enlarges the number of kin due to the fact that the second ascending and descending generations are squeezed together with the first ascending and descending consanguines. Thus, the grandparents are in the same category as the parents, and the grandchildren in the same as children. I shall return to this aspect later.

Although affinal terms do not depend on specific marriages to ex-

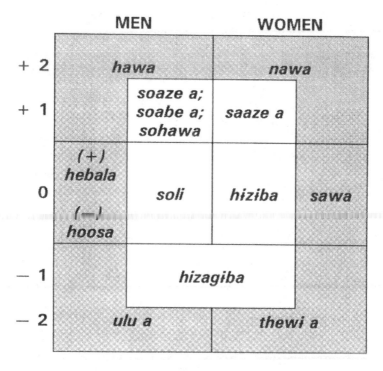

Fig. 4.1. Terms of reference—men speaking

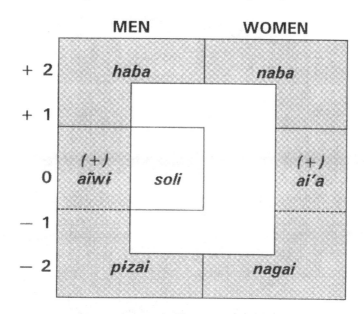

Fig. 4.2. Terms of address—men speaking

135

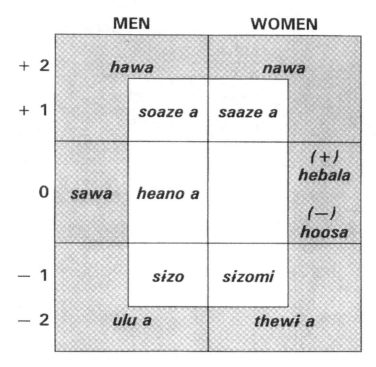

Fig. 4.3. Terms of reference—women speaking

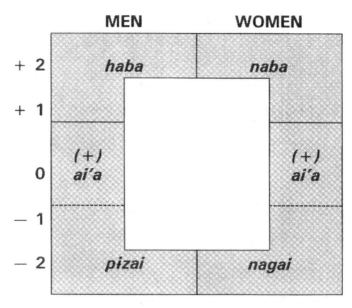

Fig. 4.4. Terms of address—women speaking

136

	MEN	WOMEN
+ 1	*pĩshia*	*pizisa*
0	*soli*	*hiziba*
— 1	*suha/pusaba*	

Fig. 4.5. Postmarital terms of reference—men speaking

	MEN	WOMEN
+ 1	*pĩshia*	*pizisa*
0	*heano a*	
— 1	*suha/pusaba*	

Fig. 4.6. Postmarital terms of reference—women speaking

ist, the Sanumá do not miss the chance to stress their marriage relations with a redundant terminology, for after they marry they apply another layer of terms to their in-laws. This redundancy, which is established whenever cross-cousins marry each other, may disappear in marriages that do not follow the golden rule. For instance, it is possible for a man to marry a woman in the "sister" or "mother" category, albeit genealogically distant. In this case, the postmarital terms come in handy to underscore the newly created relationships. These postmarital terms are shown in Figures 4.5 and 4.6.

There is yet another set of terms applied to a third person's rela-

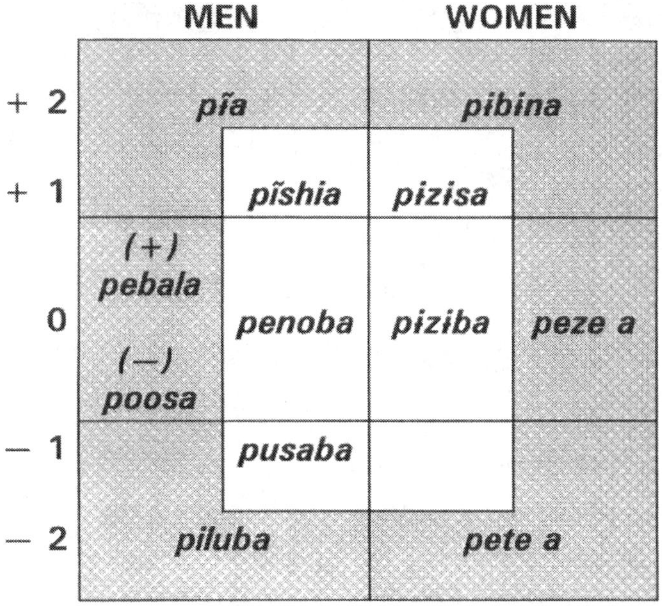

	MEN		WOMEN	
+ 2	*pĩa*		*pibina*	
+ 1		*pĩshia*	*pizisa*	
0	*(+) pebala* *(−) poosa*	*penoba*	*piziba*	*peze a*
− 1		*pusaba*		
− 2	*piluba*		*pete a*	

Fig. 4.7. Terms of reference—third person

tives, that is, relatives of the person spoken about. Figure 4.7 presents these terms. We can see that the terms for someone else's "uncle" and "aunt" are the same as the postmarital terms for one's own spouse's parents. I shall say more about this later in this chapter. Thus, the reference terms differ depending on whether one is referring to the relatives of the speaker and the listener, or to the person being spoken about. Examples: *iba hebala,* "my elder sister," *au hebala,* "your elder sister," but *kama î pebala,* "her elder sister."

When we examine these figures, we immediately notice a feature that is very typical of Sanumá kinship terminology and that differentiates it from the "classic" Dravidian type (Dumont 1953, 1957), namely, the wide range of the kin categories as compared to the affinal categories. Whereas in the "original" Dravidian system a person's grandparents and grandchildren have their own set of terms,[3] in the Sanumá system they are collapsed with parents and children, respectively. The result is that the kin are much more numerous than the affines, which is the exact opposite of what happens in the Yanomam system where the affines predominate (Ramos and Albert 1977). What the Sanumá situation seems to indicate is that affines make up a category falling under the broader rubric of "kin."

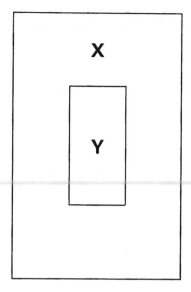

Fig. 4.8. Dumont's "encompassing of the contrary"

It is what Dumont (1980:239) calls "the encompassing of the contrary." Graphically we would have the same outcome, as shown in Figure 4.8.

The resulting hierarchy has several effects. The main one is conceptual, but there are also political and symbolic implications. In the political field, this hierarchy is most clearly seen in the position of incoming husbands. As we have seen in Chapter 3, immigrant husbands are men who have no agnatic support, who have left their village to marry, and who find themselves in a vulnerable position vis-à-vis their wife's kin. These outsiders are virtually excluded from leadership in their in-laws' village. On the other hand, the interdependence that necessarily exists between kin and affines is asserted in the symbolic fields of naming and funerals, where kin delegate to their affines certain tasks that directly or indirectly affect their own social continuity. Encompassed by the kin, the affines seem to be accessories in the former's social reproduction. It is as if they were a necessary evil, which is expressed in the rather ambiguous term *iba ai dibi*, "my other people," as husbands are to wives, and parents-in-law are to sons-in-law. Because I depend on them, they are "my people," but because they are not really *iba dibi sai*, they never stop being "others." Reflected in the kinship terminology, this dialectic is set in motion by the actual marriages. In generating alliances, marriages cast a wide net of rights and duties that go all the way from prophesying the fate of a newborn baby to conducting funerals; it is in the power of the affines to pronounce a verdict about the survival chances of a given child (see Chapter 8), and it is they who conduct the cremation of the dead. They are present and active at the beginning and at the end of life, and are vital for the reproduction of the living.

The Silence of the Affines

Another outstanding feature of the Sanumá kinship terminology is the absence of terms for certain affines, especially among women. For instance, a woman has no term of reference or address for her female cross-cousins and sisters-in-law; she has to resort to a teknonym of the "Mother of So-and-so" kind, a casual appellation, or a mere shout. As a last resort she can use *kanashimi wani*, which roughly refers to anything for which the name is not known, has been forgotten, or cannot be mentioned; in the loosest translation it would be the equivalent of "what ya call it." The term *wani*, literally "bad," or "evil," is also a term of endearment. As a rhetorical gesture that implies the opposite of what it says, this usage of *wani* resembles our habit of calling a father "my old man." Borgman characterizes this Sanumá application of *wani* as "a humble way of speaking" (1976:40).

Husband and wife do not address each other with any kinship term; *kuu maigite* (*kuu*, "to say"; *maigite*, "no"), "they don't call each other," they simply use a sort of interjection, *a'a*, when they want to attract the other's attention. As reference husbands use *iba hiziba* (my wife / my female cross-cousin), and wives, *iba heano a* (my husband / my male cross-cousin).

Male speakers also have very few terms of address for their affines. In fact, there is only one such term for male cross-cousin/ brother-in-law, *soli*, which is also the reference term for the same relatives. Otherwise, neither the ascending nor the descending generations receive any kind of term of address. Given the strong avoidance toward one's parents-in-law, this terminological silence is understandable. Before they are parents-in-law, they are one's parents' siblings of the opposite sex, and that puts them in the affinal camp in advance, so to speak. They are therefore equally avoided. When the Sanumá saw a photograph of a man lounging in his hammock, holding his baby "nephew," in Chagnon's book *The Fierce People*, they were staggered. It was hard to convince them that such a demonstration of intimacy involved a "father-in-law/uncle" and his "son-in-law/

nephew," because from a very early age people learn to avoid being in the presence of their first-generation affines, let alone engage in such close physical contact. Thus, it would not be proper for a person to address his/her father's sister or mother's brother. A form of address for them would be a contradiction in terms.

In contrast to the avoidance between consecutive generations, the relations between cross-cousins can be remarkably intimate, including practical jokes and sexual games. But they are also potentially explosive, and may involve political competition. Female cross-cousins/sisters-in-law, even—or because of—lacking a term to define their relationship, treat each other in a quiet manner and cooperate in chores, such as going to the gardens, fetching wood, or fishing, without the overstated playfulness and antagonisms that mark the interaction of their male counterparts.

Affinity, acquired at birth, is reinforced by marriage. When a man marries a cross-cousin, he continues to refer to her as he did before, *iba hiziba*. But her parents change from *soaze a* and *saaze a* into *pĩshi a* and *pizisa*, which is accompanied by an intensification of the avoidance that was already there. I don't think it is a mere coincidence that the postmarital terms are the same as those used for a third person's "uncle-aunt/parents-in-law" (see Figure 4.7 above). The symbolic distance that these terms convey is conceptually stressed, unveiling a will to social distance in the context of very close physical proximity. Within this uncomfortable closeness, marriage does not create affinity (for it was already there) but emphatically reaffirms or forges new rights and duties in the field of affinal relations such as in the institution of *suhamo*, "to do as a nephew," that is, to perform bride service.

The parents-in-law/son-in-law relationship captures the very interdependence and tension between affines which are demonstrated by silence. Marriage is a process rather than a state. In an idiom that blends antagonism and attraction, it spells out two of the most basic realms of society—the production of goods, and the reproduction of children. The avoidance between co-resident parents-in-law and sons-in-law, the epitome of this process, is something young people try to evade, but it guarantees the maintenance of a network of interactions that annuls any possibility of atomization of families and communities.

It is not by chance that opposite-sex cross-cousins who live in the same house, albeit in separate compartments, do not intermarry. As children, they treat each other as *nagai/pizai*, terms of address borrowed from the field of consanguinity, indicating intense closeness. When they grow up, although acknowledging the fact that they are potential spouses, they marry someone else. The desired village endogamy does not go as far as "house endogamy," if by "house" we mean the residence unit immediately above the domestic group. There must be a minimum of distance between potential spouses for marriage to occur, and this minimum seems to be the gap between two houses. The architectural arrangement of a Sanumá village facilitates the reckoning of this distance. Whereas other Yanomami groups congregate an entire community within the same round walls, separate Sanumá constructions foster intimacy among the co-residents of any given house, thus inhibiting the inconveniences of *suhamo*, bride service, at such close quarters. Another difference from other Yanomami societies (Albert 1985; Chagnon 1968) is that the duties of bride service are lightened not by marriage within one's community but by the search outside the residence group for ways of evading parents-in-law, e.g., by marrying orphaned or divorced women.

The absence of certain affinal terms, especially for female speakers, is one of the enigmas of Sanumá ethnography that has no equivalent in other known Yanomami groups. The reasons why men do not call their older affines by specific terms are relatively clear; an uncle may well become a father-in-law subject to strong avoidance. But why is there no term of address for spouse? And, even more intriguing, why do women have no terms of reference or address for their female cross-cousins before or after marriage, so that they must resort to a personal name, in the case of a child, a teknonym, or a simple interjection of the "hey!" type? What kind of sociological statement do these silences make? The most I can do to answer these questions is offer a tentative explanation based on the differential influence of uxorilocal residence on men and women.

While for both men and women "aunts" and "uncles" change into "parents-in-law" after marriage, the semantic load of these postmarital terms is much greater for a husband than for a wife. This is not surprising, for it is usually the man who moves into his wife's household as a subordinate son-in-law obliged to perform bride service duties. Women, in turn, may not even live near their in-laws.

The terminological difference between husband and wife is accentuated with regard to people in their own generation. A man refers to and calls his brothers-in-law by a distinct term—*soli*. A man's *soli* is an ambivalent figure who can be either a close companion in joint activities, or an opponent in domestic, economic, or political disputes. As for women, there is no term at all with which to refer to or address their sisters-in-law or, for that matter, their female cross-cousins in general. Socially speaking, this terminological void translates as easygoing and undemanding interaction between affinal women of the same generation. The female mode of residence seems to be the main reason for this.

Women stay put after marriage and are free of any special obligations toward their husband's kin. Normally a woman does not have to abdicate the company of her own kin to embark on a life of high-strung sociality with people related to her as "others." Female silence about in-laws would thus reflect a sort of "sociological indifference" regarding the relationships of a woman with her husband's blood relatives. As far as she is concerned, to interact with a husband's sister, with a brother's wife, or with any female cross cousin not married in the family makes very little difference; hence, their position in the kinship map goes unmarked. It is as if, from a woman's point of view, postmarital affinity is socially neutral, as if she acquires no in-laws at all, or, put in another way, as if the fact of her marriage does not in any significant way alter the tenor of the relationships she previously had with her husband's kin.

Here again we meet, first, with a male bias regarding social affairs (it is the men who are burdened with postmarital obligations and their attendant kinship concepts), and second, with the emphasis on consanguine relations, for no one displays such terminological ostracism toward his or her own blood relatives as women (and men to a lesser extent) do to their affines.

Affines, the Adam's Rib

The transmission of affinity from one generation to the next creates a field of ambivalence among blood relatives. Who are, after all, the affines' parents? We have first the ambivalence in the grandparents' generation. Although identified as parents, they beget both consanguines (the parents) and affines (uncles and aunts, that is, the parents' siblings of opposite sex). Something similar occurs in the grandchildren's generation. The children of sons and daughters are called by the terms for son and daughter, even though a good part of them were fathered by affines, such as cross-cousins, and may become sons-in-law.

It is, however, in the relation between opposite-sex siblings that we find the greatest ambiguity. A man's sisters are very close blood relatives until just before puberty. They play together all day long, and are part of the same remarkably ubiquitous band of children that wander about village, forest, and river. But once they are declared adults, brother and sister go their separate ways, even when they

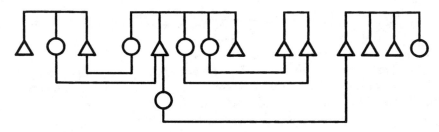

Fig. 4.9. Sibling groups at Mosonawa

continue to be co-residents. Still very attached, they no longer display easiness and intimacy in each other's presence. As the Sanumá say, men are *gili* of their sisters, that is, they feel a mixture of shame, embarrassment, and fear. They still speak to each other, and go on being mutual *iba dɨbɨ*, but their direct interaction is drastically reduced as they grow up. After she marries, a sister is placed sort of halfway between blood and affinal relatives. Although she continues to live with her parents, she is now associated with a husband, by definition an affine, and will be the mother of affines, the potential spouses of a man's children. While mother and daughter are consaguines who generate consanguines, a sister is a consanguine who mothers affines.

Here again we have affines engulfed by kin. We might, as Dumont did (1980:239–40), resort to the old Adam's rib analogy and say that, among the Sanumá, the affines come out of the kin to become entities in their own right, in opposition to their originators. An organic relationship of interdependence, albeit hierarchically differentiated, is then established between them. On the one hand, the kin are opposed to the affines in marriage. On the other hand, the kin encompass the affines by covering a much broader semantic and social field. Several kin generate affines, but no affines generate kin, if we consider that one's child is of one's own blood before it is the kinsman of one's wife. We find in the framework of Sanumá kin and affines a clear "encompassing of the contrary," as in the Adam and Eve bond. After all, this is the Western symbol for both unification and differentiation, for affinity and consanguinity, condensed by mythical language in one single dialectical relationship both contradictory and interdependent.

Sanumá brothers and sisters are the vital components for the makeup of a typical residence cluster. Figures 4.9 and 4.10 representing the sibling sets at Mosonawa and Kadimani exemplify the importance of sibling groups as backbones of a community. The larger and

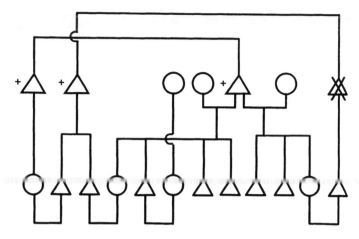

Fig. 4.10. Sibling groups at Kadimani

more sexually balanced they are, the greater are the chances of a large number of cross-cousins in the next generation and, consequently, of endogamous marriages.

Whereas other Yanomami subgroups express the ideal marriage as that between the children of "brothers-in-law" (Chagnon 1968; Lizot 1984; Albert 1985), the Sanumá idea of a good marriage is that between children of *peze díbi*, "siblings of opposite sex." The result is exactly the same, but expressed in ways that are relevantly different. With the Sanumá, it is the women who engage most enthusiastically in plans for the future marriage of their children, and their choices invariably fall on their brothers' sons and daughters. The women also aspire to have children of both sexes so as to reproduce this same pattern in the next generation.

Following the Dravidian bias of the kinship terminology, Sanumá marriages observe the inherent division between kin and affines when cross-cousins marry each other. But that is not always the case. Despite the rhetoric of preferred marriages to one's *hiziba/heano a*, this preference accounts for less than 32 percent of the total 136 marriages in my sample. Of these 32 percent, 21 percent are marriages with bilateral cross-cousins, that is, between children of two intermarried pairs of siblings. There is a difference, which seems to be merely statistical, between marriage with the maternal cross-cousin (56 percent) and with the paternal cross-cousin (23 percent). In spite of this numerical variation, I have no indication that this statistical figure corresponds to a sociological preference for the matri-

Table 4.1. Distribution of spouses per community

Community	Cross cousins	Non-cousins	Unknown connection	Non-kin	Total
Kadimani	10	—	10	7	27
Sogosɨ	3	1	5	1	10
Mamugula	7	1	—	6	14
Lalawa	10	2	3	2	17
Sabuli	—	1	11	1	13
Mosonawa	3	3	14	—	20
Kalioko	6	5	11	3	25
Colony	4	2	—	3	9
Total	43	15	54	23	135

lateral cross-cousin. What the Sanumá make very clear is that a man should marry a *hiziba;* whether she should be the daughter of his mother's brother, or of his father's sister, they never stated or implied.

If the cross-cousins are not the majority of spouses, who are the others? Table 4.1 gives the distribution of spouses by village. Cross-cousins are the children of both opposite-sex siblings and parallel cousins. The noncousins are all the rest with whom one has no clear genealogical connection. Spouses whose tie is unknown are distant classificatory relatives as, for example, members of two sibs that consider themselves to be "brothers." Unrelated spouses are those who do not recognize any previous kinship tie, no matter how distant; if we ask how they called each other before the marriage, they just say: *kuu manogite,* "didn't call." I must explain that I use the term "classificatory" to refer both to relatives with an unknown but presumed genealogical connection, and to relatives who have a clearly defined relationship, as for instance, father's father's brother's daughter's daughter, as in Figure 4.11.

When looking at marriages both monogamous and polygynous in each of the eight villages (Colony included), I counted all living residents and their deceased, divorced, and current spouses. By divorce I mean the permanent separation that results in the definitive end of a marriage.

Of 54 marriages whose spouses do not know their genealogical ties, 51 involve people from different sibs; the remaining 3 married within their own sibs. These 3, plus the case of a man who married the daughter of a parallel cousin (therefore, a classificatory daughter), are the only marriages within one's own sib in all 135 marriages recorded, that is, less than three percent.

Not ideal but perfectly tolerated are the marriages with unrelated

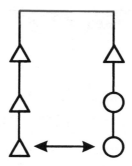

Fig. 4.11. Classificatory relationships with known connection

people, *tiko dibi*, "others." They add up to nearly 18 percent of the total number of marriages, and include those with orphaned, divorced, and refugee women, that is, cases where men can escape prolonged bride service.

The fifteen marriages with related women other than cross-cousins involve the following relationship categories:

sawa, "sister"	5 cases
hizagiba, "niece"	5 cases
thewi a, "daughter"	2 cases
saaze a, "aunt"	2 cases
nawa, "mother"	1 case

All these relatives are classificatory. In the two cases of marriage with an "aunt," the woman had been married to the man's maternal uncle. Of these fifteen marriages, only one—with a classificatory daughter—occurred within the same sib, and provoked a scandal in the community. The couple were so severely criticized that they fled the village for a while.

This raises a question regarding another feature of Sanumá marriages. None of the marriages contracted outside the same sib incited the community's censure. When I put my puzzled question about the legitimacy of Zeca's marriage to a "mother," my interlocutor laughed and said it was not the best choice, but it was all right, because he was a *higadili*, and she, an *azatali*, that is, they belonged to different sibs. Actually, it makes sense that sib exogamy wins over the definition of affinity, as, proportionately speaking, there are many more blood than affinal relatives. It would be very difficult to find an available spouse if there was no way out of a rigidly imposed cross-cousin marriage.

Strictly speaking, there are two legitimate ways to enter the marriage market: one, via transmitted affinity, concentrated on the *hɨzɨba/heano a* categories; the other, via sib exogamy. This second way allows a person to marry either within the frame of established relationships, or outside of it with *tiko dɨbɨ*, "others." This being the case, it is hardly appropriate to brand marriages with noncross-cousins as wrong. What is wrong is to marry within the same sib, and worse still to marry within the same lineage. We would then have a ranking of norms that contemplate both the observance and the evasion of cross-cousin marriage. Socially speaking, marriage with one's own cross-cousin is the most cherished option because it automatically observes the exigency of sib exogamy. There are, however, many legitimate marriages that observe sib exogamy, but do not meet the cross-cousin marriage ideal. As various sibs are in a kin relationship to each other, all their members are treated as kin, which means that if some of them intermarry, the spouses are related as kin and not as cross-cousins. It should be noted that this reckoning of intersib relationships is done in terms of category rather than genealogy. Sib exogamy is thus hierarchically more encompassing than is endogamy of the cross-cousin category. Because of this overlap between sib exogamy and noncross-cousin marriages, the distinction between kin and affines is sometimes blurred when kin marry kin. Here postmarital affinity is observed and transmitted affinity is disregarded. Again we meet with Dumont's "encompassing of the contrary" (see also Houseman 1983 about this discussion). Kin and affines remain in a hierarchical opposition but are now seen from a different angle, that of the actual marriages. For if cross-cousin marriage, the idiom of affinity, is the ideal, sib exogamy, the idiom of consanguinity, in the last analysis takes precedence at the level of actual practice. Of course, values are also forged by practices that are blessed by consensus. In the end, what matters is to marry outside one's own sib, but if it is with a cross-cousin, so much the better.

Exchanging Kinsmen

In the previous chapter, I called attention to village endogamy and its consequences for co-resident and agnatically related men. I shall now deal with the opposite situation, that is, with those who, in their marriage quest, emigrate, and by doing so trigger off a series of social and political consequences. Table 4.2 shows the occurrence of marriages in and out of the different communities. The figures refer to marriages that took place in each village after it was established.

We can see that only two communities, Lalawa and Mosonawa,

Table 4.2. Marriages

Community	Within	Outside	Total
Kadimani	10	16	26
Sogosi	1	14	15
Mamugula	4	7	11
Lalawa	10	4	14
Sabuli	3	7	10
Mosonawa	8	5	13
Kalioko	2	5	7
Colony	—	4	4
Total	38	62	100

have a larger number of endogamous than of exogamous marriages.[4] In spite of the strong wish to marry within one's own village, only about 30 percent of people achieve this ideal. The majority, usually men, move to other villages in search of a spouse. This circulation of people is bound to generate its own social effects. One of these is the intensification or, in some cases, the creation of intercommunity relations. Through time, the recurrence of intermarriages between certain communities brings about the formation of community clusters with closely connected social and political interests. Figure 4.12 shows the graphic distribution of marriages across the eight communities in my sample. Marriages contracted before the couples settled in these communities were not included. Each circle represents a community; the position of the circles follows approximately the geographic relations among them between 1968 and 1970. The numbers inside the circles indicate marriages within the community. Each line crossing from one circle to another represents one marriage between communities. The arrows point out marriages with both men and women outside the upper Auaris cluster. In some cases, all exogamous marriages resulted in the incorporation of spouses; in others, spouses came and went after separation. But for none of these communities are there exits without entries. Strictly speaking, Mamugula does not belong to the Auaris cluster, but their intense contact with Kadimani and Sogosi makes them a sort of extension of these two communities.

Let us examine which villages exchange spouses. Figure 4.12 indicates two major blocks of marriage exchange: one consists of the Sogosi, Mamugula, and Kadimani communities; the other, Mosonawa, Kalioko, Colony, and Sabuli. These blocks correspond very closely to the way these communities interact with each other. Within each block relations are very intense; across blocks they are much less constant.

In late 1970, the community of Lalawa, with the greatest incidence of endogamous marriages, was in fact socially much more isolated than any of the others, despite its central location on the Auaris-Kadimani axis. It had only four exogamous marriages: one with the Sabuli community, and three with distant Kobali villages to the south, in Venezuela. It would be a gross exaggeration to say that its members were marginalized, but their interaction with neighboring communities was clearly restrained. For instance, when they camped in the forest, or went on *wazimi* family trips, they rarely included people from other villages, a current practice in the other communities. Still in 1970, they joined Mosonawa and Azagoshi men in a raid against the Kobali accused of having caused the death of an Azagoshi woman. There were also plans for the marriage of one or two Lalawa girls with a young Azagoshi. But in 1974, they had moved downriver to a distant site after an internal rift that temporarily divided them and which threw them back into isolation. Before they moved away, they lived so near the other villages around them that when they appeared they were not considered as visitors and were never treated with the formality of *hama dibi* (visitors, guests). Although they exchanged news and goods with their neighbors, they never developed the kind of intimacy and trust that was very obvious, say, within the Kadimani-Sogosi-Mamugula cluster.

If at Lalawa more than 70 percent of the marriages were within the village, at Kadimani none were strictly endogamous, though this does not mean that there was a mass dispersal of its members in search of spouses. On the contrary, as we have seen in Chapters 2 and 3, by a stroke of luck that immensely favored the stability of the *kadimani dibi* lineage, no less than ten refugee women were incorporated into the community, six of whom were of marriageable age. In other words, these women became Kadimani residents before they became wives of Kadimani men. Besides these marriages with the refugees, there were seven other marriages of both men and women with their allies, especially from Sogosi and Mamugula.

Taken together, the communities of Kadimani, Sogosi, and Mamugula represent a virtually endogamous block having Sogosi as its intersection. Furthermore, the social, political, and ritual interaction between them is very intense. On a number of occasions, part of the communities of Mamugula and Sogosi spent long periods of time at Kadimani during our stay. There was even a plan for a joint Kadimani-Sogosi raid to bring back Homero's Venezuelan wife who had been taken away from Kadimani. But the raid never happened.

The second block of communities—Mosonawa, Kalioko, Colony,

and Sabuli—is less clear in this respect. Mosonawa has a low degree of endogamy; the Colony, due to its interethnic characteristics, is a case of its own, and the others have few marriage bonds in common. But they maintain intense contact with each other and have close kinship ties that pervade among them, particularly via the eight sisters who are spread out through four of these communities, married to men who are related to each other in various degrees of closeness. What marriage does to link Kadimani, Sogosi, and Mamugula, kin ties seem to do for the communities along the Auaris River. The marriages that take place in the Auaris cluster reinforce relations that already existed.

Depending on whether the migrant spouses are men or women, the political outcome of marriages can vary substantially. A woman who leaves her village and arrives at another as an actual or potential spouse falls into one of three categories: a refugee running away from enemies' attacks, an orphan with no family backup to claim bride service, or a headman's wife who will follow him wherever he goes. In the first case, there are rarely any alliances between the villages of husband and wife, either because they are very far apart, or because the refugee's community has been destroyed. In the second case, orphans, by definition, lack the close relatives who would stimulate a rapprochement between the communities involved, and no meaningful alliances result from such marriages. There is also the case of divorced women whose parents too are separated and living in different villages, and who have no influence over their sons-in-law's activities. It is the father-in-law/mother-in-law team that has the maximum capacity to pressure a man to perform bride service. In such cases, their daughters' virilocal marriage is of no import for the establishment of a social and political alliance. In the third case, women who marry headmen in other villages make a greater contribution in sealing alliances already extant than in creating new associations. Since marriage by abduction is rare, the only feasable way a man has to get the consent of a woman's parents to take her away to his village is by cultivating a policy of good neighborliness with them. We find a typical example at Sogosi, where the headman and his elder brother married two daughters of the old Kadimani headman. Except for these circumstances, women always stay put after marriage. It is in this condition of "mistresses of the house" that they are most apt to contribute to forging intercommunity alliances.

With men the situation is quite different. They leave their village expressly to get married. Coupled with their search for wives there is an intention to establish or reinforce a social and political association within the receiving community. No man in his right mind would voluntarily relinquish his own home to find a woman among hostile people. A minimum of receptivity is required to attract potential husbands. To move to another village with different social, political, and even ecological niches is in itself a gamble; to venture into enemy or unfriendly grounds is more than a gamble, it would be outright foolishness.

The Geopolitics of Marriage

Whenever a community sends off a number of its agnates to other villages, it casts a net of commitments that cement their mutual relationships. The communities that are caught in such a net find themselves tied up by reciprocal rights and duties that make their association much more stable than what Chagnon, for example, reports for the Yanomami he studied in Venezuela. Unlike the volatile and unpredictable alliances he describes, Sanumá relations between neighboring villages show a much greater steadiness which can be traced to the social and political consistency with which they tend to cluster into intermarrying units. The real enemies are always far away, with whom one has little or no direct contact, virtually no visiting, and about whom information channels are extremely garbled. It is with neighboring communities that one quarrels, fights, and duels, but within the limits of a carefully observed ritualization that rarely degenerates into serious violence. If a community has close relatives, especially agnates, living in other communities, hostilities between them are inhibited and belligerence is less likely to occur. From this point of view, the Sanumá are closer to the Yanomam of the Catrimani River valley; for about thirty to sixty years after splinter groups move away, they still interact as full members of the same cluster as their original village (Albert 1985).

In this sense, exported husbands operate as a kind of diplomatic corps. Although as individuals they may resent being at a political disadvantage vis-à-vis their wives' relatives, as representatives of their parents' group they maintain their ties while simultaneously planting the seeds of reciprocity in the other village where they marry and procreate. Figure 4.12 shows with a simple glance how potent marriage can be in entwining several communities together. The bonds that exist, for instance, between Kadimani, Sogosi, and Mamugula are so strong that they would render the rise of irreversible enmity an unlikely and complicated venture. The sturdy social chain that binds their members would have to be broken, a new realign-

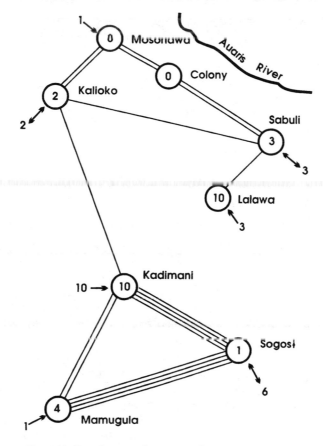

Fig. 4.12. Distribution of marriages between communities

ment of positions established on domestic and family bases would have to be made, and new community spaces would have to be opened along totally different lines. The cost would be too high.

The circulation of husbands and, to a much lesser extent, wives around communities that are socially close is also a way of guaranteeing a promise of safe conduct through the region. When we realize that the circulation of material and social goods depends on this transit, it is no wonder that the safest channel to deliver them is marriage, the institution which, at one and the same time, provides the communities with their means of reproduction and sociability.

5
Sanumá Times

The Many Faces of Time

In my attempt to convey to the reader the various facets of Sanumá time within the limitations of an Indo-European language, I have resorted to metaphoric exercises that appeal to geometrical figures, physical phenomena such as circles, arcs, pendulums, compression, and linearity, or whatever there is at hand. But at times these are quixotic gestures. How does one translate the idea of remote time, be it in the past or in the future, which derives from the single expression *sutuha?* How does one lead the reader into the merry-go-round of a life cycle that does not start with birth and does not end with death? How does one render intelligible the interdigitation of historical facts with mythical imagination, when people like us take the separation of history and myth as axiomatic? The challenge is great and the risk of miscasting the subject matter even greater. Nevertheless, I will make the attempt, based on the conviction that, after all, the most ethnography can do is to *produce* an intelligible and convincing version of what is perceived in another culture, rather than *reproduce* the original. Naturally, one hopes that what is thus produced resembles its original by means of a coherent presentation and a "reasonable" understanding, as Stocking (1968) argues.[1]

Regarding the Sanumá, it may be more appropriate to speak not of one but of several notions of time—individual, social, eschatological, and historical.[2] For each of these cases one needs to search for a metaphor as a device to translate it culturally. In a seemingly infinite series of cycles, human beings, animals, and spirits cross paths with each other, the living and the dead seem to embark on the same carousel, the natural and the supernatural fuse, what has been meets with what will be, space turns into time, and memory becomes history. In this chapter I will try to show how Sanumá times present themselves to a Western eye, not as a Western-type chronology, but

154

as an interlocked series of tos and fros, of circles that do not close, of past and present that appear to touch each other, and of trajectories that have spans and intersections.

In the course of the life cycle, nonhuman elements often cross the path of human beings. In doing so, they contribute to the construction of the person, or otherwise interfere with a person's destiny. These are spirits of game animals (*uku dɨbɨ*) that provide the Sanumá with their main criterion for establishing age sets, names, and guardian spirits for their children; alter ego spirit animals (*nonoshi*) that replicate the fate of their human counterparts; and evil spirits (*sai dɨbɨ*) that can cause damage to boys and girls undergoing puberty rites. Next, I will make some remarks about social time as revealed in the trajectory of descent groups and categories with their different timing and conjoint diachronies. I am referring to the macrotime of the sibs, the shorter cycles of the lineages, and the course taken by historical communities that are transformed into descent categories. Last, I will focus on the one hand on the sort of orbital time in which both animal and human spirits are caught, and on the other on the unfolding historical process from the time of the great metamorphoses to the time of the more recent forebears. But first I must say something about how time is inscribed in language and in the temporality of everyday life.

The Language of Time

Among Sanumá there are certain aspects of time that can be collapsed into a single category, while for us they are separate and not interchangeable. When Sanumá say "long ago," or "a long time from now," they use one term, *sutuha* (or its variant, *sutuba*). In this way, the distant past and the distant future are compressed as semantic equivalents. What is emphasized here is the equal distance that separates the speaker from what happened long ago and from what is still far from happening. Rather than arrange these two moments in the linearity that is indispensable for Indo-Europeans, Sanumá language collapses them into one single concept.

Whether an action has already been completed or is yet to occur becomes clear with verbal suffixes.[3] These suffixes, in turn, focus on aspects that, at one and the same time, reveal the timing of an action (whether it has just been completed, was completed a few hours before, or a long time ago) and the speaker's position regarding that action (whether one witnessed it oneself, or heard it from someone else). Thus, the generality of the *sutuha* adverb is counterbalanced by details as to how the speaker is related to the action described. For instance,

"Long ago the Maiongong killed Sanumá"

sutuha	nabɨ	dɨbɨ	ni	sanɨma	dɨbɨ	nia
long ago	Maiongong	the	agent	Sanumá	the	kill

ba-	-li-	-ma	
strong	direction	unwitnessed completed action	

"I married my wife long ago"

sutuha	iba	hɨzɨba	sa	po	-gubili
long ago	my	wife	I	take	witnessed completed action

Or for actions not yet taken,

"We may go to live upriver a long time from now"

sutuha	ola ham	samak	pilio	hāto	-gite
long time	upriver	we	live	perhaps	probably

"A long time from now my son will marry that woman"

sutuha	ki	suɨ	iba	ulu	a	po	-pia zalo
long time	that	woman	my	son	the	take	want with intent

One does not say "something is going to happen/will happen," but rather "perhaps something may happen," or "it is one's intention that something will happen." Seen in this light, the future seems the result more of intentionality than of inevitability.

Distant past and distant future are not the only instances that disclose this leveling of temporal categories. In the context of daily hunting we find something similar. To go hunting in the evening is *wisai hu* (*wisai*, "evening," *hu*, "to go"), and to go hunting at dawn is *wisai hu hena* (*hena*, "early"). This type of hunting is different from *namo hu*, "to go hunting during the day," and *hinomo hu*, "to go hunting in group for several days," usually for ritual purposes.

To us there is an apparent contradiction in saying "to go early-hunting in the evening!" What seems to happen is that here *wisai* ("evening") has an ambidextrous meaning. As far as I know this use of the adverb occurs only in this specific context, and it is probably motivated by the special characteristics of that type of hunting. A lone man in the dim light of dawn or dusk goes out to ambush birds that come to feed on certain trees (Taylor 1981). The hunter knows ahead of time exactly where he will go and which birds are likely to appear. He is thus circumscribed by the animals' eating habits, whether early or late in the day. Since the activity is the same, there is little to distinguish these two moments of time. Dawn dissolves into daylight, which chases away the game, whereas dusk dissolves into night, which chases away the hunter. This specific time is then defined by the action and not the other way around, for it does not exist separately from what is done, while it lasts. This perspective dissolves the apparent contradiction of having *wisai hu* applied to two opposite points in the day's time.

Sanumá indications of time proceed in two different ways: time is either given an existence of its own, as related to human activities but independent of them, or it can depend on people's options entirely. Examples of the first case are the differences between rainy season (*made pada*) and dry season (*inama*), and between day (*wakala*) and night (*mumi mumi*). Although rainy season and dry season alternate regardless of what human beings may or may not do, they are meaningful because of the human activities that are connected with them, such as the slashing and burning at the end of the dry season, or the planting at the onset of the rains. The same happens with the alternation between day and night that goes on regardless of the Sanumá's will (albeit caused by them in mythical times).

In the second case, time is divided entirely according to human behavior. The repetition of certain activities defines the various regions of a diffuse and elastic temporality. For instance, the main meal of the day is usually taken early in the evening, not because it is five or six o'clock, but because the day's activities in the fields, on the river, or in the forest have come to an end. A *sabonomo*, the ceremonial for the dead, is organized not because there is a memorial day every year, but because there are specific dead to be commemorated; the event is thus conditioned to his or her death and to the amount of food available to receive a large number of guests. It is the people who mark the occasion rather than a calendar date that constrains them to carry out specific activities.

In reckoning the microtime of daily living, one combines time with space. For example, the distance between two points in space can be measured by the number of nights' sleep, *manishi* ("after three sleeps on the way, we arrive at village X") or by the movement of the sun ("when the sun is there [at right angles with the ground, that is, noon] we will arrive at village Z"). Time is thus "spatialized." The distance the sun covers in the sky corresponds to the duration of some action on earth: traveling, grating manioc, going hunting, or working a garden.

This humanization of time is nothing new in anthropology, for at least as early as 1940, Evans-Pritchard meticulously demonstrated with the Nuer case that neither time nor space can be understood without recourse to the medium of humans. Day-to-day microtime contrasts with the macrotime of social groups and categories. With sibs, lineages, and historical residence categories we have the opposite effect, that is, a "temporalized" space—residential space transformed into patrilineality that is then passed on through the generations. Conditioned by a life cut up in minutes, hours, months, years, or even centuries, we are both fascinated and baffled by this appropriation of space and time to create a multifaceted temporality that we can only dimly perceive but perhaps never penetrate.

The calendric reckoning that is necessary for the organization of a *sabonomo* or for the preparation of a new garden makes use of lunar phases and the change of seasons. No matter how imprecise this may seem to us, accustomed as we are to written calendars, logs, and date books, the Sanumá system with its three numerical categories—one, two/several, and many—always surprised me with its infallibly satisfactory results. It never happens that a *sabonomo* planned months in advance fails to take place due to disjointed dates and guests. Everyone arrives at the set time, even those who come from very far away. It is an inseparable union of time and space that I could observe, but could not myself apprehend. It consists of particles of cognition so intangible and fleeting that one would have to be a Sanumá to be able to totally share it. I resign myself to the pleasure of contemplating and admiring its results.

What follows is a series of examples of how the Sanumá construct their temporality by bringing together or pulling apart activities, ritual states, and changing conditions in life. The result is a complex web interlocking the living and the dead, individuals and collectivities, humans and nonhumans.

Lived Time

Let us begin with the age sets. The Sanumá division of the life cycle into segments of varying timespans represents a conception of biological time that challenges our demographic methods of representation. For example, I can draw a Sanumá population pyramid using a five- or ten-year interval (see Appendix at the end of this chapter). But, although it may serve the purposes of comparative Yanomami demography, such a pyramid is built on criteria that have nothing to do with the way the Sanumá themselves divide their lives. The pyramid's artificiality has to do with the regularity of the age clusters, and with the fact that most people's ages are assessed by educated guesses rather than by a reliable register system (at least before the arrival of missionaries in specific locations). I even tried to make a demography-style pyramid using their age categories, but the result was totally unintelligible.

One problem comes from the fact that different Sanumá age clusters cover different lengths of time. Whereas one cluster lasts about two years, another covers fifteen years, and others four, so that the system is rendered incompatible with the regular figure of a Western-style population pyramid. After several attempts to diagram these subdivisions, I concluded that a circle would be the most appropriate shape to give visual coherence to the Sanumá life cycle.[4] The result is Figure 5.1.

The criteria the Sanumá use to define age sets are taken from the system of food taboos and its articulation with human fertility. As this theme was exhaustively treated by Taylor (1974, 1981), I will limit myself here to a brief outline.

In the first place, we have a division into four large population segments: "children," *ulu dibi*; the "young," *hiza dibi* (males)/*mogo dibi* (females); "grandparents," *pada*; and the "elderly," *padashibi*. Following the maturity line—children versus adults—*ulu* and *hiza/mogo* are together, separated from *pada* and *padashibi*. But, if we shift focus to the fertility line, we have *ulu* and *padashibi*, both "infertile," in the same category, opposed to *hiza/mogo* and *pada*, that is, the "fertile." But, whereas the "grandparents," *pada*, and the "elderly," *padashibi*, together span thirty years or more with no subdivisions, the "young," *ulu* and *hiza/mogo*, although taking up another thirty-year span, are divided into eight out of all the ten age sets. The "children" category includes infants, *oshidi*, toddlers and older children, *ulu*, as well as the pubescent who, in Sanumá time-reckoning fashion, are called *padashibi* as are the "elderly." In turn, the "young" comprise five age sets, according to the number of children born to them: singles, parents with one child, parents with two children, parents with three children,[5] and the mature.

All these divisions are informed by the system of food taboos regarding game. Depending on their descent group or category, most people are prohibited from eating the meat of certain animals. The combination of these taboos with one's position in the life cycle results in the classification of the population into age segments. The phases of life most susceptible to penalties for breach of these taboos go from prepuberty, *padashibi*, to mature adults, *pada daude*. The food taboos reach their peak in prepuberty, postpuberty, and first-child

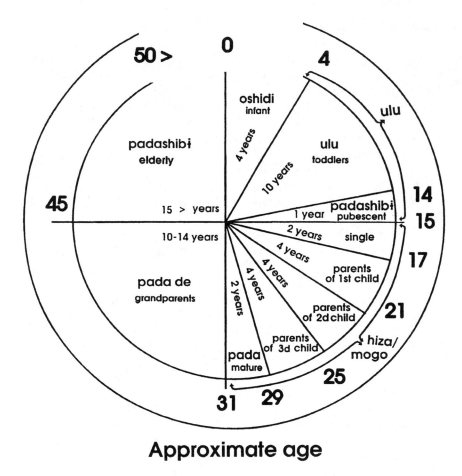

Fig. 5.1. Age sets

parenthood, after which they gradually diminish. The age set least affected is that of the "elderly," *padashibɨ*, who can eat just about anything they want. After them, the children, *ulu*, are also free to eat most meats from the time they begin to walk until prepuberty. Next are "grandparents" who observe the taboo for only a few animals.

Penalties are manifested as attacks by the spirits (*uku dɨbɨ*) of game animals unduly killed and eaten, and provoke physical symptoms of various kinds. For instance, if a prepubescent person eats wasp larvae, he or she will be covered in boils. If a husband and/or his wife, not yet grandparents, eat the meat of porcupine, coatimundi,

squirrel, rabbit, otter, or turtle during a pregnancy, the woman will
have a miscarriage.

Certain animals are more strongly governed by taboo than others.
For example, frogs and sloths are summarily prohibited to almost all
age sets, whereas tapir is permissible for nearly everybody. Moreover, the spirits of eaten animals, *uku dibi*, vary a great deal. In some
cases, it is the *uku dibi* of the entire animal that attacks the person; in
other cases, it is the spirit of just one part of the animal, such as the
teeth, the paws, or the beak. In still others, it is the spirit of something
that is usually associated with the animal, such as the worms found in
a coatimundi's hide.

One takes precautions to avoid dangerous meats in order to protect one's own health and that of one's children. The bond of substance that is established between parents and children is very directly and most strongly materialized in the food they eat. But, unlike
the relations of substance found, for instance, among the Timbira of
Central Brazil (Melatti 1976; Da Matta 1976), the precautions taken by
the Sanumá last only while the child depends on its parents for nourishment. As soon as it becomes autonomous, its parents cease to be
responsible for the food taboos that affect it. From then on, each person takes care of his or her own defense from the attacks of these *uku
dibi* spirits.

Sickness and disease resulting from breaches of food taboos are
perhaps the most frequent complaints among the Sanumá, but they
are also easily cured with "a few hours of shamanism" (Taylor
1974:66). Other causes of illness are attacks by *hekula dibi* spirits sent
by enemy shamans; attacks by *sai dibi*, evil spirits; sorcery prepared
with *alawali gigi*, magical plants; sorcery prepared with dirt contain-
ing the victim's footprints (*mazo*); the killing of the victim's spirit animal (*nonoshi*).[6] These attacks vary a great deal in virulence, but in general they are much more severe than the attacks of *uku dibi* animal
spirits, and may actually kill their victims. Death is almost infallibly
attributed to human agency, and all these pathologies are directly or
indirectly caused by human beings (Ramos 1986).

Breach of food taboos is rarely so serious as to put the offender's
life at risk, but it is sufficiently dangerous to merit precautions. The
salient role of these taboos in Sanumá life is highlighted by the fact
that they serve as conceptual tools for the elaborate classification of
the society by age. People may transgress them and risk being sick,
but it is precisely in these risks that they find inspiration to organize
themselves in age segments.

Sanumá age grading has its surprises. We have seen some, such as the uneven time spans that comprise the young and the mature. But there are other aspects worth noting, such as the association of the prepubescents with the elderly in the same category, *padashibɨ*. The time span of each is very different—one or two years for the young, and fifteen or more for the elderly. There is also an outstanding difference in their quota of food taboos—maximal for the young, none for the elderly. What is it then that they have in common? It is the fact that both are at the extreme points of the fertility line; they are the limiting cases of a social course that emphasizes life reproduction. The prepubescents are being prepared to begin their reproductive life in a year or two, a preparation which includes rigid abstinence from game meat. The elderly in turn are recognized for having already contributed their share to posterity; this recognition includes their being granted total freedom to eat whatever game they want. Drawing together the two extreme age sets into the same category (*padashibɨ*) is a powerful way to establish the difference between fertile and nonfertile human beings.

The *padashibɨ* category is one more manifestation of the bringing together of what has been with what is yet to be. This does not mean, of course, that these are interchangeable positions, and that the Sanumá see the elderly as capable of going back to adolescence, or vice versa. On the road of life, at least in its material form, there is no U turn. What this conceptual equivalence between the young and the old seems to be, then, is a condensed, and hence economical, way to underscore culturally important issues such as fertility.

In Figure 5.1 above, the age sets are distributed in a deliberately open circle. This graphic device is intended to match the idea that Sanumá age sets are attuned to the belief that life is not limited to a time stretching out on a straight line from birth to death. It is meant to call attention to what is beyond the physical substance of the human body as manifested in this world (the gap between the two extremities of the open circle is filled in in Figure 5.2 below), for the Sanumá life cycle contains both what comes before and what comes after the corporeal passage of humans through the earth. Birth and death do not isolate the person in a biological chronology; rather, one is wrapped in a complex system of interrelations with other entities such as animals and spirits.

The fate of the nonliving seems to follow the same tendency toward condensation that is manifested in language morphology (the *sutuha* adverb), in technical activities (the *wisai hu hena* hunting), and in conceptualization (the collapsing together of the *padashibɨ* age sets).

Once again we see times and occasions, for us totally separate, being compressed into the same category. The trajectory of the nonliving is yet another case of this compression, as spirits of children yet to be born are contemporaneous with souls of the already dead. The latter, *ni pole bi dibi* (or *heno pole bi dibi*) live in the south where the Sanumá ancestors, *ni pada bi dibi*, and the whites once lived, in Saula-dulia, the region of the Ocamo River in Venezuela, that is, the point of dispersal of the present-day inhabitants of the upper Auaris.

This extraordinary conception of temporality mixes dimensions of the material and the nonmaterial worlds in such a way as to raise the nagging question of the applicability of the canonic dichotomies in anthropology such as nature versus culture, natural versus supernatural, and sacred versus profane. On the one hand, there is a continual flow between human beings, animals, and spirits. On the other, those not yet born share the same place with the already dead. In this sort of limbo the living find the parameters, both eschatological and historical, for their material life. Here we shall see how animals and spirits contribute to the construction of the Sanumá person. Two other time dimensions will also be discussed — the great circuit of spirits that epitomizes eternal recurrence, and movements of people through history.

Animals, Spirits, and the Person

From their immaterial state at Saula-dulia, future members of Sanumá society become material when conceived by a man and a woman in procreation. But the constitution of a Sanumá being does not stop there. From the moment of birth, a person's life is punctuated with a number of occasions when animals and spirits will intervene in his or her fortune.

At Birth, a Name and a Spirit

The first encounter of a baby with animal spirits comes a few days after birth. Its father will go on a hunt, not to feed his family, but to find a name for the baby. The name of the species of the animal killed will be given to the child, who will also get a spirit of the dead animal, a *uku dibi* that enters its body through the coccyx, *humabi*, and stays there for life. The name may be abandoned, but not the *humabi* spirit. It protects the child from the attacks of a certain kind of evil spirit, *meini dibi*, a fearful forest entity that strikes at night and preys on children. That is why people often close off all the house entrances with mats, blankets, or branches wherever there are walls that allow for this precaution. The *humabɨ* spirit also helps the child grow.

As we shall see in Chapter 8, this naming procedure is beset with existential risks and ritual care; it generates a great deal of anxiety, perhaps because of the total intimacy that is established between child and animal, and between the social and the supernatural realms. If, on the one hand, doing the *humabɨ* hunt and giving a spirit and a name to the child is dangerous, not doing it would be worse. The Sanumá phrase is "[ilo] humabɨ thabalɨma,"[7] that is, "[a howler monkey] made the coccyx" (the name in brackets is just an example). If the coccyx is not "made," the child will be more prone not only to attacks by the *meini dɨbɨ* spirits, but to being returned to the house of the souls, *nɨ pole bɨ dɨbɨ sai a*, which means to die for the world of the living. This being so, the Sanumá owe to the animals the very continuity of society, for their children's lives depend on the death of the animal that will make their *humabɨ* spirit. True, not all babies are the object of this ritual hunt, but every family has at least one child with a *humabɨ* spirit, most often several of them. The relationship that is established by this joining of animal spirit and human body involves more than just the child and its father; it covers a whole network of kin and affinal relatives who, at another level, play important roles in the reproductive process. By means of affinal ties, a man and a woman beget children; by means of the symbolic bond between animal and child, the continuity of life is guaranteed.

Animal shadow

Not everyone has a *humabɨ* spirit, but every Sanumá necessarily has a *nonoshi*, a spirit animal, alter ego, or individual totem, to use Durkheim's term (1965:183–91). To each human birth corresponds the birth of a certain animal that becomes his or her double. Anything that happens to one will simultaneously happen to the other; if the animal dies, the person dies, and vice versa. Their processes of birth, growth, and maturation are perfectly synchronized. *Nonoshi* also means the shadow that is projected by any source of light and follows the person wherever he or she goes while exposed to the light. In turn, the animal *nonoshi* is always very distant from its human counterpart. The *nonoshi* of the upper Auaris Sanumá are far away to the south, in the land of the Kobali.

There are different sets of spirit animals for men and women. The physical characteristics of a person determine which *nonoshi* he or she will have. The most common are large birds for men, such as *kokoi*, "hawk," and *momo*, "harpy eagle," and land animals for women, such as *hanagasa*, "bush dog," *oligigi*, "snake," or *they a*, an animal similar to the tapir which I could not identify.

One does not change *nonoshi*, nor does one get it from one's parents. Each one of these animals is an individual totally committed to a specific person, even though their paths never meet. Given that the *nonoshi* is always far away, and one has virtually no contact with the people who live there, the killing of a *nonoshi* is usually accidental, but even so open to retaliation. For vengeance to take place, it does not matter whether or not the killing of the *nonoshi* was intentional. Great distances are no guarantee that no revenge will ever be taken against someone by disposing of his or her *nonoshi*. When a Sanumá is angry with another, said Jorge, he will kill his *nonoshi*, and this is very bad, *wanishala*. If the victim's relatives find out the cause of the death, they will turn into *wazu dibi*, "raiders," and set off for a revenge attack on the supposed killer of the deceased's *nonoshi*. The only raid I heard of between 1968 and 1974 was in retaliation for the *nonoshi* killing of an Azagoshi woman who, at the time, lived near the mission communities. The shamans who diagnosed her death indicated the Kobali as responsible for it.

Just as the *nonoshi* of the Auaris people are in the land of the Kobali, so also those of the Kobali are in the upper Auaris region. A long time ago, Jorge went on to say, his maternal uncle, Heitor, killed an immense harpy eagle "with legs as thick as those of a Sanumá." He gave the bird to João, a Maiongong who likes its feathers as ornaments. The Maiongong also ate it. As a consequence of this killing, a man of the *shilawa dibi*, a Kobali descent group, died. Still according to Jorge, Heitor went into seclusion (*kanenemo*) to be purified from the pollution generated by the killing. He was isolated for about twenty days. He lost weight, had a sore ear, and as his hair gave out a fetid odor, he cut it. He left seclusion after he learned from his *hekula* assistant spirits that the dead person had been cremated. I never knew whether Heitor killed the bird intentionally; since there is no evidence that he was acquainted with the victim, one may suppose that it was an accident.

Occasionally a game animal appears in a village displaying odd behavior such as coming very close and causing alarm, for it can be either an evil spirit in disguise, or someone's stray *nonoshi*. These occasions provoke great interest and long discussions, and the elders warn everyone to keep away from the beast. It is not killed, let alone eaten.

Sanumá discomfort in talking about *nonoshi* is very apparent. Some people are reticent, others give contradictory information, still others claim ignorance about it, and for a long time my data on the subject were limited to loose and vague fragments. It was not until 1974 that I got a better picture of it from Jorge. It is as if the *nonoshi* were the Sanumá Achilles heel, a sore spot that leaves them prone to accidents or attacks that cannot be averted.

The inextricably bound fates of humans and their alter spirits bring another dimension to the constitution of the person and the life cycle. This cycle not only continues after death, but is not limited to the human individual as a discrete unit. The person is complete only when it has a *nonoshi*, his or her three-dimensional shadow in animal form. Human body and distant shadow: their spaces are far apart, but their lifetime is only one, and their fates are irreversibly intertwined in the same process of life and death.

Puberty and the Seduction of the Spirits

After birth the most critical moment in a person's life is puberty. The twelve months that precede and follow it—practically the whole young *padashibɨ* phase—are surrounded with strict food taboos and special precautions against supernatural dangers. The rite of passage from adolescence to adulthood involves both boys and girls in a state of liminality that leaves the person unusually vulnerable to the action of certain evil spirits. Unlike the *meini dɨbɨ* that attack children in an ostensibly aggressive way, these puberty spirits use seduction as their weapon. Like the *meini dɨbɨ*, they are not *uku dɨbɨ*, for their origin is neither animal nor human. They are in the category of *sai dɨbɨ*, spirits that specialize in causing harm to human beings.[8]

When a girl has her first menstruation, *hogolomo*, she is hidden from the rest of the village by an enclosure (*hogolo*) put up in a corner of her house. She sits on the dirt floor for three days, consuming only water and a tiny amount of cassava bread her mother passes on, taking care not to touch her. She makes herself look as ugly as possible. With a shaven head, no apron, no ornaments, skin dirty from the smoke of the ever-lit fire, and thin from the prolonged fast, she becomes intentionally unattractive to men. All of this is to discourage the advances of *sōtenama*, evil spirits of both sexes (the male is especially fond of girls going through the *hogolomo* seclusion). Without this meticulous personal untidiness, a male *sōtenama* would surely leave his house in the mountain to the south, come invisibly to the girl's house in the still of the night, and call her with all the seduction of which he is capable. He would take her away, marry her, give her children, and she would never come back home, leaving behind her dead body.

At the end of her first menstrual period, having managed to elude the *sōtenama's* lust, the girl returns to her normal activities. Having taken a bath and put on bead ornaments and a new apron, she waits for her hair to grow back to ear length to consumate her marriage, in case she already has a husband. From then on, her periods will not be marked by anything other than just sitting on the ground. It is simply said that she is "sitting," *loa.*

In the case of boys, the telltale signs of puberty are much more diffuse. The ritual occasion is called *poko manogoshi,* "bare arm," in reference to the act of cutting off the armbands the boy wears constantly. This is also an attempt to make him unattractive. Zoca's description is as follows. The day comes when it is decided that the boy must throw away his *shinanu,* the "cotton" armbands. It is when his pubic hair begins to show. The men notice it first and say, *"wanagi!"* ("be quiet," "shut up"); then the women repeat, *"wanagi!"* At night, one of the older women throws away his armbands. His head is also shaven. The boy lies in his hammock above his mother's or grandmother's. He should not scratch himself with his own nails lest he develop wounds, *sonaga.* He eats nothing for two days; on the third day he drinks a little *nashi kōi,* cassava bread crumbled in water, and on the fourth, it is all over. If he fails to take these precautions, he, like the girls, will run the risk of being taken as a spouse by a female *sōtenama,* and then his skin would become leathery and dark like black ink. The removal of the armbands and the shaven head are also attempts to make the boy as ugly as possible so as not to attract a female evil spirit. If he keeps his ornaments, she will smell the cotton and "will leap like a chick" over the boy in order to marry him.[9]

After crossing the threshold to adulthood, the Sanumá boy gives no ostensible signs of transformation in his behavior. Decorated with new armbands and his head covered to conceal the cropped hair, he will continue to enjoy the carefree existence of adolescence for a year or two more. It is only when he takes on the role of husband and son-in-law that there is a noticeable change in his manners. Once and for all he abandons his teenager's nonchalant habits and enters the hall of the "serious" men, slowly occupying his place in shamanism, ceremonial dialogues, and in the political debates to which he has been a mere spectator and apprentice.

The Immaterial Life of Humans

Like animals and invisible beings of the forest, humans also generate their own spirits. The term *uku dɨbɨ* means image, or reflection. Loathing cameras, the Sanumá, like other Yanomami, resent having their image, *uku dɨbɨ* taken away by the big glass eye directed at them. *Uku dɨbɨ te die!* "Don't take my image spirit!" is what we hear whenever we point a camera at them. Mothers cover their infants' faces and send older children into hiding.

The person carries his or her own *uku dɨbɨ* that is passed on together with blood, flesh, bones, and other corporeal substances. Among these *uku dɨbɨ* is the *mani de*, the dream spirit (*manimo*, "to dream"). Lodged in the chest, *õshi*, of both men and women, it is regarded as dangerous, at least potentially so, because it acts independently of the person's will during sleep. It may take off and roam around causing trouble the person may not even know about, let alone control. It flies high like the large birds, *katewi*, goes to far-off lands, and is capable of killing game and even people. When the person dies, his or her *mani de* is freed from the body during cremation, returning to the house of the *nɨ pole bɨ dɨbɨ*, the souls of the dead.

The *nɨ pole bɨ dɨbɨ* are also dangerous to the living. People die, said Zeca, because the soul of a close relative, a dead father, for instance, appears in dreams offering food. The person stops eating normal food, becomes very thin, and dies. He or she then goes to the *nɨ pole bɨ dɨbɨ*'s house where there is plenty of food. But if the person continues to eat, even if he or she goes on losing weight, the souls do not insist, they say that he or she still wants to be with the living, with his or her *sanɨma dɨbɨ*. When the person stops eating altogether, it is a sure sign that the souls are feeding him or her. Through their assistant spirits, *hekula dɨbɨ*, the shamans see these souls, try to chase them away, but are not always successful. Here, too, the agent of death is a human, albeit dead.

After death all the immaterial parts of a person are returned to the *nɨ pole bɨ dɨbɨ*. The souls of the recently deceased, still very attached to the world of the living, need to be convinced to go back there for good. One of the best ways to achieve their return to the house of the souls is to drink the ashes of the person's charred bones. If, for example, the deceased's mother does not take the ashes, the soul becomes *hĩsho*, "angry", and makes her ill. The gourd where the ashes are kept after cremation must be totally destroyed lest the soul insist on staying around persuading the living to accompany it. The wailing that follows death also contributes to appease the soul and coax it into leaving for its original dwelling at Saula-dulia.[10]

Humans and animals trace their own routes through life and death, but these routes have similar contours and many junctions, even when we leave out the obvious relationship between hunter and hunted, or between the eater and the eaten. In their immateriality as spirits, "shadows," or alter egos, animals interact with humans in contexts of great symbolic power at various points in a person's life. As both material and nonmaterial beings, they are essential parts of a person's formation (in the sense of *Bildung*) over the whole course of his or her existence as both material and nonmaterial beings.

The process that transforms an infant into a child, a child into an adult, an adult into a mature person, and on into old age does not end with death or with the reduction of the physical body to ashes. In their immaterial essence, the souls of the dead, *ni pole bi dibi*, may cause physical harm to the living, as do the animal *uku dibi* spirits when food taboos are disregarded. We shall now see the course of human and animal spirits in their respective cosmological orbits.

The Eternal Recurrence of Eschatological Time

Just as there are many convergence points between animals, spirits, and people during the material life cycle of human beings, so there is a cosmological dimension where they also cross paths. Their trajectory is such as to take them back to their original state, albeit transformed. Let us begin with the animals. Taylor's (1976) fine analysis follows their fate.

Before the great metamorphosis in times that we whites call mythological, both animals and humans existed in the corporeal form of human beings, but were immortal. A series of events that Taylor identifies as antisocial acts provoked the transformation of animals into mortals with a nonhuman corporeality. As such, they are now hunted and eaten by men. If their meat is prohibited to someone who then breaks the prohibition, the animal's *uku dibi* spirit, which is a miniature copy of the live animal, may attack the offender or his/her children, causing a specific sickness. In attacking, the *uku dibi* expose themselves to total and irreversible destruction by the weapons of *hekula dibi*, the assistant spirits of the shaman who treats the sick. An unrelenting chase of the aggressive *uku dibi* ensues, as exemplified in the following passage.

> [W]hen the prohibition on anteater meat is broken and the *uku dubi* of the dead anteater inflicts the "stroke" penalty on the offender, the *uku dubi* has to be (1) tracked, (2) chased into ambush, and then (3) killed. The *hekula* of a *honama* (a grouse-like bird which feeds on the ground and can run very quickly) searches for the tracks, hunts, and then chases the anteater *uku dubi*. The *hekula* of a *kulemi* bird (long-legged and a fast runner), of an *amu una* (a fast-flying species of bee), and of an *uemigigi* (a fast-moving snake) all chase the anteater *uku dubi* into an ambush where

the *hekula* of the *maitaliwɨ* (arrow-head bamboo) and *managaitili* (mythical ancestors of a specified distant group of Yanoama) are waiting to kill it with bow and arrow. If necessary, a *paso* (spider monkey) *hekula* can then deliver the coup-de-grâce with its quarter-staff. (Taylor 1976:44)

When a vengeful *uku dɨbɨ* is thus killed, it falls down to the universe's underworld (*hidi kuoma*), and is devoured by the dwarfs (*oinan dɨbɨ*) who live there. "Thus twice-over hunted, killed, and eaten, they are totally destroyed" (Taylor 1976:45).

But people do not break food taboos all the time, and when they do, the *uku dɨbɨ* of the eaten animal may not take revenge. These *uku dɨbɨ* that escape the implacable persecution of the shamans' *hekula dɨbɨ* may try to retrieve what they lost in the primeval metamorphosis—immortality, corporeality, and human form. They leave the forest they inhabited as animals and go to the house of the *hekula dɨbɨ* of their own species, associated with a given hunting territory:

These *hekula* houses are typically in mountains, waterfalls, rivers, but not simply "in the forest." On arrival, the *uku dubɨ* will metamorphose into a *hekula*, a spirit with the appearance of a miniature human being. It is then available to be taken as one of his assistant spirits by some Yanoama shaman, necessarily someone living a considerable distance away in a totally different part of Yanoama territory.

The worst that can happen to a *hekula* is that, if it is sent to attack a human being, other *hekula* may defend its human victim by attacking and chasing it away. The extreme form of such an attack involves actual dismemberment of the *hekula*'s body. But this is only a way of establishing dominance and does not destroy the dismembered *hekula*, which will put itself back together again and withdraw. On undergoing metamorphosis from its *uku dubɨ* to its *hekula* phase, the being in question has regained a state of indestructibility. (Taylor 1976:45)

This animal trajectory obviously depends on the will of men, first in hunting and killing the prey; second, in observing food taboos; third, in destroying the spirit via shamanism; fourth, in procuring *hekula* among the surviving *uku dɨbɨ*; and fifth, in lodging them in their chests and restoring their lost corporeality, even though reduced to the condition of tenants.

This curious eschatological route of the animals seems to draw a long arch. Their life begins with three primeval features—corporeality, humanity, and indestructibility—when they live on earth as game; they lose the first when they are killed on a hunt; they lose the second and third when they live on earth as game. All there is left is the immateriality of their *uku dɨbɨ*. When the animal spirits become *hekula dibi*, humanity and immortality are reclaimed. With luck, if a shaman decides to adopt the newly transformed *hekula*, corporeality is restored as well.

This hard road of losses and gains is by and large also taken by humans within the limits of their humanness. Let us see how Taylor describes their fate.

> The spirits of dead people are already humanoid in form, but they do somewhat correspond to the *uku dubi* phase of an animal's existence in being also disposed to harm living people. Such spirits are known as *ni pole bi dibi* 'ghosts'. The ghosts typically do harm to their own surviving relatives, usually in revenge for some offense committed during their lifetimes, though it is often many years after their death before they find an opportunity to take this revenge. Ghosts can also attack their killers if ritual seclusion after the killing is not correctly observed. Disposal of the dead is normally by cremation. If the body of a dead person is incompletely cremated, his ghost can be especially dangerous: *ni pole bi dibi* are said to live in a home far off to the south in what is nowadays unoccupied territory. They can be called from there to become a shaman's *hekula* and also to live in his chest. (Taylor 1976:36–37)

As *hekula dibi*, the *uku dibi*, so far dehumanized, destructible, and disembodied, may recover their immortality, take on human form, and live again among men.

Men, like animals, lost their immortality. Their corporeal form disappears with death, and what are left are the humanoid spirits, *ni pole bi dibi*. As far as we know, these spirits do not run the risk of total destruction as do animal *uku dibi* when hunted down by a shaman's *hekula dibi*. They can, however, lose their corporeality forever, as this depends on the will of specific shamans to recruit them as their *hekula dibi*, and lend them a body by housing them in their chests. The house of the *ni pole bi dibi* at the Saula-dulia is then a reservoir of spirits that can be transformed into *hekula dibi* for living shamans.

In this reservoir are also the spirits of children yet to be conceived. This does not mean that the Sanumá espouse reincarnation in the strict sense of this term. They never associate a child with someone already dead in a direct incorporation of the deceased's soul into the infant's body, nor do they propose the return to earth of the same soul in a quest for purification. The Saula-dulia reservoir resembles rather a "memory bank" brimming with cosmological information and with eschatological resources that can be used and reused in a general and impersonal way. This eschatological memory bank, at one and the same time, stores up human spirits and recycles new Sanumá lives. Figure 5.2 attempts to capture this notion. Notice that it

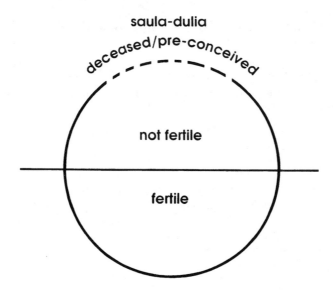

Fig. 5.2. Recycling of life and death

repeats the main features of Figure 5.1 in that it emphasizes the fertility line and the circularity of the process. But where in Figure 5.1 the top of the drawing is an open space, here we fill up that space with the souls of the dead and of the not yet born.

Agents of eternal recurrence, the *ni pole bɨ dɨbɨ* are the continuation of the life cycle as seen in its totality, that is, including both the material and the nonmaterial phases of human beings. Their "house" is the place where the living constructed a very special portion of their history. When they speak of *ni pole bɨ dɨbɨ*, the Sanumá of the upper Auaris can't help but remember that place, Saula-dulia. In this sense, the *ni pole bɨ dɨbɨ* are, as it were, the guardians of the historical origin that is kept in the memory of the living. Moreover, they give durability to the life cycle by taking over after the body's death. This continuity in time turns the material phase on earth into a short interlude of a trajectory that is infinitely longer. Like a spring, the house of the *ni pole bɨ dɨbɨ* feeds the society of the living with new spirits, those of children to be born. It is point of departure and of arrival.

The Unfolding Historical Process

Whereas the souls, *ni pole bɨ dɨbɨ*, are the agents of eternal recurrence, the long-dead elders, transfigured into ancestors, *ni pada bɨ*

dibi, are the agents of unfolding history. By means of a metamorpho-
ais, *ishiwanihioma*, they created the immediate ancestors of today's
Sanumá, and prompted a series of spatial movements that are now
part of the living experience of the inhabitants of the upper Auaris
River.

In 1973 I was taken aback by the way all this was told to me by the
junior widow of old Mosonawa, a sweet *padazoma*, or elderly woman,
who always answered my naive questions with infinite patience. We
were talking about changes in residence of the community clusters to
which her parents belonged:

—Where did the *totobidili dibi* first come from?

—From over there [south], [east of] Saula-dulia where the Kobali
now live.

—Why did they split apart?

—I don't know, the elders metamorphosed, *ni pada bi dibi
ishiwanihiogima*.

—Why did the elders metamorphose?

—I don't know, that's what the elders simply said, *ina pada dibi ku
bio gubili*. The *ni pada bi dibi* (ancestors) made the *paluli*, "bush turkey,"
cry. They shot it with their arrows and then they metamorphosed. Then
it became dark, there was no daylight, people had to light immense fires
because it was always night; then, at last, it began to get light and people
were happy. Before the bush turkey was shot, there was only daytime.
People couldn't sleep properly until the elders killed the bird. It was
huge, covering the whole sky. We metamorphosed, said the elders.

Before this transformation that brought about the alternation of
day and night, all Sanumá lived in one place, a big round house with
an internal patio. Afterward they all dispersed, *selegibazoma*. Some
went to Saula-dulia and became *saulagidili dibi*; others, such as the
kazuma dibi, went farther, beyond Saula-dulia; still others came
northward, and thus they all spread out.

—Before the metamorphosis, what was the name of the *higadili dibi?*

—*Totobidili dibi*. Later they were also called *higadili* (*higadili dibi hila
nimima*).

—What was the name of the *azatali dibi* before the metamorphosis?

—I don't know, I was too young when they metamorphosed, I don't
know.

We see here, again, mixed in the same discourse, things that we
as white anthropologists normally attempt to keep separate—history
and myth. The Sanumá historical trajectory begins with the nightly
bush turkey which, shot by sleepless men, brought about a porten-

Elderly woman feeds her pet. 1973. Photograph by K. I. Taylor.

tous transformation that echoed through the generations that followed. It is as though a command had been given, "Let it be darkness," and there was darkness. Finally men could sleep properly, and the life cycle was never the same. History was then created and is now part of the collection of social memories.

Also surprising is the manner in which my interlocutor claimed not to know about the origin of the *azatali dibi*, her own sib. She placed herself in a time frame that was not too remote (she did not say, "I don't know because I hadn't been born yet") but not recent enough to allow her to know about it firsthand. "Because I was too young," *ose kuteni*,[11] "I don't know," *taimi*. This is a very common answer in contexts such as this, where the knowledge requested could never come from lived experience, for it refers to something that happened long ago. It is as though it would make no sense to say that one does not know something because one did not yet exist, for, in a way, people always existed within the Sanumá eschatological cycle of eternal recurrence.

We can also perceive that "post-bush-turkey" history, that is, relatively recent events, is told in a sort of compartmentalized fashion. This view seems to indicate that Sanumá as a whole had a common destiny up until the point of dispersal. From then on, each community cluster would take care of its own history, casting off others to less focused regions of discourse. Indeed, this seems to be a rhetorical style for this kind of narrative, for the flow of news between villages keeps everyone reasonably informed as to what goes on within their common social universe.

In Chapter 2 we saw a little of the history of the *saulagidili dibi*, the former inhabitants of an important village cluster that, after dispersing, metamorphosed into a descent category. Their dispersal northward resulted in the Sanumá occupation of the upper Auaris and other river valleys, such as the Merevari in Venezuela. The history of these movements is described as a great migration that, like a fan, radiates out from a common and revered origin. The term *selegibazoma* is made up of a morphological sequence — *sele-gi-ba-zo-ma* — that contains the root *sele*, "to separate," and a series of suffixes that indicate various aspects of the action. Among these, it is worth noticing -*gi*-, "dynamic focus," -*ba*-, "strong degree of execution," and -*ma*, "nonwitnessed completed action" (Borgman 1976). We could then read in the word *selegibazoma* a type of separation that forced people to abandon their villages, impelled by attacks from enemies such as the Samatali, the Waiká, the Kobali, and the Maiongong.

Dispersal led to the translation of space into time. The names of old residence sites are kept as patronyms transmitted from fathers to children of both sexes. Through the medium of patrilineality they are retained as social memory not only for the generations that lived in those places, but also for those who only heard about them. In the case of the latter, this memory is implanted by instruction, not by lived experience. It is a memory of things learned and reaffirmed whenever the toponyms-turned-patronyms are evoked. We might say that, by means of this transformation of space into descent, the Sanumá emphasize events and places that are regarded as milestones in their historical journey. Saula-dulia is one such milestone. From it come unborn *saulagidili dibi* children, and to it go the souls of their dead. From it came the "fathers beyond" (*pi dibi tolea*) who, in transmitting their membership in those villages on to their descendants, infused in the latter the awareness of a highly revered common origin. As a point of reference, the place known as Saula-dulia and the entity known as *saulagidili dibi* operated as historical moorings to orient the people in the intense migrations that provoked frequent social, economic, and political turmoil and in subsequent rearrangements as they ran away from enemies and encountered new places and new peoples (such as the Maiongong and the whites) on their way north (Ramos 1980). Theirs is a case of patrilineality put at the service of memory and historical awareness, supplying the Sanumá with an idiom that is both condensed and expandable. By means of this device, spaces are delimited, horizons are enlarged, communities are consolidated, and persons gone astray are tracked down. A vast network of social connections is then cast over the newly occupied territory. Some of these connections are tighter than others, but they all still contribute to the organic chain that is the Sanumá people. The communities studied here are but one fragment of this chain, joining others in a long succession of village clusters that share a common geographical and historical flow.

Again, I must repeat, space turns into time. What began as a reference for residence resolved itself into a starting point for a time sequence via descent. It is so with lineages and it is so with historical residence categories exemplified by the *saulagidili dibi*. But unlike the lineages that submit to a structural time, or to a diachronic structure that repeats itself through time, the *saulagidili dibi* type of category operates in the key of an unfolding history which is generated by the eventful experience of a specific group of people in a given territorial space that will no longer be relived. These former residential categories are the finished product of a process of diachronization of space

having patrilineality as its apt medium. They are the nodal points of a
historical interest that has been perserved as collective memory so as
to resist the hazards of Sanumá spatial moves for the last one hundred years at least. As former centers of dispersal, these nodal points
have acquired the status of topographic ancestors, replacing the *ni
pada bi dibi*, the very elders who, albeit inadvertently, provoked the
unfolding of history. They are also the home of the souls, *ni pole bi
dibi*, watchmen of the eternal recurrence both in the cosmos and in
society. In returning to their point of origin, the souls celebrate in
their own key the importance of these sites in the flow of Sanumá life
before and after the passage of the living through this world.

Appendix

Figure 5.3 represents, for comparative purposes, the distribution of
population segments in the Sanumá villages under study, according
to Western statistical criteria. The regular age intervals sharply contrast with the irregularity of the age sets as recorded in Sanumá
ethnography.

Fig. 5.3. Sanumá population pyramid for eight communities
of the Upper Auaris region

Part 2
Names

6
Names under Erasure

Derrida's tr⨯e is the mark of the absence of a presence.
　　　　　　　　　　　　　　　—Spivak

Sanumá personal names are secret and yet some are disclosed. They are private and yet some are public. As we have seen in Chapter 2, a few, indeed very few, names are selected out of a community in order to be used as bases for teknonyms (personal names combining someone else's proper name and a kinship term) and eventually as patronyms (male names used as "surnames"). The social use the Sanumá make of their proper names betrays a sense of conceptualization so refined as to require an equally complex Western theoretical tool to put it across. A mere description of how names are concealed or exhibited might risk falling short of Sanumá refinement and incur what I want to avoid at all costs: exoticization. In an attempt to do justice to the sophistication of the Sanumá naming practices, I appeal to the sophistication of Derrida's discussion of the sign.

As Gayatri Spivak clarifies in her translator's preface to *Of Grammatology*, "In examining familiar things we come to such unfamiliar conclusions that our very language is twisted and bent even as it guides us. Writing 'under erasure' is the mark of this contortion" (Spivak 1976: xvi). A word under erasure should not be mentioned, but it has to be mentioned if the message in question is to be delivered. I might add that this situation is aggravated when we examine unfamiliar things. The twists and bends of our language become sharp and contorted to the point of jeopardizing intelligibility. One possible way out of this conundrum in cross-cultural communication is to resort to language that is so obviously alien to the ethnographic context that it jolts the reader out of his familiar grounds into the disquieting terrain of cultural translation. Just as I was startled by the language the Sanumá create with their proper names, so may the reader confront the slippage of meanings that I take to be neces-

181

sary for a better appreciation of what we are about to examine. "It is necessary to use the word, since language cannot do more" (Spivak 1976: xv).

Whereas Heidegger puts "master-words" such as B~~e~~ing under erasure, Derrida crosses out, while keeping visible, what he calls the "trace" (or track), "a word that cannot be a master-word, that presents itself as the mark of an anterior presence, origin, master" (Spivak 1976: xv). In extracting from the realm of philosophical enquiry the instrument I have been looking for to convey the import of Sanumá secrecy and disclosure of proper names, I am taking a liberty that Spivak seems to grant the antropologist.[1] Hence, just as Derrida proposes that the trace is the mark of the absence of a presence as detected in ordinary language, so do I submit that Sanumá personal names are the marks of the camouflaged presence of the nuclear family, and of the absence of desired but not yet present lineages. As such, they are used under erasure, an erasure that is phonologic rather than graphic, as it occurs in speech, not in writing. But again, if we are to accept Derrida's contention that graphics are not the indispensable stamp of writing in the broad sense of the term, and that proper names, like cinema, dance, or sculpture, represent yet another form of inscription, that is, writing *lato sensu* (Derrida 1976: 9), then I may be justified in declaring Sanumá personal names the signs that inscribe a certain type of temporality. Names are the individual traces of collectivities past, present, or future. Unsuspecting Derrideans, the Sanumá put their proper names under erasure: they are unutterable, "yet necessary to say" (Spivak 1976: xiii). Covering them over with protective silence, the Sanumá create with their names a language for a social process that is amenable to as many readings as there are readers to read it.

This chapter is about teknonymy. At first sight, this is a naming procedure that contemplates individuals rather than collectivities, and conceals personal names under the guise of name-dropping. But, as I hope will be clear, Sanumá teknonymy also oversees the shift from the many to the one, that is, from a number of closely related persons to the unity of a nuclear family or of a lineage. Here the essence, the "master-word," would be *lineage*, and its trace, someone's proper name. A private name that is made public is a name under erasure, or rather, under conceptual scrutiny; it becomes the index that points toward an entity of social magnitude; it is a tool by which society conceptualizes itself. In the interplay between the personal and the collective realms, personal names that serve as referents for teknonymy are traces or tracks, but tracks of a path yet to be trodden.

Teknonymy Sanumá-Style

To call someone "Mother of So-and-So," "Father of So-and-so," "Older brother of So-and-so," "Wife of So-and-so," or "Daughter of So-and-so," a usage known in ethnology as *teknonymy*, is neither as folkloric nor as inconsequential as it might seem. Ethnological studies have demonstrated that by thus naming people, societies may be accomplishing a lot more than simply allocating a name and a kinship term. Just to mention a couple of examples from both South America and elsewhere, the Balinese (Geertz and Geertz 1964) and the Piaroa Indians of Venezuela (Kaplan 1972) use teknonymy to go well beyond naming. For the former it is an instrument for time reckoning; for the latter it is a mechanism for reconciling contradictions between kin and affines.

The Sanumá also say things with teknonymous names. They conceal names, but they also show that not everyone's name is forever secret. When someone's name is chosen as referent for a cluster of other names such as the "So-and-sos" above, that person is being transformed into a public figure. In anticipating the emergence of a new lineage, people choose its eponym in advance, as it were. In these ways, the teknonym distinguishes itself through understatement, becoming a telegraphic and efficient way of conceptualizing a social region such as the rise of a new lineage. Teknonymy gives us precious clues to the unsaid of Sanumá society.

The traces of Sanumá teknonymy appear under various guises. While it performs its role as a naming procedure, it also takes on other performative and conceptual assignments. It is a remarkably succinct and economic way of articulating several ideas at once. By "performative" I mean the power that certain language expressions have to contribute to a *Bildung* that is fashioned by the strength of expectations emanating from the collectivity about someone specific. We have seen in previous chapters that the personal name for a Sanumá is something very confidential and secluded, and represents one of the rare regions of privacy that are granted to individuals. "Common" people have their proper name or names cloaked in secrecy as protection to their individuality; in this respect these people greatly differ from others whose names not only are well known, but are rather freely uttered by everyone and anyone. A person who is accustomed to hearing his personal name called around in the public sphere will necessarily react to this onomastic exposure in a different way from that of their name-muted companions. For instance, Sopai's mode of being in the world cannot be the same as that of, for instance, his elder brother, protected as he is by the teknonym *Sopai pebala* ("Older brother of Sopai").

Why some people are culled out of a mass of others to be taken as referents is very difficult to ascertain. Factors that may have to do with favored personality traits shroud this matter with a considerable dose of imponderability. I am, however, inclined to think that their choice is not altogether arbitrary. If Sanumá ethos typically favors extrovert behavior, the human referents of teknonymous names are particularly uninhibited and outgoing. It is as though, having heard their names publicly voiced so often, they assume the burden of a notoriety that is assigned to them rather than conquered, much less desired. Mostly men, these teknonymous personae are as if molded to be open to the collectivity, with no right to the privacy of that which is one of the most important attributes of a person, his name. If proper names contribute to forge personalities, as Mauss argues when he associates them with the notions of person and soul ([1929] 1979: 178–180), their being secret or public will obviously affect the constitution of those personalities. That is what I mean by the performative aspect of teknonymy. By calling someone's name regularly and unrestrictedly, the community produces a public figure. After all, "to *say* something is to *do* something" (Austin 1975: 12), even when the sayer and the doer are different people.

As for the conceptual aspect of teknonymy, it is revealed in the way certain personal names are associated with specific kin categories. A circle of relatives is drawn around the referent, with the result that these relatives are defined and identified as a unit in contrast to all other units. The effect is similar to that produced by concepts. In Chapters 2 and 3 we noted how important are personal names for identifying agnatic groups that stand as potential forerunners of new lineages. We shall now see how the passage from personal name to group name is brought about, and how the role of the human eponym can be stripped of onomastic privacy in order to provide a group of people with the conceptual status of belonging to something that is greater than the sum of its individual parts.

Chapter 4 showed how Sanumá kinship terminology, a version

of the Dravidian type, dissolves the nuclear family into a host of classificatory "fathers," "mothers," "siblings," "children," etc. If all we knew was the kinship terminology, we would be at a loss to identify people's progenitors in a given community of kinsmen. Although the nuclear family comes up to the surface elsewhere—in garden ownership, and in some domestic spaces, for instance—its existence and delimitation are only indirectly verbalized. The indirect trace of its conceptualization, disguised in teknonymy, demarcates the members of the nuclear family, leaving out the other co-resident "mothers" and "fathers." Thus, even though the kinship terminology addresses paternal uncles and maternal aunts as parents, parallel cousins as siblings, and "parallel children" as children of one's own, teknonymy excludes all of them. Only primary kin or spouses are included in a teknonymous cluster. In this sense, Sanumá teknonymy differs from most comparable cases in anthropological literature in that it is applied to a wider gamut of kinship categories than just "mother" and "father." For this reason, I take the Sanumá version to be a case of "extended teknonymy."

There are at least four situations in which teknonymy plays a crucial role, two involving individuals, and two, collectivities. Although the former will be mentioned, my focus here is on the latter, that is, the nuclear family and agnatic groups as social fields that receive recognition and conceptual attention via teknonyms. Before I begin to demonstrate this proposition, it is necessary to define the extended character of Sanumá teknonymy.

Proper names that are referents in Sanumá teknonymy may be combined with a number of terms for both kin and affinal relatives: "father"/"mother," "older brother"/"older sister," "younger brother"/"younger sister," "sibling of opposite sex," "son"/"daughter," "husband"/"wife." Teknonymy never employs terms for relatives that are more distant than these, and never includes classificatory relatives, such as those we would call "aunts," "uncles," "grandparents," "nephews," or "nieces." The Sanumá use regular kinship terms in teknonyms, unlike the Venezuelan Piaroa, for instance, who have a special nomenclature for that purpose (Kaplan 1972).

Not all Sanumá have teknonyms. Based on the criteria of frequency and consistency of usage both as reference and address, I can account for about a hundred cases of teknonymy in a total of approximately a thousand proper names. These hundred teknonyms were clustered around fifty-five proper names, 76 percent of which were male referents, and 24 percent female. Teknonymy is consistently widespread; I found it in all eight villages, and in forty of the forty-seven domestic groups studied.

Most often it is the names of children that are selected for teknonymous combinations, but there are instances of names of adults used for this purpose, that is to say, people whose names have been chosen after they passed through childhood. This preference for children's names is the logical result of the fact that until puberty proper names are not covered in secrecy, a situation which is expected to change when the referents grow up. But some teknonyms persist through life. In these cases, instead of being kept private, the referents' proper names are definitively launched into the public domain. Why theirs and not other names are revealed is, as I said, the result of choices that do not follow a discernible pattern. Thus appropriated by teknonymy, their names are no longer their own but their relatives', who use them as if they were social diacritics.

In this sense, the Sanumá owners of these public names play a role that is reminiscent of the New Caledonian Canaque personage as described by Leenhardt (1979). A Canaque personage is a composite of the various facets of a person as spelled out by his multiple names; "no name can cover the whole person" (1979: 156), who is thus apportioned practically as many names as the roles he plays. Some of these names are sacred—"The ancestral name, periodically restored over the generations, actualizes the former personage by investing a new person in the society with his august personality" (1979: 156)— and secret, for their disclosure may cause "emotional turmoil of the personage 'bared' by the pronunciation of the totemic name" (1979: 161).

Shifting the focus from the many names concentrated on a single Canaque person to the many names a single Sanumá person may generate for others, we have in the Sanumá case another version of the personage who is such on the strength of the symbolic power of proper names. When a number of relatives cluster around someone by using his name as an identification mark, this "person is sensed beneath the social costume, in the role of personage" (Leenhardt 1979: 162).

Let us see some concrete examples of teknonymous combinations and the range of relatives they encompass. These examples include both proper names that have been kept public, and others that have been returned to secrecy.

Oima penoba	*Hewulia pɨa*	*Aɨge pɨa*	*Sopai pɨbɨna*
"Husband of Oima"	"Father of Hewulia"	"Father of Aɨge"	"Mother of Sopai"
	Hewulia poosa "Younger brother of Hewulia"	*Aɨge pɨbɨna* "Mother of Aɨge"	*Sopai pebala* "Older brother of Sopai"
		Aɨge poosa "Younger brother of Aɨge"	*Sopai poosa* "Younger brother of Sopai"
			Sopai pezea "Sister of Sopai"

The distribution of these names on the page indicates the recurrence and diversity of their usage. The frequency of teknonyms based on a given kinship category depends, of course, on whether or not there are relatives in that category. If, for instance, Aɨge's mother was to have a daughter, she would probably be called *Aɨge pezea*, "Sister of Aɨge."

In examining the cases of teknonymy, one is struck by the realization that this is not just a clever device to help keep most names secret. Its role is of much greater consequence than a mere onomastic trick. Nor is it a metaphor that stands for something else, for the Sanumá would much rather *not* expose proper names, but, despite themselves, they *have* to if they are to put their social message across. In its highly concise and condensed form, this naming practice exposes certain aspects of the social tissue that without it might go undetected. It is yet another example of the capacity Sanumá society has for making comments about itself, using a code to decode other codes. When some names are exposed in order to conceal others (a code), they stand for the unsaid; they decode the messages behind what is explicitly said. These are codes upon codes. It is precisely this combination of exposure and concealment that renders the code known. These are the subtly implied messages that draw far more attention than messages explicitly put. They present, in Derridean terms, the trace of the essence. By overtly denuding people of their proper names, teknonymy unveils a perception about the potential of certain men to become public figures. This process, as complex as it is subtle, generates some by-products to which I will return later.

Family, the Birthplace of Teknonymy

The domestic compartment is the most concentrated region of the family, be it nuclear, polygynous, or extended. Each compartment, identified by a hearth and perhaps walls, does not, however, necessarily correspond to the totality of the family it shelters, nor does it display in a literal way the bonds that exist between families within the same communal house. There are, for instance, families that are apparently nuclear who occupy contiguous compartments, but whose social and economic interaction is so intense that it would be frankly artificial to consider them as separate units. In such cases it is more appropriate to assume that they are just one extended family of parents, children, and grandchildren spread out in more than one compartment. The reason for these changes in the occupation of the domestic space can be found in the life cycle of family groups, as described in Chapter 1. The dynamics of a family's life are best perceived along a trail that begins with a couple in uxorilocal residence, goes on to the birth of children, passes through the death of the wife's parents, with vicissitudes along the way such as divorces, premature deaths of parents or children, remarriages, or acquisition of additional spouses. In short, a family usually braves a whole series of events and/or misfortunes that make up its specific history, but also signal the properly sociological features that are common to all families.

In the ongoing process of family development, the nuclear family is hardly noticed as compared with the emphasis given to relationships that occur within the wider set of relatives in which it is inserted. This set comprises people of various generations and degrees of collaterality. Even within the strictly nuclear family, relationships often overlap. A wife, for instance, may at one and the same time be the mother of a man's children, the daughter of his mother's brother, and the daughter of his father's sister. In other words, the nuclear family is so entangled in the web of kinship that, in order to define it, it is necessary to go through relatives who are primary neither to the husband nor to the wife. Seen from the economic angle, in the phase of bride service, when the man works for his parents-in-law, it is the extended family that is in charge of supplying the domestic group with food and other goods as well as services. As for child rearing, although the parents are mostly responsible for it, to all intents and purposes it is the extended family that is actively involved in raising the children born to it. In most cases, the nuclear family lives in the shadow of the extended family that envelops it.

Diluted in the network of collateral relatives, the nuclear family is revealed as in a negative, that is, in the absence of a specific term for it in Sanumá language. From this vantage point it would seem that it has no conceptual recognition by the Sanumá, and therefore no significance as a social unit. Were it not for teknonymy with its onomastic emphasis on relationships restricted to the nuclear family, perhaps that impression would persist.

The question then is, Why is the nuclear family shown in this roundabout way? By way of an answer I turn briefly to certain attitudes and expectations of parents-in-law and sons-in-law regarding matrilocal, or uxorilocal, residence, already handled in previous chapters. From the point of view of the parents-in-law, the man who marries their daughter will never leave their home; if he does, the separation will most likely be sealed with a duel between the mother-in-law and the son-in-law, who suspend their strict avoidance so as to physically confront each other. As a result, he will go away alone, leaving wife and children behind. If we hear the sons-in-law, however, they will tell a different story: they state very emphatically that, as soon as they serve their bride service term, they will take wife and children away from the in-laws' house, for they will not live forever under their control.

What seems to happen most of the time is that a son-in-law typically has no opportunity or even motivation to move away after years as a resident in his wife's village. The farthest he usually goes with wife and children is to a hearth of his own. When he marries a woman of his own village, his decision is easy, and happy is the coincidence between his interests and those of his in-laws.

But, as we have seen, it is not always possible to find a spouse in the neighborhood. In these cases, which are not few (they can be as high as 70 percent), a man has to go against everybody's preferences and leave his village to get married. If he finds a wife in a distant village, his contacts with his own community will be limited to sporadic visits. He will go through a period of accommodation to his new village, changing from being a stranger to a regular resident. It is a long process usually riddled with tension. Slowly, as he begets children, he will be recognized as a participant member of his wife's community. In this phase, teknonymy contributes to his integration and to his permanence in his in-laws' village. By linking him to the name of a son, an in-born member of the community, teknonymy is a simple and efficient procedure in declaring this outsider a fellow member of a nuclear family and by extension of the community as a whole. Here, by the way, the role of offspring is not so very different from that in countries that grant legal status to nonimmigrant aliens.

On the other hand, the bride service duties, so convenient for the woman's parents, are a constant cause of discontent for the husband. If a man wants to shake himself free of the shackles of bride service, he will have to marry a woman with no parents to claim their rights over him. We have seen how child betrothal can exhaust a man's energy and patience before his immature wife is ready for the consummation of the marriage. Not infrequently the man gives up the girl and goes looking for a mature woman, preferably orphaned or divorced with no parents for him to work for. He then founds a nuclear family of his own.

As a phase of the developmental cycle of the family, the Sanumá nuclear family is materialized when a man, his wife, and his children are the only residents in a house compartment. In social terms, however, its existence is not fully acknowledged, and it is submerged by interests that arise from the interaction between kin and affines; in fact, it is even denied by parents-in-law who benefit from the continual permanence of sons-in-law under their roof or a roof nearby. On the other hand, the son-in-law's quest for domestic independence tends to highlight the social being of the nuclear family as a desirable possibility.

In this dialectical tug-of-war, teknonymy appears as the mediating factor which grants recognition to the nuclear family, if not in the daily life of the domestic group, at least in terms of conceptual definition as a possible alternative. By means of teknonymous combinations, the nuclear family is picked out of the wider tangle of relationships where its members are caught, and will have its moment of recognition.

Teknonymy appropriates a man's name for its referent, but maintains a very clear distinction—orientation and procreation do not mix. It is either the primary kin of one's parents and own generation who are thus pulled together, or the spouse and children, but not both. For example,

Manomashi pibɨna	"Mother of Manomashi"
Manomashi poosa	"Younger brother of Manomashi"
Manomashi pezea	"Sister of Manomashi"

Although Manomashi was married and had children, his wife and offspring were not linked up to his name in teknonymy. In turn, we have cases such as

Suli pizɨba	"Wife of Suli"
Suli petea	"Daughter of Suli"
Suli piluba	"Son of Suli"

Although Suli had father, mother, and siblings still alive after he be-

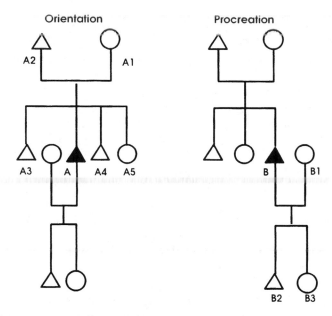

Fig. 6.1. Teknonymy in the family

came a husband and a father, his name was "lent" only to his family of procreation. Even though he had a younger brother living in his village by marriage, this brother was not known as *Suli poosa*.

Manomashi, a member of the *kadimani dɨbɨ* lineage and a resident of the Kadimani village, married one of the refugee women who were adopted by his people (see Chapter 2). In this case, the in-married spouse was the wife. Manomashi, being at home, was immersed in the daily life of his own close kin for whom he was the selected referent. With Suli it is the reverse situation. He lived in his wife's village, far away from his own. Already a mature man in the early 1970s, with children from a previous marriage, he decided to find younger wives, two sisters, and submit to yet another period of bride service for them. The use of teknonymy in his case underscored his position as husband and father in a village away from most of his kinsmen. Figure 6.1 represents these two alternatives.

As it stresses the place of the nuclear family within a larger kinship cluster, teknonymy also unveils another dimension of Sanumá social organization, namely, the rise of new agnatic groups that may come to grow into lineages. It is precisely within the nuclear family that these agnatic groups are conceived, and it is where they begin to be noticed in their earliest embryonic form. The connection between teknonymy and lineages is what we will see next.

Teknonymy and a Lineage Foretold

In Chapters 2 and 3 we accompanied the developmental cycle of the lineages, just as we had done for the family in Chapter 1. The cycle may lead either to the blossoming of a group of agnates into a robust lineage that lasts for several generations, or to its dwindling frustratingly out of existence just as it begins to emerge. In order to demonstrate how teknonymy contributes to the growth of agnatic groups into lineages, I need to recapitulate the general features of this process.

Lineages are subdivisions of the sibs. Membership to lineages is not universal. Where they occur they have a prominent role in the political life of the village, providing it with a headman and a good portion of its population. Unlike sibs, lineages are extremely vulnerable to setbacks, and their lifespan tends to be much shorter than that of the sibs. Indeed, the most outstanding feature of Sanumá lineages is their fragility. Incidents such as the death of a leader or the dispersal of agnates in marriage may destroy the chances of a future for an agnatic group. Former clusters of agnatically related men may be reduced to so many husbands doing bride service to in-laws in widely scattered villages. These men are incapable of perpetuating the lineage membership they inherited from their father. Their lineage patronym will linger, but they have no way of actualizing their membership while living away from each other. In due time, their descendants will have only sib membership.

In this sense, lineages are like edifices that may crumble even before they are totally erected. At each vicissitude, they run the risk of collapsing. The vagaries of temporality cause agnatic groups to tumble down to microscopic social particles even as they try to consolidate as full-fledged lineages. In the clash between the force toward permanence and the force against it, agnaticity survives as it can, making do with a truncated course.

When, however, a man succeeds in congregating brothers, sons, and sons' sons as his co-residents for the crucial amount of time it takes to create a coherent agnatic unit, he will be elevated to the condition of founder of this new unit, and will be publicly recognized as such by becoming its eponym.

In brooding over the phenómenon of Sanumá teknonymy, I realized that it is a tool for conceptualizing not only the nuclear family, but the lineage as well. Nearly 80 percent of the proper names used in teknonymy are male names. Despite the curtain of privacy that conceals personal names, those of certain men are picked out to become public. This occurs when their names are transformed into patronyms

Table 6.1. Extended teknonymy

Individual	Name	Kinship term
A	*Ishinabima*	mother, father, older brother, sister
B	*Sopai*	mother, older brother, younger brother, sister
C	*Aīge*	mother, father, younger brother
D	*Manomashi*	mother, younger brother, sister
E	*Ōkobidili*	mother, father, sister
F	*Palalo*	mother, father, younger brother
G	*Suli*	wife, daughter, son

as these men rise to the position of lineage eponyms, or when their names are consistently used as referents for the teknonymous names of their primary relatives. It is no coincidence that there are many more male than female name referents in Sanumá extended teknonymy. More kinship categories are attached to men's names than to those of women. Of a total of fifty-five referents, seven represent extended teknonymy. Table 6.1 gives details of these seven cases.

Of these seven cases, only D and G have children. B, still a teenager in 1974, was married to a little girl. A, B, D, and F are members of uterine groups of siblings as the result of the polygynous marriages of their respective fathers. Their mothers are the focal points of differentiation within their polygynous families. Figure 6.2 illustrates this type of situation.

As we have seen in Chapters 2 and 3, uterine sibling differentiation is one of the most common cleavage points leading to lineage segmentation, and is made concrete with the separation of one or more of these groups. In such cases, one of the brothers, usually the oldest, is selected as the reference point for the new segment that gradually drifts away from the rest. Of the seven cases in Table 6.1, D is the closest to the splitting point. The owner of the name is the oldest of a Kadimani sibling group that showed both verbal and behavioral signs of an imminent separation from their half siblings.

In the case of C, the referent was a boy about ten years old in 1974, the oldest of the three surviving sons out of several who died in infancy. He belongs to a small agnatic group of the *ōka dibi* sib, with no lineage affiliation. His father and paternal uncle occupied separate compartments of a house at the Mosonawa village. The boy's entire nuclear family was named after him.

G is Suli, the mature man mentioned above who was doing bride service for two young girls at the Mamugula village. He alone out of the seven cases of extended teknonymy had his name attached to his

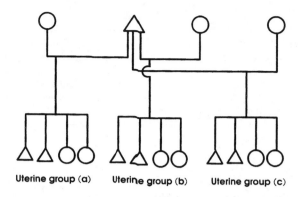

Fig. 6.2. Uterine siblings

family of procreation. In his case emphasis was given to his status as father, projecting him to his descending generation, that is, those who transform his status as father into the status of an accepted and permanent resident in the community to which he migrated.

We can read in the traces of extended teknonymy an indication of the Sanumá disposition to recognize the potentiality of certain agnatic groups to develop into something bigger and more lasting. This recognition comes mainly from the invention of a patronym that is then applied to a set of relatives that eventually outgrows the nuclear and extended family. The patronym is an anticipation that perhaps there is a lineage in the making. The collective use of a private personal name is the hint, or the trace, that the path is open to the emergence of a new lineage. In the early seventies, people referred to all of Sopai's (B in Table 6.1) immediate relatives as *sopai dibi*, "the Sopai people," thus using the same formula that is applied to full-fledged lineages, such as, for instance, *kadimani dibi*, "the Kadimani people."

It might seem rather hasty to take small children as heralds of hypothetical future lineages. But here teknonymy expresses the aspiration that in a given community at least some families may grow into mature agnatic groups with an eponymous leader. To take children as referents is to register not a de facto situation, but a *will to grow* in an auspicious future. As these children grow up, most of them recover the secrecy of their names either by having them drop from public usage, or by replacing them with new, private names. In this way, a small number of child teknonyms survive their referents' passage into adulthood. Those that persist will come in handy in situations such as the fissioning of uterine groups. Manomashi, for instance, kept his name from childhood which later in life served as a marker for his uterine siblings. In other words, what begins as wishful thinking may come true under the right conjunction of circumstances.

The owners of the personal names thus selected are, so to speak, advertised as potential leaders even before they are old enough to demonstrate any inclination or qualities for leadership, for a lineage needs a leader to push it forward. The way teknonymy foretells the possible advent of a lineage, in light of the numerous odds against it, makes one think that the materialization of specific lineages is not necessary to establish the fact or rather the expectation that lineages are bound to emerge sooner or later. It is, if you will, the premonition of a lineage not yet born.

If this is a reasonable interpretation, it means that the Sanumá themselves underline the process of lineage formation, conferring on it enough importance to sacrifice the secrecy of certain men's names for the sake of conceptualizing it. Whether the men in question come to meet the community's expectations by realizing their leadership potential is an empirical and contingent question that does not alter the message conveyed through the medium of extended teknonymy. In fact, boys whose names become referents in teknonymy and who are thus selected as eponyms-to-be rarely fulfill the collective promise of founding a new lineage, and quite often reach adulthood under a new personal name, this time protected by secrecy. What matters is that they provide the collectivity with an occasion to express a concept and a future possibility. All that is needed then is to put into practice the potential indicated by teknonymy. Since this is not achieved automatically, the use of extended teknonymy seems to operate as a reminder that a new lineage may not come now, but will, sooner or later. In this sense teknonymy represents the memory of the future.[2]

Moreover, teknonymy brings out the existence of the nuclear family precisely because it is the seed of agnatic groups and, by extension, of lineages. In cases where the name of reference belongs to the head of a family and the kinship terms are those of his family of procreation, the correlation between nuclear family and potential lineage is especially revealing. Where extended teknonymy uses a man's family of orientation, the nuclear family is equally highlighted, but from another angle. It is particularly strategic in cases of uterine brothers who share the same father. When an already established lineage shoots off collateral branches, the first step for the emergence of a dissident agnatic group, and a potential new lineage, is to have its members defined with a common diacritic. Extended teknonymy provides for this definition. By zooming in on a key individual, it features the whole sibling group that aspires for autonomy.

Situations such as the above come about as the result of polygyny. In marrying more than one wife, a man produces a potential cleavage point in the next generation. A subtle differentiation between his children is cultivated on the basis of their different mothers. This subtlety becomes blatant when political, economic, or other factors lead the sets of half brothers to split apart and gain a new social identity. Chapter 2 contains several such cases.

It often happens that the first-acknowledged forebear of a new lineage resulting from this fissioning is not its founder, but his father. In this way, all the uterine siblings of the founder are included as members of the newly created lineage, thus increasing its chances of surviving as a discrete unit. In this complex mechanism of subdivisions within subdivisions, teknonymy seems to be a sort of catalyst that fulfills the promise of new agnatic groups, by anticipating the moment of fission that is dimly sensed on the political horizon.

Teknonymy: The Password to Acceptance

On the individual level, teknonymy has other tasks to perform. First, it provides an additional and less restrained name for people whose proper names are zealously guarded, or for those who, for reasons unknown to me, apparently have no other name. It is, of course, very difficult to check whether a name simply does not exist or whether it is unusually protected from public knowledge. All I can say is that in these cases (69 percent) there were constant claims on the part of my interlocutors that the people in question simply had no name other than the teknonym. Many a time names thus hidden ended up transpiring. Among the Sanumá as elsewhere, such slips through the veil of secrecy are much more revealing than what is successfully suppressed. "Repressions that have failed," Freud wrote, "will of course have more claim on our interest than those that may have been successful; for the latter will for the most part escape our examination" (quoted in Derrida 1978: 197).

Second, teknonymy contributes to the settling down of people who live away from their close relatives in villages usually distant from their own. The most common cases occur with refugees who are forced to abandon their original villages and live elsewhere, and with people who leave their villages in search of a spouse. In both situations, people who are thus isolated from their own communities and immediate kinsmen often have their personal names used as referents in teknonyms for a husband, a wife, or a child, that is, someone who bridges the gap between the outsiders and the host community. I recorded eleven such cases—five men and six women—of immigrants who were thus integrated into their new homes. Most of them have their names combined with terms such as "husband," "wife," "son," and "daughter."

But teknonymy helps integrate newcomers in the reverse way, that is, by means of someone else's proper name. A close relative is then the referent for their teknonym. We have, for instance, *Koli a pibina*, "Mother of Koli," the name of a young orphan who was brought by an already married man (Lucio of Chapter 3) from her distant village to live as her junior wife among strangers at Auaris. Extremely shy and insecure, she began to show some signs of feeling less solitary when people started calling her little son by his personal name, Koli, and her by the teknonym based on it, *Koli a pibina*. She became a virtual extension of her child and, hence, a little more at home than before.

If we take all these different ways in which teknonymy is used, from the incorporation of outsiders, to the conceptualization of the nuclear family and the announcement of lineages yet to appear, we realize how remarkable an instrument it turns out to be in Sanumá hands. With such reduced material they effectively express a number of ideas at one and the same time. It is as if they use teknonymy as an ultrasensitive communication channel that is sufficiently potent to convey a variety of messages simultaneously. Economic and elegant, teknonymy allows the Sanumá to emit concepts without making them explicit: they say while not saying when they use secrecy to disclose meaning. In so doing, the Sanumá open up a vast field of conceptualization where they can play with a number of permutations and combinations, giving us the opportunity to interpret these as comments they make about their own social order.

Teknonymy, the Trace of Things Social

In violating the silence of certain proper names, teknonymy deprives people of their most private asset. These individuals surrender their recondite names for the benefit of their collectivity of kinsmen. In "tracing" the trajectory from individual names to group names, Sanumá proceed by means of a complex operation in which, first, they name a person; second, they prohibit the name from being publicly uttered; and third, they lift this prohibition. The name is thus liberated to be transformed into a patronym which takes on the features of a concept at the service of social ordering. The person is the trace of the collectivity. Instead of graphics, Sanumá language uses personal markers as collective notations: the *ōkobɨdili dɨbɨ* are a uterine group of brothers who carry the potential to grow into the *ōkobɨdili dɨbɨ* lineage. In this sense, the "trace" (*ōkobɨdili dɨbɨ*) is the mark of the absence of a presence (the *ōkobɨdili dɨbɨ* lineage). One should not utter the name *Ōkobɨdili*, for it is the ontological marker of a specific individual. But it is imperative to utter it, if one is to mark the potentiality of an *ōkobɨdili dɨbɨ* lineage. The passage from the individual to the collective field is thus achieved by denying a man what is most personal about him — his proper name. Among the Sanumá as elsewhere, society demands that public figures relinquish their privacy. A lineage eponym is a truly public man.

The passage from individual to collective names is also a passage from individual to collective memory. Social memory retains proper names when they are transformed into public names either of groups that formed in the past, or of those yet to come into existence; otherwise individual names, well-known or not, tend to meet their normal fate, which is to say, they fall into disuse and, eventually, into oblivion.

7
For Name-Sakes

If writing is no longer understood in the narrow sense of linear and
phonetic notation, it should be possible to say that all societies capable
of producing, that is to say of obliterating, their proper names, and of
bringing classificatory difference into play, practice writing in general.

—Derrida

The phenomenon of namesakes is probably far more widespread than
has been indicated through ethnographies. In a society of more than
130 million people such as Brazil, the constant confusion over identical proper names, despite the endless possibilities of permutations
and combinations, still creates bureaucratic misunderstandings, existential discomforts, or identity crises. Similarly, a small-scale society
as the Sanumá, with a much smaller number, if not proportion, of
onomastic alternatives, does not escape homonymy. Namesakes are
frequent, among both men and women. This chapter deals with the
ways the Sanumá avoid the problem of name redundancy so as to
identify specific individuals, what devices are used to sort out namesakes when necessary, why names are repeated in different people,
what is the place proper names have in a person's life, and what name
secrecy and its breach represent for the individual and for collectivities. First, some more about this name secrecy.

An integral part of the importance of proper names is the fact that
they are protected by privacy. Contradictory as it may sound, this
secrecy conveys much more information than if names were publicly
exposed. It is precisely because names are normally secluded in the
private sphere that, when they are deliberately and systematically unveiled, they are filled with social and symbolic meaning that brings
forth certain aspects of Sanumá thinking that might not be revealed
otherwise. Among other things, proper names are good, not exactly
to call people, but to conceptualize groups.

To pronounce Sanumá personal names in front of a stranger is
considered to be in extremely bad taste, offensive both to the owner
of the name and to his or her close relatives. Etiquette prescribes that

one should not pronounce the other's name in vain. This does not mean that the Sanumá do not know everyone's name or names. In fact, their knowledge in this field goes well beyond their immediate folk; they often know or speculate about the name(s) of distant villagers whom they have never met. Indeed, there is always a sort of gossipy curiosity about other people's names.

To avoid a breach of etiquette while preserving interpersonal communication, there are various ways to refer to or address somebody that reduce the exposure of the name while serving to summon the person's attention. Among these appellations are certain calls, such as *a'a,* the equivalent of the English *hi* or *hey,* kinship terms such as *nagai,* "daughter," *pɨzai,* "son," as well as circumlocutions that look like teknonyms but are not, as they are improvised, perhaps never to be repeated. How do I know they are pseudo-teknonyms? Because, for one thing, they are never used in address as real teknonyms are.

The Sanumá use two types of names for human beings: personal names and patronyms. Both are necessary to resolve ambiguities that result from homonymy. Patronyms are collective names of sibs and lineages applied to their respective members. Most people have both, but a few individuals seem to have only a patronym that, in their case, becomes or plays the role of a personal name. For instance, a little boy of the *sadali dɨbɨ* sib who lived in the community of Mosonawa was always called Sadali, and I never heard any other name attributed to him, either in reference or address. If he had another name it was so secret that it might as well not have existed.

The fact that patronyms are collective names does not exempt them from secrecy. One has to spend a while among the Sanumá before these names are revealed, and a while longer before they are pronounced with relative ease.

Unlike other Yanomami (Barker 1953; Chagnon 1968; Biocca 1971; Albert 1985), the Sanumá place no special taboo on the names of the dead. They are treated with the same reserve that is prescribed for the living, which makes genealogy collecting much less hazardous for the Sanumá ethnographer. Whenever I pronounced the name of someone's close relative, her or his reaction was either indifference, amused surprise, or embarrassment, but never indignation or anger, as Chagnon and Albert indicate. Sometimes, when unexpectedly I made clear that I knew a certain name, this fact would trigger whispers and giggles in my interlocutors, especially in groups of teenage girls. I was never confronted with any kind of violent reaction whenever I let them know that I knew people's names, but I was always careful to keep quiet about it in contexts that might generate uneasiness.

Perhaps the most embarrassing situation for a person is when he or she is forced to say his or her own name. The deep discomfort that this provokes was hinted at on two different occasions. When Ken Taylor and I were engaged in conversations with two or three Sanumá, the names of certain animals happened to be mentioned. Each time, there was a man whose name was either identical or very similar to the name of the animal in question. Each man asked a third person to tell us what the animal name was, even though we knew their names and could grasp the meaning of their reluctance and the juggling they had to do to get around the trap we unwittingly had set for them. They did it, not with resentment, but with funny looks and amused grins.

In general, the Sanumá do not explicitly admit that there is name secrecy. Just once was there an explanation given to us for it. Jorge, a Colony villager, said that if a person's name is known by an enemy, the latter may utter it with bad intentions and kill the victim by damaging his or her brain. This interpretation is rather similar to that reported by the linguist Ernesto Miggliazza (1964) for the Yanam of the Urarícaá River: when a person knows someone else's name he may give it to a shaman who can use it to do sorcery against the owner of the name.

Despite the efforts to keep proper names secret, everybody knows everybody else's names in a radius of several miles, covering a good many villages both friendly and unfriendly. Given this fact, one can presume that to hide names from enemies is not an easy task. But I never heard of anyone who had died of this cause. It is as if people vaguely believe in this possibility, but either do not take it very seriously, or take it as one more hazard of this world, such as the possibility of coming across a snake or a jaguar; the danger is there, but one does not agonize over it. Furthermore, given the role that personal names play in the conceptualization of social groups, it would be rather impractical to disclose these public names for one purpose and conceal them for others. In fact, secrecy is often denied, although this denial is constantly contradicted by the obvious zeal with which names are guarded from public usage. It becomes a complicated game of hide-and-seek, where the hideout is alternately concealed and disclosed according to personal and social convenience and priorities. They insist on saying that when people's names are not revealed it is because they really do not exist. On a certain occasion I asked, "What is her name?" referring to my interlocutor's sister. Her answer was simply, "She has no name," *hilo maigite*. I tried to face the problem squarely and questioned her point-blank why she was *gili*, afraid/embarrassed to pronounce her sister's name. She candidly replied that no, she was not *gili* at all, it was just that her sister really and truly had no name; if she did have one, she would have told me with no problem. This interchange happened after a long and intense interaction with this woman who was one of my best sources of information at the Kadimani village, always cooperative, friendly, and patient. But that was it, I never got to know that name . . . if there is such a name.

Name secrecy may have a magic or religious basis, but in everyday life it operates as a code of etiquette that conveys respect and deference toward other human beings, that is to say, Sanumá. It is interesting to observe, for instance, the treatment they give to whites they get to know well, such as missionaries and anthropologists: they call our names out loud at any time in any situation. My name, *Shida*, was repeated for minutes on end, especially by the children, until finally I turned my attention to them. But my other name, a teknonym—*Keni a piziba*, "Wife of Ken"—was preferred by older people who uttered it without any trace of affectation.

A sign of respect and good manners, name secrecy, when infringed, can betray moods and antagonisms. It is common, for example, to hear children shout each other's names when they get angry. In a quiet Auaris afternoon, during those dead hours when everybody is either in the gardens, or hunting, or fishing, and only a few children are left behind, two little girls were killing time in our house looking at photographs. For some reason that escaped me, they ended up quarreling with each other. Their irritation was relieved by each girl's endlessly repeating the other's name, right there under our eyes and ears. It was as if our presence was the trigger that turned an act that might have been quite innocuous, had we not been there, into an offense. The tone of their voices was similar to what one might expect from someone calling out "You bitch!"

At another time, two other girls, also preadolescent, were chasing each other around the village at Mosonawa obviously angry with each other. As they bolted past our house, they repeatedly shouted the personal name of each other's father. If I did not know their fathers' names, I would have thought they were mutually hurling "four-letter words." They offended each other with the old recourse to "calling names," in their case, literally. They could not see me inside, but it was obvious that they intended their tongue-lashing to be heard by the attendant foreigners. What would have happened if a local adult had heard them I do not know.

At Play in the Fields of Onomastics

In his incursion into the realm of Ethnology, Derrida castigates Lévi-Strauss for his insensitivity toward the predicament of name secrecy. He refers to the episode described in *Tristes Tropiques* where two young Nambiquara girls, quarreling with each other, got even by whispering the other's name in the anthropologist's ear, after which Lévi-Strauss proceeded to tap the girls for names of adults to which he had no access. When the people realized it, they reprimanded the girls, and Lévi-Strauss's source of information "dried up." Derrida points out that "it is the anthropological eruption which breaks the secret of the proper names and the innocent complicity governing the play of young girls." He goes on to say that

> the mere presence of the foreigner, the mere fact of his having his eyes open, cannot not provoke a violation; the *aside,* the secret murmured in the ear, the successive movements of the "stratagem," the acceleration, the precipitation, a certain increasing jubilation in the movement before the falling back which follows the consummated fault, when the "sources" have "dried up," makes us think of a dance and a fête as much as of war. (1976: 113)

True, but Derrida fails to see that, first, the "foreigner" need not be an anthropologist in order to serve the girls' purposes. A missionary, for instance, would have done as well. Second, the "foreigner" (anthropologist or otherwise), even at his most immanent, was also playing an instrumental role in the girls' agonistic dispute which would have been much less meaningful, or even senseless, without his presence. What they needed was a *forbidden* ear that would render relevant the breach of name secrecy. Moreover, to miss a chance of getting precious information, and hidden to boot, amounts to gaining negative points as a shrewd researcher in the anthropological trade. In this respect I find myself in Lévi-Strauss's shoes, for I too learned a great deal of personal names from Sanumá children. In field situations such as these, ethnographer and Indians were even: the Nambiquara girls (read Sanumá girls) were using Lévi-Strauss (read Alcida Ramos) as much as he (she) was using them.

What one does with that sort of information is another matter, for behind an apparently innocent game between squabbling little girls there is a not so innocent argument that hinges on the issue of differential power between a white ethnographer and her or his indigenous hosts. The anthropologist can use the privileged information she or he gets in the field either to parody exotic customs, which means playing power games at the expense of those who have no way of refuting her or him, or to contribute to an effort toward cross-cultural education and enlightenment.

The potency of proper names, especially when they are secret, is not lost on those who have as their mission in life to remake people in their own image. An example from Auaris will demonstrate what I mean. In early 1974, the local mission was run by a North American woman who played the role of nurse, dispensing medicines every morning and every evening. In contrast to the Brazilian nurse who had performed the same job four years earlier, beckoning her patients by banging on her frying pan with a stick, the North American woman saw no inconvenience in loudly calling the names of those she was treating, regardless of their age. She expected them to cross the space (about a hundred meters) from their houses to the "clinic" and wait patiently and quietly as she, assembly-line style, dispensed aspirins, cough mixture, antibiotics, merthiolate, or whatever. One day, as I heard her yell *Pokola!* (the pseudonym of a grandfather) clear across the village, I commented to neighbors who gathered at my hearth on how uncouth I found her calling habits. They agreed and added that it is in very bad taste to call adults' names, and worse still, in such a loud voice. Only children's names can be called freely, but that stops when they grow up. The white woman should not do that, but they were *gili*, afraid/embarrassed, to complain. I finally talked to her and explained what name secrecy meant to the people. She argued that since everybody knew everybody else's names, there was no point in observing such a silly habit. After much reluctance and having confirmed with Jorge, the missionaries' favorite language assistant, that what she had been doing was wrong, she agreed, under protest, to change her calling technique.

Clearly, name secrecy, and especially its violation, served the purpose of reinforcing her power in the village. *She* held the medicines, and the trade goods, and the means of communication to the world of whites through the mission radio. Why should she submit to a quaint custom of the natives, if she could show them that she had enough clout to ignore values and etiquette and, in so doing, demonstrate her superior habits. Surely, the Brazilian's frying pan banging made less of a social racket than the American's onomastic tactlessness.

In this episode I became aware of another facet of name secrecy which had already surfaced in other contexts whenever I surprised people by disclosing my knowledge of certain proper names. My zealous concern with the way adults' names were being publicly desecrated by the missionary drew amused smiles and remarks of the type: "Listen to her, she knows about these things!" More Catholic than the pope, I emphatically protested against the verbal abuse of an insensitive white foreigner. As they laughed at my indignation, it occurred to me that there is a certain dose of play in their name secrecy. Not only is it an instrument for childhood games of one-upmanship, but it can also be the subject of gossip, witticisms, and mocking with friendly whites.

Perhaps more inclined to play the mocking game than the Nambiquara, the Sanumá greeted my onomastic indiscretions with a welcome-to-the-club sort of bemused surprise. Why did they giggle when proper names were pronounced by foreigners like me, while the Yanomami threatened to kill Chagnon when he voiced personal names, especially of people already dead, and the Yanomam had to make a special effort to forgive Albert, guilty of the same offense? What is it that transforms rage into play within the same language family with a common cultural matrix?

In Chapter 2 a brief comparison was made between the Sanumá and the Yanomami/Yanomam regarding the taboo on the names of the dead. I maintained that the Yanomami/Yanomam can afford to effectively silence the names of deceased people because they had no descent units or founders whose names represent the temporal link that ties generations of agnates into common membership. If the Sanumá kept the names of their dead as suppressed as the other Yanomami, they would also be obliged to do without lineages. The legacy of the great Sanumá leaders to posterity is precisely an established collectivity that carries their personal names in the guise of patronyms. As to the names of the living, we saw in Chapter 6 how fundamental personal names are to mark out lineages that already exist or to announce those yet to come. When used in teknonymy, people's names take on the role of beacons that emit signals which forecast the appearance of possible lineages. How could this be done under a total prohibition on names both of the living and of the dead? How could the Sanumá cope with their cultural choice to demarcate agnatic collectivities via personal names, and at the same time be enraged whenever those names were pronounced? The way out of such a quandary is emblematic of the Sanumá ethos—with humor, mockery, and play. Since it would verge on the ludicrous to fly into a rage every time a lineage name was mentioned, on might as well play it cool and turn anger into humor. The uneasy giggles, smiles, and witty remarks at the sound of a personal name out of an outsider's mouth betray the discomfort that the Sanumá try rather hard to conceal.

One of the arguments used by the North American missionary at Auaris to justify her calling habits was that the Sanumá knew she knew their names. This is an important point for the understanding of name secrecy. What is objectionable is not the knowledge as such, but the use that can be made of it. Of course, in communities so small and socially so tight, it is virtually impossible not to know the names of all the people in a given region. What matters, however, is to realize that the employment of such knowledge must be limited to very narrow contexts. In a friendly gathering when everybody knows intimately everybody else, it is common to refer to people who are absent by their proper names, so long as no close relative of theirs is present. Hence, personal names are not used for address, except for children and in the case of teknonyms. And even children's names, when used in address, can have a perverse side that verges on prohibition, as with the girls who were uttering each other's and their fathers' names as forms of aggression. This being so, what are personal names for?

Between Private and Public

Besides serving as diacritics to agnatic groups, personal names identify communities and, of course, establish individual identities, even in their silent form. There is, however, a high degree of name repetition, which means that the identification of certain people requires a combinatory operation that is a little more complex than simply a unitary proper name. In Chapter 6 we saw how proper names play the role of signals for agnatic groups. In the next chapter we will see how people acquire their proper names. Here I deal with patronyms and personal names as means of individuation. But first, let us see the way in which personal names are extended to communities.

Communities are identified by the name of their leader's lineage, so that all the members of a village, whether or not they belong to that lineage, can be identified by their community's name. For example, all residents of the Kadimani community are called *kadimani dɨbɨ*, regardless of their sib or lineage membership. This produces a certain ambiguity, for both the members of the *kadimani dɨbɨ* lineage and everybody else, such as their affines, the *koima dɨbɨ*, are grouped under the same collective name, as it is applied to them by outsiders.

It is the lineage that lends its name to the community and not the other way around. Again, the Kadimani village is a good example. Before it spread out through several villages, the *kadimani dɨbɨ* lineage was located a few miles southeast of its 1970 site. At that earlier time, the community was already known as Kadimani, although the composition of its non-*kadimani dɨbɨ* members was different from what it became later. When two or three of its segments separated, the community of its main branch moved to another site but was still called Kadimani.

Given that lineage and community have the same name, one might think that one way to sort out namesakes would be the community where each one lives, but the actual cases show that this is not so. At the community of Mamugula, for instance, the leader of the local *kadimani dɨbɨ* segment was called Paso. In another village, another man had the same name; like the former, he also belonged to the *higadili dɨbɨ* sib. When people wanted to refer to the former, they would say *kadimani a Paso* rather than *Mamugula a Paso*, that is, they referred to lineage rather than to community.

Naturally, this complex interplay of personal names, patronyms, and toponyms was not revealed to me right away. At the beginning of fieldwork, aware of the taboo on proper names among the Yanomami, I naively started asking about village names, thinking that I was stepping on safe ground. The reaction was mostly silence, hesitation, evasion, disconcerted looks, and very few straight answers. Why all that mystery around what seemed to me almost a banality, a mere place name? Only later when I began to understand the role of personal names in the dynamics of descent groups did I realize why even the names of communities are protected by silence. Behind the apparent impersonality of a place name there is the name of a person who lived or lives in it. As the passage of these personal names from the private to the public sphere is not effected without qualms, it will take a total stranger the necessary time to gain a minimum of familiarity before he or she begins to hear these names pronounced with relative ease.

The ambiguity that surrounds the identification of residents by the name of the community derives from the constant interplay between the two principles that are omnipresent in Sanumá social organization—descent and residence. When they coincide, as in the cases of the members of the *lalawa dɨbɨ* lineage who resided in the Lalawa community, there is no ambiguity, because the entire lineage was concentrated in that village. In the case of the *kadimani dɨbɨ*, however, spread out as they are through various villages, one needs to specify which branch is being talked about. The same is true with the other non-*kadimani dɨbɨ* residents. In order to know which *koima dɨbɨ* is being referred to, one has to specify whether they are the Kadimani *koima dɨbɨ*, or the Lalawa *koima dɨbɨ*, for instance. About a person from the *koima dɨbɨ* sib, one can say that he is a *kadimani de koima*, "a *koima* from Kadimani," thus eliminating two possibilities: the person is neither a member of the *kadimani dɨbɨ* lineage, nor a resident of the Lalawa community.

The ambiguity in the combination of village names with descent unit names can also be resolved in the cases where there are top-onyms. A few villages have socially neutral names that come from some geographic feature, such as the Kɨsɨnabiu stream after which the Lalawa village site was named, Kɨsɨnabi-dulia. When, however, that community moved away to the Kakudu stream, it was the name Lalawa that persisted. During the Kɨsɨnabi-dulia phase, the Lalawa residents were also known as the *kɨsɨnabɨdili dɨbɨ*. There are other cases of collective toponyms, but as far as I know, this is not a universal feature among the Sanumá.

All of this makes clear that people's identification is not automatic with the mere utterance of their proper names. The same name can be bestowed, or more appropriately, inflicted on several people of different communities, sibs, and sexes. Sib patronyms seem to have an etymology that differs from that of lineage patronyms, as described in Chapter 2. Teknonyms are never transformed into patronyms—there is no lineage or sib called "The Fathers of So-and-so"—nor, obviously, are female names. Out of the nine lineage names for which I obtained a semantic explanation, five were given to founders as adults, and four in their childhood. In case the founder has more than one proper name, only one of these will be used to identify the new lineage.

Unlike personal names that are not exclusive to single individuals, neither sib nor lineage patronyms are ever concurrently repeated, as is the case, for instance, with the Shavante (Maybury-Lewis 1967). There are no two social units—sib, lineage, or community—with the same name. Descent and residence collectivities are thus "individualized" by means of a unique name, whereas individuals are lost in onomastic ambiguities. As collective entities, sibs, lineages, and communities congregate a plurality of individuals and operate as their classifiers precisely because collective names do not recur. Regarded inwardly, collective names are uniformly cast over a considerable number of people, but seen from the outside, they set each social entity apart from the others. In other words, when seen from within, patronyms act as if in the plural; when seen from the outside, they act as if in the singular. When sibs or lineages are mutually contrasted, they maintain their specificity; there is no ambiguity or confusion between them. This individuality of collectivities is a key element in the identification of homonymous people, as we will see.

Who's Who

Proper names, then, are not good indexical devices for people. The identification of specific persons can be done in a number of ways. For instance, when a person has more than one name, he or she may be referred to by one or another of these alternative names. This is an efficient way to pinpoint a person, as the chances of having two individuals with exactly the same set of names is rather remote (different from the Timbira, for example, among whom name transmission is done in blocks from generation to generation; see Melatti 1976). One can also appeal to more or less improvised teknonymous arrangements, by using the name and kinship term of someone's primary relative as an impromptu reference device. This makeshift teknonym cannot be regarded as a real proper name. It is also common to hear circumlocutions that identify certain people by means of some unusual feat (a duel), a recent event (an exceptional hunt), some physical ("the one with the light brown eyes") or personality ("the one who speaks fast") trait, or life history ("the one who used to live up on that mountain"). But, as most of these alternatives depend on chance factors, they are not trustworthy criteria for establishing a more systematic form of identification. Indeed, the Sanumá avail themselves of a more regular mechanism to achieve personal individuation, namely, the combination of a proper name with a patronym to compose a binomial with a minimum of redundancy.

Depending on where the person to be identified stands within the network of sibs and lineages, this binomial will be made up of personal name plus sib or lineage patronym. In the case of two homonyms belonging to different sibs, it is enough to mention the sib patronym to differentiate them, as, for instance, two men named Sogo, one of the *nimtali dɨbɨ*, the other of the *koima dɨbɨ* sib. One of them belongs to a lineage (*sogosɨ dɨbɨ*), but this is surplus information that is not needed to distinguish him from his namesake. All that needs to be said is *nimtali a Sogo* or *koima a Sogo* for the men to be identified. The most informative combination in this case is personal name–cum–sib patronym.

It is possible for two members of the same sib to have the same personal name. In this case, their sorting out will occur on a less inclusive level than that of the sib. The empirical cases I know of such a situation indicate that at least one of the persons belongs to a lineage. There is, for example, the case of two men named Manomashi, both of the *higadili dɨbɨ* sib. Obviously, the sib patronym here carries no information besides excluding from consideration all the other sibs. In order to specify the individuals in question, one has to bring into the picture another link in the chain, which is the lineage patronym. In this particular example, one man belongs to the *kadimani dɨbɨ* lineage, whereas the other has no lineage affiliation. It is then sufficient to say *kadimani a Manomashi* to separate the two and immediately identify the lineage member, as there is no other Manomashi among the *kadimani dɨbɨ*. The *lineage patronym + personal name* solution takes care of one man; the other is only residually identified. In order to focus on him, the alternative is to appeal to some other type of reference, such as the description of a kin relationship (*Wisa piluba*, "son of Wisa"). Chances are that no other Manomashi whose father was called Wisa will be found in Sanumá territory. By the way, this appeal to filiation is not strange to many whites. In Brazil, for instance, official identification forms require that one spell out one's father's and mother's personal names as a way to multiply the number of combinations and thus decrease the chances of confusion among homonyms. Such requirements, annoying as they may seem to us as yet another manifestation of bureaucratic fervor, have after all their raison d'être in the same principle that orients the Sanumá in their apparently informal simplicity.

Names Up and Down

As we have seen in previous chapters, one way in which new lineages may come into existence is by the segmentation of already established lineages, when a group of uterine siblings, or a dissenter, splits away from the core to start a new branch. In due course, these new segments take on an identity of their own and become known by their founder's proper name.

The twofold function of proper names is highlighted in this constant process of lineage subdivision; at one and the same time, they classify groups and persons, while articulating the social and the individual spheres.

Let us begin with personal names. Out of the possible number of names the male founder may have, only one comes to be associated with the recently formed lineage. From then on, as a lineage appella-

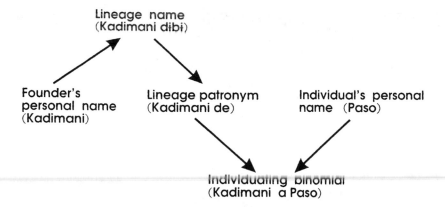

Fig. 7.1. Individual identification

tion, this name will become a collective name covering all lineage members in the form of a patronym. The naming system is thus equipped to provide labels for social groups by elevating personal names to the collective level. In turn, these labels, the patronyms, are called upon to act again at the individual level as a means of differentiating namesakes. Patronyms are then combined with their common personal name to form a binomial that in most cases is capable of setting homonyms apart. The feedback effect that results from this individualizing operation is visualized in Figure 7.1. The names in parentheses are just examples.

It should be noted that unlike the sibs, lineage patronyms do not seem to return to the pool of strictly personal names. While there are people who appropriate their sib patronym as a personal name (see Chapter 8), I have never seen the equivalent for lineage patronyms. Indeed, were this to happen, the possibility would be open for the multiple repetition of lineage names. Under those circumstances, it might then be possible for a man with such a name to become the founder and/or eponym of a new lineage; as a result, the same name would designate different lineages. Such redundancy would defeat the classificatory purpose of proper names, and I have found no empirical basis for this hypothetical situation. Recalling Chapters 2 and 3, it should be pointed out that sibs are more durable and stable than lineages, and that sib membership is universal, whereas lineage membership is not.

The point of having exclusive names for each lineage and sib is brought home when we see how these group names are used as a sort of shorthand to define collectivities in terms of their position in the

network of marriage exchanges, in food taboos, or in their association
with communities, for example. The mere utterance of a single name
is enough to immediately elicit a large amount of information. As we
saw in Chapter 2, a quick and impressionistic characterization of who
marries whom can be done only because lineage and sib names are
not repeated. The Sanumá woman who drew a marriage matrix for
me could then say in the most condensed way possible: the *kadimani
dɨbɨ* marry the *koima dɨbɨ*, but not the *labadili dɨbɨ*.

Private Names in a Public World

Some final thoughts about what I perceive to be the difference between the public and the private domains in the Sanumá symbolic
world. In the twenty-seven months I lived among them I was convinced that their private sphere is practically nonexistent in terms of
both activities and behavior expectations. If we exclude sexual intercourse, which is private only up to a point (a young couple can spend
a whole night in passionate lovemaking while the others sleep, listen,
or feel the reverberations of their vibrating hammock), and childbirth
for some women (with regard to strangers and men, except for an occasional shaman), there is virtually nothing else that cannot be done
in company. Not even the act of defecating at night is immune from
turning into a joint activity; it is very common for groups of men or of
women to leave their homes to "go to the bush" for that purpose. I
was invited several times by neighboring women to accompany them
on these physiological excursions, no doubt in part for the advantage
that my flashlight would bring to all of them.

Fights between husband and wife, for instance, attract everybody
who happens to be in the village; to a greater or lesser extent, they all
participate in the arguments and interfere directly in everything that
is said and done. This is in stark contrast to our Brazilian aphorism
that one should not get between husband and wife (a rhyming prov-
erb in Portuguese that uses the image of a spoon, *colher*, to allude to
the couple's domestic context: "em briga de marido e mulher
ninguém mete a colher"). Similarly, quarrels involving brothers,
mothers and sons, fathers and sons, mothers-in-law and sons-in-law,
deceived husbands and adulterous lovers, hosts and guests, affines,
or distant kin, are all resolved outdoors, under the cunning eyes and
accompanied by the excited speeches of men and women who are
there, above all, to preserve order, strange as it may seem to those
who have witnessed such scenes, by keeping tempers under control
and thus preventing a generalized melee.

Bodily hygiene, another sacrosanct corner of our privacy, again tends to be a social occasion for the Sanumá. People prefer to bathe with others of the same sex, with the exception of husband or wife. But, if proper decorum is kept, which is easily accomplished with appropriate postures and gestures, bathing on the river's edge or at the spring is not seen as a private act. Otherwise, cooking, shamanizing, eating, or sleeping are performed in everyone's sight, regardless of the degree of intimacy, with no discomfort at all.

If, on the one hand, there are few activities and behaviors that can be defined as pertaining to the private sphere, there is, on the other hand, a great concern to guard a person's intimacy precisely with regard to his or her proper name, in a most exemplary Maussian fashion. It is in the association of a person with his or her name (or names) that decorum is most emphatically expressed and that we come the closest to what we recognize as privacy. As we have seen, personal names are publicly exhibited by children who can turn them into insults. Moreover, it is in extremely bad taste to say an adult's name in a loud voice in his or her presence, or in that of close kin. The embarrassment that this produces can be compared to what one of us may feel when, unexpectedly, someone flings open the bathroom door and meets our nakedness.

This Sanumá nexus between name secrecy and privacy becomes all the more eloquent when we remember that the breach of the taboo on personal names is embedded in the supernatural, as name disclosure is associated with the danger of the name's being perversely used by a hostile shaman. It establishes the metaphysical character of the relationship between the human being, that is, Sanumá, and his or her personal name. Just as among us it is bad manners to intrude in other people's private life, so among the Sanumá it is extremely crude to invade someone else's personal space by showing disrespect for his or her proper name, at the risk of jeopardizing his or her welfare, if we bear with Jorge in his interpretation of the harmful effects that a violated name can have.

It is possible that the phenomenon the Sanumá call *nonoshi* (see Chapter 5) is another manifestation of privacy. This is the mystical bond that every human being has with a certain animal. The great difficulty I had in collecting data on this subject, due to the uneasiness it caused people, makes me think that this is also a very reserved area, the exclusive concern of those directly involved, that should not be discussed in public or with strangers.

In view of all this, a final comment on the private side of the Sanumá is called for. As distinct from what we decree as private, usually with reference to the individual—our bodies, our money, our neuroses—the Sanumá private domain seems to occupy a more symbolic, even conceptual, space. Their interest in preserving intimacy is not displayed in concrete activities and their consequences. Their hesitation in disclosing people's names and in identifying or commenting on *nonoshi* shows that their sense of propriety follows different paths from ours. Rather than unveiling individualities, their proper names seem to stress privacy as a region of their culture that receives no special attention in the daily affairs of social life. Like the exception that proves the rule, the breach of name secrecy says more about individuality and personal decorum than an explicit lesson in etiquette.

8
To Hunt a Name

For a long time anthropologists have been interested in demonstrating that personal names contribute to the knowledge of how a given cultural logic works. Mauss ([1929] 1979), Needham (1954, 1965), Geertz and Geertz (1964), Goodenough (1965), Guemple (1965), Lévi-Strauss (1962), Lave (1967), and Collier and Bricker (1970), just to mention a few, were concerned with various aspects of naming in several ethnographic contexts, and from different theoretical viewpoints.

In Chapters 6 and 7 I dealt with some features of the Sanumá naming system by focusing on teknonymy and the identification of homonyms. Here I will bring out yet other facets of Sanumá society through naming practices: the procedures involved in receiving a name, the semantic field of proper names, the actions and beliefs set in motion by naming, and what is disclosed between the lines of social life by this act of naming a person.

For the sake of presentation, I will divide the names according to the semantic fields from which they stem, with special attention to the ritual hunt that is carried out in order to name a newborn baby. It is especially through the latter procedure, apparently unique to the Sanumá amongst the Yanomami (Lizot 1973), that certain attitudes and expectations between kin and affines come to the fore, disclosing the otherwise veiled interplay of tension and interdependence that gives their relationships an agonistic flavor. Unlike the ritual hunt, the other ways of naming people, which are the most common, involve no special observances.

Secrecy is common to all personal names, and my data naturally reflects this. With some people I never got to know any other names besides patronyms or teknonyms. At the beginning, name secrecy was a real obstacle, but it was gradually overcome as people became accustomed to my presence. Even so, not everyone got to the point of mentioning or discussing the subject matter openly and easily. Although it was secrecy itself that aroused my ethnographic curiosity, I was always careful to observe the Sanumá rule of etiquette against pronouncing people's names in their presence. When I revealed my knowledge of some names it was always in suitable situations, such as a lively gathering of young women and children, punctuated by jokes and bursts of laughter in typically Sanumá displays of humor.

Names can be acquired at any time in life, and a person may have as many as three or even four. Multiple names, however, are not readily admitted. For some reason that escapes me, there is a strong tendency to deny that there are people with several names. Collecting data on multiple names was thus limited to what I could gather on those occasions when by chance I heard additional names referred to in conversations. Here, as in other contexts, children played the already proverbial role of precious sources of information.

The most important naming procedure is the ritual hunt that takes place after the birth of a child. It is a hunt in a literal as well as a metaphorical sense. The baby's father chases an animal and, at the same time, searches for a name. If, for a number of reasons that I will describe below, the hunt is not carried out, other names (excluding patronyms and teknonyms) may be activated, based on physical or behavioral traits, on circumstances or events at the time of the person's birth or later in life.

My information on names comes from the eight villages I studied, with special emphasis on the communities of Mosonawa and Kadimani. Over the course of nine months of collecting genealogies, I recorded about 800 to 1,000 names. As my interviews with women in particular became more and more routine, names were uttered with hardly any resistance, in part because I avoided querying my interlocutors about their own names and those of their close relatives. For the discussions that appear in this and in the previous two chapters, I concentrated on 340 names. For each name of each resident of the eight villages, including the recently deceased, I asked questions about the naming procedure, the reason for the choice of the name, the relationship between name giver and name receiver, and when, where, and in what circumstances the name was given.

When questioned, the Sanumá distinguish personal names from patronyms by saying that the former are "real names," *hilo sai* (*hilo*, "name," *sai*, "real"), and the latter, "additional names, also names," *hilo setea, hilo nãyo*. Of all the "real" names, the most complex and conventional, but less frequent, are those acquired by means of a ritual hunt. Let us turn to it now.

Hunting a Name and Making a Spirit

Childbirth can take place indoors when it happens during the night, in a garden or in the forest during the day. When it occurs outdoors, within an hour the woman returns home with the baby and sits down by her hearth. She will do no work for the next ten or fifteen days, remaining seated on the ground all day long. The verb *lo*, "to sit," in this context can be rendered as *couvade*. It also applies to women during their menstrual periods, as they sit on the ground until the bleeding stops. At night, they sleep in the hammock. During this first *couvade* phase after delivery, both mother and father are subjected to strict food taboos designed to protect the child and the mother from supernatural harm. At this stage, they are particularly vulnerable to the attack of the spirit of the prohibited game animal, if eaten in transgression of the taboo. The father must limit his activities to fishing and light work in the garden. Nevertheless, even at the risk of breaking the *couvade* taboo, he is expected to go out hunting for an animal that may be used as the child's eponym.

The overt reason for this hunt is to find a name for the baby, but, in so doing, one also gives the child a certain spirit that comes from the hunted animal. It enters the baby's body through the coccyx and stays there for life. The expression for this operation is *humabi thabalima*, "made the coccyx."[1] Translating it as "the making of the coccyx" would be closer to the original than "the making of the name," for the Sanumá phrase makes no explicit reference to name. One of the most baffling experiences in my field research was this *humabi* phenomenon. My first exposure to it was when I asked how someone was named and the answer was "——— *humabi thabalima*." I was at a loss to figure out what the relation was between it and naming, for while the immediate reply to my question about a personal name was the ritual hunt, the verbal expression of it had, in my mind, nothing to do with naming. After much bewilderment, I finally made some sense of it, once I was given an explanation that involved the existence of an animal spirit reminiscent of Durkheim's individual totemism (as is also the *nonoshi* spirit animal of Chapter 5).

While the mother is still pregnant, the baby's coccyx spirit is not in the foetus, but in the forest, in the body of an animal. People should be quiet when they walk in the forest (*Lalubalu die!* "Don't make a noise!'') so as not to disturb the baby's coccyx spirit. The coccyx is seen as one of the most vulnerable parts of the baby's body, and the coccyx spirit seems to have the quality of strengthening it. When the child is born, the father, and only he, goes out on a ritual hunt in search of an animal the spirit of which will be passed on to the child. With luck, he finds the appropriate animal, kills it, ties it up in a leaf bundle, and takes it home, all the while avoiding having direct contact with it as much as he can. Neither father nor mother should touch it, let alone eat it. Since their child's coccyx spirit is in the animal's body, to eat its meat would amount to eating their baby's own spirit. This absolute prohibition to eat the *humabi* animal is added to all the other taboos the parents must observe (Taylor 1974), and is extended to all the animals of the same species until the child begins to eat meat. The child itself does not observe any taboo regarding its eponym, unless the animal is in a forbidden category for its age group.

We should keep in mind that the father is prohibited from going hunting after the birth lest he cause back pains in the baby. It is thus at the risk of inflicting this penalty on the child that he breaks the hunting prohibition in order to meet another ritual obligation, which is the naming of his child. In this conflict of symbolic needs, a positive ritual (the *humabi* hunt) contradicts a negative ritual (the *couvade* taboo). Perhaps this is the reason why to "hunt" a name is saturated with supernatural dangers.

In the *humabi* hunt we find a theme that runs through other contexts where the Sanumá seem to create prohibitions in order to break them. Mother-in-law avoidance is broken when mother-in-law and son-in-law duel each other at the breakup of a marriage (Chapter 4); name secrecy is suspended when a person is chosen as the referent in teknonymy (Chapter 6); and hunting prohibition is halted when a father has to attend to the obligation of naming his child.

Not all children acquire a coccyx name and spirit. According to a woman who spent many hours instructing me on the subject, if one child in the family has it, there is no need for others in the same family to have it too. Another woman told me that only a couple's first child is given the *humabi* treatment. Neither statement is statistically confirmed. I found several children in the same family for whom the ritual hunt had been carried out. What those women said is nevertheless very important, for implied in their statements is a cultural double bind: the naming procedure incurs high supernatural risks, and yet it cannot be avoided. Hence, it is carried out as seldom as possible. One child per family, be it the firstborn or not, represents the idealized maximum for meeting the ritual obligation while reducing the exposure of the parents and other children to considerable metaphysical anxieties.

Possessing a coccyx spirit does not make the child visibly different from the others, and there are no apparent advantages in having it. However, said one of the women, it helps scare away the *meini dibi* evil spirits that wander about in the forest and are particularly harmful to children. A child with a *humabi* spirit is, therefore, better protected from *meini dibi* attacks than other children who do not have it.

The *humabi* naming procedure involves a series of choices that must be made at each step of the ritual hunt, even before the child is born. A set of necessary conditions must preexist the birth so that a *humabi* hunt can take place. If any of the following conditions are not met, the hunt will not happen: (a) the father is absent; (b) the father is dead; (c) the father is unable to hunt (for physical, psychological, or social reasons); (d) the father is ill; (e) the mother is ill; (f) the mother has no husband; (g) the child is illegitimate; (h) a close relative has died shortly before the birth; or (i) the community is under enemy attack.

It is only when personal and social conditions are considered to be normal that a ritual hunt is carried out. Once the child is delivered, there is a new factor to be considered—the health of the baby. If it is ill, there will be no hunt. Extreme ugliness or a physical defect is also a reason to have no *humabi* hunt, and I take this as an extension of the health factor. Given that ideal conditions of physical, psychological, and social normality are not always present, and all it takes is one flaw in the chain to prevent the ritual hunt from occurring, failure is quite frequent. In fact, the chances that it will be carried out at all are very reduced indeed. We can see how pertinent the women's rationale was for declaring that one hunt per family is enough to satisfy this ritual requirement.

When conditions are said to be normal, then the ritual hunt is performed and the child receives both *humabi* name and spirit. Only edible animals, *salo bi*, are used for the purpose. After dogs, game are the most important animals for the Sanumá. Nonedible fauna is either ignored or chased away. Among the game animals, only a few are selected for *humabi* hunts. The most common are the armadillo (*obo*), three species of monkeys (*wisa*, *ilo*, and *paso*), a kind of partridge (*pokola*), and three other birds (*paluli*, *manashi*, and *kulemi*).

It is said that some ten species of *salo bi* are not suitable for the *humabi* hunt; among these are two species of otter (*plolo* and *hadami*), a sloth (*saulemi*), coatimundi (*salushi*), one type of macaw (*kalakasa*), a kind of pigeon (*holedo*), and the largest rodent, capibara (*kazu*). In most cases the reasons why these animals are discharged as eponyms are the same given for food taboos. For example, the coatimundi (*sa-lushi*) cannot be hunted for a name and spirit because it may infest the child with worms. For this same reason, young people cannot eat its meat (Taylor 1974).

There is no pomp, ceremony, or visual/performative apparatus surrounding this ritual. It can easily go unnoticed if we are not alert to the possibility that it may happen. The father's movements are so sur-reptitious as to escape us. Add to his exaggerated discretion people's reluctance to talk about the subject, and we have a situation that is extremely difficult to ethnograph. Only once did I detect a woman at a female gathering in the act of pronouncing the name of a newborn baby by uttering the name of the animal that had been killed by its father. When I wanted to know more, they changed the subject.

The outcome of a ritual hunt is still more unpredictable than that of a normal hunt. The father may or may not find the animal, and if he finds it, he may or may not kill it. Besides chance factors, no other explanation was given to me for its failure; they simply say that there was no game, which is not very frequent. Of the hundred cases of *humabɨ* hunt on my record, only eleven resulted in the father's not killing any animal at all. When this happens, the child remains with-out a personal name, or receives an alternative name out of a number of other possibilities.

Once the *humabɨ* animal is killed, the spirit of its coccyx enters the child's body. The name may be abandoned, but this spirit stays with the person for the rest of his or her life. To kill a *humabɨ* animal does not, however, guarantee the automatic naming of the child. Even when all conditions are normal, there is still the screening of the name of the animal killed. It has to be appropriate as a personal name for that specific child, for the dead animal may have a name that is not compatible with the child's social unit. Certain descent groups ex-clude various animal names from their repertory of personal names. For instance, the names of the *honama* and *manashi* birds as well as of the *obo* armadillo are never used for members of the *kadimani dɨbɨ* lin-eage, whereas other lineages and sibs use them with no problem. These exclusions are attributed to the bad sound of the name, to pre-vious experiences when children thus named got sick and died, or simply to the fact that the group in question has not developed the habit of using such a name for its members. We would have here the opposite of what one finds, for instance, among the Iroquois (Lévi-Strauss 1962:236), and the Bororo (Cruz 1941: 203–11), where descent groups have exclusive property over personal names. In the Sanumá case, instead of property it is the prohibition that is exclusive, for there are no two agnatic groups with the same roll of prohibited names. In turn, the most common names are shared by several, or perhaps all, descent groups and categories.

If all goes well, the child at last receives the name of the dead animal. When asked why the ritual *humabi* hunt is carried out, even at the cost of breaking the *couvade* taboo, the Sanumá say, "because a name is needed," "*hilo pi ku zalo.*"[2] When asked about the reason for a specific *humabi* name, the standard answer is, for example, *paso ha humabi thabalima,* "the coccyx was made because of the spider monkey."[3]

Very rarely, however, all goes well. Of the hundred cases I collected of this naming procedure, in only forty-one did the child receive the name of the dead animal, whereas all hundred acquired the coccyx spirit. It is remarkable that after all the effort and danger involved in a man's going out on this ritual hunt in supernaturally adverse conditions, the child may end up without a *humabi* name. The baby may actually get the name, but it is highly probable that sooner or later this name will be abandoned.

Whenever an omen foretells that any harm may come to the child, when a close relative dies after the child is named, or when the name is belatedly judged to be a "bad name" (usually after the fact by an older and experienced person), it is immediately dropped. Of those forty-one cases of children who got their *humabi* names, twelve (29 percent) were relinquished, or superseded by other kinds of names. A *humabi* name can be replaced at any moment, from right after naming to some time in adult life. The reasons I heard for this were much the same as those that prevent a ritual hunt from being performed, and those that bar the naming even when the hunt is successful.

Eating the Meat and Naming the Child

The symbolic and social implications of the naming procedure based on the ritual hunt are not limited to the onomastic realm. Like other facets of the Sanumá naming system (the implicit messages of teknonymy in Chapter 6, for instance), hunting ritually for a name, in its technical and metaphorical double sense, has sociological echoes that go well beyond the mere practice of naming a baby. Embedded in the *humabi* phenomenon is a furtive commentary on the relationship between kin and affines, between generations, and between maternal and paternal relatives. In the act of disposing of the meat of the

Table 8.1. Who's who in the *humabi* name

	Kin	Affine	Total
Who eats the meat	8	22	30
Who gives the name	27	6	33
Total	35	28	63

hunted animal, and in transferring its name to the child, a conceptual stage is set for the sorting out of roles and actors in a kinship play the script of which is not quite the same as that followed in everyday life. Let us first consider the matter of who eats the meat and who names the child.

As soon as the father returns from the forest, the animal he has killed is given to a relative of his or his wife's. In most cases it goes to someone he calls *soli*, "brother-in-law" (38 percent), or, more rarely, *hebala*, "older brother" (10 percent). Less frequently, other relatives can also get the meat, such as the father's mother, and a variety of relatives amongst kin and affines. What matters is that the meat be given to someone who does not belong to the child's household. Occasionally, if one of the child's grandparents lives in the same compartment, he or she may eat the *humabi* animal.

Whoever eats the meat tests its quality. Symbolically the life of the child is represented in the state of the meat: if it is good, the child will live; if it is tasteless or too soft (a sign of bad quality), the child will die. In most cases, this judgment is in the hands—or, more literally, in the mouth—of one of the affines of both father and child. When the meat eater passes judgment on the meat, he is, in fact, pronouncing the fate of the child. One of my instructors on this subject recalled the case of a child who died many years ago after a negative verdict was given on the state of the meat of its *humabi* animal. Since bad meat means doomed child, no *humabi* name is given in those circumstances.

Whoever judges the meat rarely names the child. Eating the meat and giving the name are separate concerns and should be done by different people. One is again reminded of the Ge of Central Brazil, for whom being substance givers (parents) is incompatible with being name givers (Melatti 1976; Da Matta 1976). The name giver should be a female relative of the mother's, a child's kinswoman. By being assigned separate tasks, affines (the meat eaters) and kin (the name givers) are symbolically placed in opposite camps. Table 8.1 shows the division in numbers: the meat eaters are mostly affines, the name givers are almost always kinsmen of the child.

Table 8.2. Who's who in a non-*humabi* name

	Kin	Affine	Total
Who eats the meat	21	13	34
Who gives the name	94	36	130
Total	115	49	164

It is interesting to contrast the information in Table 8.1, which re-fers to a situation where the child acquired the name of the *humabi* animal, with that in Table 8.2 above, where the animal name was not given to the child. The data in Table 8.2 refer to situations where the father went on a ritual hunt and killed the animal and the *humabi* spirit entered the child, but the name was not given. In these cases, the father was virtually sure that his child would not get the name. He knew, for instance, that the name of the animal he had just killed was not appropriate for his agnatic group. Although the same care is taken by the parents not to touch or eat the meat, now they are no longer worried that the baby will be exposed to the supernatural dan-ger that goes with naming it after the *humabi* animal. Therefore, it matters little to make a sharp distinction between name givers and meat eaters. Here the figures do not show any significant difference between kin and affines with regard to who eats the meat. As to nam-ing, there is still a greater tendency for kinsmen to do it. One gets the impression that it is the actual bestowing of a personal name, rather than the eating of the meat, that triggers off this social play of kin and affines, a play which is made not of words but of acts, gestures, and silences.

What is the meaning of this difference between a *humabi* and a non-*humabi* name? As we saw in Chapter 7, a person's proper name is not neutral, a mere identification tag. It carries a good portion of the person's existential makeup. If used with evil intentions, a personal name can be instrumental in its owner's death. The mere uttering of an adult's name generates tension and ill feelings. How extreme, then, is vulnerability of a newborn baby who, having part of its exis-tence intimately attached to the spirit of a dead animal, is further sub-jected to having its name forever uttered whenever the species of that animal is mentioned?

One might reasonably ask why people run such risks. I have no answer to this question, and very likely the Sanumá have none either. My impression is that it is precisely because of its high risks and ten-sion that this naming technique suits itself so splendidly to portray another highly tense zone—the interaction between kin and affines.

The combination of *humabi* name and spirit would be, at the symbolic level, the equivalent of the strained kin-affine relations at the social level, no matter how veiled they may be in the daily routine of a community. There is a correspondence in the strain generated in each of the semantic fields, metaphysical and social. In their interplay, these fields project onto each other their most outstanding features, thus creating a dialectical pull between complementary opposites—animals and humans, kin and affines. The dependence on affines for the reproduction of one's own group is epitomized in their power to diagnose the fate of newborn children, particularly relevant if they are boys, in this patrilineal society. It is up to the affines to say whether the *humabi* meat is good or bad, which amounts to declaring whether or not one's group will have a chance to go on existing. In a symbolic act of cannibalism, they eat one's child's coccyx spirit. It is, as it were, a metaphoric swallowing of one's future. Affines, we saw in Chapter 4, are a necessary evil. The *humabi* naming procedure dramatizes this predicament in extremis.

Role Reversals

We can look at the *humabi* naming technique as a series of role reversals which, as Leach pointed out long ago (1961:135), mark off ritualized situations (also V. Turner 1969:166–203; Lévi-Strauss 1962:70–72). These reversals can be seen in the following way:

1. The realm of human beings is usually set apart from that of animals. People don't sleep on the ground, don't eat leaves as a matter of course, don't eat raw meat, and don't practice incest as animals do. But in the *humabi* context humans are brought into intimate contact with the animal world by the transference of name and spirit from an animal to a human. This contact is all the more extraordinary since it is conveyed by a supernatural element that differs drastically from the form in which animal substance is normally incorporated by humans, which is cooked meat. It is an animal spirit that enters the human coccyx rather than animal food that enters the human mouth.

With this reversal the Sanumá seem to be indicating one of two things: either they perceive the difference between nature and culture to be so radical that it deserves an antithetical commentary, or they see it as being so unimportant as to permit direct transit between animals and humans both at the material level (the eating of game meat) and at the symbolic level (incorporation of an animal spirit).

2. The child's father is under *couvade* prohibition from going hunting while the mother is "sitting on the ground." But he suspends the

taboo and goes out to hunt a name for his child. His role is thus twice reversed. First, owing to the birth, he interrupts his normal activities in a reversal of his daily routine. Second, he suspends this suspension and briefly resumes his role as a hunter in a reversal of the reversal (which does not, however, carry him back to daily life).

3. The difference between a normal hunt and a *humabi* ritual hunt seems to be, above all, in the treatment that is given to the dead animal. In a *humabi* hunt, the hunter should not touch the animal if he can possibly avoid it. Birds such as the bush chicken (*hashimo*) that are normally plucked on the hunting spot are taken home wrapped up in leaf bundles so as to keep them away from the direct touch of the child's parents. Neither parent should eat the animal the spirit of which enters the child's coccyx, for to eat it would mean to eat the *humabi* spirit of their own child, causing it to die.

4. In a *humabi* ritual hunt the animal is not killed in order to feed people. Here it takes on special qualities that are tested by someone who is not a member of the child's household. What is normally consumed by the hunter's family is now prohibited to them. The game animal is transformed from food into a supernatural entity, from a source of physical fulfillment to an eerie presence.

This naming practice can also be interpreted as a multiple rite of passage. On the one hand, when it is said to apply only to the first child, it signals the change of status of a young couple from being childless to being parents. This transition is explicitly acknowledged by the Sanumá in their classification of the people by age (Taylor 1974). At the same time, the *humabi* hunt seems to establish official paternity, for it is done only by the publicly acknowledged husband of the child's mother. In so doing he declares himself the baby's legitimate father. For the Sanumá a child cannot be begotten by more than one man, as is common among South American Indians. Thus, when a man goes out on a ritual hunt, he is telling the world that he is both father and genitor of the child. In addition, the newborn child is incorporated into its group as a true human being by means of its ritualized communion with the animal world. The transference, dangerously supernatural, of the *humabi* spirit into the child may be considered as a necessary step for the humanization of the new being, for part of being human is to have ramifications in the spirit world. As we saw in Chapter 5, it is said that before conception, and even right after birth, the child belongs to the world of the "specters," *ni pole bi dibi*. Moreover, after its mother's breast, the baby's most important contact with nature is through the supernatural part—the coccyx spirit—of a product of nature, that is, edible game, which will be fun-

damental to the child's future life. The complex network of relationships between humans, animals, and spirits is displayed full-size in
this ritual that is very discreet in terms of visible actions, but lavish in
social and metaphysical consequences.

Not all children receive a coccyx spirit, let alone a *humabɨ* name.
But, as some say, if only one child per family is the object of this
ritual, then the humanizing process of newborn babies becomes an
exercise in representativeness: the child for whom the ritual is performed represents all its siblings who are thus vicariously humanized
as well. Furthermore, if, as others say, it is the firstborn who must
receive the *humabɨ* spirit-cum-name, this problem is disposed of at the
first opportunity. It is worth mentioning the Sanumá belief that the
firstborn has few chances of survival. As the mother is usually very
young, just out of her puberty seclusion, so to speak, her lack of experience in childcare leads to neglect and often to the death of her first
child, *haba haba de*. The same is said about a bitch's first litter. The high
probability that the firstborn will die would thus confirm the feeling
of danger and uneasiness that accompanies this stressful naming
practice.

Children with *humabɨ* names and spirits represent their siblings
in a very different key from that of the referent in teknonymy. To begin with, *humabɨ* names, as far as I can tell, are never selected for
teknonymy: their mystically laden character seems to be incompatible
with the public exposure that is characteristic of teknonymous referents. Moreover, whereas the teknonymous referent operates in the
public sphere, the *humabɨ* referent is thoroughly hidden in the private
domain. Whereas in teknonymy personal means (proper names) are
used to define the public, in the *humabɨ* phenomenon public means
(such as hunting) are employed to construct the persona.

Other Names

If the child does not receive a *humabɨ* name, it will be named according to one of several alternatives that may or may not include animal
names, but that are devoid of any special supernatural implications.
To better present the material, I have divided these alternative naming procedures into two main categories: names based on physical
features or idiosyncratic mannerisms, and names based on events or
circumstances that occurred at the time of birth or later in the person's
life.

Although these names might be seen as nicknames, I am reluctant to use this concept because of what it means to us. Nicknames

are appellations that coexist with Christian names. Unlike the latter that constitute a set of their own and are often unique, nicknames come from common language and are not considered to be "true" names. In turn, Sanumá proper names are all derived from words in ordinary language, or modified versions of them. There is then no way of distinguishing "true" names from "nicknames." All names are *hilo*, and as far as I know, there is no specific term for nickname, besides *hilo bio*, "just a name," an expression that is little used in the context of proper names.

Idiosyncrasies and Human Archives

Of a total of 337 personal names, 127 (38 percent) refer to some physical or personality trait of their bearers. We might even make a further distinction based on the condition or state of one's body, or on some similarity between the person's habits and those of some animal. The former are usually but not exclusively acquired in infancy. They refer to a permanent state, or to a temporary condition. For instance, of a total of 63 names that invoke body parts, 10 mean "Small," 7 "Short," 6 "Brown Eyes," 5 "Big Penis," and so on. A name may also be inspired by a fleeting condition; the condition passes, but the name stays, such as "Weak," "Feverish," or "Crybaby." I found 29 such names repeated in several people. Each one of these conditions can be expressed in more than one way. For instance, "Feverish" may be rendered as Sopai or Shobi.

Some physical or personality traits are indicated by analogy to certain animals, trees, or other beings. The animals most often recalled may or may not be edible. For example, a boy was named Kazu because of his big eyes, like those of the capibara (*kazu*) rodent; another boy was called Washi because he fiddled with things, putting people's possessions in disarray, as does the monkey of that name when it is kept as a pet. A little girl was called Kudataima because she was so small as to remind people of the little *kudataima* frog. I collected 24 names of this kind.

It is also common to name someone after an unusual event, his or her birthplace, or a residence site. There are 123 (36 percent) of these names in my sample. Some of them: Waiká, the name of a boy who was born during the visit of a Yanomam group known as Waiká; Õka, the name of a baby whose family ran away from night raiders, *õka dibi*; Kokoia, the name of a middle-aged woman who, as a child, was scared out her wits by a hawk, *kokoi*.

When they refer to places, personal names can be expressed either by geographic features, or by their local inhabitants. For instance, Labadili is the name of a man who lived for a long time in the village of the *labadili dibɨ*; Mosonawa was the name of a man who was born near a *mosonawi* tree; Polalizoma, the name of a woman who was born near a waterfall, *pola*.

The 47 cases known to me of names derived from occasional circumstances seem to show a concern to record an event, a moment, or a space that for some reason acquires a special meaning to the named person or to his or her family or community. These names operate as historic records by bringing out an occasion or event that occurred at the time of the person's birth or later in his or her life. For example, the man named Lalawa acquired his name because it evoked an occurrence in his youth. In a duel with another man, he suffered a cut in his back and the wound had the shape of an anaconda (*lala gɨgɨ*). His name recalls that event. It is possible that the correlation of these names with the age of their bearers makes up a chronologic sequence to which one appeals as to a book of dates. Through his own name and that of others, a person would then be part of a memory bank of collective interest where relevant events, places, and times are preserved. Like human files, people and their names play the role of living mnemonic devices. Given the fact that the names of the dead are not immediately forgotten by the living, they help preserve a collection of experiences for the groups to which they belong for a time span that, even though limited, is longer than the person's material life on earth. One needs, however, to know the history of each person's name, for a mere mention of it does not disclose its significance.

Of all the personal names described here, the *humabɨ* names are most often replaced. The others are more rarely abandoned, although they may be added to other names, such as, for example, teknonyms.

The Name Givers

Generally, but not exclusively, names are given by relatives. Unlike the Ge peoples of Central Brazil, the Sanumá do not have a specific category of people in charge of name giving. For the non-*humabɨ* names I was able to identify the name giver in 131 cases; of these, 94 (72 percent) are kin to the name owner, while 36 (28 percent) are affines, and just 1 is not a relative.

In terms of lineage and sib affiliation, the figures are as follows: for the sibs, of a total of 127 cases on record, the name givers are from the father's and, of course, the child's sib (35 percent), or from any other sib (65 percent). For the lineages, 18 percent are from the same lineage as the child and its father, and 82 percent from another lineage. Names tend thus to be given by members of lineages other than that of the name bearer. "Mothers," either real or classificatory, are the most frequent name givers (60 percent). For those who have no lineage affiliation, no significant difference seems to exist between the name receiver's own sib and any other.

The Search for a Being

For every child that is born, the Sanumá are confronted with the problem of naming. The ritual hunt, which seems to be their canonic form of naming, is transformed into a social and existential dilemma that is brought about by heavily laden metaphysical reasons. The *humabi* ritual emerges as a model of normality. In the first place, conditions must be perfectly normal and favorable for the hunt to occur and for the child to receive the name. Secondly, the kin-affine division, which on the plane of every day life is blurred by communal living and unorthodox marriages, is dramatized and reinforced in the act of eating the meat of the *humabi* animal, and of giving the animal's name to the child. Third, the marriage link that seals the complementarity between kin and affines is emphasized, as only legitimate children of a normal and healthy couple are given a ritual name. And finally, the tacit antagonism that underlies relationships between kin and affines comes to the fore at the moment of bringing the baby definitively to the social scene. Its fate, especially if it is a boy, is symbolically put in the hands of the father's affines as they associate the quality of the game meat with the child's survival; by implication, they are declaring the fate of the child's lineage itself. The *humabi* hunt epitomizes in the most literal sense the very origin of the Greek term *onomastics: on hou masma*, that is, "being for which there is a search" (Krell 1990: 42). The outcome of this search is a new human being, a true social being that is equal to its name.

Sanumá naming also reveals a social feature that is not normally put forth, albeit acted upon in daily life. In this society where paternal affiliation is mostly responsible for group identity, the naming system seems to open a way for nonagnates to contribute to the formation of a new social being. We have seen that maternal relatives are the most frequent name givers. But the link between name giver and name receiver does not in itself generate rights and duties or any identification device. The act of naming someone in and of itself does little more than reinforce or acknowledge a relationship that is already there, but is not formally expressed. Unlike the father-son relationship, which is marked by the transmission of a patronym and membership in sib and lineage, the mother-son bond, no matter how important it may be, does not receive any formal emphasis, for the woman does not transmit any social identity marks to her children. Her contribution in this domain is in her choice of her children's names, if and when she chooses them. The fact that she usually stays home after marriage, a privileged position when compared with her husband's, is not translated into a formally recognized identity. The closest a mother gets to conferring social identity on her children is in the case of the splitting up of uterine brothers, but then she is an implicit referent rather than a conspicuous emblem for her children's social and political personae.

Again we find the Sanumá using a naming code to decode other codes, as we saw in teknonymy. The *humabɨ* ritual hunt, explicitly enacted to generate a personal name, seems to do a lot more than that in the end, considering that very often the resulting name is not even used as a personal name. A whole series of aspects, so far implicit, come to the fore when we look closely at this naming procedure. From metaphysical considerations of nature and culture, to the low-profile animosity between kin and affines, to the role of nonagnates, the hunt for a name, or the search for a being, is yet another example of how the Sanumá transform actions into conceptual messages. If Austin points out that it is possible to do things with words, the Sanumá demonstrate that it is possible to say things with deeds.

In the last three decades Brazilian names have entered the circuit of Sanumá onomastics. Unlike their own traditional names, these new appellations are not secret at all. In fact, they are doubly convenient, a welcome addition to the existing naming repertoire, as they help Sanumá maintain their "real" names concealed while providing outsiders with an identification device in the context of Sanumá name secrecy. Hence it is no surprise that "white" names have become very popular both in Auaris and elsewhere. Most often Sanumá get their white names directly from whites, sometimes on request, but typically they merely comply with the name giver's initiative.

Just as some Indian names can serve as a record of past events, so also Brazilian names introduced into Sanumá life can tell an interesting story about their contact with foreigners. The choice of Western names can have a variety of inspirations, one of the most common being the white name giver's desire to pay homage to friends and relatives. One can, however, easily detect two layers of recurring foreign names that circulate in the communities. The first, older layer (one finds them in adults as well as in children) is made up of biblical names—Paulo, Davi, Enoque, Sara, Moisés, Lucas. They are the hall-mark of missionary influence.

Although most missionaries I have known in Auaris show little respect for the Sanumá cultural dictum of name privacy, and rarely miss a chance to display their contempt by uttering people's names aloud, in the end they favor the opportunities of bringing in the Gospel via personal names. Killing two birds with one stone, they pay lip service to the Sanumá quest for secrecy and at the same time they brand them with Christian names. It is as though the road to conversion becomes shorter with the creation of a meticulous onomastic palimpsest, the application of a new coat of names over the existing ones so as to render the previous layer strategically innocuous. One is reminded of Columbus who reacted to the shock of the psychologically and culturally ungrammatical natural forces and people of the New World[4] by indulging in a naming orgy. "Like Adam in the midst of Eden, Columbus is profoundly concerned with the choice of names for the virgin world before his eyes" (Todorov 1984:26–27).

The second, more recent layer is frequently detected among the younger generation and refers to place names, most often names of Brazilian states or their human derivations—Piauí, Ceará, Paulista. These place names are common currency among gold miners[5] who use them as nicknames in part to protect their real identity from legal scrutiny, given that gold mining in Indian lands is unlawful, and miners have been subjected to repeated police raids in Yanomami territory. Like the biblical names, these epithets are not self-attributed by the Sanumá, but imputed to them by invading miners.

To call people by place names such as Piauí or Ceará is derogatory in the way that Paulista is not. Paulista is the quality—an adjective—of being from the wealthy state of São Paulo, which is by no means a disgrace, whereas Piauí, Ceará, or Maranhão are blunt noun evocations of the fact that these are some of the most undeveloped states in the impoverished Brazilian Northeast corridor. Such names are especially unbecoming as they are applied with no modification and in a quasi-collective way to the myriad of backwoodsmen who compose the gold-mining universe. These sobriquets are, we might say, the mark of an underclass. Transmitted as they are to the Sanumá, such names betray the intent to transfer onto the Indians the stigma of inferiority, in typical pecking-order fashion.

To name something or someone is to "humanize" it, which means to assume or pretend that one is dealing with a tabula rasa, an empty slate, a no-man's-land. In any case, be it land, objects, or people, such an assumption or pretense means that appropriation is in keeping with this self-ascribed humanizing mission. One way to take possession of land, goods, and souls is to stamp them with one's own branding name. Baptism, conscription, and paternalism are just some manifestations of the dominating power of naming. "[Columbus] seeks to rename places in terms of the rank they occupy in his discovery, to give them the *right* names; moreover nomination is equivalent to taking possession" (Todorov 1984: 27).[6] In the case of both missionaries and miners, to distribute white names among the Sanumá as if they were operating in a naming void is also a political act of conquest.

As Austinian as one can get, personal names are telltale traces laid bare for anthropology and history to pursue. In an outlandish fantasy of the future, were all whites to disappear from Yanomami lands and, much later, were someone minimally informed about Brazilian naming practices to visit the Sanumá, supposing they kept their Portuguese names, this stranger would have no problem identifying the kind of whites who roamed around those lands. "Tell me your name and I'll tell you what white types have tampered with your culture." For, after all, Sanumá are not the only people in this world to leave behind a trail of information disguised as personal names.

The receiving end of such disparate onomastic catharses as are those of Christians and underdogs alike, the Sanumá accept these new names with their usual derisive jesting, mockingly experimenting with possible pronunciations, some merely clumsy, others positively burlesque. They play mirror, often amusingly distorted by the reflecting surface of their sardonic tongues, to both the divine and the damned.

Part 3
Others

9
A Rumor on Stage

To the memory of Lourenço, killed by gold miners in September 1990

Scenario

In 1974 I took a trip to Auaris to study interethnic relationships between the Sanumá and the Maiongong, their Carib-speaking neighbors. During my two-month stay, I was witness to the birth, growth,
and climax of an elaborate rumor. From its inception as a remark in
casual conversation, the fervor surrounding the rumor grew with
such drama and intensity that the atmosphere often verged on de-
lirium. A whole universe of unexpected doubts, hopes, and fears on
the part of members of both ethnic groups paraded before my eyes.
The symbolic wealth of this rumor is comparable to that of the most
complex of mythic narratives of heroic sagas.

The rumor revolved mainly around a Maiongong man, Lourenço,
the leader of the Colony who enjoyed an outstanding social and political position among the Auaris communities.

As an attempt to recapture the dramatic verve so lavishly cultivated by the Sanumá, I have organized the information collected by
Ana Gita de Oliveira, my field assistant at the time, and myself the
way I subliminally perceived it, that is, as a play carried out on an
open stage where the audience were also part of the cast.

What I would like to show here is how efficient this rumor was as
a medium to convey the predicament of the Sanumá-Maiongong intertribal situation. Repeated armed clashes, mutual accusations of
treachery, raids, village burning, and kidnapping of women around
the turn of the century have gone into the production of an atmosphere saturated with suspicion and tension. Yet such volatile interaction, I argue, is due not so much to their cultural differences, as to
their shared history. In order to render the rumor intelligible, I must
briefly describe the circumstances that preceded it.

The arrival in the Guiana Shield of the Yanomami in general, and
the Sanumá specifically, brought about a resettling of the few indigenous peoples who still inhabited the Orinoco and Amazon water-

shed. The depopulation of the Carib and Arawak groups under en-slavement by rubber gatherers and other intruders made it easier for the Yanomami to occupy territories that had been emptied by the decimation of those peoples (Migliazza 1972; Arvelo-Jiménez 1974; Ramos 1980; Guss 1986). The Maiongong (also known as Yekuana or Maquiritare) were virtually the only group left in that area.

These displacements were by no means peaceful. They cost both the invading Yanomami and the invaded Maiongong a great deal of lives. Nearly a century after the last raid in memory, the mistrust that underlies Sanumá-Maiongong interaction is all too evident. Confron-tations involving disputes about theft accusations have been frequent; on such occasions, the Maiongong invariably charge the Sanumá with stealing their garden produce. The unconcealed uneasiness between them has long produced an obvious discomfort on either side when they have to be near each other for a prolonged period of time. For instance, at medicine time, set by the missionaries for both groups, Sanumá and Maiongong tend to avoid each other at the mission dis-pensary so as to spare themselves the embarrassment of a lengthy joint gathering. In so doing, the Sanumá try to dodge the jokes, the mocking and teasing aimed at them by groups of Maiongong. One person alone does not bother another; in fact one can often see a Maiongong and a Sanumá engaged in long and peaceful conversa-tion. But when in company, their interactions are punctuated by sar-castic remarks and jokes in bad taste. This is most pronounced when the victims are unaccompanied women from either party.

Despite their animosity and avoidance habits, Maiongong and Sanumá sometimes participate in joint projects and ventures. One such venture gave rise to the incident at hand. In early 1973, about ten Maiongong and five Sanumá organized a canoe trip to the town of Boa Vista where they planned to work and earn enough money to buy some of the goods that have become part of the Maiongong's regular needs, such as salt, ammunition, and clothing. Expeditions of this sort have a high cost in terms of effort and time. Navigating rivers strewn with rapids and waterfalls means that serious accidents—capsized canoes with loss of equipment and food—are quite com-mon. Even so, the Maiongong regularly set out on such trips. As for the five Sanumá, this was their first canoe expedition to the world of the whites. The journey out, downriver all the way, takes about twenty-five to thirty days, whereas the return trip, with canoes loaded up to the brim, lasts twice as long, if not longer.

The Maiongong organized these trips every two years or so. They stayed for about ten to twelve months in Boa Vista and on surrounding ranches where they were employed as menial workers. Very few chose not to return to Auaris. The general opinion was that their white employers systematically exploited them, and, for that reason, the trips south were never as profitable as they could have been. Even their canoes, although highly regarded in the region in those days before the gold rush (see Chapter 11), never brought good prices. From the point of view of the Sanumá, going to Boa Vista was a new and exhilarating experience, and they did not complain of the whites as much as the Maiongong did. Perhaps because of this fascination, at least two Sanumá men had years earlier decided to remain away in the town, or ranch, rather than go back home. Of the two, one refused to return despite desperate pleas from his father; the other, Lucio's stepson, went to school and the army in Boa Vista, got married, and had three children. Over a decade later, he left his work and family behind and returned to the Yanomami area as a gold miner and advocate of white mining on Indian lands.

The rumor presented here occurred during the return trip they had initiated in 1973 (see Map 3 for its route). The dialogues are adaptations from my field diaries from February 26 to March 20, 1974. These adaptations were done in two ways. One was to change the style of narration into dialogue form. For example, where in the diary I wrote, "João told Ana that he was very sad . . . ," now it appears as *João*: "I'm very sad. . . ."

The other adaptation had to do with the switching from one language to another. The conversations we had with the Maiongong were all in Portuguese, and their reconstruction into dialogues created no substantial problems. It was more complicated in the case of the Sanumá. My communication with them was in their own language, which raised the question of how to style their speech into writing. Perhaps the dialogues as presented here are a bit too erudite for us, accustomed to a certain distance between the oral and written language.[1] In converting Sanumá utterances first into dialogue, second into writing, and third into English, I have put them through so many mediations that it is impossible and even useless to attempt a realistic and faithful rendering. In the end I opted for a colloquial, yet grammatically correct, style, lest the informality of our casual speech give the false impression of linguistic incompetence on the part of the Sanumá. I thus take the risk of making the Sanumá dialogues perhaps a bit too competent, too "correct," hoping it will jeopardize neither message nor flow.

The rumor moves around Lourenço, the leader of the intertribal community I have been calling the Colony, created out of his and his

Map 3. The route to Boa Vista

younger brother's marriages to two Sanumá women. Their children, children-in-law, grandchildren, and some aggregates made up the Colony population of thirty-four people in 1974. Out of this total, nine were Maiongong, and seven were Sanumá. The remainder were the offspring of these two couples, neither Maiongong nor Sanumá, but a bit of both (Ramos 1980).

The Maiongong living at the Colony were not well regarded by the residents of the Maiongong village, nor did they feel at ease living among the Sanumá. Their life at Auaris carried all the ambiguities that go with a sandwiched existence between two cultural ethoses. Lourenço became the emblem of these ambiguities as the undisputed leader of the Colony, the ambiguous community par excellence. He symbolized the rather uncomfortable accommodation either group had to make to the other's presence after their long experience of mu tual hatred and mistrust.

Lourenço was in his early fifties at the time of the 1974 rumor. He had seven children with his Sanumá wife, three of whom were already married. With his Maiongong wife, deceased about four years earlier, he had four children; still very young when their mother died, they were all claimed by their Maiongong relatives and were raised by them in the Maiongong communal house. Despite a perceptible accent, Lourenço spoke fluent Sanumá and enjoyed a great deal of prestige in the Sanumá half of Auaris. He could present himself either Sanumá style, vociferous and gesticulating at the arrival of visitors, or as a true Maiongong, solemn posture, arms crossed over chest, near inaudible speech, a voice at once suave and hard coming from the height of the Maiongong self-image of superiority.

What follows is a rendition as drama of the 1974 rumor, a format that favors the present tense.

The Return of the Travelers: Tragicomedy in Seven Acts

The Cast

João. A young Maiongong man married to a Maiongong woman, lives at the Maiongong communal house some three hundred yards away from the Sanumá houses.

Dino. Lourenço's eldest son, married to a Sanumá woman, lives at the Colony, speaks Sanumá, but does not identify himself as one of them.

Dino's wife. Young Sanumá woman, married to Dino since childhood, mother of two little boys.

Kalioko. The Sanumá leader of the Kalioko community, married to two Sanumá women. A former resident of Auaris where he was a neighbor of the Colony, he now lives at a distant site.

Jorge. Young Sanumá man, does bride service to Lourenço's younger brother, lives at the Colony, and strives to become a headman at Auaris.

Albertino. Middle-aged Maiongong man, one of the leaders at the Maiongong village.

Adão. Young Sanumá man, in his second marriage, does bride service to Lourenço, lives at the Colony.

Lília. Young Sanumá woman, Jorge's sister, Kalioko's ex-wife.

Cici. Lourenço's adolescent daughter with his Sanumá wife.

Candida. North American missionary.

Augusta. Lourenço's Sanumá wife.

Alcida. Anthropologist.

Otavio. Elderly Sanumá from Kadimani village, spends some time at Auaris.

Edu. Young Sanumá, just out of his puberty rite, free and unbridled. It is commented that his real father was not the Sanumá who had married his mother, but a Maiongong.

Zeca. Sanumá man, calls Augusta "mother" by classificatory kinship, but is married to one of her sisters.

Beto. Young Sanumá searching for a wife in Auaris.

Act One

It is mid–dry season. The Sanumá village sluggishly carries on its summer routine. Several people are away on trips to other villages, or camping in the forest. The huge Maiongong communal house is quieter than usual. Only three of their adult men are around; the rest are either away in Boa Vista or in Venezuela. The Colony is also half empty as many men are away. The missionary performs her daily dispensary duties. Ana is busy interviewing the Maiongong João while Alcida talks to the Sanumá. The days slip by in placid, sunny, sleepy languor.

SCENE 1: Inside the Maiongong communal house, João is talking to Ana. Suddenly he interrupts what he is saying.

João: I'm very sad. I heard people talk out there at Lourenço's house. The Sanumá were counting the number of men with shotguns. I think they want to kill Lourenço. Just as Candida has told me that the Yanomami at Mucajaí—they call them Kaslabaia—were getting ready to kill Lourenço because they saw a Maiongong stalking around their house.

SCENE 2: Augusta hears about João's revelations and spreads them all over the village. She bursts into tears.

SCENE 3: In one of the mission houses.

Candida: It's all in their imagination. In the end the Maiongong are no better than the Sanumá in imagining ghosts, spirits, and invisible enemies. I always tell the Sanumá to stop being distrustful of the Maiongong because they too want peace, not war.

A while later, Candida speaks on the radio to the Mucajaí mission asking for news.

Candida: Over there at Mucajaí no one saw any Maiongong around, just a group of Indians with some whites going up the Mucajaí River.

Scene 4: Kalioko arrives at Auaris after a five-hour canoe trip from his new village downstream. He comes to say hello to Alcida.

Kalioko: Shida, is it true that they killed Lourenço? I heard people out at Shimatayam [a village in Venezuela about two days' walk northeast of Auaris] saying that a white man, drunk with rum, had killed Lourenço. A Waiká who had accompanied him ran away and showed up there very, very thin. So the Shimatayam people said.

Scene 5: Jorge and Dino return to Auaris after having gone down-river with some Maiongong to meet Lourenço and the others on their way back home.

Jorge: We came back because we lost a canoe that capsized in a waterfall. I know nothing about Lourenço's death. I've been away for a month, haven't heard anything. But in Mucajaí, so far away?

Dino: That's right, the canoe overturned, we lost shotguns and hammocks, but no one died or got hurt.

In the background the voices of men and women coming from a neighboring house discuss the news from Shimatayam about the Kaslabaia; they talk about the Maiongong women who long ago were kidnapped by the Kaslabaia, and also about Lourenço and his entourage.

Act Two

Nine o'clock in the evening, at the anthropologists' hearth. Dino, his wife, Cici, and her little sister arrive.

Dino: I've heard the story about the Waiká who got back to Shimatayam looking very thin and saying that my father has been killed. Maybe it is true, maybe they killed my father.

Dino's wife: It was the Kaslabaia who killed him, they are always drunk with rum.

Dino: I'm very sad, I heard it all and I cried. Lourenço is very dear, very valuable.

Alcida: It can't be true, maybe the Waiká got tired of Lourenço and simply ran away and then made up this story.

Dino's wife: That's right, that's what must have happened.

Dino: Maybe the Waiká is lazy and Lourenço made him work.

Dino's wife: Maybe Lourenço said: "I'll beat you up."

Dino: He just said it casually, he didn't mean it. That's why the Waiká ran away and spread this gossip all over. But what if it's true? What if Lourenço never comes back?

Alcida: But why just Lourenço? There are several other Maiongong on the trip, why do they only talk about Lourenço?

Dino: I don't know.

Dino's wife: Long ago the Kaslabaia killed Maiongong and stole their women, and now the Kaslabaia think Lourenço wants to kill them in revenge.

Dino: What if it's true that Lourenço won't come back?

Alcida: If it were true, what would you do?

Dino: I would be furious because Lourenço is very dear, he is worth a lot, he is very special. The Maiongong would be very angry, they might get tough and attack.

Alcida: But the land of the Kaslabaia is so far away, out there at Mucajaí. Couldn't it be the Shikoi dɨbɨ?

Dino: No, it was the Kaslabaia, all right.

Alcida: Why the Kaslabaia?

Dino: Of course, because they are *tiko dɨbɨ*, other people, because they are others.

Enter Edu.

Edu: A few days ago Jorge and I saw some strange people downriver and we thought it might be Kaslabaia men who were visiting the Walema dɨbɨ, looking for women.

Dino: If it's true they've killed my father, I'm going to make an extrastrong magic, *okoshi,* and send it downstream. Everybody from here downward will die, even white people.

Alcida: Is it Maiongong magic?

Dino: No, it's Sanumá. It'll have to be very strong, because I and the other Maiongong will be very angry.

Dino turns to the house entrance and shouts out for all the neighbors to hear.

Dino: If they killed my father, I'll make *okoshi* magic for everyone to die from here all the way down to Boa Vista.

Several men and women approach and silently sit just outside the entrance.

Dino: You, Sanumá, keep saying it's true, it's true, I'm beginning to think so too.

Dino's wife: Shida, didn't you see any Kaslabaia around here?

Alcida: No, of course not.

Dino's wife: One time Iuta's father [Lourenço's younger brother] went on a trip to Boa Vista, and, just like now, there was a story that the Kaslabaia had killed him. But he came back safe and sound. Well then, it may be a lie.

Cici: The spirit that accompanied their canoe was not a *hekula* [the shaman's assistant spirit], but a *sai de* [evil spirit]. That's what the shaman said.

Jorge (sitting outside): Lourenço's *nonoshi* [alter ego animal] is still alive, I saw it nearby.

Act Three

The Colony bursts out in mourning when a young Maiongong brings the news that Albertino has just returned from a frustrated trip to meet the travelers. He got as far as the Tucushim falls and saw no sign of them. The atmosphere gets thicker with tension and malaise.

SCENE 1: At Lourenço's house in the Colony.

Augusta (weeping): My husband is dead! My husband is really dead!

Jorge: I'm going back downriver with the Maiongong and try to find Lourenço. If we get to Tucushim and don't find them it's because they are really dead.

The weeping continues with peaks of greater intensity.

SCENE 2: At the Maiongong house.

Albertino: No one died, I got back because my son was ill. These Sanumá keep telling lies.

SCENE 3: At the mission dispensary a group of Sanumá men are chatting while the deep mourning from the Colony is heard by all, including the anthropologist.

Alcida: Albertino said that everything is fine, tomorrow the others will come back home, they got tired of waiting for the travelers from Boa Vista. Listen, just before I left Boa Vista to come here I talked to the Maiongong David and he told me they would get home after I leave Auaris. It's very far, it takes a long time to come upriver.

Zeca: (incredulous): Go tell Lourenço's wife, I say nothing because I'm *tiko* [other]. It's none of my business.

Stress mounts with waves of weeping rippling through the entire Sanumá section of Auaris, filling the air with expressions of mourning in both male and female voices, grave and shrill. People interrupt their chores in a mood of generalized hopelessness. Jorge, in a shamanic session, sends off some of his *hekula* to check whether Lourenço is alive or not. He gets a positive answer and informs the people about it. The weeping diminishes and then stops. Everybody praises Jorge for his good will.

Intermission

A month and a half goes by. Those who went downstream in search of the homebound travelers return alone. The cassava bread they carried for Lourenço's party ends up consumed in their own hunting camps. They are about thirty people, men, women, and children who arrive at the Maiongong village laden with game meat. For this reason they are welcomed with a feast that lasts more than three days. While the Maiongong indulge in a portentous binge of *cashiri* (fermented manioc drink) animated by games and dances, most of the Sanumá keep away, disappointed with the failure of yet another searching expedition.

During the feast some Maiongong women say that the airplane that supplies Auaris, coming from Boa Vista, would have flown over Waikás, an airstrip about forty minutes' flight to the southeast of Auaris; the pilot was said to have seen no signs of the travelers en route. They take this news as a sign that they did not even get to that point and, therefore, they must have been killed.

Act Four

SCENE 1: At the anthropologists' hearth Otavio chats with Alcida.

Otavio: The Maiongong here are saying that the Maiongong downriver have been killed and now they are going to kill Candida. Is it a lie?

Alcida: I don't know, I haven't heard anything. Who was the Maiongong who said that?

Otavio: Semo. I wonder if Candida is going to call other whites to come here and punish us.

Exit Otavio, enter Jorge.

Alcida: I've heard the Maiongong want to kill Candida.

Jorge: I heard that too. I heard it from Dino who heard it from João. The Maiongong are very angry because she should have reported long ago that the Maiongong have been killed, but she didn't, only now she tells it. That's why the Maiongong are planning to throw kerosene under her house and make a fire to burn her while she's asleep.

Alcida: Don't the Sanumá like Candida?

Jorge: The Sanumá do, but the Maiongong don't. It's bad to attack a woman, one shouldn't kill a woman. But I think she won't be afraid when she knows. She's strong, even though she is a woman.

The next day tall flames on the mission lawn devour piles of cut grass. Candida is angry, saying they shouldn't do that, and goes to take a closer look. She turns back with Zeca on her heels, saying that Edu did it because he was angry with her. According to her, his resentment was due to the fact that she had been rationing beads as payment for grass cutting: two measures per person. Edu tried to get more by giving some money to a little boy who had not been working for Candida. When pressed he confessed Edu's trick. He was taking revenge by burning the mounds of dried grass.

Act Five

SCENE 1: At night, at the anthropologists' neighboring hearth, Lília hears amidst whispering and exclamations the news Adão has just brought from the Sabuli community a day's canoeing downriver.

Alcida: What happened?

Lília: Adão said that Sabuli's wife died and has already been cremated, and that Lourenço is dead.

SCENE 2: In the morning at the anthropologists' hearth.

João: Adão said that the Yanomami of the Uraricaá brought the news of the death of the Maiongong. One of those Yanomami had been to Boa Vista and heard that they died while they were drunk. It's a lie, I think, isn't it? Dino came over at night to tell me, he was crying. I told him not to cry because it makes things worse. I don't believe they all died, at least some must have fled. Also Otavio and the other Sanumá visitor saw the Maiongong alive when they did shamanism. I think in a day or two they'll arrive. But in a little while the Maiongong are getting together to decide whether they'll go downriver again to meet Lourenço.

Alcida: I wonder whether the Sanumá don't like Lourenço and that's why they make up these stories about him.

João: No, they like him a lot.

The next day another expedition with several Maiongong and Sanumá departs to meet the Boa Vista travelers.

Act Six

SCENE 1: Lília brings cassava bread to her brother Angelo, the anthropologists' host.

Alcida: I dreamt that the Maiongong had arrived. What do you think of this dream?

Lília: Maybe they'll arrive, all right. I also dreamt that Orlando had got back. I dreamt about the little bird that is his sound companion.[2] The bird [*shobi a hea*] flew and flew and flew in circles over the house.

SCENE 2: The anthropologist interviews Zeca. The matter of the dream comes up.

Zeca: Your dream means that if you go to the forest you'll be bitten by a snake. It doesn't mean that Lourenço is coming back.

Act Seven

Beto brings the news that Lourenço's group is coming back, perhaps they have already reached the Sabuli village; they should arrive at Auaris in a few hours.

SCENE 1: At night Lília tells everybody that Alcida's and her dreams signal good omens announcing the arrival of the Maiongong. Tension has declined considerably among the Sanumá.

SCENE 2: At the Maiongong village.

Albertino: Beto is lying. I think the Kaslabaia have really killed Lourenço and the others because of old fights.

The Sanumá laugh, the Maiongong cry.

Commentary

Ana and I had a scheduled flight back to Boa Vista; hence we left Auaris before the end of the story. Very likely Lourenço and his traveling companions arrived within hours of our departure. Despite the gloomy atmosphere at the Maiongong village, preparations were being made to welcome them with huge quantities of *cashiri* brewed for the occasion. Not long after, I heard from the missionaries that Lourenço had arrived safe and sound, perhaps oblivious of all the drama he and his companions had precipitated. Once again history repeated itself in a combination of farce and tragedy. At each long trip to a white man's town a rumor was conceived, grew to melodramatic proportions, engaging all residents of Auaris in complicated plots and subplots, only to be dissolved into nothingness by the homecoming euphoria.

Characters and Situations

As the rumor progressed I became increasingly aware of how eager certain people were to augment the drama being generated by the rumor. The first character to come on stage was the Maiongong João, apparently the initiator of the rumor. Elsewhere (Ramos 1980) I have remarked on his concern to keep himself above the Sanumá, whom he deemed inferior beings. But at the same time, João confessed he feared them for their magical knowledge and for their alleged inclination to take up arms and attack indiscriminately and without warning. For example, João had witnessed an event that disturbed him a great deal. In the 1960s, near the old Maiongong round house, he saw a Sanumá man kill another as the conclusion of a long dispute. Alone in the village at that moment, João was a helpless bystander as the victim was being hacked to death by the murderer's axe blows. He felt so impotent as to be totally immobilized. He was too stunned to interfere, run away, look for help, or simply scream. His fear of the Sanumá was greatly intensified.

With such an image of his Sanumá neighbors, it is no wonder João was startled by the conversation he had overheard at the Colony and which brought about the rumor of the massacre. For him, and probably for many other Maiongong, the peace so painstakingly attained between the two groups depended on the Sanumá willingness to keep it. Sanumá unpredictability was for João a source of dread and insecurity. In a dangerous situation, such as the long canoe trip presented, feelings of mistrust are heightened. The Maiongong often blame the Sanumá—and the other Yanomami—for whatever harm they may suffer, even at a distance. The way João contributed to spinning the yarn of the massacre reflected two clear facets of the image he has of the Sanumá: their perennial belligerence, and their inferiority.

Another outstanding character was the Sanumá Jorge, one of the most active people in the making of the rumor. He was on the first trip downriver to meet Lourenço's party and, like his travel companions, had been away from Auaris for a month and knew nothing about the tales going around the village. No sooner was he back in the village than he enthusiastically proceeded to nurture the rumor as if he had always been there. He added fuel to the fire when he declared that, together with another youth, he had noticed the presence of strangers downriver and identified them as Kaslabaia; by so doing he contributed to heighten the already high tension in the village. But it was also he who eased the tension when it reached a peak which threatened to disrupt Sanumá daily routine; with shamanism he consoled the men and women consumed in mourning their alleged dead. Transmitting the comforting message from his assistant spirits that the travelers were fine, Jorge won the good graces of his community, and came out as somewhat of a hero.

Jorge's performance in the context of this rumor becomes more intelligible if we know about his personal ambition. In 1974 he was about twenty years old, and had already been to Boa Vista a few times to work as a language informant for the missionaries. Aware of his own skills in handling whites, Jorge began, as we saw in Chapter 3, to nourish the idea of becoming an Auaris political leader. His ambition was amply confirmed by other Sanumá and by the resident missionary of the day. Although still young, he knew how to use all his talents to impress his fellow villagers. The rumor of Lourenço's death came as a golden opportunity for him to promote himself as a strategic broker of information (his testimony about the Kaslabaia on the Auaris River) and as a benefactor of the people (shamanizing in the service of the community). He won precious points with his companions. Furthermore, being the son-in-law of Lourenço's brother, and living at the very Colony where the rumor began, he used his position to the full by first inflating and then deflating the emotional pressure that threatened to paralyze the community. This becomes all the more significant when we consider that his subaltern status as son-in-law put him in a particularly humble position vis-à-vis the Maiongong. If to be Sanumá is to be at a social disadvantage in the eyes of the Maiongong, to undertake bride service for a Maiongong father-in-law is to have a particularly sensitive political handicap. In appealing to the esoteric knowledge that emanated from his *hekula*, he was in a sense arbitrating the fate of the Maiongong, his father-in-law among them. In both metaphysical and practical terms, he was showing his world that he, too, had his reservoir of power.

A third prominent actor in the rumor was Dino, the eldest son of Lourenço and his Sanumá wife. The cultural and ethnic ambiguities of intertribal progeny were most evident in his case. By Sanumá patrilineal reckoning, Lourenço's children would all be Maiongong. The oldest sons tend to identify themselves as Maiongong, although the Maiongong do not recognize them as their equals. Of all Lourenço's children, Dino was the most affected by this ambiguity. He speaks Sanumá but with a strong accent. He would have liked to marry a Maiongong woman, but instead he married a Sanumá. If he cannot be considered a true Maiongong as he would have liked owing to his Sanumá mother, it is owing to his father, Lourenço, that he can claim to be, in his own words, a "false Maiongong," *Nabɨ de holeshi*.[3] Hence his stress on how "valuable" Lourenço was to him. In a way we might say that Dino's ambivalence regarding the rumor, sometimes believing, sometimes disbelieving the story of the massacre, symbolizes the ambiguity of his ethnic identity. He wanted to discredit the rumor because, as the Maiongong keep saying, the Sanumá are untrustworthy. But, if it was true, he would retaliate in Sanumá style, using their strong magic. However, Dino was not so Maiongong as to openly declare the Sanumá consummate liars or to ignore the value of their knowledge in the sensitive realm of magic. Nor was he so Sanumá as to believe the story of the rumor without reservations. He danced and drank at the Maiongong feast, but soon after it he wept, like the Sanumá, for his possibly dead father. Aware of the history of warfare between the two groups, he perceived very well the exceptional role his father played in the interface between them, and the dangers attributed to his contact with other Yanomami people. Although his brother and paternal uncle were also in Lourenço's company, Dino never focused his worries on anyone else besides his own father. He is the most emblematic product of an intertribal situation that still reeks of intertribal hatred, notwithstanding attempts to settle into a peaceful coexistence. Part of these efforts were the marriage alliances established by his father and uncle. The rumor revealed that Dino still suffers the consequences of past disputes that have yet to be totally resolved.

Taken as a whole, each of these two ethnic groups displayed very different reactions to the rumor. First, we notice the Sanumá inclination to fuel the rumor, but always attributing the authorship of the massacre to absent or distant actors. They resorted to the unfriendly reputation of other Yanomami living miles away who were very unlikely to have had the chance or reason to attack the Maiongong. From the moment they heard the first lines of the rumor that put them under suspicion of plotting to kill Lourenço, it was as if their major concern was to shift attention away from themselves and to people as remote as possible (the Mucajaí and Uraricaá Rivers, the Shimatayam community in Venezuela). In so doing, the Sanumá were exempting themselves from all responsibility for what might have happened or was yet to happen to Lourenço's party. By targeting distant actors they were also defusing the danger of reopening, right then and there, a new era of hostilities with the Maiongong—a constant menace that insidiously hangs over them and that everyone tries to suppress. If, on the one hand, the Maiongong fear the eruption of violence on the part of the Sanumá, on the other hand, the Sanumá still have a vivid memory of the times when the generation of their parents and grandparents suffered the effects of Maiongong shotguns. Although it is never overtly admitted, each group fears that the other might break the truce they have enjoyed for over half a century.

As to the Maiongong, from the moment the welfare of Lourenço's group was questioned, they began to reach into their store of stereotypes kept specially for the Sanumá. They accused them of lying, of reveling in hyperbole, and of causing disorder and anxiety. Moreover, it is curious that the Maiongong apprehensions surfaced at the very moments when the Sanumá showed optimism about the fate of the travelers. When the latter decided that all was in order, the former expressed their belief in the story of the massacre. Conversely, at the height of Sanumá despair, the Maiongong mocked them by stating that the whole thing was a sham. It was as though the Maiongong made it a point of honor to discredit the Sanumá, regardless of what they said.

While the Sanumá dramatized ad nauseam their reactions to the rumor, the Maiongong kept their usual dignified posture. The development of the rumor in its various phases had less effect among Maiongong than among Sanumá in part because most Maiongong were away from Auaris at that time. There is, however, another reason which impresses me (as no doubt it would Ruth Benedict) as the epitome of their cultural differences, namely, their respective public images: the retiring Maiongong versus the extroverted Sanumá.

In those early months of 1974, the Sanumá taste for drama was very much in evidence. At the critical points of the story the possibility of good news had no tranquilizing effect on them whatsoever. When, for example, Albertino returned to the Maiongong village with a sick child, he instantly set off a commotion at the Colony. It was promptly and consensually interpreted as proof that Lourenço, not having been found, was certainly dead. Albertino, however, had no bad news to report apart from his son's illness. As far as he was concerned at that moment no one had died, it was just that the trip back from Boa Vista was long and slow as expected. There was then a climate of relative serenity at the Maiongong village. But the Sanumá would hear none of it; they went on weeping, accusing the Kaslabaia, until Jorge's *hekula* appeased their misery with the irrefutable testimony of their supernatural powers.

Why go on suffering in the face of good news? Was it collective masochism or a pure taste for drama? At all critical moments I could observe during the twenty-seven months of my stay among the Sanumá I was always amazed by the way in which they cultivated dramatic or exciting situations. I was often reminded of what Bateson (1958: 148) described for the Iatmul of New Guinea, especially regarding male ethos. Part of Sanumá daily life are duels between offender and offended, between robber and robbed, between husband and wife, between betrayed husband and adulterous lover, between mother-in-law and son-in-law, and occasionally between siblings or mother and son. Hardly a day goes by without some thrilling event to stir up people's adrenalin. In a Sanumá village there is no such thing as "life's dull round" (Rivière 1969). All those occasions are lived to the full with the participation of all residents, amidst expressions of emotion bursting from all directions. In my mind these expressions are an integral part of Sanumá ontology, regardless of whether they interact with the Maiongong or with anyone else. Perhaps because the Maiongong recognize this Sanumá mode of being, they did nothing to minimize or neutralize the grief of the Colony women. They were mere spectators. When we asked them if the Sanumá women were mourning their husbands, they would smile and quietly repeat the formula: Sanumá lie all the time. Perhaps if they had known the word in Portuguese, they might have more appropriately said: the Sanumá dramatize.

Deciphering the Rumor

Like a capsule that reveals its concentration of chemicals when opened, the rumor, when analytically explored, unlocks a number of densely packed meanings. The idiom in which the rumor was conveyed allows fears, anxieties, and longings to be disclosed, longings which would be rarely manifested in the routine mode of Sanumá-Maiongong interaction. Although such feelings are not deliberately concealed, their exposure might have betrayed the tension that everyone seems to pretend does not exist. The allegoric language in which the rumor was delivered works as a protective mantle against the risks of literality, that is, of taking the word at face value with no metaphoric mediation.

The central theme of this 1974 rumor was death. But it was not death pure and simple. It was death as a result of a long sojourn in the land of whites. It was mainly the death of a Maiongong man who to a large extent adopted the Sanumá way of life. Subsequently inserted into this text were a number of subtexts that went on expanding until they encompassed the vast symbolic mesh of the Sanumá-Maiongong interethnic ventures. Let us examine some of these subtexts, following from the general to the specific: (a) the imaging of the white world by both Maiongong and Sanumá; (b) missionary-Indian relationships; (c) representations of Maiongong-Yanomami contact; (d) Maiongong-Sanumá relationships specifically; and (e) the role of the Colony in the Auaris intertribal microcosmos.

The white world. The parts of the rumor which highlighted the role of the whites were the very trip to Boa Vista and all its dangers, as well as the anonymous white man who, while drunk, allegedly killed Lourenço.

In the seventies, and perhaps even more so now, the whites were an enigma for both the Sanumá and Maiongong. They were seen either to bring benefits to the people with supplies of trade goods and medicines, or to hurt them with contagious diseases and economic exploitation. The unpredictability of whites is symbolized in the rumor by the drunken man who murdered Lourenço for no apparent reason. Presumably a Sanumá creation, this character has no precise features apart from one aspect that distinguishes him from the missionaries or the other whites known to the Sanumá: he was drunk. Drunkenness was seen as a marker of the dangerous, remote white of whom most Sanumá had heard through folkloric accounts. The Maiongong state of intoxication with *cashiri* did not belong in the same category. To be high on *cashiri* fell in the same cultural niche as being high on the *sakona* hallucinogen. The eventual and familiar outbursts of aggressive behavior during *cashiri* feasts or *sakona* sessions do not have the same frightening force as the unpredictable violence of a drunken white.

Canoe trips to Boa Vista had always been viewed as a major enterprise involving great risks both human and material. They represented a rich but uncontrollable experience, as uncontrollable or unpredictable as the actual encounter with whites. Furthermore, in those days such trips were hazardous not only due to natural dangers and to unintelligible whites, but also because travelers had to cross the territory of not always friendly Yanomami villages. Eventually the Maiongong adopted the tactics of taking along at least one Sanumá who played the multiple role of go-between, diplomat, and safe-conduct through socially inhospitable lands.

Missionary-Indian relationships. The rumor signals missionary-Indian relationships when it brings up the missionary who concealed strategic information, and the radio as an instrument that confers power to its users.

The advent of missionaries at Auaris in the mid-1960s changed the tone of Sanumá-Maiongong relationships, particularly with regard to economic exchanges. Prior to their arrival, the Maiongong played the self-ascribed role of "civilizers" for the Sanumá. In that capacity they hired Sanumá labor for a trifle, arguing that what the Sanumá learned while working was already a form of payment. With the establishment of the mission, however, both Sanumá and Maiongong were hired by the missionaries on an equal footing. According to the Maiongong, the result was that "the missionaries spoiled the Sanumá." Some Maiongong complained that when missionaries gave work to Sanumá, fewer goods went to Maiongong, goods which for them had become irreversible needs. A symbol of Maiongong resentment was the fantasy attributed to them of burning the missionary in her sleep; it is also indicated in Jorge's statement that it was the Maiongong and not the Sanumá who disliked the missionary. The bottom line is that the mission came to compete with the Maiongong for Sanumá labor with the aggravating factor that the Maiongong ended up being leveled with their "inferior" neighbors as mere menial workers for whites. Moreover, the Maiongong did not conceal their displeasure at not being themselves the main focus of missionary action (or anthropological research, for that matter).

The missionaries were seen as retaining the greatest power in the community. Such power emanated from the fact that most often they were the only source of scarce Western goods for miles around. Almost as important as this economic monopoly was their control over the radio and their exclusive access to strategic information shared by neither Maiongong nor Sanumá. From the Indians' perspective, such power might be activated at any moment either in their favor (the airplane could be called upon to take a sick person to the hospital in town) or against them (the missionary could call other whites on the radio to come to Auaris and kill Sanumá in retaliation for Lourenço's death). Such a notion of power that emanates from the radio machine appears again in the indignation against the missionary when she allegedly withheld news about the massacre. Radio and airplanes are strong symbols of the power of whites over Indians. Sanumá often gather around the missionaries' house while they speak on the radio and afterward ask them eagerly what they had been saying. Through the radio the whites can make things happen as if by magic. A communication channel that is beyond their control and understanding, the radio contributes to the Sanumá vision of whites as unreliable. Airplanes are equally regarded as potentially dangerous. They often appear in stories about white men taking revenge on Indians by dropping poisonous substances from the air.

Maiongong-Yanomami contact. The rumor focused on broad intertribal contact through (a) imputing the massacre to the Kaslabaia, singled out amongst the various Yanomami groups; (b) alluding to the involvement of distant Yanomami, such as the Yanam of the Uraricaá River; (c) referring to other Sanumá from a far-away village on the Venezuelan side of the border; and (d) invoking an alliance between the Kaslabaia and the Walema dibi against the Maiongong.

Given the history of warfare between the two ethnic groups, it is not surprising that to this day their relationships are somewhat strained. Like a volcano, their antagonism is dormant but not necessarily extinct. The reappearance of belligerence is always a possibility no matter how remote it may be, no matter that it is never explicitly admitted. Even at Auaris, where Maiongong-Sanumá interaction has been peaceful and intense, the frequent accusations of theft from the temptingly fat Maiongong gardens, aimed at the Sanumá, and the occasional confrontations between people of both groups are potential sparks that may some day ignite old turbulent fires. One has only to mention that men from both groups (and Sanumá but not Maiongong women) come to these confrontations fully armed.

The Yanam of Mucajaí, the so-called Kaslabaia (Big lips), being conveniently remote from the daily life at Auaris, and having in their curriculum vitae one major victory over the Maiongong, are the perfect representatives of the proverbially "fierce" Yanomami. At the same time, they are well suited to divert attention from the Sanumá as possible sources of aggression against the Maiongong. In the rumor the Kaslabaia epitomize the sore spot that betrays the veiled antagonism which underlies the relations between the two ethnic groups. It is curious to see in the rumor a reference made to the Yanomami of the Uraricaá River, also Yanam speakers (self-identified as Shiriana) and also involved in historic raids against the Maiongong.[4]

In a less elaborate way, the Walema dibi also contributed to the imagery of the threatening Yanomami. Their identification is not entirely clear; they might be associated with the Yanam speakers, or with the Yanomam at the Palimiu mission station on the Uraricoera River. In any case, the rumor has them as allies of the Kaslabaia for the purpose of confronting the Maiongong. Other Yanomami figure in the rumor as carriers of bad news, such as the young Waiká who fled from Lourenço's expedition and reappeared skin and bones to tell the story of the massacre.

Naturally the Maiongong know very well about the cultural affiliation of the Sanumá to the Yanomami family. That is why they take along at least one Sanumá on their trips so that they have an interpreter and mediator between them and the Yanomami.

Maiongong-Sanumá relations. The rumor stresses more specific intertribal relations in the following ways: (a) a Maiongong attributes to the Sanumá a plot to kill Lourenço; (b) Sanumá magic is invoked by Lourenço's son; (c) Sanumá shamanism is used to decipher the mystery of the massacre; (d) Sanumá spirits intervene in Lourenço's movements; and (e) the Maiongong insist on branding the Sanumá as liars.

The rumor points at an intertribal situation that is fairly stable, but which is the outcome of a past of unrest that continues to haunt everyone, especially the Maiongong. In this sense the Sanumá are not so very different from the other Yanomami in the eyes of the Maiongong. But what the rumor also shows is that the interaction between the two neighboring groups has reached a new equilibrium cemented with an intense trade of both material and symbolic goods. The interdependence thus created can be sustained only in peacetime.

The rumor underscores this interdependence mainly with regard to Sanumá magic and religious practices. In their contact situation, the role of Sanumá sorcery and shamanism is particularly salient for the Maiongong. The latter deeply fear the magical power of the Sanumá and have great respect for their shamanism. The episodes in the rumor that describe the intervention of *hekula* and *sai de* spirits on the one hand, and the use of powerful magic for revenge on the other, indicate that this aspect of the relationship between the two groups is consciously fostered. In the magico-religious realm, Sanumá overshadow Maiongong, who acknowledge this superiority, albeit reluctantly.

The constant reference Maiongong make to Sanumá untruthfulness is one of the most frequently heard stereotypes in Auaris. The Sanumá respond largely by ignoring it; they seem to feel neither offended nor misunderstood, but simply indifferent. After repeatedly observing the Sanumá reaction to this type of criticism both by the Maiongong and by the missionaries, I reached the conclusion that their concepts of truth and falsity follow logical directions quite different from those of the Christian morality the Maiongong appear to have adopted at least as a convenient adjunct to their judgment of the Sanumá. I have no detailed data on this subject matter, but it seems that the truth/lie dichotomy acquires a much greater flexibility in Sanumá usage than in ours. Depending on the context, what is true today can turn into a lie tomorrow and vice versa. If one removes from these two concepts the notion that they are absolute, what is left is no more than a matter of interpretation, dictated by specific circumstances. Truth would then become a relative proposition just as it seems to be for the Sanumá.

The ethnic ambiguity of the Colony. The Colony has a place of honor in the rumor due to Lourenço, its distinguished leader. As the main protagonist of the rumor, Lourenço had his special position in Auaris dramatically spotlighted, a focus that spilled over onto his entire community. Because he married a Sanumá woman he was not considered a true Maiongong by the Maiongong themselves. On the other hand, his fluency in the Sanumá language and culture notwithstanding, the Sanumá unquestioningly identified him as a Maiongong. In founding the Colony, he showed great leadership skills that were recognized far and wide. His leadership was to a certain extent reinforced by his ability to deal with whites. Although he spoke no Portuguese, missionaries, anthropologists, and occasional white visitors often requested his services as a guide or as a knowledgeable source of geographic and social information about the region. Due to his singular position in Auaris, he was often the target of criticisms by local public opinion. In the rumor, public opinion manifested itself in the form of the imaginary attack on his life. Although other Maiongong and Sanumá were on the same trip, he alone was the focus of all commentaries. His outstanding role in the rumor can clearly be attributed to his unique situation, that of a Maiongong married to a Sanumá, operating in both groups yet belonging to neither, and retaining the leadership of a community which is precisely the product of both groups brought together. He became the symbol of this encounter with all its ambiguities. The Colony was the concrete manifestation of these ambiguities. It was the collective version of the personage named Lourenço.

Rumor as Allegory

In sum, this rumor, "a representation that 'interprets' itself" (Clifford 1986:99), is an allegory of interethnic worlds. An extremely condensed narrative, it captures the essence of things that are normally dulled by familiarity. By using imagery that mixes the plausible and the improbable, the said and the unsaid, the rumor renders three-dimensional those implicit regions that are normally flattened out by the conventions of everyday living. With its inherent anonymity, improvisation, and allegoric overtones, the rumor is an informal mode of commenting on certain areas of social life. In the case of the Maiongong-Sanumá sociability with its sore past and relatively mild present, there is always a susceptible zone for the gathering of tension. If, however, this tension is openly aired, the scenario is set for the possible eruption of old grievances. In this context, the rumor is a useful safety valve with the added benefit of offering a spectacle similar to what we know as psychodrama. Were it not for the absence of rehearsals, it might be taken for a theater without backstage where actors and audience create the script as the drama moves along.

Auaris is not the only place in the ethnographic world to provide examples of rumors such as this. Among various specimens of this remarkable narrative genre, Raymond Firth (1967) speaks of the constant rumors that go around Tikopia communities in high-pressure situations. Mariza Peirano (verbal communication) saw a similar reaction among fisherman of the Brazilian Northeast whenever a storm generated anxiety in the people on shore who had no information about those out at sea. More recently, Wilson Trajano (1993) has described the role of rumors in the effort at nation building in Guinea-Bissau. Curiously enough, in all these cases the role of radio communications is specifically emphasized.

Rumors such as these frequently occur in situations of social ambiguity, of uncertainty as to the fate of people in danger, and of failure in the usual means of communication. This is not to say that rumors themselves are conveyors of news, as has been suggested (Lienhardt 1975); in fact, they should not be confused with the proper channels, both formal and informal, that exist among the Maingong and the Sanumá (Ramos 1980). Rather than being "objective" reports of something that happened, rumors are hyperbolic representations of a given reality as it is perceived by those who live it. They reflect a wide range of social, mental, and emotional moods, such as anxiety, bewilderment, stereotypes, misgivings, and fears. Ingenious artifacts that they are, rumors are informal, improvised, and collective devices to ventilate those moods that are bound to occur in touchy situations. Given their often allegoric character, rumors have the capacity to bring out problems without risking serious conflicts, as might be the case if more direct and explicit means of communication were used.

The sad irony of this rumor is that, like an eerie prophecy, it foretold Lourenço's murder by white men more than sixteen years before it happened.

10

The Sanumá's Others

"We are gathered here to show you that we are people too."
—Indian leader Marcos Terena in his closing speech at the
Brazilian Senate, First Meeting of Indigenous Peoples, 1982

Until mid-1987 most of the ten thousand Yanomami in Brazil could still be considered a rare case in South American ethnography with regard to degree of contact with the West. The Yanomami are the largest monolingual indigenous population in the Americas that still maintain much of their traditional lifestyle. Until then, most Yanomami had been spared the destructive effects of chaotic contact with outsiders, apart from localized invasions mainly on the outer fringes of their territory. In August 1987, however, came the vertiginous advance of tens of thousands of prospectors in one of the most rampant instances of gold rush in this century. While expansion of other economic activities had been averted thanks to the difficulties of access to the region that straddles the rain-forest-covered mountains of the Orinoco-Amazon watershed, for gold miners these were no barriers. They possessed small aircraft, helicopters, giant hoses, heavy machinery, and a craving for gold not easily intimidated by forest, mountain, waterfall, wilderness, or diseases, much less by Indians, protective laws, and repeated protests for the defense of ecology and indigenous life. Until 1987 it was possible to say that the Yanomami in Brazil still represented a preciously rare exception to the majority of cases of violation of basic human rights of Indian peoples the world over. They were then a living example of a society capable of extracting sustained livelihood from the Amazon environment using means of subsistence not yet tampered with by modern technology, or interfered with by overpopulation. With the massive assault of gold prospectors spread over their lands like a cancerous growth out of control, many Yanomami communities lost their hunting and fishing grounds, their gardens and source of drinkable water, their health, peace, and prospects for the future.

Although the Sanumá were not at the vortex of the gold rush, they have nevertheless felt the shock waves that reached them in the form of contagious diseases that spread through the countryside like wild fire. Smaller groups of gold miners reached out into their lands, and, although they never stayed for very long (concentration of gold in Sanumá country is smaller than elsewhere), that was enough to bring illness and insecurity into Sanumá life (see Chapter 11).

From another point of view—that of ethnic identity—the Yanomami as a whole, and the Sanumá specifically, also represented a rare case. The sharp contrast between *Indian* and *white,* imposed upon practically all existing indigenous populations in the continent, has only recently been introduced among them.[1] The emergence of the *Indian/white* categories is already perceptible in the Yanomami most intensely exposed to encroachment by road construction and agribusiness (IWGIA 1979; Ramos et al. 1985).

This chapter is based on a paper I wrote in 1982, when the notion of *Indian* had not yet invaded the lands and minds of the Sanumá. What follows is a reflection on what I have learned from the Sanumá way of capturing otherness before the advent of the concept of *Indian* as it was hatched in the nest of interethnic inequality. The Sanumá have given me the unique opportunity—I can see it now—to understand the process of category formation, and the transition from a set of traditional concepts to an alien system of classification regarding the distinction between "us" and "the others." Finding themselves, until the mid-1980s, without the experience of what is conventionally meant to be "Indian," Sanumá offer the possibility of filling in the gap that so often faces the anthropologist who gets to an indigenous group "too late." What usually happens is that by the time anthropological work is done, the group has already lost all memory of what it was like to be other than what the white man says they are—*Indians.*

Here I focus primarily on the contrast between the politically laden *Indian/white* dichotomy and the various Sanumá ethnic categories. Rather than political statements, the latter are social and cultural markers. The passage from one to the other, imposed by the politics of contact, begins to catch up with the Sanumá as they get increasingly exposed to agents of Brazilian society, such as miners, army personnel, and health teams. They too no doubt will tread the road first of self-effacement, and then of self-determination, like so many other indigenous peoples before them. Like them the Sanumá will probably end up by transforming the concept of Indian from villain to ally, that is, a political platform against subordination and forced assimilation. From victimized "Indians" they are likely to become politicized Indians, no longer in quotation marks (Ramos 1988). By examining the differences between Sanumá and white strategies of alterity I want to emphasize the radically distinct logic that informs each system of classification — the intraethnic and the interethnic.

Indian/White, a Political Statement

The politically laden category *Indian* and the category *white* (or *civilizado*) are always mutually exclusive. One can never convert one into the other. There are virtually no circumstances in which it might be possible to lump together *Indian* and *white* in the same grouping, such as occurs with the Sanumá *tiko* category. This is because *Indian* and *white* represent the ultimate polarity in the context of interethnic contact. There is always, of course, the hypothesis of an exceptional occurrence such as a war between nations for which *Indians* might be recruited. During the Paraguayan war in the nineteenth century, for instance, Terena men fought on the Brazilian side. Situations such as this might have the effect of blurring ethnic differences, but only momentarily, while the stimulus lasted. Even this, however, is questionable, judging by North American examples of Indians and blacks during World War II and the Vietnam War. Whatever solidarity linked them to white soldiers did not seem to cross ethnic and racial barriers.

The political dimension of interethnic contact is encapsulated in the very conceptual antinomy that pitches *Indian* against *white*. The power relations originating in the interethnic arena reflect the unquestionable political supremacy of the *whites* as well as their sheer capacity to dominate the *Indians*. In other words, the *Indian/white* contrast is, above all, a political expression, for it cries out power, articulated in the form of a linguistic imposition dressed up in stereotypes, prejudice, and discrimination. It is a flagrant example of how coercive language can be. It signals the profoundly unequal position of *Indians* and *civilizados* in the centuries-old arena of interethnic contact.

To first grasp the Sanumá identity categories and then contrast them to the trenchant *Indian/white* dichotomy can help us understand how violent the imposition of the label *Indian* can be to a people who consider themselves as "people," as whole, complete, and legitimate "human beings." To be human is to *be* fully in the world. To be an *Indian* is a historic misfortune for someone who happens merely to *exist* on the face of the earth at the mercy of an interethnic reality that has been forged by whites. Far from being a piece of metaphysical musing, to speak of the passage from "being in the world" to merely "existing in the world" is to speak of a radical transformation in the life of indigenous peoples. It catapults them from a state in which to be is an incontestable right, to another in which, in order to exist, one has to first deny one's own being. Self determination, once a given by the mere exercise of an identity culturally recognized, becomes a scarce commodity. One can recover it by seizing the opponent's weapon, that is, the very notion of *Indian*. From being a derogatory word *Indian* is metamorphosed into a password to ethnic legitimacy. It is a weapon in the battle for the recognition that *Indian* is equal to *white*, not by similarity, but by equivalence. But even in this political scenario—and perhaps more so here—the *Indian/white* distinction remains sharp and discrete, for now it is the Indians themselves (again without quotes) who want to maintain the ethnic differences.

Ethnic Contrasts

Linguistic studies divide the Yanomami into at least four main language groups—Sanumá, Yanomam, Yanomami, and Yanam (Migliazza 1967, 1972). The degree of mutual intelligibility varies among them. Sanumá language seems to be the most distant from all the others. Each language in turn has a number of dialectal variations.

This linguist's classification does not necessarily coincide with the way each Yanomami subgroup sees the matter. In the first place, not all Yanomami know about the existence of all the other Yanomami. The groups on the edge of their vast territory, such as the Sanumá in the north and the Yanomam in the south, use, if at all, a general and diffuse term to refer to those who are conceived as living many miles away. Second, social and geographic proximity is a much more significant factor in local classifications than are language considerations. For some Sanumá on the Brazilian side, for instance, the Yanomam once known as Parahuri and now as Tucushim are much closer than other Sanumá of remote communities in Venezuela. It thus seems that direct contact is socially more relevant than linguistic similarity pure and simple.

The way differences and similarities are articulated among the various social segments in the Sanumá universe, including the whites, gives an idea of the flexibility and relativization with which different peoples are thought about in that universe. I shall begin with the most general of Sanumá categories and work my way into the most specific, with the reminder that the inverse order might be equally acceptable.

At the most inclusive level of contrast, the Sanumá distinguish between human and nonhuman beings. "In contrast with such other beings as 'evil spirits' (*sai dibi*) and 'edible fauna' (*salo bi*), 'human be-

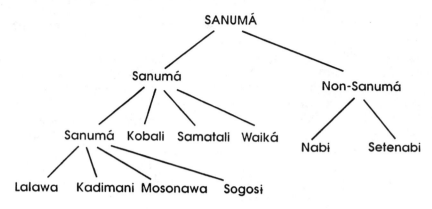

Fig. 10.1. Identity categories I

ings' are known as *sanima dibi'* (Taylor 1974:62). I refer to this wide category as SANUMÁ in capital letters. Within it a further distinction is made between "Sanumá" and "non-Sanumá." We might translate these terms as, respectively, "people like us" and "other people." Contained in the "Sanumá" category is a series of concepts related to the Sanumá themselves and to people like them. The latter are not quite "like us" because they display one or more of especially three features: different language, region, and lifestyle, as, for example, the Kobali, Samatali, and Waiká. At this same level of contrast, "non-Sanumá," or "other people," are the non-Yanomami primarily represented by Maiongong, called Nabi, and by whites, called Setenabi.

Within the "Sanumá" category, that is, "people like us," we find a large number of distinct yet related terms, such as names of villages and names of descent units (lineages and sibs). As we have seen in Chapter 7, communities usually take the name of a resident lineage group (Lalawa, Kadimani, Mosonawa, etc.). This, in turn, produces yet another contrast level, that of lineages within the same community. For example, the *kadimani dibi* and *wanabidili dibi* lineages are part of the Kadimani village. For my purposes here it is not necessary to go into the details at this capillary level of contrast, already discussed in Chapter 2. Visually we would have the arrangement shown in Figure 10.1.

One has to first examine certain Sanumá concepts that are noted for their plasticity; they are sufficiently flexible as to allow the speaker to change levels of contrast and points of reference according to specific need or convenience. For instance, someone may refer to his or her own family as *iba dibi*, "my people," or as *kamisamak*, "we"; by contrast, other families are *ai dibi*, "others." This same person may then refer to his or her own community or lineage, including both his or her own family and other families, as *kamisamak* (or *iba dibi* depending on whether the emphasis is on the group or on the person); the contrast is now made with regard to other communities or to other lineages which are then *ai dibi*. But he or she may bring together his or her community and other neighboring ones and refer to all as *kamisamak*, in opposition to other sets of distant communities, and so on in an ever more inclusive series of contrasts.

There is, however, another term, *tiko dibi*, which expresses otherness most clearly. It contrasts any "we" to any "non-we." This flexibility comes precisely from its capacity to be applied to different contrast levels. Behind the notion of *tiko dibi* is a remarkable attitude of refined cultural relativism and social tolerance toward what is "different." It is an attitude hard to find in the national milieux that surround the Sanumá, not to speak of the omnipresent intolerance that pervades *Indian/white* contact. The importance of this concept will be pointed out later.

Let us go back to the category of "people like us." In its most comprehensive sense this concept includes the Sanumá of the upper Auaris River as well as the Kobali, Samatali, and Waiká. Who are these people? The exact limits of each one of the last three categories are vague to me, as they also appear to be for the Sanumá themselves. What seems certain is that none of these terms is a self-denomination. These people consider themselves to be *sanima dibi*. The term Kobali is used in reference to a cluster of villages to the south of the Auaris valley. The residents of the Kadimani community, for instance, kept a relatively intense contact with them (perhaps once a year) and were well-informed about them. The term carries a slightly pejorative connotation, indicating backwardness. But it can also be used as a signpost to mark off the distance between communities that are actually quite close. For example, the residents of the communities around the Auaris mission used to refer to the Kadimani to the south as Kobali, while the latter not only denied their *kobali-ness*, but in fact passed it on to other communities to the south of them. A revealing episode took place during a trip Ken and I took, alone and on foot, from Kadimani to Auaris. It was an unheard-of adventure in the Sanumá experience with whites. As we reached the mission airstrip, exhausted after an erratic nine-hour walk through the forest, the Sanumá welcomed us with a mixture of disbelief, teasing, and admiration. They warmly called us Kobali dibi! We had passed the test of "humanity," but did not yet measure up to their own standards.

The term Samatali refers to people who live to the southwest of the upper Auaris. They are more remote than the Kobali. The history of the upper Auaris Sanumá has a phase, some three generations back, of warfare with the Samatali. At that time the Sanumá lived in the region of the Ocamo River in Venezuela. Like the Kobali, the Samatali seem to speak the Sanumá language, but there are great dialectal differences between them.

Within the Kobali and Samatali categories there are named subdivisions consisting of communities or community clusters such as the Kobali Hogomawa and Omawa, or the Samatali Hazatagɨdili. There are, however, other groups that are not part of these categories, like the Shikoi and the Walema of the Parima River, southeast of Auaris. Furthermore, other categories referring to former residence clusters that became dispersed have maintained their identification capacity by being transformed into descent categories. It is the case of the *saulagɨdili dɨbɨ*, *pasotogɨdili dɨbɨ*, and *totobɨdili dɨbɨ* described in Chapter 2. So as not to overload the text, I will leave these out of this discussion and limit myself to the categories that appear in Figure 10.1.

The Waiká seem to be all Yanomam speakers originally from the region of the Surucucus Mountains in the heart of Yanomamiland. The Waiká community that is closest to the Sanumá of the upper Auaris was known as Parahuri in the 1970s. They are now identified as Tucushim (see Chapter 11). In the 1960s and 1970s they were located about six or seven days' walk southeast of the mission. While the Kobali are regarded as backward and the Samatali as bellicose, the Waiká are seen as ill-bred and reckless in terms of trading etiquette. Relationships between them and the Sanumá are cordial but tense. When an important man from the Sabuli community died, the Waiká were accused of having caused his death with sorcery. They provoked great commotion in that village when they showed up at his death ceremony without invitation. Sanumá and Waiká use their own languages when speaking to each other; given the mutual intelligibility, it is unnecessary to adopt either the one, the other, or a third language as lingua franca.

All these categories refer to people with whom the Sanumá of the upper Auaris have maintained tense relations marked by sorcery accusations, hostile shamanism, and even armed attacks.

Sanumá language allows for the same terms to be contrasted in different ways along different lines of interest. Some of the identities encompassed by the "Sanumá" category can be grouped with others in the "non-Sanumá" if the situation so requires. For example, re-

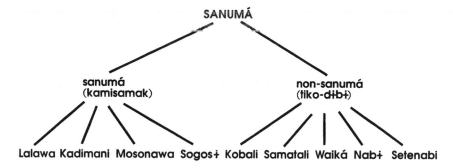

Fig. 10.2. Identity categories II

garding food taboos, raiding (Taylor 1977), or marriage practices, if what matters is to sort out the Sanumá proper (*kamisamak*, "we") from the rest, then all the other components of the more inclusive *Sanumá* category, that is, Kobali, Samatali, Waiká, as well as the "non-Sanumá" Nabɨ and Setenabi, become *tiko dɨbɨ*. We would thus have the arrangement shown in Figure 10.2.

Sanumá Relativism

The malleable character of the *tiko dɨbɨ* concept makes room for a certain amount of interchange between the various identity categories, because the terms are reducible to each other. Of course, this does not mean that a Maiongong or a white person may turn into a Sanumá the same way as a Lalawa is a Sanumá. But it is not impossible for Maiongong or whites to be embraced together as Sanumá. Granted this would be a rather remote possibility requiring very special contexts or circumstances; for instance, were a particular danger to affect Sanumá, Maiongong, and/or whites at the same moment in the same place (such as the imminent threat of an enemy attack) they might be brought together in terms of a common, albeit fleeting, identity. This was actually what happened when Ken and I were living in Kadimani and were pulled into the tumult provoked by a mild raid on the part of Sogosɨ villagers (see Chapter 2). But I must insist that the common identity created by that event was as ephemeral as the event itself.

The important thing is to emphasize that the logical operation by means of which it is possible to join together Sanumá speakers, other Yanomami, other indigenous groups, and whites indicates that these categories are not irreversibly antagonistic. Transitivity between terms is the major difference between Sanumá identity categories and the *Indian/white* contrast generated by interethnic contact. This distinction results from radically different historic, mental, and emotional processes.

It is worth comparing the Sanumá classification with that of the Carib-speaking Pemon in Venezuela (Thomas 1982:18). The latter distinguish several categories of "whites" as well as of "non-Pemon" Indians. They have a long history of contact and have learned to distinguish various types of whites. Their main criterion is language, but they also consider activities, such as that of the missionaries. Experience with otherness has in both cases led to a wider range of categories. By contrast, the response of whites to alterity, at least indigenous alterity, is to simplify differences: Sanumá, Maiongong, Pemon, or whoever, are trapped in one single pigeonhole—*Indians*.

When we compare the identity categories of the upper Auaris Sanumá with those of the Catrimani Yanomam (among whom I spent three and a half months in 1975), we notice a variation that reflects their different interethnic experiences. Whereas the Sanumá reserve the term Nabɨ for Maiongong and other indigenous groups,[2] the Yanomam use the same word to refer to any "foreigners," particularly whites. This distinction has to do with the historic experience that each group has had with other Indian groups.

For over a century, since the days of warfare and of geographic expansion, the Sanumá have had very intense contact with the Maiongong. To them, non-Sanumá people, they applied the term Nabɨ. Much later, in the 1950s and 1960s, white travelers and missionaries came into contact with the Sanumá. For these strangers the Sanumá reserved the term Setenabi, probably of Maiongong origin (Guss 1986:415 gives *Iaranavi* as the Yekuana word for "white"). The linguistic criterion, however, is of minor importance in the Sanumá distinction between these two categories. It is the "ways of life" that count. Whereas the *Nabɨ dɨbɨ* are regarded as arrogant, *cashiri* lovers, guilty of incest, makers of an elaborate technology, more familiar with whites (besides being nonspeakers of Sanumá), the *Setenabi dɨbɨ* stand out for their skin color, their clothes, their constant habit of writing, their religious worship (*deusɨmo*, "to make God"), their unpredictability, and, ultimately, for being the desired source of Western goods. Furthermore, whites speak no Sanumá, or talk like children when they do.

The Yanomam, in turn, use the term *Nabɨ bɨ* to refer to whites, their "others" par excellence, as they have no similar experience of close and long contact with other non-Yanomami indigenous people.

Having perceived the gap that separates *Indians* from *whites*, the Sanumá translated their dissimilarity into the distinction between Nabi and Setenabi. It is as if, by so doing, they foretold what was to come: the fateful opposition between *Indian* and *white*. Such opposition thrives not in their familiar intertribal medium, but in the context of social inequality traditionally unknown to the Sanumá, and incompatible with the subtlety with which their ancestors designed their concepts for cultural relativism.

The meaning underlying the Sanumá category of *tiko dibi* is neither inherently political, nor an expression of the will to power. The identities conveyed in the concepts of Kobali, Samatali, Nabi, and Setenabi are rather social and cultural, marking distance or proximity as well as features that are unique to each category. They do not in themselves refer to any distribution of power relations. Naturally, there may be an antagonistic, if not agonistic, bent in the relationships between several of these categories, but they depend on the balance of allegiances at each given moment, and may be easily rearranged. These relationships have no built-in quest for hegemony, with the notable exception of the missionaries. It is true that the Sanumá-Maiongong interaction has a component of inequality, at least in ideological terms — for the Maiongong the Sanumá are inferior and annoying; for the Sanumá the Maiongong are arrogant and demanding. But neither group tries to politically subjugate, nor ethnically negate the other. In contrast, the missionaries who operate among both groups, regardless of how enlightened and tolerant they may be as individuals, have as their ultimate goal to transform the *Indians* into Christians. In the Maiongong-Sanumá interaction, *tiko* is a legitimate, useful, and permanent category, whereas for the missionaries the Sanumá are "different" only until they accept the Gospel. When that time comes, so the missionaries hope, then Christian faith will have the power to erase differences, rendering *tiko* as an obsolete and unwanted notion.

The discussion of the Sanumá *tiko* concept points to the remarkable difference that seems to exist between indigenous and Western interethnic ideologies. Whereas the West is closed upon itself, regarding otherness as an undesirable condition, indigenous worldviews are typically open to real or virtual human alternatives. The openness of the Sanumá *tiko* on the social plane is manifested elsewhere as a trademark of indigenous experiences with alterity (Ramos 1980). Lévi-Strauss (1991) has demonstrated this point, this "openness to the Other," on the cosmological plane of myth analysis.

The Impact of the Indian/White Opposition

The category "other" is as deeply rooted in both individual and collective conscience as is the category "self." A change in the basic
meaning of these categories will necessarily trigger a profound mental
and emotional dis- or reorientation. This is precisely what happens
when indigenous peoples are forced to abide by the *Indian/white* political key imposed on them by the national societies that enclose
them. Naturally, concepts of this import are not empty slates. They
are socially created and shared; they have denotations and connotations which transcend whatever individual interpretations may be
elaborated. They slip into people's minds not only via cognition, but,
and primarily, through affect, contributing to forge a culturally recog-
nizable *Bildung*. A Sanumá person, not yet familiar with the Portuguese language, in meeting members of the national society, will
soon realize that the word *Indian* as uttered by Brazilians has a meaning that is not quite the exact counterpart of what he means by Setenabi, his term for *white*. This Sanumá, however, will need a great
deal of exposure to the effects of interethnic contact before he can
grasp all the nuances and implications of the *Indian/white* opposition,
particularly its political dimension. He will not fathom that he has entered into a relationship of domination from its weakest end until his
most basic rights begin to be systematically violated, and his essence
as a legitimate other denied him. It is then that the full weight of the
Indian/white antinomy dawns on him. He begins to understand that
the string of stereotypes hurled at him along with the word *Indian* is
only a cue to the somber and inescapable reality of contradictions that
interethnic politics engender and for which there is no possible resolution. He will learn to decode from *Indian* the array of adjectives such
as dangerous, dirty, treacherous, lazy, or irrational that he unknowingly carries around with him. A new stage is then set up for him
where he will have to face an essential impasse, an aporia with no
way out: in order to be accepted by the whites he will have to renounce his *Indian* condition. But, even if he attempts to do it, he will
never stop being *Indian* because the *whites* will never forgive him for
his Indianness. Obviously, this unbearable conundrum can only produce an overwhelming emotional and mental confusion, if not an outright existential collapse via alcoholism or any other type of escapism.
For there is nothing in this person's previous cultural experience that
prepares him to face such an insoluble problem. While before he
handled concepts of social classification that not only allowed but actually encouraged otherness as part of the "natural order of things,"

now he finds himself excluded from this order of things. Worse still, he finds out that there is no such order. Even this is destroyed by contact. He will have to build another anew.

Land and Language

Whether an indigenous group will be able to resist the pressures to give up its ethnicity is in large part determined by its success in retaining two things: its own language and its territory. A linguistically coherent community is much better equipped to keep its deepest categories of thought and values alive than a group that has lost its language and has no good command of the imposed national idiom. As we know, "mere words are not enough to understand a way of thinking" (Cardoso de Oliveira 1983:132). Even if an Indian group or individual can communicate in Portuguese, this does not mean that he can perceive all the subtleties and multilayered meanings of its concepts. He is left in a limbo of ignorance and bewilderment.

Similarly, there is no question about how important it is for indigenous societies to retain their territories. With their own adequately sized lands, they will have a chance to hold together and preserve their ethnic integrity. This is a necessary condition for the maintenance of their language which is the appropriate medium of expression for their own concepts and categories of perception and understanding. Language means tradition, the passing of knowledge and affect along the generations, which means continuity through time. Territory means coexistence, shared experience, which means continuity in space, which in turn means social and cultural coherence.

Both positive and negative examples can be found in Brazil. For instance, the Shavante and Kayapó, despite all the vicissitudes of half a century of intense contact with whites, have managed to preserve a considerable portion of their original territories and are two of the most successful indigenous societies in the country in maintaining and defending their ethnic identities. Part of their interethnic strategies is to intentionally use their own languages as a political vehicle to impress Brazilian authorities. By contrast, a number of indigenous groups in the Northeast of Brazil have lost their original languages altogether as one the consequences of loss of territory and disintegration of their traditional way of life. Interestingly enough, the Patasho in the state of Bahia have made a special effort to learn the language of the remotely related Mashacali in the state of Minas Gerais with the purpose of adopting it as their own. Portuguese, the only language they speak, is not regarded, with good reason, as the most appropriate means to communicate legitimate otherness to the society that engulfs and dominates them.

The *Indian/white* antinomy is now filtering into the Yanomami universe. They have not yet fully experienced, let alone understood, the political power of the whites' discourse of contact. How great will be the disruption that the imposition of the *Indian/white* dichotomy symbolizes will depend on whether or not the Yanomami succeed in retaining what is their due, guaranteed by Brazilian laws: their own land and the right to continue to be as they have been for time immemorial—a truly linguistic world of self-determined communities.

11
The Age of Gold and Misery

Undermining a Homeland

The largest indigenous people in the Americas to retain their traditional way of life, the Yanomami have been caught in the trap of fast and mindless development schemes, both governmental and private. The result has been social turmoil and a staggering death rate. Most of the troubles the Yanomami have faced have originated on the Brazilian side of the international border with Venezuela. Road building, agribusiness, and mining have brought the Yanomami in contact with Western-style expansion. Whereas in previous decades of this century only the outer villages had been affected by the activities of isolated groups of Brazil nut gatherers, jaguar skin hunters, and other small scale ventures, the 1970s and 1980s brought an avalanche of intruders that ultimately spilled over into the entire Yanomami area from its fringes to its innermost, still isolated recesses.[1]

In the early 1970s, the military government in Brazil turned its attention to Amazonia as a target for the implementation of megaprojects that characterized the decade. Considered to be a region segregated from the rest of Brazil and, therefore, escaping the control of central state power, Amazonia became the focus of huge development schemes as part of the National Integration Plan. A network of roads, of which the Transamazon is the most notorious example, was conceived to bring the region into direct contact with the more developed south, and with neighboring countries, such as Venezuela, Colombia, Peru, and Bolivia. The Perimetral Norte Highway, planned to run east-west above the equator, parallel to the Transamazon, was meant to reach the Colombian border and thus give Brazil access to the Pacific coast. Less than 250 kilometers were opened through thick jungle, of which more than 200 are in Yanomami land. Construction began in 1973 and was discontinued in early 1976 allegedly for lack of funds. Leading nowhere, the Perimetral Norte succeeded in deplet-

271

ing the southern portion of the Yanomami population at an unprecedented rate.

A Road to Nowhere

The opening up of the Perimetral brought hundreds of men and machines into the Ajarani and Catrimani River valleys which up until then had been largely isolated from the outside world. Where access had been difficult and very limited, after construction it became easy to travel deep into the Indian area. From the town of Caracaraí to the first Indian settlements was now less than an hour's drive.

A multitude of workers in poor health poured into a number of small Yanomami communities, offering food and drink, seducing the women, and spreading a plethora of contagious diseases. One year later, prostitution and begging were sorely visible. But worst of all was the rampant effect of microbe dissemination.

The Yawarib cluster of Yanomami communities was the first to be affected by the road. Their population was estimated to have been around a hundred. By August 1975, they were down to about eighty people some broken up into four tiny settlements, others living with another Yanomami subgroup, and still others living as nomads on the road. Not only were they killed by influenza, pneumonia, and measles, but they also had their social life seriously disrupted. Table 11.1 shows the disintegration of the Yawarib.[2]

Further west at km 130, another Yanomami community, Opikteri, was also severely affected by the invasion. In 1974 they had built a traditional-style roundhouse for 58 people, about an hour's walk to the south of the road, having abandoned their previous location 10 kilometers inland. Most of their young men spent that year's dry season hunting jaguars for a Brazilian adventurer, and thus they failed to make new gardens at the appropriate time. Their old fields, still yield-

Table 11.1 Yawarib losses

Settlement	Before the Road	After the road (August 1975)		
		Dead	Dispersed	Remaining
Nainashiuteri	26	7	—	19[a]
Arapishi	22	8	9	5
Castanheira	24	5	5	14
Kilometer 33	20	2	2	16
Kilometer 32	10	?	?	9
Total	102	22/23	16/17	63

[a] Yawarib living at Opikteri village

ing, were said to be too far away. It was easier to get food from the construction camps. Most of the Opikteri turned to a life of "roadside nomadism." They simply drifted from one work camp to another, covering distances of 50 kilometers or more. They developed the habit of standing side by side across the road, making a human barrier to force drivers to stop in order to get food, clothes, or just an idle ride to nowhere in particular.

Unlike the Yawarib, the Opikteri were spared the measles epidemic of mid-1974, for they had benefited from the vaccination program carried out by the Catholic missionaries at Catrimani before the road came. But they also had serious health problems. Besides infant malnutrition, the group as a whole had suffered at least one major influenza epidemic which escalated to seven cases of bronchitis and two of pneumonia. The latter were taken to a hospital in Boa Vista, along with a woman who had contracted tuberculosis.

I visited the three at the "Indian ward," an infirmary sponsored by the National Indian Foundation (FUNAI) within the main hospital, and was shocked. The "ward" was just a small room with three bare, filthy, and torn mattresses on the floor, a Yanomami lying on each. The tuberculosis patient was so thin that a nurse, obviously inexperienced, could not get the needle into her vein for the application of blood serum. The liquid was collecting under her skin, producing a big lump. The woman was too weak to sit up. Not knowing a word of Portuguese, she waited helplessly for someone to do something about it. The door was wide open, and a crowd of curious onlookers just stood there staring at the Indians. After a week of treatment, the three Opikteri patients were discharged and sent by FUNAI to the Catrimani mission, miles away from their villages further up the new road. The woman with tuberculosis continued part of her treatment at the mission. The last time I saw her was again in Boa Vista for a checkup. She had gained weight and seemed much better. She died shortly afterward.

Even among the protected Yanomami at the Catrimani mission the spread of infectious diseases was alarming. Catrimani is a Catholic mission established in 1965 and run by the Italian Order of the Consolata. The missionaries' concern with providing medical assistance was crucial to seeing the Catrimani Indians through repeated flu and measles epidemics. In the first fifteen months of road construction, the Catrimani villagers suffered fifteen flu epidemics. Four people were treated at the mission for pneumonia, ten for bronchitis, and twenty-five for common colds.

In June 1974, the first symptoms of measles appeared at Catrimani, caught from two infected road laborers. The entire village came down with it before vaccines were sent from town. There were two miscarriages but no one died of it then. Upriver, however, away from the immediate attention of the missionaries, at least seven people died.

Not only the massive presence of road workers, but the road itself became a health hazard to the Indians. It was easy, for instance, to take the sick to Boa Vista and back again. On one such occasion, after construction had been abandoned, a little boy caught measles while in hospital. Before the disease manifested itself, he was returned home to his community, one of four virtually uncontacted Yanomami villages on the headwaters of the Catrimani River. No less than 50 percent of their population perished in the epidemic that followed, including some of their most important headmen. Slowly, the survivors regrouped into one single community and moved closer to the road. They became the residents of the Demini village where FUNAI had set up an outpost using the buildings left by Camargo Corrêa, the construction company.

The road, while it lasted, also attracted the curiosity of town people who took to driving west on weekends to "have a look at the Indians." These tourists increased even more the chances of contamination with diseases that until then were unknown to the Indians. Indifference and ignorance on the part of the whites, who failed to have themselves vaccinated or simply to keep away when they had a cold, played a big part. As a consequence, they increased the incidence of diseases to which they, whites, were resistant, but which could be lethal to the Indians.

Millions of dollars were wasted on a road that fell short of its purpose and destination. All it achieved was the conquest of a portion of the Yanomami through death, social turmoil, and land expropriation.

Hand in hand with road construction was a vast colonization project for the Apiaú and Ajarani areas. A previous measles epidemic (1967–68) had killed an estimated hundred Yanomami who lived at Apiaú; eight years later, they were reduced to thirty survivors. With insufficient people to maintain an autonomous community, they abandoned Apiaú. Some of them joined the villages in the Mucajaí River valley, while others roamed what was left of the Ajarani communities. In 1992, when I flew from Boa Vista to Toototobi in the state of Amazonas, the pilot and I were bewildered by the hundreds of miles of menacing reddish-brown skies. What had been the homeland of the Apiaú Yanomami was going up in gigantic columns of smoke as regional settlers burned the forest for cattle ranching.

Similarly, the Yawarib of Ajarani, the first Yanomami to be hit by the Perimetral Norte Highway, after losing many of their relatives, also lost their land to Brazilian colonists. Now, consumed by alcohol, they live as a favor on the "properties" of these new settlers. Epidemics prove once again to be efficient instruments for creating empty lands for white occupation.

In 1975, while road construction was under way in Amazonia, the government launched the RADAMBRASIL Project, a region-wide mineral survey. Their reports on the Yanomami area described very poor soils, and recommended that over 40 percent of it in Roraima and 20 in Amazonas be declared as areas of permanent protection. But they also announced a wealth of minerals, all the way from radioactive materials to tin ore, gold, and diamonds. The Icomi mining company immediately invested in research in the uplands around Surucucus, but did not pursue exploration. That same year the first eight placer miners appeared in Surucucus searching for cassiterite. A year later they numbered five hundred. Serious conflicts with the Yanomami generated enough pressure from concerned public opinion abroad for the minister of the interior to order the miners expelled. They left behind a trail of venereal diseases and tuberculosis. But it would be another four years before the gold fever besieged the whole Yanomami territory.

Gold Fever

The price of gold increased seventeen fold from 1970–1980, before
peaking spectacularly at US$ 850 pre troy ounce in 1980.
                                        —Gordon MacMillan

It started in 1980, when five thousand *garimpeiros* rushed to the area known as Furo de Santa Rosa in the upper Uraricoera River valley. They occupied an area of twenty thousand hectares within Yanomami land inhabited by nearly two hundred Indians of the Shiriana (Yanam) subgroup. Six months after the invasion, malaria began to afflict the Shiriana, causing some deaths and generalized anemia. The invaders moved up the tributaries of the Uraricoera, coming close to the FUNAI outpost at Ericó. Their numbers began to decline in 1986 when most *garimpeiros* were driven out by the federal police, but the area was never totally cleared of invaders. A diffuse *garimpeiro* population coming from other parts of the country and from the evacuated Indian areas were stationed in towns such as Boa Vista awaiting the right moment to return to the Yanomami area. The great majority of these people were either underemployed or unemployed, small holders who had lost their lands, or urban workers who had lost their jobs. Victims of the country's grossly unequal land and income distribution, these migratory human masses have been pushed off into Indian lands by the shock waves created by underdevelopment (Monbiot 1991; MacMillan 1993).

In February 1985, a mining entrepreneur gathered sixty *garimpeiros* in Boa Vista, supplied them with automatic guns, dressed them in combat fatigues, and flew them up to Surucucus. Backed up by local politicians, they launched an assault on the FUNAI outpost and for five days held their position, until the federal police removed them and arrested their leader.

The following year, the air force enlarged a small three-hundred-meter-long airstrip in the hilly region of Couto de Magalhães, just east of Surucucus. It had served Protestant missionaries who paid occasional visits to the local Indians, and later the small outpost built by FUNAI. The military turned it into a wide, one-kilometer-long landing strip for no apparent reason, as they had no plans for that site, but only for Surucucus, Auaris, and Ericó. Declaring the strip to be a national security area, they had the Indian communal house within it destroyed and went away. The operation was part of a secretly drawn up plan by the military—the Northern Watershed Project (Projeto Calha Norte)—to occupy and develop the north frontier zone. The plan was to establish military outposts at strategic locations that would serve as bridgeheads for future settlement projects. To fill up the area with Brazilian colonists was their idea of inhibiting foreign craving for Amazonia.[3]

As the military took command of Surucucus, in August 1987, tens of thousands of *garimpeiros* poured into the now vast Couto de Magalhães airstrip which became known by the traditional Yanomami name, Paapiú. The national security area was soon filled with shacks covered in bright blue tarpaulin, typical of *garimpeiro* camps. From it the invaders radiated out to virtually the entire Yanomami territory. The gold rush had begun in earnest.

While masses of *garimpeiros* continued to enter the area unbridled, medical doctors, Catholic missionaries, anthropologists, and other researchers were expelled by the military and by FUNAI, at that time acting as an executive arm of the former. For more than two years there were no accurate reports of what was happening to the Yanomami. All we knew was that devastating malaria epidemics were killing the Indians en masse, and malnutrition was rampant. The Yanomami were totally deprived of health care precisely when they most needed it. Some journalists managed to evade surveillance, went into severely struck areas, and brought back horrifying pictures. The macabre spectacle of Yanomami decimation then began. Scenes of extreme malnutrition filled newspapers and the TV screen—cachectic men, women, and children, bearing a distressing similarity to the cadaverous images of the worst famines in Africa; corpses of Yanomami men abandoned in jungle trails; or arrogant and patronizing *garimpeiros* handing over bags of rice and canned food to begging women and children while showing their scorn by comparing them to monkeys.

In two years an estimated 23 percent of Yanomami had been killed by malaria or by *garimpeiro* bullets. By June 1989 the flood of bad news from the area had so swelled that a group of congressmen organized an inspection trip to Paapiú, still the center of *garimpeiro* dispersal. They were staggered by the chaotic scene produced by a continuous stream of aircraft coming and going, with countless *garimpeiros* drifting along the muddy airstrip, small groups of prostitutes sitting on gigantic hoses, Yanomami of all ages roaming around, all of it under the unbearable noise of engines that stopped only after sunset. In the meantime, the Yanomami communal house, rebuilt a short distance off the airstrip, sheltered a dismayed community of people still mourning their dead while others withered away with malaria and its attendant anemia. Under the deafening racket of aircraft, we heard from the Indians reports about huge muddy craters that had been carved out of garden plots and enormous chunks of forest, bisecting trails between villages, and contaminating streams, thus killing the fish and causing a shortage of drinking water. The infernal noise of machinery scared game away, aggravating even more the intense food crisis that debilitated the Yanomami. Their accounts also made it amply clear that the government, represented by FUNAI, was there not to protect the Indians, but to make sure these would not get in the way of the gold orgy. FUNAI employees and members of the military police also stationed at Paapiú were said to deal in gold acquired as bribes from *garimpo* owners.

From then on, several steps were taken to curb the invasion and its catastrophic impact on the Yanomami. In Brasilia, the attorney general's office (Procuradoria Geral de República) filed an appeal to have the 9.5 million hectares of Yanomami territory officially recognized.[4] In October, a federal judge ordered the executive to interdict that area and remove from it all non-Indians who were there illegally.

The reaction to the judge's order was as quick as it was bold. *Garimpeiro* bosses, owners of airplanes, of stores, and others involved in gold traffic immediately took dozens of sick Indians out of the area and dumped them in Boa Vista hospitals and in the Casa do Indio, a sort of hostel run by FUNAI to accommodate Indians who came to

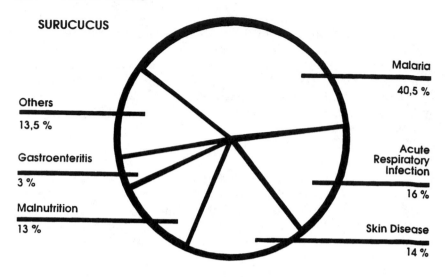

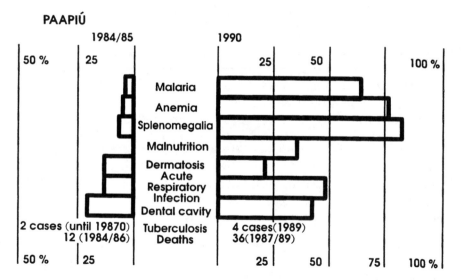

Fig. 11.1 Incidence of diseases at Surucucus and Paapiú after 1987. *Source:* Ação pela Cidadania 1990:31.

town for medical treatment or just on a visit. The invaders were thus transferring to FUNAI and the government the accusatory attention they had been getting from public opinion. In November, more than two hundred Yanomami crammed the poorly run Casa do Indio, virtually without medical assistance, hungry due to insufficient food, impotently watching their children die of malaria and starvation.

But in this case as in many others, dialectics did its work, for out of sickness and death came the prospect of remedy. The appalling conditions to which the Yanomami were subjected attracted to Boa Vista an unprecedented number of foreign and Brazilian journalists. They stayed in town long enough to document the arrival of hordes of *garimpeiros* who were being removed from the Indian area. Boa Vista was virtually under siege. Hair-raising sequences of angry masses of squalid men defying the chief of the federal police, or setting fire to the bishop's garden, saturated the news hours of national TV networks. The country and the world were shocked.

Brazilian government responded to the intense pressure from abroad, including the UN and the OAS, by creating a long-overdue emergency health program to cope with the Yanomami problem that was getting out of hand. All medical doctors and anthropologists who had been banned from the area were urged to join the effort. The first reliable figures about the spread of diseases were collected in early 1990. The charts in Figure 11.1 give an idea of the proportion of this epidemiological calamity.

The 1970s tragedy of the four upper Catrimani communities which, having lost half of their people in a measles epidemic, were regrouped in one single village, has been repeated manyfold in the central part of Yanomami territory. Now the scourge was no longer measles, but malaria of the worst kind, *Plasmodium falciparum*. In the regions of Paapiú and Surucucus, where malaria had been virtually absent, some communities had an incidence as high as 91 percent, most of it *falciparum*. "In Paapiú, 43 percent of the individuals on record lost from one to seven close relatives (parents, children, or siblings) between 1987 and 1989" (Ação pela Cidadania 1990:32). Entire communities were devastated by continuous waves of malaria epidemics, and the few survivors were compelled to join distant relatives, often in socially strained conditions, as in the following case.

> The former Moshala people, now Thireitheri, who in early 1990 inhabited six communities, were reduced to 127 survivors; after years of enmity with the Homoshitheri, they are trying to establish alliances with them by having their widows marry Homoshi men, and finding families to take care of their orphans—70 percent of their children lost either father or mother. (Fundação Nacional de Saúde 1990:69)

Between 1987 and 1990, 13 percent of the children in the regions of Paapiú and Surucucus lost either their father, mother, or both. Orphaned Yanomami children began to appear in Boa Vista, as FUNAI employees, among others, took them as foster children. This practice, apparently humanitarian, occurs in the context of a great deal of prejudice on the part of the regional population toward the Indians. It is very common for Macushi children, for instance, to be raised by white families as servants. On the other hand, the larger the number of Yanomami children taken away, the harder it will be for the decimated communities, and for the Yanomami as a whole, to recover their demographic balance.

Malaria epidemics are not the only Yanomami killers. From the onset of the gold rush, there have been repeated conflicts between Indians and miners with casualties on both sides, but with a lot more Yanomami deaths. Numerous clashes occurred, not including those that went unreported or uninvestigated. Three are well-known: at Paapiú, at Olomai, and at Hashimu, totaling twenty-two Indians killed.

The Paapiú killings occurred when the first invaders arrived at the airstrip enlarged by the air force. When the Indians reacted negatively, the miners murdered four of the local men, including an important leader, cut up the bodies, and left them visible to intimidate the rest of the community. There was no more resistance until 1992 when one Indian and several *garimpeiros* were killed after a squabble that escalated into shooting.

In September 1990, Lourenço (of Chapter 9), the Maiongong headman at Olomai on the Auaris River, was killed at point-blank range by a group of five *garimpeiros*. In the shootout that followed, his youngest son was fatally wounded, a third Indian (Zeca of Chapter 3) was hit with a volley of lead pellets, and three *garimpeiros* were killed.

Nearly three years later, sixteen Hashimu villagers of the upper Orinoco valley in Venezuela were murdered by a group of heavily armed Brazilian *garimpeiros*. The brutality of the killings shocked the world. The victims, mostly children, were beheaded and pierced through with knives. The case was defined as genocide, and both Brazil and Venezuela joined efforts to punish the criminals. This event put the Yanomami back onto the media's front pages; Boa Vista was again swarming with journalists, who greatly contributed to the garbled renditions of the case in the absence of reliable reports before the sequence of events was minutely reconstructed by the survivors of the massacre. It also had far-reaching repercussions in the political management of the indigenous issue in Brazil. The president of FUNAI was fired for having exaggerated the number of dead at Hashimu, and the Ministry of Amazonia and the Environment was created in response to a new flare of international pressure regarding the protection of the region and its inhabitants.

The cause of all these deaths was basically the same: accumulated conflicts over badly managed trading arrangements between Indians and miners. This pattern is well summarized by Bruce Albert.

When gold miners first enter the Yanomami area, they arrive in small groups. Since they are few in number, they feel endangered by the more numerous Indians and try to buy their goodwill through the liberal distribution of food and goods. For their part, the Indians have little or no experience with Whites and consider this attitude to be a demonstration of generosity that they would expect from any group that wishes to establish bonds of neighborly alliance. At this early stage of cultural misunderstanding, the Indians do not yet feel the health and ecological impact of the mining activities. . . . As the number of gold miners increases, it is no longer necessary to maintain the initial generosity. The Indians turn from being a threat to being an annoyance with their incessant demands for the goods that they are accustomed to receiving. The gold miners get irritated and try to shoo them away with false promises of future presents and with impatient or aggressive behavior.

At this stage of the contact, the Indians begin to feel the rapid deterioration of their health and means of subsistence caused by gold mining. The rivers are polluted, hunting game is scared away by the noisy machinery, and many Indians die in constant epidemics of malaria, flu, etc., all of which tends to destroy the economic and social fabric of their communities. Due to this situation, the Indians come to see the food and goods given by the miners as a vital and indisputable compensation for the destruction they have caused. When this is refused, a feeling of explicit hostility wells up within them. Thus they arrive at a deadlock: the Indians become dependent upon the prospectors just when the latter no longer need to buy the former's goodwill. This contradiction is at the root of all the conflicts between Yanomami and gold miners. From there, the possibility of minor incidents degenerating into open violence increases. And since the disparity in force between the prospectors and the Indians is enormous, the scales always tip against the Yanomami. This type of situation clearly shows the extent to which the logic of gold mining repels the participation of the Indians and even their mere presence. Because they use mechanized techniques to extract gold, the miners have no interest in the Indians as a labor force or anything else. From the miners' point of view, they are, at best, a nuisance, and at worst, a threat to their safety. If gifts and promises do not get rid of them, then the solution is to intimidate or even exterminate them. (Albert 1993; translated by Paul Little)

In the last fifteen years, the Yanomami have gone from being an exotic and fierce people to becoming a symbol of indigenous peoples on the verge of extinction. Catapulted into the mass media circuit, they have unknowingly played the role of political badge in campaigns for human rights and environmental preservation. "As this century comes to a close, Brazil and the world follow on newspapers and television the genocide of one of the largest indigenous people of the Amazon forest" (CEDI 1991:172).

BOX 1: The Massacre of the Yanomami of Hashimu

. . . On June 15, the situation came to a head and led to a quick succession of tragic events. A group of six Hashimu youths arrive at a different storehouse in the area to ask for food, trade goods and, perhaps, to take back their shotgun, as was suggested to them by their elders. They are only given a little food and a scrap of paper with a note to be delivered to another storehouse upriver, with the promise that they will be given more things there.

At the next storehouse, they find a group of miners playing dominoes. They are received by the cook who reads the piece of paper, throws it into the fire, and harshly sends them away with a few items of food and clothing. The slip of paper reads: "Have fun with these suckers." Piqued by this message and encouraged by the cook, the miners even think of killing the six youths right there and then, but give up, fearing that other Indians might be hiding nearby. They decide to attack them along the trail that leads back to the Indians' village.

After walking for less than an hour, the Yanomami stop to eat the food they received. As they eat, six armed miners arrive and invite them to go hunting for tapir and then visit a nearby storehouse. The Indians mistrust the invitation and refuse at first, but finally accept upon the miners' insistence. Miners and Indians alternating, they all walk single file along the trail, led by a Yanomami.

Shortly afterward, the last Yanomami leaves the trail to defecate, gives the Indians' only shotgun to another Yanomami, and tells the others to go on ahead. But the miners stand still. Suddenly, one of them grabs the arm of the Indian with the gun and shoots him at point-blank range in the stomach with a sawed off two-barrel shotgun. Three other Indians are shot at by the other miners. One of the assassins later tells a friend that one of the boys knelt down with his hands over his face, trying to escape death, and begged: "Miner, my friend!" He was summarily executed with a shot in the head.

Upon hearing the shots, the Yanomami who was in the bush jumps into the Orinoco River nearby and escapes. The eighteen-year-old who led the file also tries to run away, but is surrounded by three miners who, standing in a triangle, shoot at him as if they were taking target practice. Thanks to his agility and to the thickness of the jungle, he dodges the first two shots, but is wounded by the third. As the miners reload their guns, he gets away and also throws himself in the Orinoco. Still stunned by his wounds, he tries to hide by submerging himself up to his nose. From this position, he sees the miners bury the three victims (the body of the fourth was never found; mortally wounded, he probably fell into the river and was swept away by the current). While searching for the bodies, one of the miners turns and walks toward the river where he sees the hidden boy; he goes back to get his gun, but the youth manages to escape.

Meanwhile, the other survivor arrives at the Hashimu community with news of the murders. Two days later, he returns with a group of men and women to the locale where their relatives were shot. Along the way they run into the injured boy who tells them what he saw, including the spot where the bodies were buried (this custom is considered by the Yanomami to profane the dead). They dig up the three corpses, look in vain for the fourth, and take the remains to be cremated at a place an hour-and-a-half walk into the forest. They collect the charred bones needed to officiate their funeral rites and return home.

During the following days, they organize a ritual hunt which precedes the ceremony of preparation of the mortuary ashes (the bones are crushed and stored in gourds sealed with beeswax). After the hunt, (which lasts for a week to ten days), three allied villages are invited to come: Homoshi, Makayu, and Toumahi. Upon finishing the preparation of the ashes, a group of warriors get together to go on the traditional raid of vengeance against the murderers. It should be emphasized that Yanomami tradition demands that violent deaths be avenged in raids where the targets are men, preferably those who committed the previous murders. Women and children are never killed.

On July 26, after a two-day walk, the war party camps on the outskirts of the mining encampment. At ten o'clock the following morning, under a steady rain, they come close to the kitchen of a storehouse where two miners are chatting around the fire. One of the Yanomami slips away and from behind a tree fires his gun at the men. One of the miners is struck in the head and is killed instantly; the other escapes, but is wounded in the side and buttocks. The warriors continue their revenge by splitting open the skull of the dead man with an axe, shooting arrows into his body, and, before fleeing, grabbing everything in the storehouse, including shells and the dead miner's shotgun.

Preparing for the Attack

The Indian attack infuriates the miners. They bury the body in the kitchen, abandon the storehouse, and carry the wounded man to an airstrip two days' walk away. Then they begin to plan their retaliation. Two meetings are held where they decide once and for all to put an end to the problems with the Indians, by killing all of the inhabitants of the two Hashimu communal houses, a total of eighty-five people. They recruit men from all around and gather arms and ten boxes of shells. The entire operation is sponsored, if not commissioned, by the four main owners of prospecting rafts in the region. These four men, some of whom are well-known figures in the state of Roraima, are João Neto, rural landowner, his brother-in-law Chico Ceará; Eliezio, also the owner of a supply store; and Pedro Prancheta, the author of the note. They free their workers, supply them with ammunition and guns, and host their preparatory meetings for the attack. Fifteen heavily armed miners (with 12- and 20-gauge shotguns, .38 caliber revolvers, machetes, and knives) set out on the trail to carry out their plan. Among them are several of the men who participated in the murder of the Hashimu youths, along with four gunslingers contracted to guarantee the safety of the owners.

Meanwhile, the inhabitants of Hashimu leave their houses and camp for five days in the jungle at a safe distance from the community to guard against any counterattack by the miners. Since they are expecting an invitation from the community of Makayu for a celebration, they head in the direction of this village. On the way there they spend the night in their own houses. The next morning, they continue their trip and stop at an old garden between Hashimu and Makayu. As they wait there for a formal invitation brought by messengers from their hosts, as is the custom, three young warriors go back to the miners' encampment to attack them once again because they are dissatisfied with their previous attempt at revenge. The leader of this party, the brother of the missing dead youth, has particular reason to avenge his brother's death, precisely because his body was never found, thus precluding a proper funeral. They arrive at the edge of a gold digging and, protected by the noise of the machinery, slip up and shoot at one of the miners working there. The man, who senses the Indians' presence at the instant of the shooting, protects his head, and is wounded in the arm that served as his shield. The three youths escape and join their Hashimu relatives at the old garden where they are camped.

This attack occurs while the fifteen miners are en route to the Hashimu community, a two-day walk from their encampment. The Indian youths and the miners miss each other on the trail only because on war expeditions the Yanomami avoid trails and hike through the dense brush. Upon arriving at Hashimu, the miners find the houses empty. They look around, find the trail that leads to the old garden, and set out in search of the Indians.

On the previous day at the old garden, the Hashimu people received the formal invitation from Makayu messengers. Since they are at war with the miners, they decide to shorten that visit to a minimum. Only men and a few women without children will accompany the messengers to the community, leaving at the garden the women with children, along with three older men. These people are left behind for two reasons: they do not walk as fast as the others, and women and children are never attacked in war raids. The three young warriors who attacked the miners also stay behind to rest.

The Massacre

In the morning of the following day, most women in the camp go out to collect wild fruit far away from the old garden. They take along nearly all the children; the old leader of one of the communal houses also accompanies them. Nineteen people stay at the camp, including the three warriors who are still resting.

A few hours later, around midday, the miners arrive at the camp and close it off on one side. Children play, women chop firewood, and the others rest in their hammocks. One miner fires a shot and the others begin the shooting, as they advance toward their victims. In the middle of the hail of fire, the three warriors, an older man, a middle-aged woman, two six- or seven-year old children, and a girl of about ten years of age manage to escape thanks to the complex distribution of the shelters and the thickness of the underbrush typical of old gardens. The two small children and one of the warriors are wounded by buckshot in their face, neck, arms, and sides; the older girl receives a serious wound in the head from which she later dies. From their hiding place, the Indians who escaped continue to hear cries muffled by the sound of gunshots. After a few very long minutes, the miners stop shooting and enter the shelters in order to finish off anyone still living. Machete blows kill not only the injured but also the few who have not been hit; they mutilate and dismember the bodies that are already riddled with buckshot and bullets.

In all, twelve people are killed: an old man and two elderly women; a young woman who was a visitor from the community of Homoshi; three adolescent girls; two baby girls, one and three years old; and three boys between six and eight years of age. Three of these children were orphans of parents who had died of malaria. The woman from Homoshi, of around eighteen years of age, is first shot from a distance of less than ten meters and then again from a distance of two meters. A blind, elderly woman is kicked to death, while a baby lying in a hammock is wrapped in a cloth and pierced through with a knife.

The miners realize they have not exterminated all of the people of Hashimu. Thus, as a preventive measure, they take away the two shotguns that were in the shelters, shoot off a flare to dissuade anyone from following them, and return to the empty communal houses where they spend the night. The next day they pile up the Indians' household gear left behind and fire volleys of gunshot into them. Then they set fire to both houses and quickly head back to their mining sites. Several weeks later, they hear on National Radio the news of the massacre. They hike for two or three days to the landing strip of Raimundo Nenê. They threaten to kill anyone who informs on them, indicating that any miners who talk "will receive the same treatment that the Indians did." They fly to Boa Vista, the capital of Roraima, and from there most of them scatter all over the country.

(—Excerpts from the report by Bruce Albert, translated from Portuguese by Paul Little)

The Chronicle of a Demarcation Postponed

The lands traditionally occupied by the Indians are designated for their permanent possession where they have the exclusive right of usufruct to the resources found in the soil, in rivers and in lakes.
   —Brazilian Constitution of 1988, chapter VIII, article 231, paragraph 2

From 1968 to 1991, no less than fifteen proposals for the demarcation of Yanomami lands were drawn up by different groups and organizations. Most of these proposals defended the need to have a large, continuous area, encompassing as many communities as possible, that would meet the Indians' material and cultural needs in the present and in the future. In contrast, two of the governmental proposals, one by FUNAI in 1977, the other by the National Security Council over a decade later, devised a series of small, separate areas with corridors between them open to white occupation. Both these attempts to cut up the territory into what was sarcastically called "the Yanomami archipelago" came after the RADAMBRASIL survey had revealed that desirable minerals were buried in the Guiana Shield, homeland of the Yanomami.

In response to the 1977 FUNAI attempt to chop up the Indians' land into twenty-one small pockets, a group of people concerned with the survival of the Yanomami, still reeling from the impact of the decimation caused by the foundered Perimetral Norte Highway, created in 1978 the Committee for the Creation of the Yanomami Park (CCPY), a nongovernmental organization that immediately launched a major campaign in Brazil and abroad against the attempt to expropriate the Indian lands. As an alternative, the committee offered proposal no. 12, an area of 6.5 million hectares, based on the deficient survey carried out by FUNAI in 1977, according to which the Yanomami population in Brazil amounted to less than 8.5 thousand (IWGIA 1979:99–170). The campaign progressed and created unprecedented repercussions; the twenty-one-island project was shelved.

During the first Brazilian civil government since 1964, the military bargained for their maintenance of power in Amazonia. Soon after Vice-President Sarney took office as president in April 1985, information that the National Security Council was secretly preparing the Calha Norte Project was leaked to nongovernmental organizations. A year later, it was implemented. One of its aims was to "discipline" the problem of Indian lands in the 150-kilometer-wide strip of international frontier between Brazil and its northern neighbors. This military notion of discipline materialized as a single mold through which all Indian lands in the region would be reduced to small parcels separated from each other by areas that would then be opened to development. Starting at the northwest end of the Brazilian Amazon, the military cookie cutter was to slash its way through the whole area as far as the Atlantic seashore. The Yanomami were right in the line of fire.

In 1987–88, the military organized a work group ostensibly under the leadership of FUNAI, to carry out another survey of the Yanomami area. They concluded that their population in Brazil was nearly ten thousand people, most of them in the state of Roraima. But, against the recommendation of the anthropologists who participated in the work group, the military rejected the idea of a continuous area. Instead, they proposed nineteen separate islands, thus reducing to a mere 30 percent (2.5 million hectares) the area that only three years before had been recognized by FUNAI as Yanomami. Indeed, in 1985, FUNAI, with CCPY's technical aid, presented a proposal for the demarcation of 9.5 million hectares, but that was before it was sucked into the Calha Norte Project as its executive branch for indigenous affairs.[5]

The nineteen-area proposal was about to be legalized when the Yanomami health problems resulting from the gold rush hit the mass media, thus creating a national and international scandal. By that time the new constitution had been ratified, and the rights of indigenous peoples to the land they effectively occupy were guaranteed. Even so, and in defiance of the 1989 judicial order to interdict the Yanomami area and to evict the invaders, President Sarney signed decrees creating three *garimpeiro* reserves inside the 9.5 million hectares. This was done in February 1990, on the eve of the inauguration of President-Elect Fernando Collor.

Sarney's initiative yielded to lobbying pressure of those interested in maintaining their lucrative dividends from gold mining. The beneficiaries of Sarney's protective measure were neither the masses of dispossessed menial workers who slaved away at the *garimpos*, nor the state economy. Nearly 90 percent of the gold extracted from Yanomami lands had been smuggled out of the country in connection with drug trafficking. (A telling report broadcast in 1989 by the largest TV network in Brazil traced the gold route from the huge craters opened in Paapiú, Homoshi, and other Yanomami sites all the way to Israel and the United States, after a laundering operation in Montevideo, the capital of a country that produces no gold at all).

A few days after his inauguration, President Collor staged a visit to Surucucus and, right then and there, ordered the federal police to remove the *garimpeiros*, confiscate airplanes, empty out fuel drums to immobilize machinery, and blow up clandestine airstrips. The forty-five thousand placer miners in the area were reduced to about two thousand, according to FUNAI. But once the pyrotechnical effect of all this subsided, the miners quietly returned, quickly filled up the holes made in the landing strips by dynamite, and resumed their operations. By mid-1992, they were up to some eleven thousand. Once again the "Operation Free Jungle," which had feebly begun after the 1989 judicial order, was reactivated, and in September 1993 FUNAI estimated that only about six hundred *garimpeiros* were still in Yanomami lands, mostly on the Venezuelan side of the border.

During the Collor administration (cut short by his impeachment in October 1992), the Calha Norte Project lost much of its impetus, but was by no means terminated. In fact, the military have secured funds to continue the construction of outposts on the frontier, complete with housing for servicemen and their families, schools, banks, and supply stores.

As planners of the cookie-cutter model, the military have always opposed the designation of a large, continuous area for the Yanomami. But the pressure they put on Collor had much less influence on him than the urgency generated by international organisms, especially the UN and the organizers of the Rio-92 Earth Summit. On November 15, 1991, despite some belated moves to avert it, the decree of demarcation was finally signed after nearly a quarter of a century of frustrated attempts.

The Field Revisited

1968–1970. Americans conquered the moon, the undeclared war in Southeast Asia continued to consume thousands of lives, the military were wreaking havoc with Brazilian citizenry, but in Auaris my research went on reaping the benefits of an ethnographic heaven. Data poured into diaries and notebooks amidst beautiful meadows, spectacular hills, cozy streams, fantastic tropical storms, and a tranquil routine broken only by frequent exciting episodes that are part and parcel of Sanumá sociality.

This beatific scenario was to be lovingly cherished in my memory, for it is no longer there. Apart from the short period, late 1990, of a sentimental reencounter with the Sanumá after a seventeen-year absence, my returns to the field were beset by the misery of entire Sanumá communities consumed with malaria and its disruptive effects.

November of 1990 marked my return to Auaris. After three years of frustrated requests to FUNAI for authorization to go back to the field as a researcher, I finally received it and went to Roraima for a couple of months. I planned to go down to Olomai and reconstruct the incidents that led to Lourenço's death. While still in Boa Vista, I met three men who had been directly involved in the shooting at Olomai—a son and a son-in-law of Lourenço's who were brought to town to testify to the federal police, and Zeca who was being treated for shotgun wounds. We were all on the same flight back to Auaris.

At the old Mosonawa community adjacent to the mission there were still visible signs of a *sabonomo*, the ceremony in honor of the dead, for a young man who had died of snakebite a few months before. Lourenço's widow, daughters, and their families were all there. Having been told their version of the tragedy, I remained in Auaris to

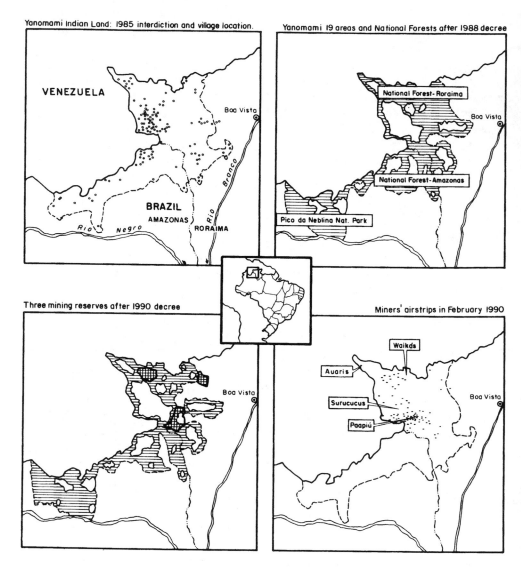

Map 4. Yanomami area under siege. *Source:* Ação pela Cidadania 1990:16.

update censuses and collect other versions of the killings at Olomai
(Ramos 1991).

A quick look at the federal police files on the case revealed that
Lourenço and his people had been caught in the cross fire between
two rival *garimpeiro* gangs. Lourenço had been charging for landing

fees. As time went by and the *garimpeiros* became more confident that the Indians would not bother them, they neglected to make the payments as arranged. Lourenço complained. One of the gangs, pretending to be on his side, advised Lourenço to confiscate the other gang's backpacks the next time they came to the airstrip. He did so. As it turned out, one of the backpacks had over two kilos of gold. A few days later, five men came at the break of dawn; four hid behind a clump of weeds, while the fifth called out to Lourenço, shook his hand in greeting, and discharged three bullets into his head and chest. Lourenço died on the spot. Lourenço's youngest son was shot (he died a few hours later at the Auaris mission). Zeca, who was there on a visit, was also wounded, and three *garimpeiros* were killed. The police files indicate that one gang used Lourenço's credulity to get the other involved in serious trouble.

Back in Auaris, Zeca's condition worsened. During most of the five weeks of my stay in the village, he lay in his hammock, subdued at the best of times, in agony at other times, provoking constant bursts of wailing on the part of his family, and occasionally of the entire community. The dozens of lead pellets lodged in his head and body rendered him doomed in the eyes of his fellow villagers and in his own eyes, at least when the pain increased and, once again, he cried for painkillers.

In the three years of contact with *garimpeiros*, the Sanumá of the upper Auaris had learned to extract gold by rudimentary means. While I was there from November 1990 to January 1991, several men were away in Venezuela working in a *garimpo* known as Shimara Woche. That was also the destination of a dozen or so *garimpeiros* who used the Auaris airstrip as their gathering point.

There had been a few cases of malaria that were uneventfully treated by the nurse at Auaris, but several deaths in Sanumá villages in Venezuela were reported to the missionaries. In February 1991, however, an outbreak of malaria spread through the whole Sanumá area, perhaps most severely on the Brazilian side. Five people died at Olomai, including Lourenço's widow, his youngest pregnant daughter and her husband, and two children of his youngest son, killed in the September shooting.

By that time the National Health Foundation had been created and, within it, the Yanomami Health District, designed to provide permanent health care to the Indians. One of the most active and dedicated doctors engaged in the fight against malaria among the Yanomami, Ivone Menegola, called me to accompany her medical team to Olomai as interpreter and cultural go-between. After a long wait at

Surucucus, the FUNAI and military base in the heart of Yanomami territory, we were taken to the airstrip at Olomai by an air force "Squirrel" helicopter. The once-thriving community that Lourenço had originally founded near the mission at Auaris (the Colony), and later relocated downriver near the mouth of the Olomai stream, was deserted, the abandoned houses already collapsing, and the airstrip overgrown and blocked up with tree trunks. The survivors were precariously camped on the wedge of land that divides the Auaris from the Olomai, about five kilometers upstream from the airstrip. We waited for them to meet us and take us to the camp by canoe. As she came up the riverside landing, one of Lourenço's daughters (Cici of Chapter 9) cried to me that her people had died, and that at the camp people were ill. Her husband (Edu of Chapter 9), who had flown with me from Boa Vista, had malaria stamped on his face. During the three days we stayed at Olomai, 103 slides were examined, corresponding to the total population of three clusters of houses along the lower Olomai. The result was 25 percent malaria positive (42 percent *falciparum*, 50 percent *vivax*, and 8 percent mixed). We heard that in the community of Kodaimadiu, a tributary of the middle Auaris, three people had died of malaria a few days before our arrival, and the others were very ill. We were also told that at Shikoi, a village cluster of about 150 people, the health situation was equally serious. But we had to wait at Olomai for the return of the helicopter to take us to the mission at Auaris. As our team was reduced to a minimum—one doctor, one microscope technician, and one anthropologist—there was no way to fill the demand that came from all around. And so, through our whole stay in Sanumá country, we continued to hear about more deaths at Kodaimadiu and other places. We left Olomai with the unsettling sense that more cases of malaria would appear in our absence, as the disease had not run its full course.

We landed at the mission on March 18 and headed for the thatched house the Sanumá had built for me four months before. As we chatted with the helicopter crew, Jorge, now a plump mature man, still intent on headmanship, called me over to a neighboring house where a group of men were gathered. In a solemn atmosphere, Jorge spoke to me in the formal tone of the intercommunity ceremonial speech. He asked me to mediate a request they wanted to put to the air force crew: to rescue the body of a young man from the Kadimani village who had died and been buried at Waikás, a Maiongong village and *garimpo* site on the Uraricoera River. They needed the body in order to give it a proper funeral. Until that happened, his

Table 11.2. Malaria in Auaris

| | March 18 April 15, 1991 | | | | |
	Falciparum	Vivax	Both	Total	Population
Sanumá	42	22	7	71	237
	59%	31%	10%	30%	
Maiongong	34	16	1	51	147
	67%	31%	2%	35%	

relatives would be tormented with the need to appease his specter, which can be done only with cremation and manifestations of grief.

I felt extremely touched by the vote of confidence I was being given and did my best not to disappoint them. It was not the air force crew but the missionary pilot who, some ten days later on one of his rounds through the mission stations in Yanomami country, agreed to take the deceased boy's father and a Maiongong man who knew where the body had been buried. The single-engine Cessna brought the father back to Auaris carrying the remains of his son reduced to a small bundle wrapped in a piece of cloth.

Work on collecting blood samples began the day after we arrived at Auaris. The missionaries had been away since early February, in spite of the epidemic that killed people in Olomai. During the next thirty days, malaria cases appeared continuously among the 147 Maiongong and the 237 Sanumá around the mission. Every day new statistics had to be compiled as positive slides piled up. The small but constant occurrence of new cases demonstrated to us two things: the necessity to carry out an active search in the whole population, whether or not there were visible symptoms, and the need for the medical teams to remain in the same place for the time it takes the disease to spread through all its residents. Table 11.2 shows the incidence of malaria in both groups.

One week after we arrived at the mission, messengers from Kadimani brought news about the serious condition of their relatives. They were spread out at different summer camps, as is the custom in the dry season. Some were near the *garimpo* site at Shimara Woche, others were on the other side of the Kisinabi Mountain on the border with Venezuela, and others around old fields closer to the mission. We gave the messengers instructions to open a clearing for helicopter landing where the very sick were camped, and called Surucucus on the radio for help. Days went by before it came. With Indian guides on board, they searched for the camps, but could find no one. Again the messengers came with worse reports. Two girls had died, and the others were extremely thin and had no strength to walk all the way to the mission. But then, on March 27 in the afternoon, the first group from Kadimani reached our house. It was a desolate Indian file of emaciated people, many in the last stages of undernourishment, leaning over sticks, or being carried on the backs of the stronger. They dragged themselves to my house and collapsed on the dirt floor, many of them burning with fevers of over 100 degrees. More of them kept coming the next days.

The week that followed was consumed by a frenzied rhythm of taking blood samples, recording information such as approximate age, height, and weight, giving medicine for fever, for malaria, and for anemia, and the worst part, finding food from our meager resources and those of the local Auaris residents to feed 133 hungry people. I told them to come for help any time of the day and night, so many times I was awakened by someone pulling on my hammock strings, telling me her baby had a high fever, or that she and her child were hungry, could I give them some banana or cassava bread. My mind simply refused to accept that those were the same lively people with whom I had lived for months on end and from whom I had learned so much. The headman's senior wife, my old friend who had spent countless hours sitting by my side teaching me Sanumá culture, was scrawny beyond recognition. Little seven-year-old Alusoma, her naked body reduced to bones, shaven head, and bulging, frightened eyes on a face disfigured by malnutrition, arrived half dead. With no strength left in her fleshless limbs, she had to be carried. Her mouth exuded a foul odor, and she was past wanting food. She had *falciparum* in a very advanced stage. It was agony to force her to take the bitter malaria pills and to eat tiny portions of food while she weakly cried in protest.

We then decided to order food from Boa Vista. Fifty-kilo sacks of manioc flour and rice, frozen chicken and fish, cans of sardines, and cans of milk to last at least a week were flown in, but were consumed in just a few days. Many other food supplies were ordered during the weeks the Kadimani stayed at the mission. The ordeal of dispensing manioc flour is engraved in my mind as the epitome of dispair. With my head nearly buried inside the sack, suffocated by dozens of bodies leaning over me and countless hands demanding that their bowls, mugs, pots, plates, and plastic bags be filled up, I could not see whose hands they were. At the end of each session, twice a day, I heard complaints about unfair distribution. Competition between Kadimani and Auaris people became increasingly bitter, as the locals insisted on being equally served the Boa Vista food the "thin people" (*nomi dibi* as they took to referring to the Kadimani) were getting. Quarrels between the two groups became more frequent as the weeks went by and the sick began to recover. Had the team been staying with the Kadimani in their own village, distributing to them alone the foodstuffs from town, much intercommunity acrimony would have been avoided.

The figures of the Kadimani epidemic were unbelievable. In a population of 133 people (21 of them from other villages closely associated with Kadimani, such as Mamugula and Sogosi of Chapter 2), there were 151 cases of malaria, or 114 percent of the population. This means that some people were cured of one type and immediately infected with another. Of this total, 71 percent were *falciparum*, 18 percent were *vivax*, and 11 percent were both together. Added to the highly advanced stage of the disease was a crippling anemia and acute undernourishment. A young mother stopped producing milk due to malnutrition; we had to feed her baby with powdered milk. It turned out she also had tuberculosis; after months of treatment at the Casa do Indio in Boa Vista, she died back home about a year later.

Severe anemia was evident not only in their feeble appearance, but also when the medical team, instead of getting a drop of red blood for the microscope slide, drew a diluted pinkish liquid. Such cases needed blood transfusions. Nine transfusions were done right there with local donors who were free of malaria at the moment; despite the precarious field conditions, all these patients survived. A little boy died in my house on arrival. His father, the important Kadimani headman, was himself fighting both *falciparum* and pneumonia.

Ten patients were sent to the Boa Vista public hospital, three of whom died there for lack of proper attention. The bodies were returned to their relatives. At each airplane that arrived with a coffin, bursts of wailing filled the air around the mission grounds as the dead bodies were carried to the small hangar near the dispensary where the Kadimani were uncomfortably camped. Their poignant collective crying intensified all the more the visual depression of the "thin people." The weeping of the Kadimani families over their dead relatives, returned to them by faceless whites from miles away, became a repeated echo of an unspeakable tragedy that did not result in their extinction only thanks to the coincident presence of the medical team right then and there. Deadly *falciparum* would have wiped out the Kadimani in a matter of weeks, leaving a handful of survivors at loose ends searching for a community willing to receive them.

The calamity that befell the community of Kadimani in March and

April of 1991 lays bare the trauma that a generalized epidemic can cause, when only three or four people are well while more than a hundred are prostrated. The effects have long been known.

> At least a wide proportion of deaths . . . are due to the abrupt halt in productive activities by the simultaneous collapse of the whole community, which for an Indian tribe means doom, since they don't have a storage system that would allow them to have a food supply that could see them through such crises. (Ribeiro [1956] 1970:278)

The factors that led the Kadimani people to such disaster were twofold: malaria infestation due to the circulation of *garimpeiros* in the area, and an exceptionally long lean period between harvests. The Kadimani were now located in the corridor between the Auaris airstrip and the Shimara Woche *garimpo* in Venezuela, and for a few years they had been exposed to the presence of *garimpeiros* who either camped or passed through their village, gardens, and hunting grounds on their way to the *garimpo*. Furthermore, the conjunction of at least three factors kept them from opening new gardens, while the old were at the end of their yield. Two successive years with unusually short dry seasons reduced the period of slash-and-burn that requires weeks of dry weather before the planting of crops. At the same time, the community moved to a new site without having first made new gardens. Apparently house building absorbed all the work force that should also have gone into garden making as well. But the decisive factor seems to have been the attraction of food ready and easily acquired from *garimpeiros*. Rice and canned sardines encouraged the Indians to postpone the hard and slow work of food production. The result was a whole community on the brink of starvation and, therefore, highly vulnerable to the assault of *falciparum* that raged through it like wildfire.

By May 1991, the Kadimani people were back in their new village on the edge of the Walobiu stream, surrounded by maturing gardens, and Auaris returned to a quieter routine of sporadic cases of malaria among both the Sanumá and the Maiongong population.

It was at that time that a group of military officers and engineers landed at the mission to go on a trek in search of a convenient waterfall that might be tapped as power source for the installation of the Auaris Calha Norte outpost. A year later the work of enlarging the airstrip was under way. The construction teams brought in the first TV set Auaris had ever seen. Groups of Sanumá youths and, more discreetly, Maiongong women began to frequent the barracks of the military construction company. I heard the first complaints of sexual abuse of both Indian women and boys on the part of the workers. The atmosphere was heavy with the clouds of dust that deafening bull-dozers raised out of the strip, a smothering symbol of the new era that was engulfing the Sanumá. Whenever aircraft landed or took off, the air became solid with a thick red curtain that choked up whoever ventured near. The Calha Norte Project had come to Auaris.

Box 2: Davi Kopenawa Speaks

Today white people are interested in supporting the Indians because the Indians have greater knowledge of the earth, the forest, and the planet. White people are interested in taking our knowledge for themselves, in borrowing our words because their knowledge is worth very little. White people talk a lot but they know nothing. So now white people come after us, because they are interested in hearing our words.

The forest where I live is beautiful, and only when I am there can my mind be at peace. When I am in the city I get nervous. Only when I am near my relatives do I have calm thoughts. Before, I didn't know this word "politics," I learnt it from white people. Now I am beginning to understand your word "politics." I began to think correctly about it. First, I had it wrong. I used to ask myself: "are the whites good people? Are they friends?" I don't think this way any more. I think there are many bad politicians, who want to make us forget our language and send white men to work in our lands. This is why they try to deceive us, saying: "When you are a white man, you are going to have money! You are going to live in the city among white people! You are going to drive a car!" They are lying, and anyway, I don't want to live where white people live. I want to live in our Yanomami land. I want to live where I really belong, in my own land.

FUNAI and the government closed the borders of our lands. But the people who don't like us are very numerous. All these gold miners, who have no land, no house, and no money, are coming back to our lands. They're increasing again and want our gold. When they've taken this gold they will give it in turn to other, rich and powerful, white people. These people — far, far away — ask for it, and the number of gold miners on our lands increases again. I am very worried again. "Are FUNAI and the government going to defend our land? Are they really going to defend it?" This is what I am asking myself. But they're not going to. If they had been serious, the gold miners wouldn't have come back. FUNAI has no money. FUNAI, which does defend us, hasn't got any money, and the gold miners are increasing again. You, abroad, are going to have to give FUNAI money, so they can really help us.

When the gold miners arrived we were worried, because they were a people we didn't know. The Yanomami didn't know who the gold miners were. Then they tempted us with their goods and the Yanomami began to grow bad. The gold miners came looking for gold in the ground; they were very poor. Their chiefs who sent them had ordered them to work in our lands. These gold miners invaded our lands and we began to get ill. We got malaria. We were all ill with the white people's malaria epidemic that these gold miners brought to our lands, the *shawara*. This is why none of us now wants these gold miners in our forest.

When the gold miners came, some Yanomami were, unwisely, happy to have them around. They were thinking, without knowing them: "Maybe the gold miners are good people." They liked their food. The gold miners began to lure them with rice, manioc flour, and old clothes. The Yanomami didn't think much of the old clothes, but the gold miners kept giving them some of their food and they were happy to eat it. They stopped working their plots of land and planting their own food. Soon, all of them grew very ill. Then they began to die, all the old people died, and the Yanomami were very frightened. These Yanomami had no goods to trade; they were isolated, they didn't have machetes or knives, which is why they came to the gold miners' camps in the first place. If they had had enough of these things, they wouldn't have come anywhere near the gold miners.

Our people are ravaged by epidemics, they are ill, many of us are dying. To defend our lands against the gold miners, we spoke to the government, but they didn't respond. We were angry, and so we went to New York, where some white people's elders live, where there are people who are involved with what happens in our lands. I went there to speak to some important people. It is from there that the call for gold from our land comes. They ask for it, and the gold miners, Brazilians, New York want gold, too, so I went to tell them that this is bad and to put them right about it.

City life is awful, it's so noisy. You can't hear anything. It's impossible to hear the voices that we hear in the forest. The noise of motors drowns everything. It fills the ears. This is why I don't say, "cities are

good!" They are noisy, full of fumes and disease. You can't hear anything, and people can't speak clearly. We Yanomami don't think cities
are good. In our forest, we don't make such a noise. We remain silent,
because we are listening to the forest. We hear the macaws and tou-
cans when they talk, the howler monkeys when they scream, the spider monkeys when they shout all at once. When the forest creatures
speak, it is the only thing worth listening to.

"Five hundred years" . . . In our language we only say "a very long
time go" . . . "Five hundred years" ago, as you put it, is when the
white people arrived here, after Yoasi [a demiurge] sent them back
from their country to the place where they were created [in Yanomami lands]. They came back across the waters. Other peoples,
like the Yanomami, were living here. The white people, the Portuguese, came and killed these people with their guns and epidemics.
When they killed them, they used to take off the skin to show it to
other white people. They killed the Indians, and while the bodies lay
on the ground, they skinned them with knives. Then the whites
showed these skins to their chiefs. This is what the spirits of these
dead people say when we see them in our shamanic trances. A long,
long time ago, the white people didn't live here, but we did. We have
always lived here, in our forest. When the white people came, they
shot the Indians and caused them to die of epidemics. So, I am not at
peace. We are not at peace.
— Excerpts from the interview filmed by Geoffrey O'Connor during
       Eco-92 Earth Summit in Rio de Janeiro, translated from
       Yanomam by Bruce Albert, published in March 1993
              in *Urihi* 16, Bulletin of the CCPY,
          Comissão pela Criação do Parque Yanomami

It was also in 1991 that a group of Auaris men who returned from a
visit to Shikoi brought the news that the residents of another village
cluster, Hogomawa, had been killed by poisonous gas sprayed over
them by *garimpeiro* airplanes. Their bare bones were said to be strewn
all over the ground. The visitors heard the story from the three surviving women who fled to Shikoi. I transmitted it to Boa Vista, asking
the local headquarters of the National Health Foundation to have the
case verified, but nothing was ever done. The Hogomawa communities, the epitome of remoteness and isolation in the 1970s, had been
ravaged by intense *garimpeiro* activity near an airstrip known as Dicão,

on the border with Venezuela, halfway between the mouth of the Auaris and Surucucus. In September 1990, the Venezuelan National Guard arrested nine Brazilian *garimpeiros* at Dicão and confiscated twelve kilos of gold. According to an Auaris Sanumá, the Hogomawa lived by the Madoú River in a total of twenty houses divided into four residence clusters. A rough estimate places the population at approximately two hundred people.

The following year I accompanied another medical team, this time to the communities of Olomai, Tucushim, and Shikoi, all in the middle Auaris region. But before leaving Auaris, we paid a visit to Kadimani. There was a *sabonomo* ceremonial in course for one of their several dead relatives. Many of the men were taking hallucinogen and shamanizing, and children were running about, but there were people down with a new bout of malaria. Mission personnel who accompanied us took blood samples from all the villagers and their guests and assumed responsibility for the treatments. With a catch in my throat, fighting off tears, I hugged little Alusoma, perky and healthy, under her mother's loving glance. I could now see what her face looked like, pretty and vivacious, all smiles and sweetness.

With members of a new team—Dr. Maria Stella de Castro Lobo of the Federal University of Rio de Janeiro, microscope technician Olivier Parisot of the French Médecins du Monde organization, and Tomé, our Maiongong assistant—I flew back to Olomai by helicopter on March 27. But it was a very different Olomai. A short distance upstream from the mouth of the Olomai, the village site was a pleasant, spread-out clearing near an inviting stretch of crystal-clear stream that in the dry season exposed its pebbled bottom and smooth black rocks.

The community's composition had changed substantially. None of Lourenço's descendants lived there anymore; they were scattered along the middle Auaris as usually happens upon the death of an important headman. The three residence clusters we had visited the year before were now grouped together. After the previous medical visit in October, twelve people had died of malaria, which means a 13 percent loss in nine months. Our own blood search of the eighty people present at Olomai indicated that malaria epidemics were far from controlled; 60 percent were positive, of which 67 percent were *falciparum*, 32 percent *vivax*, and 1 percent mixed. A pregnant woman had a premature baby who died a few days later. Some children were beginning to show the typical symptoms of advanced anemia that results primarily from *falciparum*.

We postponed the date of our departure from April 6 to April 14, in part to attend to the residents of the distant Halaikana community,

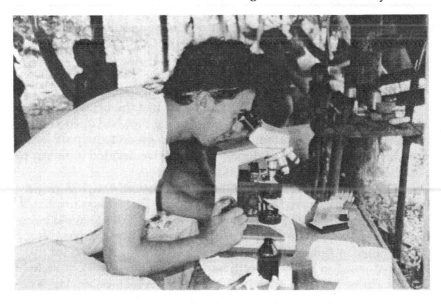

Olivier Parisot of Médecins du Monde at the microscope in the village of Olomai. 1992. Photograph by the author.

closely related to Olomai, who also came down for malaria treatment. The other reason was lack of transportation, as the air force helicopter set aside for the Yanomami health program was out of service for an indefinite period of time. We had to mount a canoe expedition in order to go down to the community of Tucushim, three and a half days' paddling through countless rapids and waterfalls.

The Tucushim people occupied two sites: a temporary camp just below the Nosamo waterfall, and a full-size village a short distance downstream from the camp. I visited the village, but could see only the newly built empty houses and a large garden on the hill at the back. Its residents were away on a visit to the Aracaçá communities to the north.

At the camp we found again a high incidence of malaria. Of the thirty-four residents present, 62 percent were infected. During the previous rainy season (from June to November), five people died. I was able to identify them, but there were also an unspecified number of children who had died at the community downstream.

The *Tukushimdili dɨbɨ*, as the Sanumá call them, are Yanomam speakers whose language is heavily influenced by Sanumá. Traditionally they occupied the zone between Surucucus and Auaris, and belonged to a much larger group of villages located near the Tucushim falls from which their name derives. For reasons still unknown, the original group was decimated in the 1960s, and the survivors scattered along the Auaris and Parima river basins. To this day, the Auaris Tucushim consider the Parima branch as their close relatives, even though they pay each other no more than sporadic visits.

After a week at the Tucushim camp, we had the helicopter, back in action, take us to Shikoi. But, as the clearing they had opened three months before was deserted, and we had no guide to help us locate the people in the middle of the thick jungle, we decided to return to Auaris. Shikoi would have to wait until May.

We heard that the National Health Foundation was changing directors and the future of the Yanomami Health District was uncertain. We were thus advised to go back to Boa Vista in order to avoid being trapped by amorphous political and administrative changes. Tomé stayed home in Auaris, Dr. Stella went back to Rio, and Olivier and I were marooned in Boa Vista waiting to continue our work at Shikoi.

For the next twelve days I tried to recruit a medical doctor to accompany us back to the field, but not a single one was available. In the end I requested the health attendant at the mission in Auaris to come with us to Shikoi. Finally, on May 13, the four of us—Olivier, Mimica (the attendant), Daniel (the Kadimani headman's son), and I—landed on the Shikoi clearing.

Several Indians waved as the helicopter approached. They were exultant to see us finally appear after the many messages they had sent to us at Auaris. We set up camp in one of the derelict shelters left by the previous medical team on their February visit, and set to work on collecting everybody's blood with the same monotonous results. Of a total of 135 slides collected, 61 percent were positive, of which 65 percent were *falciparum*, 30 percent *vivax*, and 5 percent mixed. Since the last time they had been treated, a mere three months before, five children had died. And before that, another thirty-two people had been lost apparently to malaria.

Due to such brutal loss of members, the Shikoi residents, following a Yanomami pattern, avoided concentration in more permanent villages. They lived in temporary shelters, moving frequently through the forest. While we were at the clearing, they were preparing a *sabonomo* for the dead.

The first days of treatment were intense and tiring. Some people, adults and children alike, refused to take the medication and caused me to upbraid them constantly as to why, after all, they had called us so insistently. A young woman, about three months pregnant, infected with malaria, had a miscarriage. Amidst her excruciating screams of pain, we felt with full force the impotence and insecurity of being in such a situation without a medical doctor.

Again, we prolonged our stay at Shikoi for longer than planned due to lack of transportation. Three days after we settled in, we were informed that the air force had removed their helicopters from Surucucus, and that their collaboration with the Yanomami health program had been discontinued. In other words, we were stranded in the middle of nowhere for more than ten days, during which I had ample opportunity to be infected by malaria which manifested itself back home in Brasilia.

Working conditions were anything but easy. Although it was pleasing and educational to interact with the members of the various teams with whom I worked, the strain we were often put through added to the already distressing task of trying to stop the bleeding of Sanumá lives caused by virtually uninterrupted epidemics. The support we got from the Yanomami Health District in the early days rapidly dwindled as national and local politics interfered by replacing dedicated people with others whose qualification and/or commitment was wanting. Let me illustrate how this deteriorating situation affected us in the field.

The canoe trip from Olomai to Tucushim, although it added a flavor of adventure to an otherwise tedious or depressing work, meant a loss of precious time, not to speak of the risk of accidents, and the tension generated by those risks. We loaded two dugout canoes to the brim with fourteen people and about three hundred kilos of cargo that included a collection of cardboard boxes with medicines, a big metal trunk with food supplies and trade goods, the microscope case, the two-way radio set and its two batteries weighing twenty-four kilos each, a fifty-kilo sack of manioc flour and another of rice, plus backpacks and assorted pieces of luggage. The Auaris River is jammed with rapids of various depths and lengths, and has two or three major waterfalls. At each one of them we either braced ourselves before plunging in, or had to stop, unload the canoes, carry all the gear over rocks, and either float the canoes over the turbulence, drag them over a sea of boulders, or portage them up and down steep hills, only to start all over on the other side with the reloading before continuing, fortunately, downstream. As we began to relax, a faint murmur announced the approach of another interruption, another stop, more unloading, carrying, reloading, and so on for three entire days. On one occasion, misjudging the negotiability of a rapid, the crew dispensed with unloading the larger canoe. They hit a rock sticking out of the whirlpool past the main barrier of white water, and the

Health team and crew leave Olomai for Tucushim. 1992. Photograph by the author.

canoe began to sink. During the short paralysis that froze us who stood on the river's edge, we watched in disbelief the row of cardboard boxes, backpacks, microscope case, even the big red trunk placidly floating down the quiet backwater that followed the turbulence. Everything was safely recovered, except a few kitchen utensils and the sacks of manioc flour and rice, our provisions in case the Tucushim people were undergoing a famine like the Kadimani. In a moment of enviable lucidity, a crew member snatched the radio out of the sinking canoe at the very last minute. Both batteries dropped to a three-meter depth under water, and it took a full hour for a group of three or four men diving repeatedly, including Olivier, to retrieve them. The cardboard boxes disintegrated, and we had to place countless medicines in makeshift containers. Inexplicably, both radio and batteries continued to serve us well till the end of the trip. For three nights, blissfully dry, we slept in the open air, camping on beaches that made the middle course of the Auaris look like a superb ecological postcard, complete with a rather ethereal full moon. Between the waiting at Olomai and the long canoe trip, we lost more than a week of our tight schedule.

Getting out of Tucushim also presented its difficulties. The local airstrip the Auaris missionaries had once opened up but never used

Fording the rapids. 1992. Photograph by the author.

was too short and unsafe for airplanes (which hadn't stopped *ga-rimpeiros* from using it years before). We had, then, to leave again by helicopter. On the assigned day, the air force crew could not find us, despite the fact that the air strip was clearly visible on a sharp curve of the Auaris River. We had to wait for the next day, having to lug our gear to and from the camp, some two hundred meters away. Through the radio we added more details as to our location and were asked by the helicopter pilot to make a big bonfire to produce smoke as a beacon. A few hours later, we were found.

But the worst experience was to come at Shikoi. The news that we had been abandoned at the clearing by the air force was not exactly welcome. Living conditions at Shikoi were by far the worst I had experienced. Access to water supply was painfully hard, as it was limited to a trickle that ran at the very end of a long, steep, and muddy path at the bottom of the hill. Our shelter had a slanted dirt floor which made stepping about quite uncomfortable; its old and sloppily repaired roof leaked and cut short many a night's sleep. And the entire area was swarming with insects, including the fearful anopheline mosquitoes; the Indians identified the characteristic sound emitted by scorpions somewhere in the middle of our luggage, but could not locate them; once or twice, we were startled by a snake moving across our floor. The idea of being trapped in such a place with no supplies, no food, and amidst a group of Indians who expropriated our clothes as their chance to replenish the tatters they had acquired from the *garimpeiros* was far from appealing.

For about ten days we heard on the radio that the military were withdrawing their support from the health program and "Operation Free Jungle," that more and more *garimpeiros* were reentering areas such as Homoshi, and that no one knew how to get us out of Shikoi, for the new director of the local National Health Foundation was not willing to find an alternative to the air force transportation.

The stalemate in the arrangements to rescue us led me to request that our situation be transmitted to the attorney general's office in Brasilia: I feared that such delay would eventually put our safety at risk. Moreover, there was the question of my being called back to the university to resume my oft-postponed teaching duties (the academic term had begun in mid-March). A few days later we heard that the Health Foundation in Boa Vista was hiring the only private helicopter available to fly us back to town. Three days passed before that was to happen.

The rescue operation was a folly of its own. The helicopter left Surucucus at seven in the morning and spent all day going from airstrip to airstrip allegedly looking for us, despite the fact that the pilot had in his hand the map we had given the air force crew who brought us in with the precise location and coordinates of the Shikoi clearing. We could hear the roar of the engine, but caught no sight of it. We made a huge fire for the proverbial smoke sign. We asked the FUNAI outposts whether they had seen the helicopter, and we even talked to the pilot who expected us to provide technical details about aerial navigation, all to no avail. All day long we waited, gear on the clearing, ready to go. We were repeatedly called on the radio by Health Foundation people, FUNAI people, and the military at Surucucus, Boa Vista, and even Manaus, who wanted to know where we were. Apparently, the air force crews who flew to Shikoi before did not leave any information of their flights once they were completed. The radiophonic chaos went on in the scalding sun of the clearing, under the amused and perplexed eyes and remarks of dozens of Indians, while columns of smoke went futilely up to the empty skies.

It was 5:30 in the evening when the pilot finally saw us as the sun was about to set. It was a "Squirrel," and so I imagined he would take two trips, one of them, obviously, the next day. But no, the pilot was adamant. It was either one trip now, or no rescue at all, for he was in a hurry to go back to Belém the next morning. I protested, fighting to be heard under the hellish noise and agitation of the blades, but as I saw my companions board the helicopter, I had no choice myself. The four of us, plus 180 kilos of cargo, along with the pilot and his companion, were jammed into the tiny space of the aircraft. The luggage compartment was near overflowing; the big red trunk was placed on the back seat and we sat on it. Olivier, six feet tall, was doubled over in foetal position with his neck pressed against the ceiling, his long legs folded in an impossible way (if inadvertently he had stretched his right leg he would have pulled open the door); Daniel, hugging a styrofoam box, was leaning up against the co-pilot's back; Mimica, leaning forward, held onto the pilot's chair; I, crouched against the left-hand door, clutched at the loose end of the idle security belt, while we were all tightly squeezed against each other. Contrary to his promise of testing the weight of the helicopter before taking off in earnest, no sooner were the doors closed than the pilot darted off, just missing the treetops. It was the longest half hour in my recent memory, as I tried to shift position to avoid cramps, watching the daylight fade away over the forest. It was dark when we landed at Surucucus. For weeks afterward I was haunted by the memory of the trash bags we had to leave behind, exposing the Indians to a multitude of used lancets and soiled wads of cotton wool from the many blood drops we drew for microscope slides.

The pilot had taken eleven hours and forty-five minutes to do a job that should take, at the most, two laps of a half-hour each. He charged all those unnecessary extra hours, at about two thousand dollars an hour, to the National Health Foundation whose director, in turn, complained that I had forced him to do something that had no urgency at all, for, he said, we had the radio and, therefore, were not isolated. I must point out that in this case, unlike that of Olomai and Tucushim, there was no other way to come or go short of a weeklong walk through extremely difficult trails going up and down a score of steep hills, carrying an overwhelming amount of weight, even when we reduced our gear to the most valuable items—radio, batteries, and microscope.

Ironically, on the very day we were caught in the blazing Shikoi clearing waiting to be rescued, President Collor solemnly ratified the demarcation of the Yanomami Indian Area in a festive ceremony in Brasilia.

The irregular and irresponsible way in which our medical teams were treated, both by the Health Foundation and by the military whose duty it is to help assist the Yanomami in the recovery of their health and of their lands free of invaders, reveals a lot more than simple morosity or lack of sympathy for whites like us. By exposing the health teams to such ordeals, these authorities are, in fact, condemning the Yanomami to neglect.

In the devasted Yanomami "malaria-scape" the Sanumá have a tragically prominent place. The impressive rise in the population of Kadimani and mission communities was dangerously close to being reversed by one of the most intense health crises recorded among the Yanomami as a whole.

The upper Auaris had been considered a low risk area in terms of malaria epidemics due to its location far from the center of *garimpeiro* activities. There was no great concentration of invaders as in Paapiú, Homoshi, or Shidea to the south, nor was there severe damage to the environment. Nevertheless, until late 1991, the recorded number of deaths by malaria was about 60 for the Sanumá as compared to 110 for the Yanomami as a whole (Fundação Nacional de Saúde 1991: 105a, table XVII). These figures confirm that the propagation of malaria does not depend on a large number of infected individuals:

> There have been numerous instances in which malarial epidemics, some of which have claimed thousands of lives, began after one or more individuals harboring *Plasmodium* entered an area where anopheline mosquitoes and susceptible hosts coexisted in large numbers. (Reff 1991:106)

One single medical team was available to attend nearly one thousand people scattered in very dispersed communities, and thus, a great portion of Sanumá population was left at the mercy of *falciparum*. In twelve months, 6 percent of Sanumá lives were extinguished by malaria. It is much too heavy a toll for a people painstakingly attempting to grow and maintain control of a territory that is ever on the brink of expropriation. Malaria, it would seem, has the potential to produce the much heralded demographic voids of Amazonia, an important ideological piece in the politics of conquest (Ramos n.d.). Apiaú and Ajarani are examples of how epidemics (in these cases mostly measles) can wipe out indigenous populations and leave the terrain free for colonization. One has only to ponder the following:

> No doubt the Plymouth colonists had prepared themselves for hard confrontations with the natives . . . , but by the time they had begun building their homes alongside the still-intact cornfields of Patuxet the following month, they were given ample reason to believe that Providence had,

for their sake, all but cleared the entire countryside of its native population. (Sanders 1978:300)

After 1992 malaria subsided in the Yanomami area, thanks to the removal of the majority of gold miners and the repeated treatments, even though not as extensive as they should be, in a number of community clusters. This decline in the incidence of malaria may be a hopeful sign that a certain amount of recovery is under way. However, since it is far from being eradicated, the disease may enter another explosive phase at any moment under similarly favorable conditions. It has gone from endemic to epidemic and even pandemic levels, and now it seems to be ebbing down to being endemic again. It all depends on the commitment of the Brazilian government to maintain the policy of respecting the Yanomami right to exclusive use of their lands and of providing them with constant medical assistance. If the country complies with the protecting legislation and if dedicated people are allowed to continue their work of preserving Indian lives, then the Yanomami will have a chance to recover and decide on their own future.

Box 3

Comissão pela Criação do Parque Yanomami – CCPY
Rua Manuel da Nóbrega 111 cj.32 – 04001-900 São Paulo SP – Brazil – Tel. (+55.11) 289.1200 / Fax 284.6997

Update 74   **February 5, 1994**

INVASION BRINGS NEW THREAT TO SURVIVORS OF MASSACRE

As clandestine gold-miners (*garimpeiros*) once again pour into the Yanomami Area, armed miners are now operating a short distance from the village where the survivors of the Haximu massacres have taken refuge.

Members of the Haximu community arrived last week at the CCPY health post of Tooto-tobi to warn of the presence of *garimpeiros* some four hours' walk from the village of Makos, where the survivors have been living since they fled after the atrocities of June-July 1993. The messengers, who were visibly frightened, described the *garimpeiros* as armed and equipped with mechanised mining machinery.

Before this latest invasion, the surviving members of the Haximu community had shown signs of overcoming the trauma of the massacres. Following the period of ritual mourning over the ashes of the dead, they had once more begun to plant manioc gardens and to organise collective hunting expeditions. Now, with the renewed *garimpeiro* invasion of Yanomami territory gathering pace, the threat of violence once more hangs over them and over the other communities of the area. Miners are entering the area both along the rivers Apiaú and Catrimani (see **Update 73**) and via the clandestine airstrips which litter the area.

In Boa Vista, capital of Roraima (the state within which most of the Yanomami's territory lies), the signs of renewed *garimpeiro* presence are everywhere. Local newspapers have commented on increased activity in the gold trading houses, the light planes which serve the illegal airstrips once more crowd Boa Vista airport, and more *garimpeiros* are arriving by the busload. The rumour that the area has been declared open to mining has spread like wildfire with the relaxation of official vigilance.

In late January a *garimpeiro* aircraft was destroyed by the Federal Police inside the Yanomami Area, but the official presence in the area remains limited. Government Indian agency Funai claims it is short of funds for control of the invasion, has no helicopters to transport its personnel and is receiving little cooperation from the Federal Police. The violence which pervades the mining camps has already made its presence felt; on January 24 a *garimpeiro* was murdered by a colleague inside the Yanomami Area after they argued over a packet of cigarettes.

There are also disturbing rumours that *garimpeiros* have been giving shotguns to some groups of Yanomami and stirring up inter-community disputes, in the hope that those who oppose the invasion can be destroyed indirectly.

CCPY urges all those concerned about the renewed threat to the Yanomami with the return of miners to their territory to write or send a fax to the Minister responsible for Amazonia: Excelentíssimo Senhor Ministro Rubens Ricúpero Ministério do Meio Ambiente e da Amazônia Palácio do Planalto, Anexo 2 Brasília – 70150–900 – DF – Brazil Fax (55) 61.226.9871

In Brief . . .

• **TV Farce:** An extensive report broadcast on the national news of the powerful *TV Globo* network on January 24 provided one of the most extreme examples of the black propaganda which is increasingly deployed to undermine public support for indigenous peoples' rights in Brazil. Filmed on board an aircraft which he claimed was flying over the Yanomami Area, Globo journalist Marcos Losekan "denounced" the non-existence of villages whose presence had been used by Funai to justify demarcating an area rich in minerals as indigenous territory. His claims of a plot by "foreign missionaries and NGOs" to undermine Brazilian sovereignty over the region were seized on by local politicians and the pro-mining press in Roraima as "proof" of what they had long argued. Unfortunately for Losekan's lies, Funai subsequently obtained not only a statement from the pilot confirming that the aircraft never in fact flew over Yanomami territory at all, but also a copy of a receipt proving that the flight was paid for by a prominent *garimpeiro* boss. Such is the power of Globo, however, that even when these documents were passed to the press no newspaper questioned the story.

• **Mining lobby:** With Brazil's Constitutional Review finally under way, the pressure to open the Yanomami Area to mining is growing. The government's Mineral Production Department has hosted meetings including both mining companies and indigenous rights groups which left the impression that at least the larger mining companies are likely to secure access to indigenous areas. The current acceleration of the *garimpeiro* invasion may well represent an attempt to create a *fait accompli* which would guarantee informal-sector miners access as well.

• **Militarisation:** A Bill submitted to Congress by the government on February 3 proposes that all activities in frontier zones (such as the Yanomami Area) receive the prior approval of the military-dominated National Defence Council, part of the Strategic Affairs Secretariat. If the Bill is passed into law, the military would also have an effective veto on the presence of NGOs in these areas.

I share with the other whites who have had the privilege of living among the Yanomami the profound distress of having to witness the unfolding of a process that is usually spared contemporary ethnographers. Typically the anthropologist arrives among his or her Indian hosts when these have already gone through the worst; what the ethnographer sees are the ruins of what there used to be, while he or she is interested precisely in what was. I had always imagined that watching the effects of uncontrolled contact on the Indians you study was something that happened only to other people, like the loss of a dear one. I didn't expect to be around, only ten years after my immersion into an autonomous and healthy culture such as I found among the Sanumá, to see one of the worst examples of cultural devastation in the recent history of Brazilian Indigenism. It is one thing to be aware of the global and irrevocable process of Western domination that engulfs all indigenous peoples. It is another thing to observe the sordid details of the here and now—the cynicism, the cooption, the murder or the neglect—that go into the making of this domination. When we see in close-up the aerial pandemonium at Paapiú, the near extinction of a whole village at Auaris, or the brutality of the Hashimu murders, we, Yanomamists, end up developing a pathos of our own. The mental and emotional effect of these catastrophes is stunning: in a diffuse state of disorientation we either pretend none of it is happening, or try desperately to find a brilliant idea that will bring light to the end of the tunnel. This is a rather difficult experience to convey to others who have not gone through something similar; there are times when we have the sensation of speaking to a void. We fall into an idiom of our own that seems to protect us like a safety belt. We are the involuntary receiving end of the shells that bounce off the interethnic commotion ablaze on the Yanomami front.

Epilogue

Remembering, forgetting, and recalling belong to the historical
constitution of man and are themselves part of his history and his
Bildung. Whoever uses his memory as a mere faculty . . . does not yet
possess it as something that is absolutely his own. Memory must be
formed; for memory is not memory for anything and everything. One
has a memory for many things, and not for others; one wants to
preserve one thing in memory and banish another.

—Gadamer

As I watched disaster upon disaster befall the Sanumá, I noticed how
reluctant I was to turn it all into ethnographic data. My disinclination
to generate fieldnotes was not, at least consciously, for purist or moral
reasons. I did not feel then as I do not feel now, that because people
are under stress they should not be asked to provide information.
Data (obviously relevant to the situation) collected under such gruel-
ing circumstances can be valuable for no other reason than to gather
support for the defense of their human rights, or to "set the record
straight." No, my problem was not one of ethnographic conscientious
objection. It was an unexpected distaste for the activity of focused
gathering and recording of data, *inscription*, as Clifford (1990) calls
it. Apart from demographic and medical records, practically all my
annotations of that period took the form of "headnotes" (Ottenberg
1990). In lieu of sheets of paper, I stored information in my own
memory. Fortunately, this ethnographic paralysis has not erased
what I regard as anthropologically interesting data.

I was able, for instance, to check whether my previous analysis
stood the passage of time. I was especially concerned with the thorny
issue of Sanumá "lineages." The original idea still held, but the degree of their fragility was even higher than I had described.

Take the Lalawa group. In 1989, my interviews with the missionary Donald Borgman had already indicated that they were undergoing considerable changes. Then, in 1992, I reencountered the descendants of the old leader reunited in Olomai. As I identified one by one
the current Olomai residents who had replaced the dismantled community founded by Lourenço, in my mind I was restoring the old
group much as an archaeologist puts back together the sherds of a
broken pot. They were the same, yet different. Our amiable hosts at

313

Olomai were, indeed, the sons, daughters, and grandchildren of old Lalawa, but now, together with new in-laws and other co-villagers, they made up a community that had very little resemblance to the gloomy atmosphere of the Lalawa group of twenty years before. They were no longer referred to as Lalawa dibi, as I discovered back in 1990 at Auaris when I asked about them and got roars of laughter for an answer, the Sanumá way of changing an uncomfortable subject.

The notes in Chapter 2 account for the changes of the Lalawa group from 1974 to the late 1980s. Some of its members had joined Lourenço's community at the Olomai airstrip, while others had moved upriver on the Auaris to become the Halaikana dibi. After Lourenço's death, new alignments began to take shape. His sons and daughters dispersed in a number of temporary arrangements, while the Lalawa descendants reassembled in a new village not far from the mouth of the Olomai stream. By 1991 they were divided into the Olomai and the Halaikana branches. Whereas the latter had as their acknowledged leader Lalawa's oldest grandson, the Olomai branch seemed undefined in terms of political leadership.

As far as the Kadimani lineage is concerned, the passage of time has not altered its political structure. Typically, the village went through many different sites in nearly two decades, but its leadership was still in the same hands. They were now only two hours' walk from the mission, and, no doubt due to the medical assistance they got from it, their population increased dramatically. The number of children under thirteen was impressive. Whereas in 1970 they were 52 people, now their population was up to 112, that is, a 115 percent increase. Considering that a good proportion of the children are the offspring of Kadimani men, it is no surprise to find this lineage alive and well. However, the thought that came ever so strongly to my mind, as I saw the Kadimani people consumed with malaria, is that such a demographic growth achieved in the course of decades can at any moment be drastically reversed in a matter of weeks. Not even the solid Kadimani is immune to the menace of depopulation.

As the Kadimani moved closer to the cluster of communities around the mission, their interrelations grew increasingly tense. As we saw in Chapter 11, the special attention the Kadimani received from the medical team during their health crisis triggered a great deal of resentment that had been accumulating between them and the mission villages for the last five to ten years. One symptom of their veiled antagonism is the lack of intermarriages between them despite their new proximity.

Population growth among the members of the old mission cluster has been even more spectacular. In 1970, all the mission residential segments together added up to 94 people. In 1990 that figure had jumped to 237, that is, a 152 percent increase. Equally revealing is the fact that they were no longer tightly concentrated around the mission. What had been a dense group of households became a long string of eight communities on both banks of the upper Auaris.

The issue of leadership at Auaris is as muffled as before. In the absence of politically strong older men, the younger generation seems to have assumed the responsibility of making political decisions. Jorge, the self-proclaimed headman, has seen his already weak position steadily deteriorate, especially since the death in late 1990 of his only daughter. He was so intensely grieved that he burned down the solid house his Maiongong father-in-law had recently constructed and which he had shown me with great pride. By mid-1992, he had not rebuilt his life, and was still moving from house to house among his relatives. He is also severely criticized for having willingly sheltered *garimpeiros* on their exploratory passage through Auaris, and entertained their friendship in the face of all the troubles they have caused.

In contrast to the political and demographic prosperity of the Kadimani, the community of Kalioko suffered such intense setbacks as to render it unfeasible. My last visit to them was in 1974. Shortly before, their village had been relocated to a site roughly four hours by canoe downstream from the mission. At that time, there were forty-three residents under Kalioko's leadership. In 1977, a malaria epidemic killed both his wives and several other people. As discussed in Chapter 3, it was his senior wife who provided the strongest connecting kinship link which gave social coherence to the group. With her death, that chain collapsed. The villagers dispersed mainly through the mission communities. Kalioko himself ended up marrying a young girl from the former Auaris cluster, and submitted to the bride service obligations toward her father, an old man who died in 1989.

Slowly but steadily, Kalioko is regaining his political position. His children by his deceased senior wife, most of them young men, live in his community or do bride service nearby. Traits that have distinguished Kalioko as a quiet, responsible, and wise man have been enhanced, and, again on the strength of his character, he is once more reconstructing with different people what he lost.

But now he faces political rivals such as Angelo, Jorge's younger brother. Angelo's strategy has been to build a large family, surrounding himself with sons and sons-in-law. In 1992 he had eight children—five boys and three girls—by two wives, had brought in as a third wife an extremely subdued young woman who had lost her parents and husband in Venezuela, and was trying to coerce Lourenço's widowed daughter-in-law to be his fourth spouse. With this social capital, Angelo has projected himself as a forceful man whom people fear rather than respect.

In turn, Jorge does not conceal his disappointment at his wife's failure to give him more children. In a moment of defiance of missionary morals, he attempted to keep a young unmarried woman from the defunct Azagoshi community as his junior wife as a way to increase his progeny. His efforts failed due to the girl's rebellious sense of freedom. Jorge is the father of two prepubescent boys.

There have been noticeable changes in the political map of Sanumá intergroup relations. For example, Shikoi, which twenty years ago was little more than a mere name to most communities of the upper Auaris valley, has become a meaningful social reality, especially for the Kadimani and the mission villages. Some people at Auaris have taken to visiting Shikoi country on some sort of vision quest for deceased relatives. One man (Lucio of Chapter 3) assured me that the dead no longer return to the Saula-dulia region in Venezuela, as before, but now go to the territory of the Shikoi. Mutual visits are rather frequent between Shikoi and Auaris, despite the long distance that separates them. Now that the Shikoi have entered the sphere of political influence of the upriver villages, they are also included in the roll of potential enemies, ōka dibi, who attack by blowing magic dust at their victims. A flurry of such accusations permeated long conversations among Sanumá at Auaris, Kadimani, and elsewhere. The Shikoi were said to attribute the death of a headman's wife to an attack by magic from the Kadimani leader. The leader's son, Daniel, who was our guide on two health trips, was indignant as he heard this story told by returning visitors from Shikoi. His most vehement argument was: how could his father possibly be engaged in magic making when he was prostrate with malaria at the mission? When we left Auaris that year, insistent rumors had it that the Shikoi were coming upriver to attack the Kadimani.

By now most Sanumá know that malaria kills people due to contagion from infected mosquitoes, and that the spread of epidemics is a legacy of the gold rush. But this knowledge does not dispose of the residue of indeterminacy which got the Azande to elaborate on their theory of witchcraft (Evans-Pritchard 1937). The Sanumá need to have an explanation as to why A or B died of malaria while others did not. In this sense, malaria has made its way into the geopolitics of intercommunal life as a powerful catalyst for shaping and reshaping political allegiances. Not only the living but also the dead can become important points of articulation between groups, even when this articulation is manifested through animosity. Each person who dies has the potential to bring together communities that might have remained distant were it not for the accusations of sorcery that a death can provoke. From this point of view, malaria, the Sanumá "second spear," takes on unsuspected social overtones.

The urge to write ethnography is about making the *then* into a *now*. In this move from then to now, the making of knowledge out of experience occurs. Both movements, from here to there and from then to now, converge in what I called presence. This is the way I would define the process of othering.

—Johannes Fabian

Had I published this book in the early 1970s when I finished my Ph.D. dissertation on which it is based, there would probably have been no verbal tense inconsistencies. The *then* and the *now* were not as disjointed then as they are now. Although all writing is necessarily retrospective, the issue of verbal tenses would not have arisen. Now, more than twenty years later, I wrestle with a problem I have created for myself: to define the proper tone of this book. It has grown out of a traditional ethnographic-present mode, but since so much has happened in the intervening years between conception and publication, I could not pretend that nothing had occurred. How then to describe permanence in a context of change? How to sort out what goes into structure from what will pass as ephemeral conjuncture? When I wrote the original version of *Memórias Sanumá* I was already aware that from the moment the book went into print it would be lagging behind events. Because I have covered a lot more temporal ground in this English version, this feeling has grown stronger. The incongruities that still remain in terms of time reference unveil my inability, or rather unwillingness, to pasteurize the messiness of historical events, especially in view of the speed and force with which they have hit the Yanomami lately. The *now* keeps bouncing back to the *then*, as I lace the ethnographic analysis with notes indicating *post factum* changes.

On the other hand, bringing the *then* to the *now* has its advantages. Temporal distance allows one to develop a critical dimension regarding previous analyses as well as the sensory experience of the field. Both can then be digested together as elements of a new interpretation. Without the long process of mulling over my 1970s analysis of Sanumá society, I would not have been able to move beyond it. Similarly, without the passage of time that smoothed over the sharp and unmediated sensations of lived experience, I would not have been able to separate myself from these sensations and observe them dispassionately, thereupon transforming them into useful thinking tools. In other words, what one loses in freshness and immediacy one gains in perspective and seasoning. The sense of the "real" is relativized, once more demonstrating one of the most attractive aspects of anthropology: its capacity to render the relevance of what is lived independent of the moment when it is lived. An anthropological account does not, after all, pretend to be a faithful portrait, a factual report of what "really happened" at the very time when it happened. Anthropological narrative permits one to capture fleeting moments of the past or the present, tap their significance, and thus consign to them a lasting interest. Sanumá society is no longer what it was in 1974, but this does not mean that what I did apprehend of it has lost its ethnographic pertinence. In this sense, ethnography telling is comparable to storytelling:

> The value of information does not survive the moment in which it was new. It lives only at that moment; it has to surrender to it completely and explain itself to it without losing any time. A story is different. It does not expend itself. It preserves and concentrates its strength and is capable of releasing it even after a long time. (Benjamin 1969:90)

As in storytelling, the ethnographer's fleeting moment acquires a permanence that is forsaken in other fields, such as journalism, for instance. That does not always mean, as Fabian asserts in the epigraph, that the ethnographer's present tense has the effect of "othering," reducing the Other to a historically deprived being. The complexity of grasping historical consciousnesses quite different from that of Western history is not resolved by the simple device of applying the past tense to one's narrative. "Bluntly put," say the Comaroffs, "a truly historical anthropology is only possible to the extent that it is capable of illuminating the *endogenous* historicity of all social worlds" (1992:24; emphasis in the original).

This brings me to another aspect of the enthnographer's métier which strikes me as a double-edged sword, that is, the search for the "native philosopher."

The double rewriting of my dissertation in book form, first in Portuguese and now in English, has stirred in me a profound admiration for the subtlety and sophistication of my Sanumá interlocutors. Projected against the backdrop of physical and temporal distance, the simplistic image I had first developed in the field of their performance as sources of ethnographic information changed to an uncompromising intellectual respect. The last paragraph of the introduction to my 1972 Ph.D. dissertation exposes the green days of my Sanumá understanding.

> Working with Sanumá informants meant that almost every interview session was a succession of painstakingly elicited information which was highly specific in nature. It was very difficult to get informants to make generalizations that were not too vague or to make analytical statements of any kind. Whereas statistical norms were relatively easy to get at, ideal rules were obtained with great difficulty due to this seemingly non-analytical character of Sanumá thinking. (Ramos 1972:21)

Apart from reflecting a certain anthropological climate of the day, the passage reveals much more about my own mindset than about the Sanumá way of thinking. Without premeditation or hurry, their counterargument to my simplistic outlook came as an unexpected lesson in humility: many of my questions got simple answers because, as I have already mentioned, my "informants" knew my language limitations and gauged their speech to match my capacity to comprehend. If she had said more, confessed a woman dedicated to instruct me in things Sanumá, I would not have understood.

The ethnographer's expectation, or dream, is to find the "philosopher of the tribe," perhaps in the fashion of an Ogotemmêli (Griaule 1965). What this expectation does not contemplate, however, is that "philosophy" is a direct result of the distancing the members of a society develop about themselves. In projecting such an expectation on the people of a culture like the Sanumá, we reveal an ambivalence of which we are not quite aware. While we admire the spontaneity, integrity, and harmony of their way of life, at the same time we hope that someone will come to us to dissect the yeses, the nos, and the perhapses of their own culture. In 1974 I interviewed Jorge, who aspired to headmanship, by converting his contacts with whites into a political asset. He showed himself to be a caustic critic of certain Sanumá customs. I began to think about the issue of self-questioning when later I pondered those encounters with him. What goes into the making of a native philosopher? How is his or her philosophical road paved? The seed of distancing may be sowed by missionaries or any other agents of change, but it is the anthropologist, the spawner of distancing *par excellence*, who often nourishes that seed to germination. In his eagerness to unveil what is implicit, he (as often as she) asks the unaskable, planting doubts about what is taken for granted. In so doing, the ethnographer projects a way of being Western that has neither precedent nor nexus for the people. The very respect for and emulation of the local culture the ethnographer often demonstrates become themselves an impetus for questioning on the part of his or her hosts.

I didn't have these thoughts back in 1974, much less in 1968. They came to me with my bitter but essential experience with activism in the political field of interethnic contact. By observing and interacting closely with the "philosophers" of the nationwide indigenist movement in Brazil, I learned to appreciate what I had clumsily called Sanumá "non-analytical thinking." The price these Indian leaders have paid for acquiring a critical conscience has been loss of lives, land expropriation, breach of human rights, and negation of their legitimate ethnic identity. The Sanumá, like the other Yanomami in Brazil, who until a few years ago were spared this painful process, are now on the threshold of its somber prospect.

Notes
Bibliography
Acknowledgments
Index

Notes

Introduction

1. Pondering the impact of interpretive anthropology, Behar (1993:308) says: "Women readers [of *Writing Culture*] in the profession were knocked off their feet with the power of something like a tidal wave. . . . When [they] stood up again . . . they came back with a series of critical readings and creative works that are unraveling the original project of writing culture. . . ."

2. First published in English in the Venezuelan journal *Antropológica*, in 1979, and then in Portuguese in the book *Hierarquia e Simbiose*, in 1980.

Chapter 1. Sanumá Spaces

1. Smole (1976) argues that these savannas were created by the intensive and prolonged use of slash-and-burn fires.

2. Strictly speaking, the Yanomami population in Brazil is yet to be totally known. Several surveys have been made, but none of them covered all the communities. In 1977, the National Indian Foundation (FUNAI) carried out an aerial survey during the rainy season with the result that many places could not be visited. At that time they counted 8,400 Yanomami living in 203 dwellings. In 1987/88, an interministerial group (National Security Council, FUNAI, Agrarian Reform) carried out the most extensive survey to date, reaching the figure of 9,910 Yanomami in both states — Roraima and Amazonas. The outcome of that survey was the official delimitation of nineteen small and isolated areas adding up to less than 2,500 square kilometers, less than one fourth of the traditional Yanomami territory in Brazil. For further details see IWGIA 1979, and Albert 1992.

3. Toward the end of 1968, Ken Taylor came down with hepatitis. The Sanumá attributed his illness to the fact that, months earlier, he had eaten rare venison. They reached their diagnosis through shamanism.

4. For a comparison with the economic activities of the Sanumá of the Ventuari river in Venezuela, see Colchester 1982.

5. More details about the Shikoi will be found in Chapter 11 and in the Epilogue.

6. There is another form for the Yanomam term *yano*, viz., *yahi teri*,

323

meaning people who like spending most of their time at home, inside their *yano* (verbal information by Bruce Albert). In terms of acoustic comparison, *yahi* is even closer than *yano* to the Sanumá *sai*.

7. A similar concern with the dynamics of household reproduction is spelled out in T. Turner 1979a.

8. The use of the past tense here indicates that things are no longer as they used to be. The Sabuli village lost its leader and eponym, and its interaction with the mission communities became much less intense after 1974. In turn, the Lalawa village has disintegrated, giving way to new arrangements, and the Kadimani people have moved closer to the mission. These changes are discussed in Chapter 11 and in the Epilogue.

9. See Fock 1963; Maybury-Lewis 1967; Rivière 1971; Harner 1972; Urban 1986.

10. Marcus Colchester (1982) found even fewer cases of killings among the Sanumá of the Ventuari in Venezuela.

11. The other two were Mucajaí and Surucucus. In 1975, the latter was transferred to Palimiu on the Uraricoera River, while a part-time station was set up at Paapiú on the hills of Couto de Magalhães, and a new station was opened at Olomai, an extension of the Auaris mission. Since then the Paapiú and Olomai mission stations have been closed down (see Chapter 11).

12. I use pseudonyms except for people whose personal names are normally used in public.

13. The various ramifications of the Sanumá-Maiongong contact can be found in Ramos 1980.

14. In the Sanumá language, the toucan "cries" (*mazubi ĩkĩbalo*). Dusk, associated with the toucan's cry, is recognized as a melancholy time also by the Catrimani Yanomam, as Bruce Albert tells me.

15. I visited Shikoi in 1992 and could attest to the difficult conditions of their geographic location (see Chapter 11).

16. Our experience contrasts with Colchester's (1982), according to whom the Venezuelan Sanumá who live farther away from the missions are more aggressive than those more directly influenced by the missionaries.

17. It turns out that those refugees belong to a group they call Magula, who are the remnants of the Máku, an indigenous society considered extinct due to raids and intermarriage with the Sanumá (Migliazza 1972).

Chapter 2. Time as Space Organizer

1. This is a distinction not very different from that made by Western philosophy for an "ontologic" being (equivalent to *dɨbɨ*) and an "ontic" being (similar to *bɨ*). There is an intermediary term, *gɨgɨ* (two, several), between the singular *de/a* and the plural *dɨbɨ/bɨ* (many), that is used for both ontologic and ontic beings, but I never heard it applied to sib members. The term *bɨ* is also used as an adjective, "very," as in *toita bɨ*, "very good"; in this context it corresponds to the Yanomam *mahi*.

2. In order to distinguish residence groups from descent units with the same name, I use the former with capital initial and no italics, and the latter with italics and lower-case initial.

3. Chagnon describes the threats he suffered for having pronounced names of dead people among the Venezuelan Yanomami. Bruce Albert did not conceal his surprise at the ease with which the Sanumá speak openly of the names of the dead. The Sanumá treat the dead as they do the living, with no special precautions regarding their names. In Albert's experience that would be impossible among the Yanomam.

4. The ambiguity that surrounds the data presented for the Yanomami is not sufficient to keep us from concluding that their system is, above all, cognatic (Lizot 1984; Chagnon 1968).

5. Compare this with the figures in Geertz and Geertz (1975:74–76) showing a situation similar to that of the Sanumá.

6. In his doctoral dissertation, Marcus Colchester (1982) criticizes the use I made of the terms sib and lineage as the unnecessary result of conceptual imposition. Among the Sanumá of the Ventuari valley, he did not preceive these differences and considers that there are only what he called "local descent groups." He does not, however, recognize that this too is the result of a conceptual imposition. For him, every Sanumá belongs to just one of these local descent groups. It is intriguing that, at various points in his work, Colchester refers to more than one name for the same group (for instance, "the *tokolodɨbɨ* are also *Apiamdɨbɨ*" [1982:180]. He also criticizes my Ph.D. analysis (Ramos 1972) on the basis of an apparently inattentive reading. I insist now as I did then that, in the absence of lineages, the Auaris Sanumá are not left empty-handed, for they always retain their sib affiliation, regardless of being lineage members or not.

7. In principle, political leaders are also subject to the custom of uxorilocality. It is up to them to gain the privilege of skipping both bride service and residence with their parents-in-law. As distinct from many Amazonian societies, especially Tupians, where the political leader has the right to virilocality, for the Sanumá it is not a given but has to be gained. For further details see Chapter 3.

8. In February 1989, I obtained the following information from Donald Borgman about Hanisho. Still in the 1970s, the old Lalawa headman died while his community lived by the Kakudu stream on the middle Auaris River. Under Hanisho's leadership the entire group, by then called *hanisho dɨbɨ*, moved to the banks of the Auaris at a site known as Halaikana (the name of an evil spirit like a giant anaconda); their name changed to *halaikana dɨbɨ*. When, around 1980, Lourenço, the Maiongong head of the Colony, opened up the Olomai airstrip on the middle course of the Auaris, the *halaikana dɨbɨ* joined him in his new village, but slowly they began to leave Lourenço's house. Some went to the hills about a half-hour walk away and became known as the *palɨkɨdɨlɨ dɨbɨ* (people of the mountain's chest). Finally, their dispersal was completed, and Hanisho lost his leadership to a younger brother. Borgman had not heard of him again. In 1992 I met him at Olomai, a semi-senile old man with no traces of his former prestige.

9. The Sogosɨ village also suffered with the move of one of the brothers and his family to another place (personal communication by Donald Borgman). Even imprecise, this piece of information points to the constant tendency for residence groups to split apart.

10. Information obtained from Donald Borgman shows that the *ōkobɨdili dɨbɨ* had moved away from the Mamugula community, and were back at the Ōkobiu stream.

11. The *kadimani dɨbɨ* nucleus continues to be a strong agnatic group living in the region of the Walobiu stream. News of February 1989 had it that its two oldest brothers are still together and that the community is filled with small children (personal communication by Donald Borgman). In 1991 they were on the verge of extinction due to a malaria epidemic (see Chapter 11).

12. *Pɨ̄ a*, "father"; *nomazoma*, "died"; *pilubɨ dɨbɨ*, "sons"; *selegɨbazoma*, "dispersed."

13. *Pɨzɨba*, "wife"; *mi*, "absence"; *kudio*, "stay"; *maigite*, "no."

14. *Sami*, "one"; *kutenɨ*, "due to."

15. Like several communities that split up between 1974 and 1989, Mosonawa also separated into various segments. With the exception of a few families, Jorge's included, nearly all former residents now live elsewhere along the Auaris River. The expectation that Jorge had in 1974 of being a headman faded away as people disbanded upriver (verbal information by Donald Borgman). It is possible that the search for better hunting and agriculture grounds have led the Auaris people to move away. It is also possible that it is only a temporary situation, and that they will reunite in the future. It certainly makes clear how flexible and mobile Sanumá residence groups can be when we look at them after a time span even as short as a decade.

16. That baby grew into a healthy young man who in 1992 was still single, living at Kadimani with his father's kin.

17. *Ulu*, "child"; *tha*, "to make"; *-wi*, "agent".

18. The Sanumá word *shibinabi* seems to derive from *shibo*, "to carry." But, according to Bruce Albert, in the Yanomam language the equivalent word for *shibinabi* is *shimunabi*, whereas to carry is *ihibu*. Interesting as this linguistic comparison may be, it does not provide conclusive evidence as to the ultimate meaning of the Sanumá word for pregnant.

19. See, for instance, Pollock 1985 for a description of the Culina case.

20. Zeca's sardonic remark: "Women like to have baby boys so that they can play with their penises"!

21. *Tiko dɨbɨ hākobo; tiko dɨbɨ*, "others"; *hākobo*, "to hug while lying in the hammock."

22. About the movements of the Sanumá and other Yanomami see Colchester 1982; Chagnon 1968, 1974; Migliazza 1972; Smole 1976; Albert 1985.

Chapter 3. Diachrony and Leadership

1. The main feature of the Balinese *dadia* is thus summarized: "[A]n agnatic, preferentially endogamous, highly corporate group of people who are convinced, with whatever reason, that they are all descendants of one common ancestor. . . . [O]ne of the most interesting, and from a theoretical point of view most challenging, features of the dadia as a kingroup is its contingency, the fact that it does not necessarily form whenever there is a large

enough group of agnatically related kinsmen. There are many Balinese who have recognized patri-kinsmen who never organize themselves, never incorporate into a dadia. . . . [P]erhaps half the population remains outside of corporate kingroups" (Geertz and Geertz 1975:5, 73).

2. In rural Turkey the situation is thus described: A lineage "consists of a number of households, the heads of which are descended patrilineally . . . from a common ancestor generally three or four generations back. . . . Yet not all household heads are members of lineages, nor do all lineages that could be defined genealogically constitute significant social groups. . . . The villages . . . contain some who have no wish to belong to lineages, and some who have no lineages to belong to. Between them they cover perhaps half the population of Elbasl and rather less than half that of Sakaltutan . . . All households aim to grow and proliferate . . . : the large, patrilineal joint household which on the death of its head splits into a number of simple households, each seeking in turn to grow again into a large joint household" (Stirling 1965:27, 169, 247, 120).

3. Notice the difference between the Sanumá situation and that, for instance, of the Shavante as described by Maybury-Lewis (1967:169). Among the Shavante, the members of a dying lineage are incorporated into another so as not to leave people without lineage membership. Shavante and Sanumá offer, then, two distinct cultural solutions to the same problem created by the hazards of history—either relocate unattached people, or leave them lineageless.

4. It is interesting to notice that the Yekuana, as the Maiongong are known in Venezuela, also follow the procedure of dispersal in times of crisis, such as the death of a leader, or an enemy attack (Arvelo-Jiménez 1973, 1974:190).

5. I am grateful to Ken Taylor for having pointed out to me this important aspect of the Sanumá political system, namely, dispersal as a kind of buffer zone for the redimensioning of village leadership.

6. The dispersal of the Mosonawa community into several segments along the upper Auaris River is an example of these tactics, albeit a procrastinated one. It clearly shows the leadership crisis that has troubled that community for nearly two decades.

7. It was Eduardo Viveiros de Castro who, in a relaxed conversation over a drink, pointed to similar positions in a number of dissertations (Ladeira 1987; Lea 1986).

8. I met Zeca again in 1990. He had been wounded by gunshot during an incident involving white gold miners (see Chapter 11) and, as a consequence, was manifestly dependent upon his wife. His eldest son, a twenty-three-year-old rebellious young man, was still living with his parents after a frustrated marriage. The tension and frequent quarrels between father and son unveiled a dimension of Zeca's marriage that I had not preceived before—a positively oedipal relationship with the woman he once called "mother."

9. Many years later, this son returned to Auaris, got married, and had children. After a while of living together with his mother and Lucio, he quarreled with the latter and expelled him from his mother's house. Once more

Lucio took refuge in the forest (personal communication by Donald Borgman, February 1989).

10. Notice the Turkish equivalent: "Most of those who are not committed lineage members are among the poorer and less powerful stratum of village society" (Stirling 1954:27); or in Bali: "the remaining families outside the leading dadia play decidedly secondary parts in local political affairs, and the only way they can get their voices heard is by alliance with one of the stronger kingroups" (Geertz and Geertz 1975:72–73).

11. Compare this with, for instance, the Ge situation: "The difference in prestige and authority between male heads of extended-family households and young husbands who have not yet established their spheres of dominance beyond the level of their own families of procreation is a striking feature of public political life in all Gê societies" (T. Turner 1979b:160).

12. Again in Turkey: "The successful man with more than one married son transmits all his property but he cannot pass on his social position as a senior elder and head of a large and wealthy household. Thus, although his material wealth is passed on, his power and prestige are dissolved by his death. . . . the system works to prevent a stable hereditary hierarchy" (Stirling 1965:121).

13. *Ina*, "thus," "so"; *pada dɨbi*, "old ones"; *kuu*, "say"; *shinomo*, "as usual," "always."

14. The Sanumá *kaikana* comes from the Maiongong *kahitshana* which in turn derives from the Spanish *capitán* (Arvelo-Jiménez 1974:190).

15. *Hila*, "to argue," "to fight"; *lotete*, "strong."

16. It is interesting to notice the difference between Sanumá and Yanomam leaders. Among the latter, there is a type of speech, *hereamu*, the hallmark of a good village leader, uttered in the morning to exhort the villagers to carry out the day's working agenda. There is no *hereamu* equivalent in the upper Auaris.

17. *Wa*, "you," "your"; *sɨmɨga*, "ear"; *komi*, "full," "whole"; *ki*, "there"; *ha* "direction"; *konɨnɨ*, "go back."

18. In 1990, as a young man and father of three boys, this younger brother died of snakebite.

19. Sogosɨ's success in dodging bride service is partly due to the fact that his father-in-law is no longer living, and in part to the fact that his mother-in-law already has a resident son-in-law. But it may be, above all, due to his ability to impose his own choice of residence after marriage. His case is one of the few in which a man conquered the right to live virilocally thanks to his daring and political vigor.

20. In 1980, a former missionary at Auaris sent me a letter with the news that both of Kalioko's wives had died in a malaria epidemic. Demographic surveys that were carried out afterward both by the National Indian Foundation (FUNAI) and the nongovernmental organization dedicated to the defense of the Yanomami (CCPY) failed to record Kalioko's village. It was only in February 1989 that Donald Borgman told me that Kalioko's group had been dissolved and that he was now residing with one of the fragments that had separated from the Mosonawa village; he was back to stage one, doing bride

service to an old man of the ōka dibi sib. The vulnerability of his situation was quickly tested and his project failed, at least for the time being. With the death of his senior wife, one of the strongest links in the chain of residents, his community disintegrated and was no longer an autonomous unit. Here again we have an example of dispersal provoked by a crisis; but unlike the cases of agnatic groups that lose their headman, here the pivot of the crisis was an outstanding woman whose importance grew with her death, as indicated by the subsequent disappearance of Kalioko's village. More about Kalioko in the Epilogue.

21. Dibi, "they"; hila, "quarrel"; ha, "because"; die, "don't!"; kuu, "say."

22. In this respect the Sanumá are similar to the Ge: "a man with three sons-in-law is not thereby counted more prestigious or higher in status or authority than one with two sons-in-law, or for that matter than one who has no sons-in-law (for example, a man who had only sons, and therefore has only daughters-in-law as junior affines)" (T. Turner 1979b:160).

23. Information obtained from Donald Borgman in February 1989 has it that Jorge had lost his drive for leadership, while his brother was the headman of one of the various segments that resulted from the splitting apart of the Mosonawa village. Jorge is just another resident of what was left of Mosonawa. Perhaps its fragmentation is, in part, a response to all those ambitions and vocations. More about these brothers can be found in the Epilogue.

Chapter 4. The Marriage-Go-Round

1. Indeed, he married a woman from a far-away village in Venezuela.

2. That marriage ended in a definitive separation when the husband moved to Venezuela after having endured too much aggression on the part of his in-laws (information from Donald Borgman, February 1989). In 1992, I met him with his new family as a resident at Olomai.

3. For a discussion of the "classic" or "original" status of the Dravidian system, see Trautmann 1981.

4. It is worth noting what happened to Lalawa, the most autonomous community in terms of the marriage market, with most of its marriages occurring between only two descent groups. In the 1980s, it suffered serious and sudden setbacks. After the death of its leader, its headmanship changed hands twice, the community moved away, and, via intermarriages, Lalawa became associated with Lourenço's Colony. It lost its autonomy and political independence when it fused into Lourenço's community in its new location at Olomai. A while later, it fragmented into several local groups. What could have been its strong point—the capacity to enact the ideal village endogamy—taken to extremes, ended up bringing about its demise; it is reasonable to think that the intense social "inbreeding" led to the community's implosion. As to the Mosonawa residents, they also split up into three or four groups living along the Auaris River upstream and downstream from the mission (verbal information from Donald Borgman, February 1989). More will be said about these groups in Chapter 11 and in the Epilogue.

Chapter 5. Sanumá Times

1. In his critique of history studies, Stocking proposes a dichotomy between understanding and judgment. He declares that understanding is an attempt to capture the "reasonableness" of what would be short of the "rationality" established by today's standards of judgment (1968:5). If the historian's intention is to apprehend rationality through time, the anthropologist's must be to grasp it through space, i.e., coeval cultures. It is, in other words, an exercise in relativism.

2. Several anthropologists have been concerned with how to handle multivaried notions of time. Pocock (1964), for instance, declares himself puzzled with what he found in India, defying anthropology's theoretical versatility.

3. For a detailed treatment of Sanumá verbal suffixes, see Borgman 1976.

4. I was greatly helped by Ken Taylor in this task.

5. Notice that the canonical number of three children is regarded as marking the likely end of bride service.

6. As far as I know, the sociological and political effect of the *continuum* of virulence inherent in these practices as described by Albert (1985) for the Yanomam do not have a precise correspondence among the Sanumá, who seem to carve out their sociopolitical province on the basis of a balance of forces that I would call "sociological" rather than "magical." One should, however, consider the possibility that these differences may be due to the personal inclination of the ethnographers in question.

7. *Humabɨ*, "coccyx"; *tha*, "to make"; *-ba-*, "strong"; *-li-*, "direction"; *-ma*, "unwitnessed completed action."

8. *Sai dɨbɨ* is also applied to nonedible animals and plants.

9. There is another female *sai de, henona*, that lives in the water. It comes up to the surface always looking for a youth, *hisa de*, and dives again when it is seen.

10. There are some variations on the death theme not only among the various Yanomami subgroups, but also between different subregions of the Sanumá, as attested in Colchester (1982).

11. *Ose*, "young," "immature"; *kuteni*, "due to."

Chapter 6. Names under Erasure

1. "Lévi-Strauss's anthropologist seems free to pick his tool; Derrida's philosopher knows that there is no tool that does not belong to the metaphysical box" (Spivak 1976:xix).

2. See Kastenbaum (1977) for an interesting discussion of the notion of memory of the future.

Chapter 8. To Hunt a Name

1. *Humabɨ*, "coccyx"; *tha*, "to make"; *-ba-*, "emphasis"; *-li-*, "action focus"; *-ma*, "unwitnessed completed action."

2. *Hilo*, "name"; *pi ku*, "to think," "to want"; *zalo*, "because."

3. *Paso*, "spider monkey"; *ha*, "because," "due to"; *humabi*, "coccyx"; *thabalima*, "was made."

4. Hulme (1988) brings out the shock that hurricanes (in contrast to tempests) produced in the discoverers of America.

5. They are also common among rural migrants who become menial laborers in the big cities.

6. See also Seed (1992) for an analysis of European powers' rituals of possession of the New World.

Chapter 9. A Rumor on Stage

1. I must stress that the gap between spoken and written language is wider in Portuguese than in English. In this sense, rendering the information into English dialogues was an easier task than it was in the Portuguese version.

2. *Hea*, a complex concept for the non-Yanomami, means the sound counterpart of a person or animal. Just as *shi* is the visual sign, the "glow" of something, as, for instance, the rainbow is "the snake's glow," so also *hea* foretells its counterpart with a specific sound.

3. *Nabɨ de*, "Maiongong"; *holeshi*, "lie", "false."

4. In 1985, during a short trip to the village of Ericó on the Uraricaá, I met a pair of siblings who were said to be the children of Maiongong parents, but they did not live according to the Maiongong style (Ramos et al. 1985).

Chapter 10. The Sanumá's Others

1. I understand that the term *índio* has been banned by Indian societies in South America (in Ecuador, for instance) for its discriminatory connotations and replaced by terms such as *nativo*. For my purpose this change does not alter the fact that a marked dichotomy is created with the category "white," regardless of what label its counterpart may be given.

2. Postcards of upper Xingu Indians were shown to the Sanumá, who identified them as Nabɨ.

Chapter 11. The Age of Gold and Misery

1. For the history of Yanomami contact with whites, see Migliazza 1972; Albert 1985, 1992; IWGIA 1979.

2. Details of the impact of the Perimetral Norte road on the Yanomami can be found in IWGIA 1979.

3. On the effect of the Calha Norte Project on the Yanomami, see Albert 1992 and Ramos 1990a.

4. An agreement between the attorney general's office and the Brazilian Anthropological Association guaranteed that cases involving Indian rights would be based on expert reports. I was appointed to provide the attorneys with the justification for the demarcation of 9.5 million hectares of Yanomami land (Ramos 1990b).

5. The intricacies of the Calha Norte Project regarding the Yanomami land issue are described in Albert 1992.

Bibliography

Ação pela Cidadania
1990   *Yanomami: A Todos os Povos da Terra.* São Paulo: CCPY/CEDI/CIMI/NDI.
Albert, Bruce
1985   *Temps du sang, temps des cendres. Représentation de la maladie, système rituel et espace politique chez les Yanomami du Sud-est (Amazonie brésilienne).* Doctoral Dissertation. Paris: University of Paris X.
1992   Indian lands, environmental policy, and military geopolitics in the development of the Brazilian Amazonia: the case of the Yanomami. *Development and Change* (Sage, London) 23:34–70.
1993   The massacre of the Yanomami of Haximu. Portuguese version published in *Folha de S. Paulo*, October 3.
Arvelo-Jiménez, Nelly
1973   *The Dynamics of the Ye'cuana ("Maquiritare") Political System: Stability and Crisis.* IWGIA Document 12. Copenhagen: IWGIA.
1974   *Relaciones Políticas en una Sociedad Tribal.* Ediciones Especiales 68. México: Instituto Indigenista Interamericano.
Austin, John L.
1975   *How to Do Things with Words.* Cambridge: Harvard University Press.
Bakhtin, Mikhail
1981   *The Dialogic Imagination.* Austin: University of Texas Press.
Barker, James
1953   Memoria sobre la cultura de los Guaika. *Boletin Indigenista Venezolano* 1:433–90.
Bateson, Gregory
1958   *Naven.* Stanford: Stanford University Press.
Behar, Ruth
1993   Introduction. Women writing culture: another telling of the story of American anthropology. *Critique of Anthropology* 13 (4): 307–25.
Benjamin, Walter
1969   *Illuminations.* New York: Schocken Books.
Biocca, Ettore
1971   *Yanoama.* New York: Dutton.

Borgman, Donald M.
1976   Gramática pedagógica Sanuma Yanomámi (Sanuma – Português).
        Mimeo. Boa Vista: Missão Evangélica da Amazônia.
Cardoso de Oliveira, Roberto
1983   As "Categorias do Entendimento" na formação da antropologia.
        Anuário Antropológico 81, 125–46.
CEDI
1991   Povos Indígenas no Brasil 1987/88/89/90. *Aconteceu Especial* 18. São
        Paulo: Centro Ecumênico de Documentação e Informação.
Chagnon, Napoleon A.
1968   *Yanomamo. The Fierce People*. New York: Holt, Rinehart & Winston.
1974   *Studying the Yanomamo*. New York: Holt, Rinehart & Winston.
1988   Life histories, blood revenge, and warfare in a tribal population.
        Science 239:985–92.
Civrieux, Marc de
1980   *Watunna. An Orinoco Creation Cycle*. San Francisco: North Point Press.
Clastres, Pierre
1974   *Society against the State*. New York: Urizen Books.
Clifford, James
1986   On ethnographic allegory. In *Writing Culture*, ed. J. Clifford and G.
        Marcus, 98–121. Berkeley: University of California Press.
1990   Notes on (field)notes. In *Fieldnotes*, ed. R. Sanjek, 47–70. Ithaca:
        Cornell University Press.
Colchester, Marcus
1982   *The Economy, Ecology, and Ethnobiology of the Sanema Indians of South
        Venezuela*. Doctoral Dissertation. Oxford University.
Colchester, Marcus (ed.)
1985   *The Health Survival of the Venezuelan Yanoama*. IWGIA Document 53.
        Copenhagen: IWGIA.
Collier, George, and Victoria Bricker
1970   Nicknames and social structure in Zinacantan. *American Anthropolo-
        gist* 72:289–301.
Comaroff, John, and Jean Comaroff
1992   *Ethnography and the Historical Imagination*. Boulder: Westview.
Cruz, Manoel
1941   Dos nomes entre os Bororos. *Revista do Instituto Histórico e Geográfico
        Brasileiro* 175:185–211.
Da Matta, Roberto
1976   *Um Mundo Dividido*. Petrópolis: Vozes.
Derrida, Jacques
1976   *Of Grammatology*. Baltimore: Johns Hopkins University Press.
1978   *Writing and Difference*. Chicago: University of Chicago Press.
Dumont, Louis
1953   The Dravidian kinship terminology as an expression of marriage.
        Man 54:34–39.

334 Bibliography

1957   *Hierarchy and Marriage Alliance in South Indian Kinship.* Occasional Paper of the Royal Anthropological Institute 12. London.
1980   *Homo Hierarchicus.* Chicago: University of Chicago Press.
1983   *Affinity as Value.* Chicago: University of Chicago Press.

Durkheim, Emile
1965   *The Elementary Forms of Religious Life.* New York: Free Press.

Evans-Pritchard, E. E.
1937   *Witchcraft, Oracles, and Magic among the Azande.* Oxford: Clarendon Press.
1940   *The Nuer.* Oxford: Clarendon Press.

Fabian, Johannes
1991   *Time and the Work of Anthropology.* Philadelphia: Harwood Academic Publishers.

Firth, Raymond
1967   Rumour in a primitive society. In *Tikopia Ritual and Belief.* Boston: Beacon Press.

Fock, Niels
1963   *Waiwai: Religion and Society of an Amazonian Tribe.* Ethnographic Series 8. Copenhagen: Danish National Museum.

Fortes, Meyer
1958   Introduction to *The Developmental Cycle in Domestic Groups,* ed. J. Goody, 1–14. Cambridge: Cambridge University Press.

Fundação Nacional de Saúde
1991   *Primeiro Relatório do Distrito Sanitário Yanomami: Avaliação das Atividades e Diagnóstico de Saúde.* Boa Vista: Coordenação Regional de Roraima.

Gadamer, Hans-Georg
1975   *Truth and Method.* New York: Crossroad.

Geertz, Clifford
1968   *Islam Observed.* Chicago: University of Chicago Press.

Geertz, Hildred, and Clifford Geertz
1964   Teknonymy in Bali: parenthood, agegrading, and genealogical amnesia. *Journal of the Royal Anthropological Institute* 94:98–108.
1975   *Kinship in Bali.* Chicago: University of Chicago Press.

Goodenough, Ward H.
1965   Personal names and modes of address in two Oceanic societies. In *Context and Meaning in Cultural Anthropology,* ed. M. E. Spiro, 265–76. New York: Free Press.

Griaule, Marcel
1965   *Conversations with Ogotemmêli.* Oxford: Oxford University Press.

Guemple, D. L.
1965   Saunik: name sharing as a factor governing Eskimo kinship terms. *Ethnology* 4 (3): 323–35.

Guss, David
1986   Keeping it oral: a Yekuana ethnology. *American Ethnologist* 13 (3): 413–29.

Harner, Michael J.
1972   *The Jívaro.* New York: Doubleday Anchor.

Houseman, Michael
1983   La relation hiérarchique: idéologie particulière ou modèle général? In *Différences, Valeurs, Hiérarchie*, 299–318. Paris: Éditions de l'École des Hautes Études en Sciences Sociales.

Hugh-Jones, Christine
1979   *From the Milk River.* Cambridge: Cambridge University Press.

Hugh-Jones, Stephen
1979   *The Palm and the Pleiades.* Cambridge: Cambridge University Press.

Hulme, Peter
1986   *Colonial Encounters.* New York: Methuen.

IWGIA (International Workgroup for Indigenous Affairs)
1979   *The Yanoama in Brazil 1979.* IWGIA Document 37. Copenhagen: IWGIA.

Kaplan, Joanna Overing
1972   Cognation, endogamy, and teknonymy: the Piaroa example. *Southwestern Journal of Anthropology* 28 (3): 282–97.

Kastenbaum, Robert
1977   Memories of tomorrow. In *The Personal Experience of Time*, ed. B. S. Gorman and A. E. Wessman, 193–214. New York: Plenum.

Koch-Grünberg, Theodor
[1917]
1979   *Del Roraima al Orinoco.* Vol. 1. Caracas: Ediciones del Banco Central de Venezuela.

Krell, David Farrell
1990   *Of Memory, Reminiscence, and Writing on the Verge.* Bloomington: Indiana University Press.

Ladeira, Maria Elisa
1987   *A Troca de Nomes e a Troca de Cônjuges. Uma Contribuição ao Estudo do Parentesco Timbira.* Master's Thesis. Universidade de São Paulo.

Lave, Jean C.
1967   *Social Taxonomy among the Krikati (Gê) of Central Brazil.* Ph.D. Dissertation. Harvard University.

Lea, Vanessa
1986   *Nomes e Nektrets Kayapó. Uma Concepção de Riqueza.* Doctoral Dissertation. Museu Nacional, Rio de Janeiro.

Leach, Edmund
1954   *Political Systems of Highland Burma.* Boston: Beacon Press.
1961   *Rethinking Anthropology.* London: Athlone Press.

Leenhardt, Maurice
1979   *Do Kamo. Person and Myth in the Melanesian World.* Chicago: University of Chicago Press.

Lévi-Strauss, Claude
1948   *La vie familiale et sociale des Indiens Nambikwara*. Paris: Société des Américanistes.
1962   *La pensée sauvage*. Paris: Plon.
1991   *Histoire de lynx*. Paris: Plon.

Lienhardt, Peter A.
1975   The interpretation of rumour. In *Studies in Social Anthropology. Essays in Memory of E. E. Evans-Pritchard*, ed. J. H. M. Beattie and R. G. Lienhardt, 105–31. Oxford: Clarendon Press.

Lizot, Jacques
1973   Onomastique Yanomami. *L'Homme* 13 (3): 60–71.
1975   *Diccionario Yanomami-Español*. Caracas: Universidad Central de Venezuela.
1976   *Le cercle des feux*. Paris: Éditions du Seuil.
1984   *Les Yanõmami centraux*. Paris: Éditions de l'École des Hautes Études en Sciences Sociales.
1985   *Tales of the Yanomami*. Cambridge: Cambridge University Press.

MacMillan, Gordon
1993   *Gold Mining and Land Use Change in the Brazilian Amazon*. Ph.D. Dissertation. University of Edinburgh.

Mauss, Marcel
[1929]
1979   A alma, o nome e a pessoa. In *Mauss*, ed. R. Cardoso de Oliveira, 177–80. São Paulo: Ática.

Maybury-Lewis, David
1967   *Akwe-Shavante Society*. Oxford: Oxford University Press.

Melatti, Julio Cezar
1976   Nominadores e genitores: um aspecto do dualismo Krahó. *Leituras de Etnologia Brasileira*, ed. E. Schaden, 139–48. São Paulo: Companhia Editora Nacional.

Migliazza, Ernesto
1964   Notas sobre a organização social dos Xiriana do rio Uraricaá. *Boletim do Museu Paraense Emilio Goeldi*, Série Antropologia, 22.
1967   Grupos lingüísticos do Território Federal de Roraima. In *Atas do Simpósio sobre a Biota Amazônica*, Antropologia, 2:153–73.
1972   *Yanomama Grammar and Intelligibility*. Ph.D. Dissertation. Indiana University.

Monbiot, George
1991   *Amazon Watershed*. London: Michael Joseph.

Needham, Rodney
1954   The system of teknonyms and death-names among the Penan. *Southwestern Journal of Anthropology* 10:416–31.
1965   Death-names and solidarity in Penan society. *Bijdragen Tot De Taal-, Land- en Volkenkunde* 121:58–76.

1972   *Belief, Language, and Experience*. Chicago: University of Chicago Press.

Ottenberg, Simon
1990   Thirty years of fieldnotes: changing relationships to the text. In *Fieldnotes*, ed. R. Sanjek, 139–60. Ithaca: Cornell University Press.

Pocock, David F.
1964   The anthropology of time-reckoning. *Contributions to Indian Sociology* 7:18–24.

Pollock, Donald
1985   Looking for a sister: Culina siblingship and affinity. *Working Papers in South American Indians*, no. 7, ed. K. Kensinger, 8–15. Bennington: Bennington College.

Ramos, Alcida Rita
1972   *The Social System of the Sanumá of Northern Brazil*. Ph.D. Dissertation. University of Wisconsin.
1979   Personal names and social classification in Sanumá (Yanoama) society. In *Peasants, Primitives, and Proletariats*, ed. D. L. Browman and R. A. Schwarz, 191–205. The Hague: Mouton.
1980   *Hierarquia e Simbiose. Relações Intertribais no Brasil*. São Paulo: Hucitec.
1982   Entre pais e esposas: a propósito de regime desarmônico e suas conseqüências. *Anuário Antropológico 80*, 63–76.
1986   A viagem dos índios. Maldição ou bênção? *Humanidades* 10:69–75.
1987   Reflecting on the Yanomami: ethnographic images and the pursuit of the exotic. *Cultural Anthropology* 2 (3): 284–304.
1988   Indian voices: contact experienced and expressed. In *Rethinking History and Myth*, ed. J. Hill, 214–34. Urbana: University of Illinois Press.
1990a   An economy of waste. Amazonian frontier development and the livelihood of Brazilian Indians. In *Economic Catalysts to Ecological Change*, 161–78. Working Papers, 39th Annual Conference, Center for Latin American Studies, University of Florida, Gainesville.
1990b   Terra e sobrevivência cultural Yanomami. *Urihi* 13. São Paulo: CCPY (Comissão pela Criação do Parque Yanomami).
1991   The prophecy of a rumor. The clash between Indians and miners in Yanomamiland. MS.
n.d.   O papel político das epidemias. O caso Yanomami. In *Grupos Étnicos en Riesgo de Extinción*, ed. M. Bartolomé. Quito: Abya-Yala (in press).

Ramos, Alcida Rita, and Bruce Albert
1977   Yanoama descent and affinity: the Sanumá/Yanomam contrast. *Actes du XLIIe Congrès International des Américanistes*, 2:71–90. Paris: Société des Américanistes.

Ramos, Alcida Rita; Marco Antonio Lazarin; and Gale Gomez
1985   Yanomami em tempo de ouro. Relatório de Pesquisa. *Série Antropo-*

logia 51. Brasília: Departamento de Antropologia, Universidade de Brasília.

Reff, Daniel

1991   *Disease, Depopulation, and Culture Change in Northwestern New Spain, 1518–1764.* Salt Lake City: University of Utah Press.

Ribeiro, Darcy

1956   Convívio e contaminação. Republished In *Os Indios e a Civilização*, 272–307. Rio de Janeiro: Civilização Brasileira, 1970.

Rivière, Peter

1969   *Marriage among the Trio.* Oxford: Clarendon Press.

1971   Political structure of the Trio Indians as manifested in a system of ceremonial dialogue. In *The Translation of Culture*, ed. T. O. Beidelman, 293–311. London: Tavistock Publications.

Rosaldo, Renato

1980   *Ilongot Headhunting, 1883–1974.* Stanford: Stanford University Press.

1989   *Culture and Truth.* Boston: Beacon Press

Sahlins, Marshall

1963   Poor man, rich man, big-man, chief: political types in Melanesia and Polynesia. *Comparative Studies in Society and History* 5:285–303.

1981   *Historical Metaphors and Mythical Realities.* Ann Arbor: University of Michigan Press.

1985   *Islands of History.* Chicago: University of Chicago Press.

Sanders, Ronald

1978   *Lost Tribes and Promised Lands.* Boston: Little, Brown.

Seed, Patricia

1992   Taking possession and reading texts: establishing the authority of overseas empires. *William and Mary Quarterly*, 3d ser. 49:183–209.

Smole, William J.

1976   *The Yanoama Indians. A Cultural Geography.* Austin: University of Texas Press.

Spivak, Gayatri Chakravorty

1976   Translator's preface. In J. Derrida, *Of Grammatology*, ix–xc. Baltimore: Johns Hopkins University Press.

Stirling, Paul

1965   *Turkish Village.* London: Weidenfeld & Nicolson.

Stocking, George W., Jr.

1968   On the limits of "presentism" and "historicism" in the historiography of the behavioral sciences. In *Race, Culture, and Evolution. Essays in the History of Anthropology*, 1–12. Chicago: University of Chicago Press.

Taylor, Kenneth I.

1974   *Sanuma fauna: Prohibitions and Classifications.* Monograph 18. Caracas: Fundación La Salle de Ciencias Naturales.

1976   Body and spirit among the Sanumá (Yanoama) of north Brazil. In

Medical Anthropology, ed. F. X. Grollig and H. B. Haley, 27–48. The Hague: Mouton.

1977   Raiding, dueling, and descent group membership among the Sanumá. *Actes du XLIIe Congrès International des Américanistes,* 2:91–104. Paris: Société des Américanistes.

1981   Knowledge and praxis in Sanuma food prohibitions. In *Food Taboos in Lowland South America*, ed. K. Kensinger and W. Kracke, 24–54. Working Papers on South American Indians 3. Bennington College.

Thomas, David J.

1982   *Order without Government*. Illinois Studies in Anthropology 13. Urbana: University of Illinois Press.

Todorov, Tzvetan

1984   *The Conquest of America*. New York: Harper & Row

Trajano Filho, Wilson

1993   Rumores : uma narrativa da nação. *Série Antropologia* 143. Brasília: Departamento de Antropologia, Universidade de Brasília.

Trautmann, Thomas R.

1981   *Dravidian Kinship*. Cambridge: Cambridge University Press.

Turner, Terence

1979a   Kinship, household, and community structure. In *Dialectical Societies*, ed. D. Maybury-Lewis, 19–217. Cambridge: Harvard University Press.

1979b   The Gê and Dororo societies as dialectical systems. a general model. In *Dialectical Societies*, ed. D. Maybury-Lewis, 147–78. Cambridge: Harvard University Press.

Turner, Victor

1969   *The Ritual Process*. Chicago: Aldine.

Urban, Greg

1986   Ceremonial dialogues in South America. *American Ethnologist* 88 (2): 371–86.

Viveiros de Castro, Eduardo

1986   *Araweté. Deuses Canibais*. Rio de Janeiro: Jorge Zahar/ANPOCS.

Weber, Max

1978   The sociology of religion. In *Economy and Society*, 1:399–634. Berkeley: University of California Press.

Acknowledgments

As always my first thanks are to the Sanumá people whose joie de vivre has passed the most rigorous of tests. What could I have done without the fabulous help of Bruce Grant, who spent countless of his precious hours going over my unpolished English? My gratitude to him cannot be overstated. I am also grateful to Paul Little for his language assistance with the last pages of the manuscript. I am pleased to have had the chance to incorporate Donald Pollock's useful suggestions particularly for Chapters 2, 3, 4, and 8. Special thanks go to my department colleagues Wilson Trajano Filho for the dedicated reading of portions of the book, Mariza Peirano for many profitable intellectual interchanges, and especially Julio Cezar Melatti, who so unselfishly gave his time and patience to the cause of turning my clumsy attempts at computation into a professional job. To Cristina Sá, who voluntarily joined in the last push to prepare the final version of the manuscript, my warm thanks. George Marcus' sympathy and encouragement are greatly appreciated.

Index

Aesthetic judgment, 130, 219
Affinal relationships, 80–90 *passim*, 132–53, 215, 221–24, 229
Afterlife: beliefs in, 162–63, 166, 167–72, 283–84, 293, 330*n10*
Age sets, 158–63, 225
Albert, Bruce, 4, 200, 205, 281, 323*n6*, 325*n3*, 326*n18*, 330*n6*
Avoidance: between co-wives, 38, 62; of mother-in-law, 38–39, 128–30, 189, 218; intertribal, 236

Bateson, Gregory, 250
Behar, Ruth, 323*Intro.n1*
Borgman, Donald (missionary), 7, 44, 140, 313, 325*n8*, 326*n10*, 328*n20*, 329*n23*
Bororo Indians, 220
Brazilian Anthropological Association (ABA), 331*ch11n4*
Bride service, 39–40, 97, 98, 108, 109, 114, 121, 128, 189, 239, 315, 328*n20*, 329*n2*; dodging, 40, 77, 121–22, 128–30, 142–43, 151, 190, 191, 248, 325*n7*, 328*n19*

Camping: grounds, 21, 23, 36, 37, 284–85, 301, 304; family, 22, 25, 27, 36–37, 85, 116, 150, 240, 293, 302; mentioned, 63
Canaque society: 186
Canoes: 33, 46, 49, 52; long distance travel by, xviii, 44, 51–52, 116, 236, 241, 245, 247, 252, 301, 303–4, 315. (*see also* Travel); value of, 237; mentioned, 22, 292

Catgory formation, 259–70
Celibacy, 130–31
Ceremonial dialogues, 104, 111–12
Chagnon, Napoleon, 140, 152, 200, 205, 325*n3*
Children: rearing of, 5, 326*n16*; betrothal of, 39, 74, 128, 190 (*see also* Marriages); number of, 40, 314, 326*n11*, 330*n5*; games of, 42; prematurely weaned, 50, 54, 132, 326*n16*; claims on, 77–78, 106; playing with, 326*n20*; neglect of, 106; names of, 186, 204, 217–28; quarrels between, 202, 203–4, 206, 213; death of, 278, 280, 285–86, 301–2, 315; orphaned, 278–80, 286
Clastres, Pierre, 124
Clifford, James, 313
Colchester, Marcus, 324*nn10, 16*, 325*n6*
Collor, Fernando (President of Brazil, 1990–1992), 288, 307
Columbus, Christopher, 231, 232
Comaroff, John and Jean, 318
Comissão pela Criação do Parque Yanomami (CCPY), 287, 309–11, 328*n20*
Community: definition of, 32; ties between, 41, 90, 99, 125–26, 148–53, 263–64, 300–302, 314; name of, 67, 325*n8*, 117, 206–8, 264, 302; power in, 77, 102, 109–26, 235; historical, 91–95, 155, 173–77, 264, 301–2; destruction of, 272–74, 278–79, 292, 299–302, 309, 313, 315; dispersal of, 325*nn8, 9*, 326*n15*, 327*nn4, 5, 6*, 328*n20*, 329*n4*. *See also* Village

Conflicts: internal, 45, 327nn8, 9, 113, 129, 131, 150, 152, 212, 246–247, 257, 295; provoked by whites, 310
Cosmological transformations, 169–75
Couvade, 217, 218, 221, 224–25
Cremation, 165, 168, 171, 245, 283, 293. See also Mortuary ceremonies
Culina Indians, 326n19
Cultural relativism, 263, 267

Death, causes of, xv–xvi, xviii–xix, 44–45, 78, 105, 106, 113, 289, 294–95, 300, 316–17, 328nn18, 20
Demography, 21, 46, 158–59, 177, 280, 287, 308, 314–15, 323ch1n2
Derrida, Jacques, 14, 181–82, 187, 199, 203, 330ch6n1
Descent group membership: in sibs, 57–66, 69, 71–73, 80–81, 97, 108, 192, 193, 207–8, 210, 211, 229, 325n6; identifying features, 59, 79, 220, 262–65; in lineages, 67–77, 80–81, 92, 97–98, 108, 114–15, 117, 191–96, 207–8, 210, 211, 229, 313, 325nn4, 6, 326n11; in Bali, 70, 96, 100, 326n1, 328n10; in rural Turkey, 70, 96, 327n2, 328nn10, 12; fissioning, 75–76, 81–87, 92–94, 97–101, 193–96, 210; fragility of, 326n11, 329n4, 192; solidarity of, 90; in historical residence categories, 91–95, 173–77, 264; formation of, 96–103, 124–25, 192–96, 197, 205; in Shavante society, 327n3
Development, 271–75, 287, 308–9, 331ch11nn2, 3, 5
Diachronic structures, 101, 109–10, 125, 176
Diseases: traditional, 160–61, 169–70; caught from whites, 251, 259, 272–75, 281, 291–96, 298, 299. See also Epidemics
Division of labor, 30–32
Divorce, 127
Dravidian kinship, 132–43, 185, 329n3
Dreams, 168, 245–46
Dumont, Louis, 132, 139, 144
Durkheim, Emile, 164, 217

Ecology: regional diversity of, 19; seasonal variation of, 21–22; social

importance of, 26–32, passim; defense of, 258; natural barriers of, 258; destruction of, 277, 281, 308, 323ch1n1
Epidemics: measles, xv, 272–74, 308; malaria, xvi, 7, 272–79, 281, 286, 291–96, 298, 300–303, 308–9, 315–17, 328n20; influenza, 273, 281; political force of, 275, 308–9; records of, 278–79, 289; social consequences of, 278–80, 296
Ethnic identity, 259–60
Ethnographic style, 3–4, 7–15 passim, 56, 181–82, 235, 237, 239, 317–20, 323Intro.n1, 330nn1, 6
Ethos: female, 10; male, 10, 44–45, 250; cultural, 238–39, 250
Evans-Pritchard, E. E., 158

Fabian, Johannes, 317, 318
Family: phases of, 39–40, 58, 98, 188, 324n7; membership to, 58, 69; definition of, 184–91, 195, 197; incorporation in, 189–92, 196–197. See also Names, teknonyms
Feasting, among the Maiongong, 244, 246, 248, 252
Fertility, as classificatory feature, 159–62
Fieldwork: return to, xv, xvii–xx, 289–95, 313–20; in retrospect, 4, 312, 317–20; conditions of, 5–13, 263, 289, 290–95, 303–8, 311–12, 324n15
Firth, Raymond, 256
Fishing: 23, 30, 36, 40, 123, 141, 202, 217, 258, 277
Food taboos, 159–62, 169–70, 217, 323n3; mentioned, 212, 218, 220, 265
Fortes, Meyer, 96
Freud, Sigmund, 196

Gadamer, Hans-Georg, 123, 313
Gardens, age of, 22–23, 25–26, 35–36, 46, 52–53, 158, 272–73, 285, 296; division of labor in, 23; produce of, 23–26, 28, 36, 43, 46, 53, 236, 253; shape and composition of, 23–32, passim, 52, 53; historical importance, 92; time for work in, 157, 158, 272–73, 296, 310; theft of, 253; destruction of, 258, 277; ecological effects of, 323ch1n1
Gathering, 23, 30, 36, 40, 46

Ge Indians, 101, 161, 209, 222, 228, 328n11, 329n22

Geertz, Hildred and Clifford, 325n5, 96, 100, 109

Genetic reckoning, 77–80

Hallucinogens: used in hunting, 28–29; used in shamanism, 11, 104, 111, 121; mentioned, 11, 252

Headmanship, 97, 98–99, 102, 110–19, 121–26, 255, 314, 315, 325nn7, 8, 327nn5, 6, 328n16, 329n4; potential, 194–95, 316

Heidegger, Martin, 182

Hospitality, 56, 60

Houses: types of, 34–35, 50–51, 53, 323n6; building of, 36, 277, 296, 315; occupation of, 36–39, 50–51, 53, 114, 142, 188, 190, 193, 301; destruction of, 276, 286, 292, 315; count of, 323ch1n2

Hulme, Peter, 331ch8n4

Human rights, 258, 282, 287–89, 297–98, 308–11, 331ch11n4; activisim in, 320

Humor, sense of, 10, 103, 119, 121, 205–6, 216, 232, 236, 314

Hunting: skills, 10, 114, 115, 119, 123; collective, 22, 43, 310; types of, 27–30, 156–57; and scarcity of game, 36, 281; alter ego animals, 44–45, 165; grounds, 46, 49, 258; mentioned, 23, 26, 36, 37, 40, 79, 220. See also Ritual, of naming; Ritual, hunt

Incest, 64, 105

Interethnic relations, differential power in, 253, 258–261, 331ch10n1, 268–70, 281, 297–300

Intertribal: tension, 13, 324n13, 121, 235–57, 267; historic warfare, 47, 55, 242, 249, 253–54, 264, 266; communication, 239, 248 (see also Language); stereotypes, 248–51, 255, 257, 263–67

Iroquois Indians, 220

Judicial measures, 277, 331ch11n4, 288, 309

Kastenbaum, Robert, 330ch6n2

Kayapó Indians, 269

Killing: of Indians by whites, 225, 241, 251, 257, 277, 280, 282–86, 290–91, 299–300; of whites by Indians, 280, 283, 291

Land: invasions of, xviii, 4, 21, 258–59, 286–89, 297, 308–9, 309–10; importance of, 269–70; rights, 269–70, 286–89, 298, 331ch11n4; demarcation of, 286–89, 297, 307, 311, 323ch1n2, 331ch11n4; on international border, 287, 311

Language: learning, 5, 67, 106–7, 119, 255, 269, 297, 319; subgroup variation in, 19–20, 41–42, 261, 301, 324nn1, 14, 326n18; intertribal communication, 106–7, 239, 248, 264, 301; borrowing, 111, 266, 301, 328n14; monolingualism, 258; power of, 260–61, 267, 268–70, 297

Leach, Edmund, 101, 224

Leenhardt, Maurice, 133, 186

Legitimacy of children, 225, 229, 240

Lévi-Strauss, Claude, 13, 124, 203, 267, 330ch6n1

Life: histories, 103–8; cycle, 158–77 passim; 225–26

Macushi Indians, 280

Magic plants (alawali): 25, 37, 49, 105, 113, 161

Maiongong: 4, 13, 32, 40–41, 44, 46–48, 55, 93, 111, 116, 119, 120, 175, 176, 235–57, 262, 265, 280, 292, 293, 294, 300, 302, 315, 325n8, 327n4, 328n14, 331ch9n4

Makiritare. See Maiongong

Marriage: and extra-marital relations, 23, 45, 90, 114, 131; intertribal, 32, 48–49, 121, 149, 237–39, 248–49, 255–56, 331ch9n4; child betrothal, 39, 74, 128, 190; noncanonic, 60, 63, 104–5, 146–48, 240, 327n8; expected, 64–66, 98, 128, 145–46, 212; break up of, 78, 218; polygynous, 98, 105, 106, 124, 127, 193, 196, 239, 315–16; political role of, 124, 139, 149–53; stability, 127; serial, 127, 239, 329n2; description of, 128

Mashacali Indians, 269

Mauss, Marcel, 184

Maybury-Lewis, David, 327*n3*
Media coverage, 276–78, 280, 281–82, 288, 310–11
Medical teams, 276, 278, 291–95, 300–308 *passim*, 314, 316
Migliazza, Ernesto, 201
Migrations, 45, 48, 92–95, 114–16 *passim*, 148, 173–77, 235–36, 266, 322*n22*
Military, 259, 271, 277, 286, 292, 305–8, 311, 323*ch1n2*; and Calha Norte Project: 276, 287–89, 296–97, 331*ch11nn3, 5*
Mining, 231–32, 235, 275, 331*ch8n5*; gold rush, xv–xix *passim*, 4, 258–59, 275–86, 288, 297–98, 305, 309–12, 316; Indians working in, 237, 291; camps, violence in, 277, 280–86, 282–86, 299–300, 310; and gold smuggling, 288; political pressure for, 288; reserves, 288; prohibition of, 288, 306, 309–10; lobby, 288, 311
Missionaries: influence of, xvii, 46–48, 54, 119–21, 244–45, 273–76 *passim*, 316, 319, 324*n16*; as sources of information, xx, 7, 44, 159, 246, 252, 291, 313, 328*n20*; number of, 45–47, 324*n11*; opinions of, 131, 204–5, 255; power of, 204, 230–32, 236, 252–53, 267, 313; mentioned, 8, 13, 51, 76, 119, 133–34, 202, 239–40, 266, 293
Mortuary ceremonies, 43–45, 157, 158, 168, 264, 283, 284, 289, 300, 310. *See also* Cremation
Mourning, 103–4, 243, 251, 277, 291
Myth and history, 173–75, 235

Nambiquara Indians, 124, 203, 205
Names: secrecy of, 12, 56–59, 68, 116, 181–83, 194, 197, 199–207, 215, 218, 230, 324*n12*, 325*n3*; of Maiongong origin, 55, 111; patronyms, 57–60, 62, 69, 92, 95, 176, 181, 194, 198, 200, 205, 206–9, 215, 216, 229; of sibs, 57–60, 94–95, 173–75, 325*n6*; meaning of, 59–60, 63, 209, 227–28; teknonyms, 62, 68–69, 98, 142, 183–98, 200, 202, 205, 206, 208, 209, 215, 226, 228; of lineages, 68, 182, 184, 194, 198, 325*n6*; multiple, 196, 200, 209, 216; homonyms, 199, 207–12; giver of,

222–24, 228–29; nicknames, 226–27, 231–32, 331*ch8n5*; Christian, 227, 230–32; as historic records, 228
National Guard (Venezuela), 300
National Health Foundation, xviii, 291, 299, 302, 306, 307
National Indian Foundation (FUNAI), xvi, 277–78, 280, 286–89 *passim*, 292, 297–98, 306, 310, 311, 323*ch1n2*, 328*n20*
"Native philosopher", 318–20

Patasho Indians, 269
Patrilineal reckoning: 32, 57, 60–80 *passim*, 158, 176–77, 192, 229, 248; and succession, 113–15, 125
Peirano, Mariza, 256
Pemon Indians, 266
Person: components of, 14, 60, 68, 103, 155, 163–69, 171–72, 175, 183–84, 186, 195–98, 201, 213–14, 217–21, 223–24, 226–28, 229–30, 245, 331*ch9n2*; categories of, 58
Personage, 184, 186
Piaroa Indians, 183, 185
Pocock, David, 330*ch5n2*
Political leadership, 69, 73–77, 85, 97, 109–26, 255, 295, 328*nn10, 11*; succession to, 85–86, 99, 110–26; and qualities of a leader, 110–15, 117–23; without lineage affiliation, 116–19
Pollock, Donald, 326*n19*
Population: decrease, xv–xix *passim*; 272–86, 294–303, 308–12; in the Guiana Shield, 236, 308, 314, 324*n17*; increase, 314–15
Power and authority, 102, 110–26, 235, 255; 328*n19*, 329*n22*; striving for, 119–22, 239, 247–48, 292, 315, 319, 326*n15*; loss of, 325*n8*, 328*n12*, 329*n23*
Privacy, 212–14; of personal names, 14, 39, 51, 58, 60, 68, 116, 181–84, 197–98, 213–16, 231

Raiding, 44–45, 150, 165, 265, 283, 316, 324*n10*; intertribal, 235–36
Regional subgroups: Shikoi, xviii–xix, 32, 41, 51, 73, 85, 242, 264, 292, 299–307 *passim*, 316, 323*n5*, 324*n15*; Kobali, 41, 44, 51, 82, 113, 150, 164, 165, 173, 175,

262–67 passim; Samatali, 42, 74, 75, 84,
92–93, 117, 175, 262–67 passim;
Hogomawa, 42, 88, 264, 299–30;
Tucushim, 261, 264, 300, 303–4, 307
Ritual: of puberty, 114, 155, 166–67; of
purification, 165; of naming, 215, 216,
217–26, 229; hunt, 283
Rosaldo, Renato, 6
Rumor(s), 13; regarding interethnic
conflict, birth of, 235, 247, 248;
recurrence of, 246, 310, 316

Sahlins, Marshall, 102
Sarney, José (President of Brazil,
1985–1990), 287, 288
Seed, Patricia, 331n6
Sex ratio, 45, 79, 97, 98
Sexual behavior: impotence, 105;
abstinence, 132
Shamanism: reputation of practicing, 45,
114–15, 123, 255; frequency of, 54;
skills in, 104, 107, 109, 110, 111,
114–15; political use of, 120, 123, 243,
245, 247–48; curing by, 161, 169–70;
mentioned, 299, 323n3
Shavante Indians, 208, 269, 327n3
Siblings: solidarity among, 85, 131;
cleavage point among, 81–87, 230;
confrontations between, 87–91;
terminology of, 134–38, 143–45;
representatives of, 226
Smole, William, 323ch1n1
Socialization, 5; intertribal, 106–7, 110–11
Sorcery: acusations of, 45, 264; sorcerers
(ōka dibi), 49, 54; types of, 161, 242;
fear of, 246, 248, 255, 316–17
Spirits: as alter ego, 44, 113, 120, 155,
161, 164–66, 213–14, 243; assisting
shamans, 79, 104, 161, 165, 168–71,
242, 243, 247, 248, 250, 255; of game
animals, 155, 161, 163–64, 166, 169–71,
217–26; evil, 155, 161, 163–64, 166–67,
219, 242, 255, 216, 330nn8, 9; human,
163–64, 167–69, 316, mentioned; 13,
22, 23, 27, 58, 154
Spivak, Gayatri C., 181–82
Spouses: behavior of, 127, 140–41; age
of, 128, 130–32, 212
Stirling, Paul, 96
Stocking, George, 154, 330n1

Storytelling, 318
Streams: social importance of, 22–23, 34,
49, 91
Supernatural attack, 120, 201; danger of,
217–24, 250

Taste for drama, 10, 49, 87–89, 235–46,
250
Taylor, Kenneth, 4, 8, 9–10, 11, 169–71,
201, 323n3, 327n5, 330n4
Terena Indians, 258, 260
Time: reckoning, 154–158, 299, 330ch5n2
Trading: goods, xvii, 8–9, 29, 236, 244,
251, 266, 298, 303; with missionaries,
8, 46–47, 204, 244–45, 251–52; with
anthropologists, 8–10, 51; with
Maiongong, 25, 46–47, 254; intertribal,
29; etiquette, 43–44, 264;
intercommunity, 52, 123; with miners,
281, 290–91, 298
Trails: social importance of, 23, 52;
destruction of, 277; mentioned, 282,
285
Trajano, Wilson, 256
Translation, xvii–xix passim, 7, 9, 262,
281, 286; problems of 43, 53, 133, 140,
154, 181, 217, 237, 331ch9n1
Travel: to other villages, 21, 51–52, 63,
104, 240; to white man's land, 119,
121, 157, 236–57 passim; mentioned,
266, 272
Turner, Terence, 102

Uxorilocal residence, 62, 70, 97, 188,
189, 230, 325n7

Village: definition of, 32, 34; mobility,
36, 45, 46, 91–94, 116, 296, 300,
313–15, 324n8, 325n8, 326nn10, 15;
visiting, 41, 283; composition of, 45–55,
62, 116–17, 300, 314, 324n8; physical
set–up of, 47–54, 142, 300; dispersal,
61, 82, 84–85, 86, 91–99 passim, 119,
163, 173, 175–76, 264, 314, 315; name
of, 67, 91–95, 200, 262; endogamy, 70,
90, 97, 128, 142, 144–52, 189, 329n4;
formation of, 116–19, 325n8;
disintegration of, 119, 313–14; 324n8,
325n8, 328n20; contact between,
125–26, 293–96, 314, 316–17, 330n6;

Village (*continued*)
incorporation into, 196–97, 315, 325*n8*, 329*n4*. *See also* Community
Visitors: rituals, 42–44, 111 (*see also* Ceremonial dialogues); frequency of, 51, 157, 301, 316; hospitality toward, 63, 150; fear of, 111
Viveiros de Castro, Eduardo, 327*n7*

Weber, Max, 43
Whites: emulation of, 119–22, 255, 316, 319; original residence of, 163; names of, 230–32; contact with, 230–32, 251–52, 258–61, 268–312 *passim*, 315, 331*ch11n1*; traveling to land of, 236–37, 243, 251, 327*n9*; working for, 236–37, 272; opinions about, 237, 251–52, 262, 266, 297–99; conflicts with, 257, 275, 277, 281, 289–91; prejudice of, against Indians, 259–61, 268–70, 277, 280, 312, 331*ch10n1*; invasion by, 271–86, 288–89, 309–12;

disruption caused by, 272–300, 308–312, 327*n8*; account of origin of, 299; mentioned, 176, 202, 241, 265
Work: for missionaries, 76, 119, 244–45, 247, 252–53; for other whites, 236–37; for the Maiongong, 241, 252

Xingu Park, 331*ch10n2*

Yanomami Health District, 291, 301–4 *passim*
Yanomami language family and subgroups: xv–xix, 4, 6, 7, 11, 14, 19–21, 34–36, 40–45, 56–57, 59, 67–68, 79, 104, 111, 122, 138, 142, 145, 152, 158, 167, 200, 201, 205, 215, 227, 232, 235–36, 240–42, 245–51 *passim*, 253–54, 258–59, 261–67, 270–89, 297–99, 302, 307–12, 317, 323*nn4, 6*, 324*nn1, 17*, 325*n3*, 328*n16*, 330*n6*, 331*ch11nn1, 2, 3*
Yekuana. *See* Maiongong

New Directions in Anthropological Writing
History, Poetics, Cultural Criticism

George E. Marcus
Rice University
James Clifford
University of California, Santa Cruz

General Editors

Nationalism and the Politics of Culture in Quebec
Richard Handler

*The Pastoral Son and the Spirit of Patriarchy: Religion, Society,
and Person among East African Stock Keepers*
Michael E. Meeker

Belonging in America: Reading Between the Lines
Constance Perin

*Wombs and Alien Spirits: Women, Men and the Zār Cult
in Northern Sudan*
Janice Boddy

*People as Subject, People as Object: Selfhood and Peoplehood
in Contemporary Israel*
Virginia R. Domínguez

Sharing the Dance: Contact Improvisation and American Culture
Cynthia J. Novack

Debating Muslims: Cultural Dialogues in Postmodernity and Tradition
Michael M. J. Fischer and Medhi Abedi

*Power and Performance: Ethnographic Explorations through
Proverbial Wisdom and Theater in Shaba, Zaire*
Johannes Fabian

Dialogue at the Margins: Whorf, Bakhtin, and Linguistic Relativity
Emily A. Schultz

Magical Arrows: The Maori, the Greeks, and the Folklore of the Universe
Gregory Schrempp

After Freedom: A Cultural Study in the Deep South
Hortense Powdermaker
With an introductory essay by Brackette F. Williams and
Drexel G. Woodson

Dancing with the Devil: Society and Cultural Poetics in Mexican-American South Texas
José E. Limón

To Remember the Faces of the Dead: The Plenitude of Memory in Southwestern New Britain
Thomas Maschio

Sanumá Memories: A Yanomami Ethnography in Times of Crisis
Alcida Rita Ramos

Fragments of Death, Fables of Identity: An Athenian Anthropography
Neni Panourgiá

The Lost Drum: The Myth of Sexuality in Papua New Guinea and Beyond
James F. Weiner